THE CAMBRIDGE COMPANION
TO SHAKESPEARE ON SCREEN

The *Cambridge Companion to Shakespeare on Screen* provides a lively guide to film and television productions adapted from Shakespeare's plays. Offering an essential resource for students of Shakespeare, the *Companion* considers topics such as the early history of Shakespeare films, the development of 'live' broadcasts from theatre to cinema, the influence of promotion and marketing and the range of versions available in 'world cinema'. Chapters on the contexts, genres and critical issues of Shakespeare on screen offer a diverse range of close analyses, from the silent cinema films to the BBC's *Hollow Crown* series. The *Companion* also features chapters on the work of individual directors – Orson Welles, Akira Kurosawa, Franco Zeffirelli, Kenneth Branagh and Vishal Bhardwaj – and is supplemented by a guide to further reading and a filmography.

Russell Jackson is Emeritus Professor of Drama in the University of Birmingham. He has published widely on Shakespeare, film and theatre and has worked as textual consultant for many film and theatre productions of Shakespeare's plays, including those directed by Kenneth Branagh and Michael Grandage. Among his most recent publications are *Theatres on Film: How the Cinema Imagines the Stage* (2013), *Shakespeare and the English-Speaking Cinema* (2014) and *Shakespeare in the Theatre: Trevor Nunn* (2018).

CAMBRIDGE
COMPANIONS TO
LITERATURE

THE CAMBRIDGE
COMPANION TO
SHAKESPEARE ON SCREEN

EDITED BY
RUSSELL JACKSON
University of Birmingham

CAMBRIDGE
UNIVERSITY PRESS

University Printing House, Cambridge CB2 8BS, United Kingdom

One Liberty Plaza, 20th Floor, New York, NY 10006, USA

477 Williamstown Road, Port Melbourne, VIC 3207, Australia

314–321, 3rd Floor, Plot 3, Splendor Forum, Jasola District Centre, New Delhi – 110025, India

79 Anson Road, #06–04/06, Singapore 079906

Cambridge University Press is part of the University of Cambridge.

It furthers the University's mission by disseminating knowledge in the pursuit of education, learning, and research at the highest international levels of excellence.

www.cambridge.org
Information on this title: www.cambridge.org/9781108421164
DOI: 10.1017/9781108367479

© Cambridge University Press 2020

First published 2020

A catalogue record for this publication is available from the British Library.

Library of Congress Cataloging-in-Publication Data
NAMES: Jackson, Russell, 1949– editor.
TITLE: The Cambridge companion to Shakespeare on screen / edited by Russell Jackson.
DESCRIPTION: Cambridge ; New York, NY : Cambridge University Press, 2020. | Series: Cambridge companions to literature | Includes bibliographical references and index.
IDENTIFIERS: LCCN 2020015725 (print) | LCCN 2020015726 (ebook) | ISBN 9781108421164 (hardback) | ISBN 9781108367479 (ebook)
SUBJECTS: LCSH: Shakespeare, William, 1564–1616 – Film adaptations – History and criticism. | Shakespeare, William, 1564–1616 – Television adaptations – History and criticism.
CLASSIFICATION: LCC PR3093 .C363 2020 (print) | LCC PR3093 (ebook) | DDC 791.436–dc23
LC record available at https://lccn.loc.gov/2020015725
LC ebook record available at https://lccn.loc.gov/2020015726

ISBN 978-1-108-42116-4 Hardback
ISBN 978-1-108-43155-2 Paperback

CONTENTS

CONTENTS

CONTENTS

ILLUSTRATIONS

CONTRIBUTORS

VICTORIA BLADEN, University of Queensland

JUDITH BUCHANAN, St Peter's College, Oxford

MARK THORNTON BURNETT, Queen's University, Belfast

DEBORAH CARTMELL, De Montfort University, Leicester

ANNE-MARIE COSTANTINI-CORNÈDE, Université Paris Descartes/Université Sorbonne Nouvelle – Paris 3

KINGA FÖLDVÁRY, Pázmány Péter Catholic University, Budapest

SARAH HATCHUEL, Université Paul-Valéry Montpellier 3

PETER HOLLAND, University of Notre Dame

RUSSELL JACKSON, University of Birmingham

PETER KIRWAN, University of Nottingham

COURTNEY LEHMANN, University of the Pacific

PATRICIA LENNOX, New York University

ANTHONY GUY PATRICIA, Concord University

EMMA SMITH, Hertford College, Oxford

PETER J. SMITH, Nottingham Trent University

POONAM TRIVEDI, Indraprastha College, University of Delhi

NATHALIE VIENNE-GUERRIN, Université Paul-Valéry Montpellier 3

RAMONA WRAY, Queen's University, Belfast

PREFACE

The Cambridge Companion to Shakespeare on Film appeared in 2000, followed by a revised second edition in 2007. Changes in the techniques of production and distribution make it appropriate for the present *Companion* – a new work rather than a revised version of its predecessors – to address itself to Shakespeare 'on screen', rather than 'on film'. Rather than attempt to encompass the whole of the constantly widening range of screen adaptations, in the chapters that follow, the contributors to this *Companion* suggest a diversity of critical and historical approaches to particular productions.

NOTE ON REFERENCES

Unless otherwise indicated, references to Shakespeare's plays are to the one-volume *Complete Works* edited by Stanley Wells and Gary Taylor, 2nd edition (Oxford, Oxford University Press, 1988).

RUSSELL JACKSON

Introduction

Although 'film' remains in common usage as a generic term, digital technology has made it inaccurate when applied to work no longer shot, edited or distributed on chemically coated celluloid. The 'photochemical era' has ended, and rapid developments in the distribution and consumption of audio-visual products have reduced distinctions between what is viewed in the home and what is seen in public.[1] This *Companion* takes as its remit feature-length productions, both those commonly perceived as 'delivering' the plays, and those that appropriate them as the starting-point for work that makes no such claim. These are all to some degree adaptations, but some are more adapted than others: consequently the first group of chapters focuses on the various ways in which screen versions of Shakespeare's works have figured in a changing media environment.

Part I Adaptation and Its Contexts

In all the audio-visual media the relationship between emotional intimacy and a wide view of the context of the action remains significant. The older style of television production, dominated by studio-based staging (sometimes with filmed inserts) and editing between a limited number of cameras, has given way to techniques closer to those of the cinema. Across the visual media, digital technology has changed the choices available in aspects ranging from focus, the scope of images and editing to the use of Computer-Generated Imaging (CGI) to create complex and expansive environments for action. Nevertheless, screen adaptations still have to accommodate such characteristic techniques of the playwright's theatre as soliloquy, the reporting of offstage action, the 'turns' of clowns and heightened and rhetorically organised speech. In Shakespeare films from before the advent of synchronised sound, discussed by Judith Buchanan in Chapter 1, the viewer encounters a range of techniques developed by filmmakers anxious to translate these elements of the plays into their new medium. Spoken dialogue did not simply overcome these challenges, and study of the 'silent' cinema reveals a rich variety of responses to them. Since the early 1930s the history is not so much one of movement towards a goal ('now we can do it properly') as a widening of the range of possible approaches: a continuum rather than a success story. There is no definitive way of making a 'Shakespeare film', let alone an exemplary production to serve as some sort of gold standard.

Despite the increasing availability of Shakespearean product for individual consumption, many productions gain from being viewed on a large screen in the company of an audience. However, 'opening wide' – simultaneous initial distribution to a large number of multiplexes – is usually reserved for films that aim for 'blockbuster' status. Cinema release remains a requirement of the annual Academy Awards competition, but it is not unusual for films to have only a brief initial exposure of this kind. In recent years, the streaming of theatre performances to cinemas has added to the range of Shakespeare on screen. Critical and theoretical questions raised by this 'Shakespeare "live"' are discussed by Peter Holland in Chapter 3.

The plays have been seized on with a variety of cross-fertilisation strategies comparable to the cherry-picking of source materials in the playwright's own theatres. In Chapter 2, Deborah Cartmell considers adaptation in relation to the promotion of films, in which perceptions of closeness or distance from a source text play a significant role. Rather, then, than answer the question as to whether Olivier's 1944 *Henry V* 'does justice to the play' more fully or faithfully than Kenneth Branagh's 1989 film, reference to their common source is more properly employed understanding the task the films' makers have undertaken. Especially when a popular play is in question, Shakespeare films inevitably participate in the industry culture of reboots and remakes. Many of these present themselves as revisiting both the plays and earlier versions of them in terms of current social and political concerns – or at least of current popular culture. Baz Lurhmann's *William Shakespeare's Romeo+Juliet* (1996) was in part a response Zeffirelli's *Romeo and Juliet* (1969), displacing the earlier film's appeal to the an earlier generation of the 'youth' audience. Samuel Crowl observes that Lurhmann 'recasts Shakespeare as a secular saint, and *Romeo and Juliet* as a revisionary film'.[2]

Although Shakespeare film can be a 'prestige' commodity, attracting generous spending in production and distribution regardless of limited expectations for box-office profits, the pressures of the marketplace are hard to avoid, even for independent filmmakers who assemble finance from a range of sources, and they apply as much to broadcast and cable television and streaming platforms as to the cinema. For this reason, work produced beyond the immediate scope of Hollywood (which encompasses many films made outside the United States) has a distinctive value, addressed directly in this *Companion* by Chapter 4 on 'World Cinema' by Mark Thornton Burnett, in Victoria Bladen's survey in Chapter 7 of versions of two 'Tragedies of Love', *Romeo and Juliet* and *Othello* and in Poonam Trivedi's discussion in Chapter 18 of the films of Vishal Bhardwaj.

Part II Genres and Plays

The chapters in Part II take questions of genre as their starting-point. In offering Shakespearean products, distributors commonly invoke movie genres, and although the categories used by the editors of the 1623 Folio have no particular significance in their decisions, 'Comedy', 'Tragedy' and 'History', remain influential. Nevertheless, these categories, the media themselves and for that matter 'Shakespeare' – the works and their cultural significance – cannot be regarded as stable entities. In the film industry, techniques of production have both informed and responded to changing audience expectations. Film financing, both within and beyond the Anglophone commercial mainstream, commonly depends on perceptions of a project as both similar to and different from what is already in the marketplace. As Steve Neale points out in *Genre and Hollywood*, 'Genres do not consist solely of films. They consist also of specific systems of expectation and hypothesis which spectators bring with them to the cinema and which interact with films themselves during the course of the viewing process'.[3]

Although with rare exceptions 'Shakespeare films' have situated themselves (or been placed by producers) within a niche market, their makers usually hope to reach as wide an audience as possible, either through the attraction of established stars or kinship with such popular film genres as musicals, romantic comedies, 'teenflicks' and 'action' or costume dramas. Some categorisations common in academic study lack general currency: Michael Almereyda's *Cymbeline* (2014), released without great success under the revised title of *Anarchy: Ride or Die* – even the play's name would have been incomprehensible to the wider public – could hardly have been presented as a 'late romance'. Viewers attracted by DVD box's citation of a reviewer's comment that it was a 'mash-up' of the television series *Sons of Anarchy* and *Game of Thrones* can only have been dismayed by its failure to match up to either. (There are only a few deaths, and hardly any riding.) Unlike the same director's *Hamlet* (2000), his

Cymbeline lacked the support of a source with a clear narrative trajectory and a centuries-old track record across the popular media. The lesson to be learned is that for an adaptation to work, it is important to have both kinds of strength in the source, especially if the audience for a particular kind of genre film is being courted.

Part III   Critical Issues

Increased attention to productions in terms of their degree of responsiveness to contemporary social and political issues is reflected in three chapters addressing questions of race (Chapter 11), sexuality and gender politics (Chapter 12) and violence (Chapter 13). The work done by productions in present-day society intersects with the politics *within* a given play. Analyses of (for example) the sexual politics of *King Lear* or *The Taming of the Shrew* co-exist with the strategies and influence attributable to performances of them, and commentary on the latter has to take account of the extent to which they aim to adopt or take issue with attitudes expressed in the original text. These chapters raise questions that measure the distance between the plays and their modern audiences and adaptors. In films of *King Lear*, what response is made to the underlying misogyny that arguably inhibits acceptance of the more elevated values associated with tragedy? How do filmmakers work with – or around – racial attitudes that are at issue in *The Merchant of Venice* and *Othello* but whose expression in these plays may sit uncomfortably with modern sensibilities? (And how do they engage with the plays' scrutiny of prejudice in ways that do not patronisingly imply that somehow excuses must be made for them?) What is the relationship between treatments of comic and tragic violence in, respectively, *The Taming of the Shrew* and *Coriolanus*, and in the case of the former, where are the lines that must not be crossed?

Part IV   Directors

Part IV includes chapters devoted to five directors: Orson Welles, Akira Kurosawa, Franco Zeffirelli, Kenneth Branagh and Vishal Bhardwaj. The selection does not imply that others (for example, Julie Taymor and Grigori Kozintsev) are somehow excluded from a privileged club: their films receive detailed attention in other chapters. In the case of Olivier, although his work does not receive a chapter of its own, he might be said to haunt commentary on several of the other filmmakers. Although they do not concentrate exclusively on traits that tend to identify the directors as creative personalities, underlying these chapters is the question of who (or what) should be credited.

Since its first formulation by the filmmakers and critics of the French 'new wave' in the 1950s, the validity of *auteur* theory, which examines the inner coherence of films in terms of authorial control, has been both contested and defended with vigour. A film is both a collaborative work, and the product of its society, to be viewed historically (its cultural moment) and in terms of the cultural and ideological work it does. Sometimes this can seem a straightforward task: Laurence Olivier's *Henry V*, proclaims its propagandistic agenda. But in other cases the connection is not so obvious: the same director's *Hamlet* (1948) and *Richard III* (1953) spoke to and of their time in a less obvious manner. However, despite the actor-director's presence in all of them, Olivier's films are remarkable more for their dissimilarity from one another than any sense of being a coherent *oeuvre*.

Even when such factors are taken into account, engagement with productions in terms of a director's track record remains a valid approach shared by many writers on film, as well as by the public at large and commentators outside the academic community. From an 'industry' point of view, as David Bordwell has pointed out, in Hollywood 'the classic studio system maintained fruitful, sometimes tense, balance between directorial expression and genre demands'. Arguably, though, this has been fragmented, apparently producing a polarity between 'big-budget genre films … and small "personal" films that showcase the director's sensibility'.[4] But, as Bordwell acknowledges, this analysis may not be sustainable in the case of many directors who have moved successfully between the two poles.

'Shakespeare': The Brand Survives

In recent years, as if to reinforce the hold of the 'Shakespeare' brand on the popular imagination, the dramatist himself has appeared as a character on cinema screens, whether as a lover (*Shakespeare in Love*, 1998), an untalented hack lending his name to a better qualified aristocratic author (*Anonymous*, 2011) and even in troubled but eventually serene retirement (*All is True*, 2018). In the animated comedy *Gnomeo and Juliet* (2011), the garden-gnome hero is exceptional among adaptors of the plays in making his way to the statue of Shakespeare in Stratford-upon-Avon to argue for a happier ending. (His wish is granted.)

Meanwhile, the plays have also acquired a new sphere of existence, in adaptations and critical interventions on the Internet. Strictly speaking,

'Shakespeare' and the plays, beyond copyright restrictions and not owned by any one commercial entity, do not constitute a franchise of the kind that entails 'the [commercial] exploitation of an intellectual property across multiple cultural contexts'.[5] But their status is in many ways analogous, and Shakespeare-branded products take their place alongside other material in twenty-first-century 'Convergence Culture', with its opportunities for participation and – counterbalancing them – control of product on diverse media platforms.[6] Like the cinema and video productions discussed in the chapters that follow, this new manifestation of 'Shakespeare on screen' is a continuation of a long tradition in which the story-worlds and characters of the plays and subsequent variations on them had already circulated in older media, with Shakespeare's texts themselves participating in their own day in this ongoing process of making and remaking.

Notes

1. Stephen Prince, *Digital Cinema* (Rutgers University Press, New Brunswick, 2019), 3. See also Barbara Klinger, *Beyond the Multiplex. Cinema, New Technology and the Home* (Berkeley and Los Angeles, University of California Press, 2006).
2. Samuel Crowl, *Shakespeare at the Cineplex: the Kenneth Branagh Era* (Athens, Ohio University Press, 2003), 119.
3. Steve Neale, *Genre and Hollywood* (London, Routledge, 2000), 31.
4. David Bordwell, 'Superheroes for sale' in David Bordwell and Kristin Thompson, *Minding the Movies. Observations of the Art, Craft and Business of Film Making* (Chicago, Chicago University Press, 2011), 21–33 (28).
5. Daniel Herbert, *Film Remakes and Franchises* (New Brunswick, Rutgers University Press, 2017), 86–7.
6. A key work on this development is Henry Jenkins' *Convergence Culture. Where Old and New Media Collide*, 'updated' edition (New York, New York University Press, 2008). This rapidly expanding sphere of 'digital Shakespeare' demands is receiving scholarly attention in its own right. See Stephen O'Neil, *Shakespeare and YouTube. New Media Forms of the Bard* (London, Bloomsbury, 2014), and Bruce R. Smith, *Shakespeare|Cut. Rethinking Cutwork in and Age of Distraction* (Oxford, Oxford University Press, 2016).

PART I

Adaptation and Its Contexts

I

JUDITH BUCHANAN

Shakespeare and the Film Industry of the Pre-Sound Era

The arrival of the film industry's sound era in the late 1920s quickly
consigned silent film to being 'yesterday's thing'.[1] As a result, the cans
containing gently crumbling or spontaneously combusting prints of silent
films were not a mainstream archiving priority for some time. In relation
to the considerable corpus of Shakespeare films made in the pre-sound
era, the results for the surviving archive were grim. Through
a combination of neglect, loss, disintegration and wilful destruction, of
the approximately 300 silent Shakespeare films originally made before
1927 (when the first talkie was released), only approximately forty now
survive.[2]

Given the non-survival rates for silent film in general, however, the
fact that, significant losses notwithstanding, so many *have* survived is
testimony to the very high numbers initially made.[3] For all the seeming
oddity of the project to represent material from the world's greatest
dramatist in a form shorn of the spoken word, the production rate for
Shakespeare films in the pre-sound era makes of it more than just an
eccentric sideline: in both commercial and cultural terms, something
about the collaboration between Shakespeare and silent film clearly
worked.

The films that survive constitute a corpus of varied, funny, touching,
illuminating, beautiful and sometimes wonderfully silly work. They range
from the filmed record of a celebrated theatre production to the film conceived as an autonomous piece of cinema; the brief citational allusion to the
full-blown drama; live action to animation; the narratively precise retelling
of a Shakespeare tale to a skittish borrowing from it; the historically placed
production to the radical update. The majority of silent-era Shakespeare
films were released by production companies in Britain, the United States,
Italy, France, Germany and Denmark. Collectively, they are revealing both
about the priorities of the film industry of their moment and of the broader
history of Shakespearean performance on screen. Moreover, even the films

now lost can contribute to the wider story about this body of work: the impulses that inspired them, what they achieved, how they were exhibited and received and the nature of their legacy. In this chapter, I consider in broadly chronological order a representative sample of films selected from across the era.

*

1899–1906: Shakespeare in the Film Industry's Pioneering Years

In September 1899, the British Mutoscope and Biograph Company used their open-air London studio to shoot brief scenes imported from prominent actor-manager Herbert Beerbohm Tree's London stage production of Shakespeare's *King John*. The short (c. four-minute) resulting film constituted the first Shakespeare moving picture ever made. It was exhibited in the UK and internationally through the Autumn and Winter of 1899 as part of the varied Biograph moving picture programme of sketches, actualities and sporting news. Given how popular Shakespeare was to become both as a story pool to feed the film industry's voracious hunger for material and as an efficient indicator of cultural legitimacy for an industry regularly in need of a reputational boost, it is no surprise that the film industry should have reached so early in its own life for Shakespearean material. It was to do so again – both regularly and with a self-conscious pride in aligning itself with culturally elevated material – throughout the pre-sound era, and, of course, with undimmed enthusiasm through to the present day.

The surviving scene from the *King John** film[4] depicts a poison-wracked John (Tree himself) writhing in pain, mouthing inaudible words, desperately stretching out his arms and then collapsing histrionically back into his chair on the point of death (Figure 1.1). Even in its brevity, it provides rare and valuable access to a significant Shakespearean actor-manager of his moment. What it does not do is attempt narrative coherence as a piece of story-telling. As exhibited on variety bills in London, it will have served most efficiently as a sample advertisement for the full theatre production that was showing concurrently at Her Majesty's Theatre. As exhibited further afield (both in Britain and in abroad), it offered access to a celebrated contemporary Shakespearean production for the appreciation of the masses unable to attend the London show in person. In this respect, it was driven by some of the same aspirations that underpin the international live theatre broadcast programmes of today.

Figure 1.1 Herbert Beerbohm Tree as King John in the first Shakespeare film (BMBC, 1899), *Play On!* DVD (BFI).

The 'brief excerpt' approach of the *King John* film was in step with the industry's filmmaking impulses in relation to adaptation more generally. In these early years, short cameo references to literary and dramatic works were typically privileged over full narratives. Literary or theatrical subjects cinematically exhibited were, therefore, enjoyed primarily as momentary visual 'quotations' from known works, and 'read' partly through the processes of recognition and narrative supplementation on the part of picture-goers. This approach produced a clutch of short Shakespeare-related films in cinema's first decade, typically of between one and three minutes each: Sarah Bernhardt's 1900 *Hamlet* duel scene; Georges Méliès' 1901 *Le Diable et la Statue* featuring Veronese lovers Roméo and Juliette and a Shakespeare-evocative balcony scene; a 1902 *Burlesque on Romeo and Juliet*, distributed by Edison, with another Shakespeare-imitative balcony scene; Edison's 1905 *Seven Ages of Man*; the American Mutoscope and Biograph Company's 1905 Macbeth-Macduff fight scene;* Méliès' only mildly Shakespearean 1905 *Le Miroir de Venise* (*Une Mésaventure de Shylock*); Charles Urban's 1905 storm scene from Tree's stage production of *The Tempest*; and Messter's 1907 *Death of Othello* from the Verdi opera (with synchronised sound). Each of these fleeting Shakespearean film vignettes was designed to generate in its audience the pleasure of recognition, while depending on an audience's familiarity with the original to conjure broader narrative context.

The Transitional Era (c.1907–1913)

By c.1907,[5] however, the impulse to provide sample visual quotations from a Shakespearean (or other literary or theatrical) source had ceded to a desire to tell a fuller, autonomous narrative in moving pictures. At the start of this period, there was typically only one reel (approximately 10–12 minutes of projection time) available in which to tell the story. To shoe-horn the entirety of a Shakespeare tale into the one-reel format, a significant degree of selection and compression was, therefore, necessary. Sub-plots and peripheral characters were omitted while the films tended to focus on creating a connected sequence of the best-known dramatic moments from the plays. Such imagery was already well peddled, familiar to many from artistic representations, edition illustrations, vaudeville sketches and the variety of other popular forms in which Shakespeare was disseminated in the late nineteenth and early twentieth centuries. Thus it was, for example, that in 1908 the American production company Vitagraph was specifically commended for the editorial selections determining its one-reel release of *Julius Caesar* which omitted all but 'the vital scenes', thereby clarifying the story while avoiding narrative inefficiencies.[6] The action of such vigorously truncated versions of Shakespeare necessarily moved swiftly from one dramatic highlight to another, implicitly establishing (or confirming) a 'best of', summary form in which the plays could circulate manageably and (more or less) intelligibly.

Structuring the story as a medley of strung-together 'moments' rather than as a consistently advancing narrative ensured that, even after 1907, many films still depended upon an audience's familiarity with the original, or upon access to other sources of information beyond the film, to make sense of its narrative segues.

The years 1907–1912 saw a significant increase in the number of Shakespeare films being made annually. In 1907, there were just three focused Shakespearean releases: *Hamlet* and *Shakespeare Writing Julius Caesar*, both by Méliès, and *Othello* from Italian production company Cines. Encouraged by the story-telling possibilities that these releases opened up, in 1908 there was then an explosive flurry of Shakespearean releases in both Europe and the United States. In America, this included Lubin's *Julius Caesar*, Kalem's *As You Like It*, Biograph's *The Taming of the Shrew** and seven Shakespeare titles from Vitagraph. In Europe, the same year's Shakespearean releases included *The Tempest* (Clarendon),* two *Othello*s (Nordisk and Pathé), two *Hamlet*s (Cines and Milano) and two *Romeo and Juliet*s (Cines and Gaumont). Nineteen hundred and nine saw a further fifteen Shakespearean releases on both sides of the Atlantic and 1910 saw twenty-two more (some of which were parodies). More individual Shakespeare film titles were released between 1908 and 1910 than in any equivalent period before or since.[7] One-reelers were still being produced in these years, but as the industry's first decade was left behind, increasing numbers of two- and then three-reelers (of c.20–45 minutes screening time) also began to appear on the varied moving picture programmes of the period. These aided story-telling possibilities considerably by providing more space in which plot complexities and character detail could be explored.

Across this period Shakespeare films were increasingly celebrated for their status as autonomous vehicles for Shakespearean story-telling rather than seeking validation through their relationship to acclaimed theatrical performances. There were, however, exceptions. Frank Benson's Shakespeare films with the British Co-operative Cinematograph Company (of which only the 1910 *Richard III** survives) deliberately identified themselves as compressed records of particular performances at the Stratford Memorial Theatre and of Benson's own hyper-physical, emphatically gestural acting style. The American Vitagraph Company's many Shakespeare films produced from 1908 onwards, however, were more of their moment in having no genesis in a stage production. They simplified the action and presented whistle-stop narratives, offering a version of high culture to the masses in easy-to-digest chunks, punctuated by plot-explanatory inter-titles. Although most were considered actively edifying, Vitagraph's *Macbeth* (1909) courted controversy for what was considered its excessively gory murder scenes. As a result, cuts were required to satisfy the Chicago censors. Attracting the attention of the censors in this way temporarily called into question the insistent, and frequently expressed, contemporary claims made about Shakespeare's 'improving' influence.

Across these transitional years, a debate about adaptational method was played out – both in theory and in practice – between the contradictory pulls of cinematic freedom and theatrical reverence. Some argued that inherited theatrical values were a stifling influence on cinema's uninhibited engagements with its own film 'language'; others thought an adherence to the codes and conventions of a theatrical heritage signalled a sustained allegiance to the medium of the material's source in needful ways. The argument was made manifest both in the pages of the trade papers and through the various modes of Shakespearean filmmaking practised in the era.

The years 1908–1909 proved to be key years of vacillation for Shakespearean cinema in deciding whether to embrace a set of cinematic codes or to re-assert a stubborn theatricality in styles of presentation. As this tussle was played out, sometimes both impulses – to produce an innovative and fluid piece of cinema on the one hand and to contain the will to innovate on the other – were illuminatingly co-present within a single film, as if in fraught testimony to some of the broader debates being conducted in the industry around them. The Clarendon Film Company's *The Tempest* (dir. Percy Stow, 1908),* for example, exhibits a medium-savvy delight in its capacity to evoke beautifully choreographed, tense drama through its own simple but effective arsenal of special effects (layers of evocative superimposition, oddly angled shots, impressionist and dynamic edited sequences, savage lacerations made directly on to the film print to create suggestive streaks of lightning). And yet every expression of cinematic adventurousness in this film is countered by another of cinematic conservatism (shallow sets, theatrically blocked entrances and exits, cluttered frame composition, stage-bound performance trickery). For all its undeniable charm, therefore, the film emerges as a document in stylistic indecision, poised between embracing and rejecting the cinematic resources it finds at its disposal in ways that, from the perspective of Shakespearean filmmaking of just a few years later, would seem notably coy.

In the USA, early film production company Thanhouser followed Vitagraph in regularly including Shakespearean subjects amongst its output of prestige films, from *A Winter's Tale* (1910)* and *Romeo and Juliet* (1911) to *Cymbeline* (1913)* and the looser adaptation *Two Little Dromios* (1914). The company's real triumph, however, came in 1916 with a feature-length *King Lear** starring the eminent Shakespearean stage actor, Frederick Warde. Warde had also made a 1912 multi-reel *Richard III** with the Broadway Film Company, and, to mark its release, offered himself as guest lecturer to accompany its exhibition in the venues that could afford his distinguished services.

Live Lecturers for Film Shows

In this respect, Warde was participating in what Charles Musser has termed the era's 'craze' for live lecturers.[8] Even into the transitional era, one of the supplementary sources of information on which audiences depended to help a film make sense, was the presence of a live film 'lecturer' or 'explainer' in the exhibition venue. Where present, it was his (I know of no accounts of female lecturers) job to explain and enliven the moving pictures by means of a running commentary: setting the scene, voicing the parts, smoothing over narrative ellipses and making the drama *live*.[9]

Though on offer for many types of films, the usefulness of live lectures for Shakespeare films in particular was frequently asserted. In 1908, one prominent film lecturer maintained that picture-goers for Shakespeare shows came away 'delighted after seeing the pictures *and hearing them competently explained*' (my italics).[10] The quality of such lectures varied significantly, depending on the erudition, articulacy and performance power of the lecturer, but the practice of hiring a lecturer of some description was common on both sides of the Atlantic across the film industry's transitional years.

By 1913–1914, production companies had become nervous about, in effect, sharing responsibility for the impact of their releases on the picture-going public with a range of unknown lecturers employed locally in the place of exhibition. In order to avoid the risk that a weak or maverick collaborating lecturer might yet compromise the quality of their film, production companies needed to ensure that their films could tell their own stories clearly without supplementary commentary. Embedding autonomous responsibility for the exposition of the work within the work itself indicated the maturation of the industry and the honing of the art form. Until the coming of commercial sound films, live musical accompaniment would always still be needed, of course, but eliminating the need for a local lecturer undoubtedly made exhibition a simpler business too. As popular, and sometimes as narratively necessary, as he (see above) had been through the transitional era, by 1913 the figure of the lecturer had become, in effect, an industry anachronism.

The Shakespeare Tercentenary of 1916

With the demise of this intermediary, films had to shoulder their own story-telling obligations without external assistance. The result was a developmental advance for the industry and, in particular, for its approach to adaptations. By 1916, the global film industry was very well-established and boasted a healthy back catalogue of Shakespeare titles. Nevertheless, film industry people in Britain were not considered sufficiently 'establishment' to be included in the official plans for the Shakespeare Tercentenary commemorative events of 1916 marking 300 years since Shakespeare's death. In response to the snub, James M. Barrie made *The Real Thing at Last* (sadly now lost). This was a skittish film that wittily compared, and unsparingly lampooned, the making of a British and an American film of *Macbeth*.[11] The many stories to emerge from the pre-production planning and then the set of the Triangle-Reliance *Macbeth*, in which Herbert Beerbohm Tree starred, provided additional fodder for Barrie. The Tree film was, for example, known to include a lavish set-piece spectacle for the coronation of Macbeth, a highly dramatic fight between Macbeth and Macduff, 'wild dances' and (wonders!) some 'special large greyhounds'. Barrie gleefully made hay with the overblown ambition of the project. Tree himself, by contrast, was clearly very taken with the Hollywood process, reporting in an on-set interview that it was 'quite wonderful ... how many things can be done in pictures for the Shakespeare tales that cannot be done on the stage'. While, however, Tree believed that audiences would find in the film 'a dramatic narrative of great power',[12] upon release, critics were not persuaded.

By contrast, reviews of the two *Romeo and Juliet* films,[13] released concurrently in October 1916, were overwhelmingly enthusiastic. The Metro release starred Beverly Bayne and Francis X. Bushman, Hollywood's premier screen idols of the moment (Figure 1.2). More notably yet, the Fox version starred the sexually charged screen vamp Theda Bara as Juliet, in an unexpected but commercially savvy piece of bravura casting (Figure 1.3). Bara reported, with a finely tuned instinct for self-promotion, that the Juliet she played was 'no Sunday-school girl'.[14] Given the simultaneity of their releases, the two pictures were immediately received as artistic competitors. Moreover, the abrasive needle between their respective production companies turned a commercial competition into a high-profile public spat.

Unsurprisingly, in market terms the public rivalry proved far from an encumbrance, boosting sales for both pictures. Although critical preferences varied, both proved a huge commercial success and both were declared a triumph. Exhibitors across the United States even had to order in additional prints of both pictures to satisfy the audience demand by which they were pleasurably assailed. The power of the central performances, the sets, costumes, quotations selected for title cards and, inevitably, the sensual appeal of the Fox Juliet (seen snuggling little

16

Figure 1.2 Beverley Baines and Francis X. Bushman, *Romeo and Juliet* (Metro, 1916).

Figure 1.3 Theda Bara and Harry Hilliard, *Romeo and Juliet* (Fox, 1916).

birds, murmuring in her sleep, kissing the bottle of poison sensuously and later extracting it from her cleavage) were all very warmly received.

The following year, both films were honoured: the Metro film by the National Association of the Motion Picture Industry, the Fox film through being included on the programme for the prestigious annual Stratford-upon-Avon Shakespeare Festival. This represented a double rite of passage for Shakespeare films. Though often popular with audiences, lauded for their educational worth and celebrated for their contribution to the industry's campaign for cultural respectability, Shakespeare films had not often attracted plaudits specifically from cineastes. In sum, therefore, 1916–1917 was a significant coming-of-age moment for silent Shakespearean cinema.

The 1920s

Alongside the production of full-blown, cinematically conceived feature films, short Shakespearean scenes from significant theatre productions were still being recorded for cinema exhibition through into the 1920s. The central impulse behind these was both to generate a lasting record of acclaimed theatrical moments and, in doing so, to give widely dispersed cinema-going audiences access to stage stars and a theatrical experience that would otherwise be exclusively enjoyed by high-paying theatre audiences. Such filming projects both remembered the very early days of filmmaking and anticipated the live theatre broadcast programmes of today. In Summer 1924, for example, Pathé included a one-minute recording of the balcony scene from the Birmingham Repertory Company's production of *Romeo and Juliet** as part of their Living Paintings series (Figure 1.4).[15] The production, directed by H. K. Ayliff and shot on stage in London's Regent Theatre, featured John Gielgud as Romeo and Gwen Ffrangcon-Davies as Juliet. Together they had been the toast of the 1924 London theatrical season in what Ffrangcon-Davies remembered as a 'thrilling time'.[16] Given his subsequent profile, it is Gielgud, in his first ever film appearance, who now claims the attention. Of the two of them, though, in 1924 Ffrangcon-Davies was the better known. The film sequence is even-handed in its balance of attention but it is Ffrangcon-Davies who is privileged by the double framing: the arch of her balcony window (part of the expressionistically lit set) frames her fetching stage presence and the cinematically inserted gilt picture frame adds an additional layer of privileging containment to the entirety of the filmed action.

The conceit of the picture frame signalled the series' central conceptual drive: a promotion of cinema as a medium of animated paintings, or 'moving pictures'. Gielgud had expressed disappointment with his own performance as Romeo in the stage production: 'I had neither the looks, the dash nor the

Figure 1.4 Four stills from the Living Pictures *Romeo and Juliet* with Gwen Ffrangcon-Davies and John Gielgud (Pathé, 1924).

virility to make a real success of it, however well I spoke the verse.'[17] Given this, the sad irony for him must have been that it was not his verse-speaking but his pictorial qualities alone (showcased through a stylised reaching up towards the balcony and a suggestive intimacy with the sleeve lowered down to him by Juliet) that this precious surviving film sequence touchingly remembers.

By contrast, Danish film star Asta Nielsen's ease in communicating wordlessly is palpable in the remarkable 1920 German film adaptation of *Hamlet*,* directed by Svend Gade and Heinz Schall. The film's surprising central premise was that *Hamlet* was, in fact, a woman, for reasons of state disguised as a man, to protect the Danish throne. This moved the tradition of Hamlet being a part suitable to be played by a woman (a tradition inherited from the nineteenth-century stage), to the character itself now being understood as female. The Nielsen adaptation drew on multiple sources,[18] including the idiosyncratic Hamlet regendering theory of an American researcher named Edward P. Vining.[19] As Nielsen's emotionally burdened Hamlet acknowledges her womanhood keenly in her own private self while making bravely tortured efforts to deny it to the world, an additional plot thread of thwarted desire (Hamlet for Horatio) is added to the existing complexities of the Shakespearean drama.

As a film of the Weimar era (made within a year of Wiene's *The Cabinet of Dr Caligari*), it is no surprise that the 1920 *Hamlet* should have been significantly inflected by expressionist aesthetics. Its dramatic stone arches plunge characters in and out of shadow while repeatedly drawing attention to light-demarcated spaces. The dramatic taper-lit grand staircase seems ironically to highlight how far removed from the world of romance is the sensitively tragic Hamlet who descends it. As Elsinore's architecture draws her irresistibly into positions in which the fettered quality of her life finds graphic expression – in particular on thresholds and by casement windows looking out – the production's visual scheme not only illustrates but seems to sympathise with her plight. At their most expressive, therefore, the film's sets do not only frame this Hamlet's strikingly elegant and dignified form: they also underscore her tortured predicament by giving visual representation to her emotional and political separation from those around her.

The stylish minimalism of Nielsen's performance stands out the more in the context of the film's other performances – performances which embrace cartoon villainy (Eduard von Winterstein's iniquitous Claudius), self-pitying complicity (Mathilde Brandt's Gertrude), caricatured silliness (Hans Junckermann's muddle-head Polonius), dull prettiness (Lilli Jacobsson's Ophelia) and lumbering obviousness (Heinz Steida's thick-set Horatio). As a performance that combined high pathos, wry comedy, nuanced observation and fierce intelligence, Nielsen was much lauded in Europe and the United States of America upon the film's first release. Her witty and unmannered performance coupled with the production's design strengths have, in fact, made of the 1920 *Hamlet* the film that has been enjoyed by the largest number of contemporary audiences for silent Shakespeare since.

The German film industry's next feature-film contribution to the evolving story of Shakespeare on silent film was Dmitri Buchowetski's 1922 film of *Othello*.* This specifically courted the interest of Shakespeareans by casting theatre stars Emil Jannings and Werner Krauss as Othello and Iago respectively. Frequently, the sets in this production too are thoughtfully employed to frame and comment on the action. Most striking of all is the set for Desdemona's bedroom whose structural design, statuary, scale and lighting make the space directly evocative of a cathedral. This architectural symbolism finds its apotheosis when Othello makes his slow and self-consciously priestly way to Desdemona's sleeping form laid out upon her spiritually lit, altar-like bed. There he strangles her violently in a quasi-liturgical sacrificial rite (Figure 1.5). To observe the scale, solidity, depth of

Figure 1.5 Othello (Jannings) strangles Desdemona (Ica von Lenkeffy) on her altar-like bed, *Othello* (1922).

perspective, varied edit and overall visual design of this sequence is also to remember, by contrast, the shallow stage, cluttered blocking, rushed action, fixed camera position and lack of focal variety of the early Shakespeare films. Despite a distractingly high performance register at times, therefore, the 1922 *Othello* is a film that provides a useful gauge of the industry's technical, aesthetic and narrative progress and, most significantly, of its desire to incorporate its visual thinking sensitively into the central interpretive conception of a film adaptation.

*

In 1929, Sam Taylor claimed that his film of *The Taming of the Shrew*, starring Mary Pickford and Douglas Fairbanks, was not just the first Shakespeare film of the sound era, but the first Shakespeare film *tout simple*.[20] The implication was clear: that the silent Shakespeare films that had preceded could not qualify as Shakespeare films at all and were not, therefore, worthy of consideration in any history of Shakespearean filmmaking.

A run of Shakespearean scholars agreed. 'There was little point in tackling Shakespeare seriously until the movies could speak', wrote

Laurence Kitchin in 1966.[21] Roger Manvell considered the films 'absurd little charades'.[22] Robert Hapgood maintained it 'hard to see' the attraction of silent Shakespeare films which, he claimed, could only possibly be of interest 'as a curiosity'.[23] Even Robert Hamilton Ball, who undertook the first important study of silent Shakespeare films, referred to the objects of his own study as 'inadequate' and 'ridiculous'.[24] Most damning of all was Jack Jorgens' summary account of the first fifteen years of Shakespearean filmmaking:

> First came scores of silent Shakespeare films, one- and two-reelers struggling to render great poetic drama in dumb-show. Mercifully, most of them are lost ...[25]

For anyone with an interest in this cultural history, this celebration of films lost makes for difficult reading.

Disparaged by Shakespeareans, the films have fared little better at the hands of cineastes. Too often, they have struck cineastes as inherently anticinematic, burdened by the memory of a literary wordiness that they cannot slough off even in silence and, as a result, unable fully to embrace the cinematic resources on offer. In the face of antagonism from both directions, the position of silent Shakespeare films has not just been that of an idiosyncratic curio: it has been awkwardly and provocatively liminal – caught between a Shakespearean world and a filmic one and apparently perfectly placed to disappoint both.

In their first moment of exhibition, however, silent Shakespeare films were more often feted for their cultural ambition, edifying social effects and delicacy in execution than mocked for their formal oddity or cultural presumption. And having survived to be part of our cultural landscape today, they are now enjoying a renaissance of interest from public audiences, students, academics and creatives – and as more than entertaining curiosities. Alongside the recent run of DVDs and online releases that are feeding the interest,[26] multiple musicians, actors and filmmakers have brought their own creativity to bear on interpreting the films anew for contemporary audiences around the world.[27] In Douglas Hickox's 1973 feature film *Theatre of Blood*,* a montage of violent deaths excerpted from silent Shakespeare films constituted the film's self-consciously witty opening sequence. In Kit Monkman's 2018 feature film *Macbeth*,* however, the central inclusion of the one-reel 1909 Italian film *Macbeth* (Figure 1.6) as a flickering projection being watched attentively by the porter in the privacy of his lodge (Figure 1.7) engages with the old film not merely as risible oddity but as something both historically charged and creatively purposeful.[28]

Figure 1.6 Lady Macbeth (Maria Caserini) sleepwalking, *Macbeth* (Cines, 1909).
Image courtesy of Library of Congress.

Figure 1.7 The porter (Dai Bradley) watches the 1909 *Macbeth* film observed by Lady Macbeth
(Akiya Henry), *Macbeth* (dir. Kit Monkman, 2018).
Image courtesy of GSP Macbeth and Viridian FX.

From Tree's histrionic death in the 1899 *King John** and the impish delight of Gladys Hulette's Puck making mischief in the 1909 Vitagraph *Midsummer Night's Dream** to the provocative casting of Theda Bara in the 1916 *Romeo and Juliet** and the impressively grand configuration of space in the 1922 *Othello:** the silent-era witnessed Shakespeare films of dynamism, invention, wit, visual drama, emotional weight and interpretive import. If a 'mercy' *is* to be identified in this history, it is not, as Jorgens would have it, that most early Shakespeare films are lost, but rather – given the fate of the majority of films of the era – that not quite all of them are.

Notes

1. It is conventional to term films 'silent' that were made before the talkies. This, however, is actively misleading since the films were never silent at the point of exhibition (being accompanied by live music as a minimum).
2. Some of the specific losses are acute. These include: Georges Méliès's 1907 *Le Rêve de Shakespeare* (*Shakespeare Writing* Julius Caesar); three out of four of Frank Benson's recorded stage productions from Stratford-upon-Avon (1910); Vitagraph's *An Indian* Romeo and Juliet (1912), in which Shakespeare's star-crossed lovers are culturally translated into a Mohican princess and a Huron brave; J. M. Barrie's skittish *The Real Thing At Last*, Herbert Beerbohm Tree's *Macbeth* and both Hollywood *Romeo and Juliets* (all 1916). It should, however, be noted that intermittently films believed lost resurface. The count is, therefore, always subject to revision as new titles come to light.
3. David Francis (former Head, Motion Picture, Broadcasting and Recorded Sound Division, Library of Congress) estimates that only 10 per cent of the films produced in the USA before 1929 still exist.
4. All films that are available on DVD or for digital download are marked with an asterisk. See 'Filmography'.
5. Here I follow the periodisation taxonomy proposed in Charles Keil, *Early American Cinema in Transition* (Wisconsin, University of Wisconsin Press, 2001).
6. *New York Dramatic Mirror* (12 December 1908), 6.
7. Films in this period were, however, short (one- and two-reelers): the greatest number of overall titles does not, therefore, equate to the most overall Shakespearean film footage released.
8. Charles Musser, 'The Nickelodeon era begins', in Adam Barker and Thomas Elsaesser, eds., *Early Cinema: Space Frame Narrative* (London, British Film Institute, 1990), 256–73 (264).
9. On live lecturers, see Buchanan, '"Now, where were we?": ideal and actual lecturing practices in early cinema', in A. Davison and J. Brown, eds., *The Sounds of Early Cinema in Britain* (Oxford, Oxford University Press, 2012), 38–54.

10. W. Stephen Bush, 'Shakespeare in moving pictures', *Moving Picture World* v.3, n.23 (5 December 1908), 446–7.
11. See Judith Buchanan, *Shakespeare on Silent Film: An Excellent Dumb Discourse* (Cambridge, Cambridge University Press, 2009), 191–202.
12. *Pictures and the Picturegoer* 9.105 (19 February 1916), 483–4.
13. See Robert Hamilton Ball, *Shakespeare on Silent Film* (New York, Theatre Arts, 1968), 235–41; Buchanan, *Shakespeare on Silent Film*, 202–16.
14. Theda Bara, 'How I became a film vampire', *Forum* 62 (July 1919), 83–93 (92).
15. The series was included in *Eve and Everybody's Review*, a cinemagazine directed by Fred Watts. It ran in cinemas 1921–1933.
16. Aged 97, Ffrangcon-Davies discussed this 'thrilling time' on BBC Radio 4's 'Desert Island Discs' (1 September 1989).
17. Quoted in Benedict Nightingale's obituary for Gielgud, 'Theater: remembering the still, simple beauty of Gielgud's art', *New York Times* (28 May 2000).
18. Screenwriter Erwin Gepard, in discussion with Nielsen, drew not only on Shakespeare, but on a twelfth-century Saxo-Grammaticus Nordic saga and on the 1704 German drama *Fratricide Punished*.
19. Edward P. Vining, *The Mystery of Hamlet* (Philadelphia, J. B. Lippincott & Co.,1881).
20. See Deborah Cartmell, 'Sound adaptation: Sam Taylor's *The Taming of the Shrew*', in D. Cartmell and I. Whelehan, eds., *Blackwell Companion to Literature, Film and Adaptation* (Oxford, Wiley-Blackwell, 2012), 70–83 (76).
21. Laurence Kitchin, *Drama in the Sixties: Form and Interpretation* (London, Faber, 1966), 142.
22. Roger Manvell, *Shakespeare and the Film* (London, J. M.Dent, 1971), 17.
23. Robert Hapgood, 'Shakespeare on film and television', in Stanley Wells, ed., *The Cambridge Companion to Shakespeare Studies* (Cambridge, Cambridge University Press, 1986), 273–86 (274).
24. Ball, *Shakespeare on Silent Film*, 302.
25. Jack Jorgens, *Shakespeare on Film* (Bloomington, Indiana University Press, 1977), 1.
26. See 'Filmography'.
27. See, for example, the interpretive work of Shakespeare's Globe's musicians for *Play On!* and the disseminating work of, Silents Now: silents-now.co.uk
28. See Judith Buchanan, 'Collaborating with the dead, playing the Shakespeare archive', in Bernadette Cronin and Nikolai Preuschoff, eds., *Adaptation as a Collaborative Art: Process and Practice* (Basingstoke, Palgrave Macmillan, 2019).

2

DEBORAH CARTMELL

Adaptation and the Marketing of Shakespeare in Classical Hollywood

From the earliest period of film, Hollywood identified with Shakespeare. In an advertisement in *The Moving Picture World*, 1920, film is celebrated as the realisation of a Shakespearean dream, a concept that persisted beyond the silent era as can be seen in the marketing of a 40-volt projection arc lamp in 1948: 'The Strong Mogul' alongside a picture of Shakespeare under the caption of 'Builders of the Theatre'. The suggestion in both these advertisements is that film is the new Shakespeare.[1] These advertisements, almost thirty years apart, articulate what has become a cliché in popular discussions of Shakespeare: that film is today what Shakespeare was in the early modern period and if the playwright were alive today he would be living in LA and making movies.

In spite of the declared synergies between Shakespeare and Hollywood film, it took Shakespeare a long time to be successfully translated into a Hollywood movie. If we count success as both critical and commercial, it was twenty-four years before a Hollywood Shakespeare film gained both critical and box-office success in the sound era. The 'straight' adaptations included British actors in an effort to appease those who believed that the British 'owned' Shakespeare and American stars to imply that Hollywood, too, could have a major share in the playwright. In the early era of sound, accents were of particular importance, especially to those who believed that Shakespeare had to be spoken in an English accent.

Swinging from exaggerated claims of fidelity to audacious disrespect for the author, promotions of the films are referred to as 'exploitation' and 'showmanship', terms that, I suggest, can be recognised as analogous to 'adaptation' in the 'Classical' Hollywood era, between the 1920s and the 1950s, during which production, distribution and marketing were dominated by the 'major' studios. Shakespeare's place in Hollywood was eagerly sought after, from the beginnings of the sound era (effectively from 1929 onwards), but until the beginning of the 1950s, it remained noticeably uncertain. This chapter considers how the ways in which we talk about the adaptive process owe much to marketing, especially what was termed 'exploitation' in the pre-war period and 'showmanship' in the post-war era. This is a key element in the way that adaptations were both conceived and received in Classical Hollywood. This chapter will focus on the advertisers of Shakespeare adaptations, who in their eagerness to please everyone reveal some of the underpinning strategies for adapting Shakespeare in Classical Hollywood, invoking synergies between translation, adaptation, commercialisation, exploitation and showmanship.

Rather than looking at the films, I am going to look at the ways in which the film adaptations were talked about, not by their critics or reviewers but by their promoters: voices that we do not often value and whose boasting about the brilliance of the films is at odds with the inferiority complex characteristic of adaptation studies. As Christine Geraghty in *Now A Major Motion Picture: Film Adaptations of Literature and Drama* (2007) boldly looks at film adaptations outside of their source texts,[2] I would like to experiment by looking at adaptations through marketing – and by marketing, I am using a concept from the first half of the twentieth century before the Internet, normally about appealing to as many people as possible, often reduced to a notion of appealing to the lowest possible denominator, 'dumbing down', making unrealistic promises akin to 'fake news'. In a short opinion piece for *Literature/Film Quarterly*, I suggested that it is time to read adaptations historically and take seriously the 'clapometer' effect – to coin a term from a British television talent show to denote what is the most popular.[3] Rather than looking at what the author intended – which is of course 'fidelity', the bane of adaptation studies – we should reflect on what the audience were perceived to want.

Film as the New Shakespeare and Films of Shakespeare

In 1936, Allardyce Nicoll suggested, while acknowledging that the Shakespeare films of the sound era had not fulfilled their potential, that film was the 'new Shakespeare' insofar as its conditions were like those of a Shakespeare play, appealing to all levels of audience, commercially driven and restricted by censorship. Shakespeare on film potentially could be more 'Shakespearean' than a production in Shakespeare's own time.[4] Hollywood shared this vision; as Russell Jackson observes, after the coming of sound, Shakespeare films were 'presented as the fulfillment of a dream, either of the medium's capabilities or even the playwright's fancies, unfulfilled by his own inadequate theatre'.[5]

The film critic André Bazin, writing almost twenty years before Roland Barthes' influential essay, 'The Death of the Author' (1967), accounted for the refusal to regard adaptations as serious films or as serious readings of literary texts due to an unwillingness to let go of the need for an author, an 'individualist conception' of the 'author' and the 'work' that he points out, only became legally defined at the close of the eighteenth century ('Adaptation, or the Cinema as Digest' 1948).[6] The need to have a single creative genius, especially behind a Shakespeare film, for some time seemed to separate the good from the bad, the serious from the flippant, the highbrow from the lowbrow and the faithful from the blasphemous.

Shakespeare-and-film criticism has historically put the plays first, focusing on a single play's journey through cinema, and numerous examples could be cited of criticism that restricts itself to a single film, links films in relation to dramatic (rather than cinematic) genre, or focuses on a single director, normally, Laurence Olivier, Orson Welles, Grigori Kozintsev, Franco Zeffirelli and Kenneth Branagh. These approaches all imply a need for a single creative genius behind the productions: either the director or Shakespeare himself.

Douglas Lanier has considered Shakespeare's presence in advertising and the 'conviction that advertising's appropriation of Shakespeare corrupts Shakespeare's art' and this 'is a cultural belief widely shared, borne of a post-Romantic faith in poetry's transcendent autonomy of the marketplace',[7] but restricts his survey to the use of Shakespeare as a symbolic commodity to promote products other than film. Emma French has written on film marketing from 1989 to the new millennium in *Selling Shakespeare to Hollywood*, considering how filmed Shakespeare at the end of the twentieth century 'prompts cultural anxiety about high culture adaptation' and how 'a complex hybrid of veneration and irreverence arises out of such anxiety in the marketing of Shakespeare, the balance within which becomes crucial for commercial success'.[8] John Madden's 1998 *Shakespeare in Love* and Baz Luhrmann's 1996 *William Shakespeare's Romeo + Juliet*, the most commercially successful Shakespeare films to date, scored highly in the box office, according to French, due to a rhetoric of reverence and irreverence, a combination of fidelity and flippancy. I would also suggest that the films' popularity is due largely to the ways in which marketing is embedded into the narrative.[9] There has been little research into the significance of marketing of Hollywood Shakespeare films in the first half of the twentieth century, film marketing described in E. S. Turner's *The Shocking History of Advertising* as the 'rawest' of all,[10] the tactics of which markedly veered from excessive reverence to extravagant claims regarding the historic significance of the film to what was considered shocking and defiant impertinence. This chapter considers how adaptation studies owes much to the marketing of film adaptations and its paradoxical mixture of the most extreme claims to fidelity with blatant expressions of betrayal.

Marketing Shakespeare in Hollywood

Reading Shakespeare adaptations historically shifts the focus from the play or director to the audience and involves a consideration of the marketing strategies surrounding the films. This requires a reading of what Gérard Genette calls 'paratexts', usefully summarised by Robert Stam as 'all the accessory messages and commentaries which come to surround the text such as posters, trailers, reviews, interviews with the directors, and so forth'.[11] An historical approach to Shakespeare adaptations also includes consideration of the frequency of certain types of films over a given period. If we discount Orson Welles' 1948 *Macbeth* as outside the mainstream, post-sound Classical Hollywood only managed to produce four full-scale studio feature length treatments of Shakespeare.[12] The surprisingly small number suggests that the promotion of these films failed to attract their targeted audiences. The imprint of 'Shakespeare's name' and the consequent insistence upon authenticity persisted; but while the films were both critical and box-office disappointments, the brashness and inventiveness of the marketing of the movies seems to have inspired the more lucrative and numerous Shakespeare offshoots of the period.

Three of the four mainstream 'straight' Shakespeare films were released in the pre-war period. These were marketed as the 'first' films of Shakespeare, in spite of their silent predecessors.[13] It seems that the early promoters of Shakespeare film required sound, or Shakespeare's words, for them to be 'truly' Shakespearean, and the way that the words were spoken dominated much of the films' criticism. These films in the early sound era include *The Taming of the Shrew* (dir. Sam Taylor, 1929), *A Midsummer Night's Dream* (dir. William Dieterle and Max Reinhardt, 1935) and *Romeo and* Juliet (dir. George Cukor, 1936). The plays were chosen to display the stars' hitherto unknown verbal skills, with some winners and some losers. Among the stars in these prestige productions were Douglas Fairbanks and Mary Pickford (*The Taming of the Shrew* – 'Hollywood Royalty' making their first appearance together), James Cagney, Mickey Rooney and Olivia de Havilland (*A Midsummer Night's Dream*), Norma Shearer and Leslie Howard

(*Romeo and Juliet*). The Shakespearean roles offered opportunities to show off both the stars' acting credentials and the studio's cultural aspirations. Unfortunately, the appeal to too wide an audience (fans of the stars and potential Shakespeare enthusiasts) resulted in poor box-office figures; and while the films flopped and today seem, to many, stilted, stagey and conservative, the marketing of these films is charac-terised by extreme claims to the historic significance of these movies, the fidelity of the productions and, paradoxically, a joyful irreverence to the language of the text. The marketing of the first talkie, *The Taming of the Shrew*, claimed that the film would be an improvement on the play. The pressbook (the term for an illustrated guide to marketing for exhibitors of the film) even brings Shakespeare back from the dead, to join 'Mary and Doug' for tea, where he gives the movie (described as the 'first' film adaptation of his work) the warmest approval, authenticating it as worthy of the author. However, *The Taming of the Shrew* is greeted in *Photoplay* as 'swell entertainment' with the reassurance that 'it isn't Shakespeare'.[14]

What is striking today in the advertising of these movies is the insistence on Shakespeare's approval as well as the striking contrast between the seriousness of the films and the irreverence in the promotional materials. The extravagance of the claims promoting the films is shocking to an audience today, such as in the poster for *A Midsummer Night's Dream* asserting that the movie is: 'THE MOST IMPORTANT PRODUCTION EVER DONE IN TALKING PICTURES'. In contrast, *Shake Mr Shakespeare* (1936, dir. by Roy Mack), a short promotion of the 1935 *Midsummer Night's Dream*, offers musical renditions of Shakespeare's plays presented in a dream sequence to a screenwriter who has been charged with adapting all of Shakespeare. For me, this is a minor master-piece full of ingenious contemporary musical adaptations of Shakespeare's plays and much more watchable than the film it promotes. Shakespeare is marketed, for the same film, in *Photoplay* as a 'newcomer named Bill Shakespeare'. *A Midsummer Night's Dream* is advertised as a film that would 'have delighted the Bard'.[15]

A year later, *Romeo and Juliet* is celebrated for its fidelity and for surpassing all other versions in its 'sheer physical beauty'. It is regarded as a milestone akin to *Birth of a Nation* and *The Jazz Singer* in its translation of classic art into screen entertainment and as the culmination of Shakespeare's art. Its director George Cukor claimed that 'Shakespeare wrote his masterpieces for the screen'.[16] The film promo-tion claims now, 'after five hundred years [*Romeo and Juliet*], has for the *first* time been transformed in all its beauty and breathless excitement to a medium perfected for its reception – the motion picture screen'.[17] In the short (or as it refers to itself 'miniature') made to accompany Cukor's *Romeo and Juliet*, *Master Will Shakespeare* (1936 dir. Jacques Tourneur), Shakespeare is depicted as an aspiring screenwriter, making his way to London, depicted as the Hollywood of the sixteenth century. The short concludes with Shakespeare reflecting on *Romeo and Juliet* (which we are informed is his favourite play) with the film's soundtrack in the background with the not so subtle message that if he were alive today, he would be writing for the movies. In the marketing of these films, Shakespeare is made into a product to be consumed and exploited, and audiences of these movies were cheated with fake news, promises that were not delivered, adaptations that presented themselves as not the real thing, but better.

Variety ran a column entitled 'Exploitation' in which activities for film promotion are suggested and 'exploitation' is significantly a feature of the pressbooks, often featuring several pages under the heading 'Exploitation' which offer ideas as to how to promote films to local audiences, involving activities around the movie theatres, installations and images to promote the films. 'Exploitation' is a useful term to apply to Hollywood's approach to adaptation of this period, on the one hand insisting upon the accessibility or the contemporariness of the films and, on the other hand, declaring that the movies would be what Shakespeare would have produced himself. Robert Stam has listed the numerous ways of discussing translations of literary texts with words such as 'infidelity', 'betrayal', 'deformation', 'violation', 'bastardisation', 'vulgarisation' and 'desecration'[18] and the general bad press that adaptation or translation into the new media has received throughout the twentieth century. Implicit in all of these terms of abuse is exploitation – or commercialisation – the attempt to turn the text into a product, an approach which the trade magazines and the pressbooks actively embraced. Rather than 'loss', what Stam describes as resulting from 'the prior valorisation of historical *anteriority* and *seniority*', film exploitation adopts a rhetoric of 'gain', wildly insisting upon the triumph of the movie which completes or perfects the source text.[19] In the pre-war period, Hollywood tried but failed to exploit Shakespeare in these three prestige productions. By the 1950s 'exploitation' had been translated to 'showmanship' but with the same commercialising tactics to promote the films to local communities, including tie-in books, bookshop displays, walking books, posters of the stars and fashion accessories, possibly making explicit what was implicit in the films themselves.

In response to the box-office failures of the 1930s, the following decade is dominated by more 'serious' renditions of Shakespeare, aloof from the Hollywood pizzazz of their predecessors: Laurence Olivier's British films *Henry V* (1944) and *Hamlet* (1948) and Orson Welles' low budget *Macbeth* (1948). Olivier's *Henry V* ushered in a new period of Shakespeare movies with a focus on a single director/star (a surrogate Shakespeare), very much as Welles was to establish himself in America. Rather than marketing Shakespeare as a collaborative product, as in the Hollywood productions, these films succeed through their emphasis on a single creative genius – Olivier and Welles. A poster for *Hamlet* in *Variety* (5 January 1949) gives all the credit to Olivier, his name dwarfing that of Shakespeare and with Olivier's image alone, with sword aloft, promoting the film. In her study of Laurence Olivier, Jennifer Barnes describes how Olivier as actor-director-producer usurps Shakespeare, as in a *News Chronicle* cartoon in which two American studio executives describe Stratford-upon-Avon as 'the birthplace of the guy who writes the movies for Larry Olivier'.[20] While the previous decade loudly celebrated Shakespeare exploitation or appropriation by Hollywood, the 1940s made no major Hollywood film of Shakespeare with the exception of Orson Welles's *Macbeth* which was made by Republic Pictures, on 'Poverty Row' in Hollywood, on a limited budget of $700,000.[21] While bruised by the failures of the 1930s Shakespeare films, the major studios sneaked Shakespeare into the movies in offshoots such as the war comedy, *To Be Or Not To Be* (1942), directed by Ernst Lubitsch at United Artists, starring Jack Benny, John Ford's western *My Darling Clementine* (Twentieth Century Fox, 1946) and *A Double Life*, George Cukor's film noir drama about an actor who is 'taken over' by the role of Othello (Universal, 1947).

Hollywood's determination not to repeat the mistakes of the 1930s can be seen again in the following decade, with Shakespeare making unheralded appearances in offshoots rather than in explicit cinematic renditions of his works, such as the western, loosely based on *King Lear*, *Broken Lance* (1954, dir. Edward Dmytryk for twentieth Century Fox), *Macbeth*, turned into a gangster movie, *Joe MacBeth* (1955, dir. Ken Hughes for Columbia Pictures filmed in the UK), *Othello* as western, *Jubal* (1956, dir. Delmer Daves for Columbia Pictures), and *The Tempest* as sci-fi fantasy, *Forbidden Planet* (1956, dir. Fred McLeod Wilcox for MGM). Three other notable English-speaking films, Welles' *Othello* (1951), Renato Castellani's *Romeo and Juliet* (1954) and Olivier's *Richard III* (1955) were produced outside of the Hollywood system. 'Straight' or 'faithful' Shakespeare seemed to have no place in Hollywood, but the success of Olivier's 1944 *Henry V* and, in particular, the Oscar award winning *Hamlet* in 1948, revealed that Shakespeare movies had a place elsewhere.

Shakespeare Arrives in Hollywood

Two Hollywood films were released by MGM in 1953, *Kiss Me Kate* and *Julius Caesar*, the latter identified by Robert F. Willson Jr. as the best of the Hollywood Shakespeare movies and the last Shakespeare film of the Classical Hollywood period (156). The films represent the opposite ends of the adaptation spectrum, the 'so-called' 'loose' and 'straight' adaptation. *Kiss Me Kate* recalls the Hollywoodisation of Shakespeare in the early 1930s in the irreverent marketing of the playwright. *Julius Caesar* draws on the tradition of reverence, recalling both Olivier's *Henry V* in its political and theatrical representations and *Hamlet* in the black-and-white depth of focus and statuesque *mise en scène*. The film was shot in black-and-white to remind audiences of the wartime newsreels of mass Fascist rallies,[22] seeming to emulate Olivier's chorus in *Henry V* whose commentary on the action emulated the newsreels shown in picture houses during the war and also the depth of focus of his black-and-white *Hamlet*. The only other films explicitly referred to in the 1954 British *Julius Caesar* pressbook are Olivier's *Henry V* and *Hamlet*,[23] inviting viewers to forget the earlier Hollywood attempts at Shakespeare and compare the American movie with its successful British predecessors. *Julius Caesar* and *Kiss Me Kate* represent two Hollywood approaches to Shakespeare film – exploiting both a tradition of irreverence and reverence. Both films look backward to Shakespeare's previous Hollywood representations, drawing on the explicit attempts to Hollywoodise Shakespeare (*Kiss Me Kate*) and to prove that Hollywood could produce serious Shakespeare (*Julius Caesar*).

Kiss Me Kate (dir. George Sidney), based on the 1948 Broadway musical by Samuel and Bella Spewack with music by Cole Porter, seems to pay tribute to the 1930s marketing of Shakespeare by Hollywoodising *The Taming of the Shrew* in its blatant commercialism and exploitation of Shakespearean language. The film owes much to the early Shakespearean spoof adaptations, especially Norma Shearer and John Gilbert's hamming up of Shakespeare in MGM's *Hollywood Revue* of 1929 and the all-dancing and singing, 1936 *Shake Mr Shakespeare*, as well as harking back to Douglas Fairbanks and Mary Pickford's 1929 *Taming of the Shrew* in which fans would be voyeuristically watching the breakdown of a famous Hollywood marriage. As Taylor's *Taming* implicitly combined two stories – that of the real life story of the married actors, Fairbanks and Pickford, playing together for the first time and that of Petruchio and Katherine, *Kiss Me Kate* parallels a divorced couple playing the roles of their Shakespearean counterparts. Shakespeare's name is absent from the trailer and the opening credits.

Rather than Shakespeare, the pressbook, unrelentingly focuses on Kate being spanked by Petruchio – 'A SPANKING SPECTACULAR NEW MUSICAL!' – and on the film's technical innovations (colour and 3D).

Hollywood in the 1930s displayed a certain nervousness in the casting of Shakespeare films in the translation of Shakespeare into American vernacular and played safe in using both American and British actors. Audiences in the 1930s, as Allardyce Nicoll demonstrates, still referred to these films as 'talkies' and would be alert to the voices of the actors, expecting British actors to inhabit the parts. The Shakespeare films would be the first time some in the audience had seen Shakespeare or had seen Shakespeare radically cut, the first time some would have heard a British or American actor speaking Shakespeare. The novelty of sound had yet to disappear and a speaking film was still something to marvel at. *Julius Caesar*, while addressing an audience more acclimatised to different accents and fully accustomed to sound, likewise, mixes British and American actors in the tradition of Hollywood Shakespeare. But by the 1950s, the British accent had become firmly associated with deviance and villainy, probably initiated by Charles Laughton's performance in *The Private Life of Henry VIII* (Alexander Korda, 1933), followed by his type-casting as the villain in his later Hollywood films, establishing a pattern for the casting of male British actors to follow.

Influenced by Orson Welles's modern dress version of the play, referencing Mussolini's rising fascism (which was produced by John Houseman, also producer of the MGM movie), *Julius Caesar* attracted actors at a quarter of their usual salaries. With little confidence in its commercial success, the budget of the film was confined to $2,070,000.[24] The choice of *Julius Caesar*, as stressed in the pressbook, was due to its relevance, described as Shakespeare's 'most modern play': 'Dictatorship versus free society, power politics, much action, totalitarian purges – these are forces all too familiar in the world today.'[25] Made at the time of the Hollywood blacklist, motivated by anti-communist sentiment, the film boldly addresses the topical issue of free speech. Elia Kazan, who directed Marlon Brando in his breakthrough role in *A Streetcar Named Desire* (1951), had just released names to the House Committee on Un-American Activities, to the shock of those who knew him, including Brando. Choosing such an overtly political play was daring enough, but the most notable and boldest decision was the casting of Marlon Brando as Mark Antony.

There were several reasons for the choice of Brando: his contemporary appeal, his reputation as an actor who breaks the usual mould and his American identity, clinched in his extraordinary performance two years earlier in *A Streetcar Named Desire*. The decision to cast Brando (originally it was to be offered to emerging British actor Paul Scofield), in fact, dominated the film's publicity and reception to such an extent that it became identified as Brando's *Julius Caesar*, much in the same way of Olivier's 'ownership' of *Henry V* and *Hamlet*. It is a film that does not belong to the writer/screenwriter/director, but to the star.

Brando's identification with the uncultured American seems to be key to the vision of the movie. The director Joseph L. Mankiewicz allegedly stopped Brando trying to imitate British Shakespearean performances: 'You're trying to copy the goddamn Limeys! Let's work on this together goddamn it.'[26] The choice of Gielgud was equally strategic. The press-book includes an article entitled 'OUR GREATEST SHAKESPEAREAN ACTOR: John Gielgud as Cassius', in which we are informed why Gielgud finally chose to act in a Hollywood film. Referred to as 'our foremost Shakespearean interpreter', he is claimed to explain why he changed his mind about going to Hollywood and filming Shakespeare:

> 'Among all Shakespeare's plays "Julius Caesar" is probably the best suited for filming. It's a play of action, with a minimum of soliloquizing. Mankiewicz assured me the film version would be faithful to Shakespeare, emphasizing character rather than spectacle', Gielgud related, 'and I had faith in him'.

The presence of Gielgud 'authenticates' the film as a Shakespearean vehicle. Finally, the choice as Brutus of James Mason, who was regarded as one of the most popular stars in Britain before he made his way to the USA, serves as foil to Brando in both physical stature and in the oratory competition at the heart of the film, a contest in which Brando unequivocally wins. The American Brando, as in the poster promoting the movie, towers over the British Mason.

Unlike *Kiss Me Kate*, *Julius Caesar* pronounces its Shakespearean credentials: the opening credits of Joseph L. Mankiewicz's film announce 'William Shakespeare's Julius Caesar' (no other writer's name was to be included in the screen credits),[27] placing Shakespeare in the forefront for the first time in Hollywood after seventeen years of suppression. The pressbook reveals how the play required a minimum of cutting 'and not a single word of "additional dialogue"'. This recalled the credits allegedly attached to Sam Taylor's 1929 *Taming of the Shrew*, in order to emphasise 'the vast strides made by Hollywood in the past few years' with the suggestion that this film is 'pure Shakespeare'.[28] A review in the pressbook surveys the cast, director, producer, cameraman and culminates with 'The screen play is by a certain gentleman of Stratford – William Shakespeare himself. Nothing has been added to the play's original dialogue.' *Master Will Shakespeare*, used in conjunction with the last Hollywood mainstream film, the 1936 *Romeo and Juliet*, was revived to promote the film, perhaps in recognising the brilliant audacity of the short and alluding again to Shakespeare's conquest of Hollywood. The poster for the film reflects the overall marketing strategy, a strategy that draws on the lessons learnt from the previous Hollywood feature films of Shakespeare's plays: a statuesque Brando towering over the other characters played by James Mason, John Gielgud, Louis Calhern, Edmond O'Brien, Greer Garson and Deborah Kerr. It also suggests the dominance of an American/Hollywood culture – as epitomised by Brando, quintessential American heart-throb and seemingly uncultured bad boy – over those British pretenders, Mason, Gielgud, Garson and Kerr.

The 'SHOWMANSHIP' section of the British pressbook, the new version of the 'Exploitation' section of earlier pressbooks, reveals that 'GIANT BOOKS' of the 'novel' are available: 'a pretty girl could hold a copy in such a way that the title is plainly seen and tour town, get into bus queues, "wait" outside factories during the lunch hour, etc.' Compared to earlier pressbooks, the 'showmanship' feature is relatively restrained, but the British pressbook does include 'The "JULIUS CAESAR HAIR STYLES' originally featured in *The Hairdressers' Weekly Journal* which pictures women modelling 'the Mark Antony', 'the Cassius', 'the Brutus' and 'the Casca', juxtaposing the models with the newly styled hair against their counterparts in the film.

For some this Hollywood conquest of Shakespeare worked. According to the review in *The New York Times*, it surpassed Olivier's *Hamlet* ushering in the coming of age of Tinseltown and almost lived up to the press book's hyperbolic marketing: 'M-G-M's JULIUS CAESAR is acknowledged as the greatest box-office attraction ever created from a Shakespeare play'.[29] While credit was given to the rest of the cast, Brando received the lion's share and was nominated for his third Academy Award. Shakespeare in Hollywood seemed to have arrived, if somewhat late. Kenneth S. Rothwell, writing almost fifty years later, concurred: 'The likes of this remarkable performance will rarely be seen again'.[30]

For the first time in Hollywood's Classical Period, the marketing and targeting of the film seems to have paid off and for the moment, at least, Mankiewicz's *Julius Caesar* was 'the new Shakespeare' and Shakespeare had finally arrived in Hollywood. But *Julius* Caesar's success is in no small measure due to its borrowings from previous advertisements of Shakespeare films in persuading a doubting public of its worthiness, focusing on authenticity, irreverence and relevance while assigning its success to a single creative genius. And this time, the creative genius behind the production who sells Shakespeare to Hollywood was neither the director nor Shakespeare, but the star. The key ingredients in Hollywood exploitation and showmanship can be summed up by foregrounding contemporary relevance, authenticity and paradoxically its opposite, irreverence, having a controlling/creative presence dominate the film, and implying that the film triumphs over both Shakespeare and British culture in general.

Conclusion: Shakespeare, Film, Exploitation and Marketing

Perhaps we should not discount the 'clapometer' effect, but embrace exploitation, showmanship or commercialisation as something to be recognised in adaptation studies, an approach that focuses on the consumer rather that the author, the adaptation not as interpretation but as product, not as something to be admired but as something to be sold. The epigraph of Gary R. Bortolotti and Linda Hutcheon's article, 'On the Origins of Adaptation', from the 2002 film *Adaptation*, sums up the notion of adaptation as exploitation: 'Adaptation is a profound process, which means you try and figure out how to thrive in the world'.[31] I have tried to follow a lineage of descent from the 1929 *Taming of the Shrew*, the first full-length Shakespearean 'talkie', to the 1953 *Julius Caesar*, hailed as the 'greatest ever production of Shakespeare'. Through trial and error, the Hollywood studios increasingly commodified Shakespeare by trying to figure out the key selling points of a successful adaptation.

It is worth remembering that 'adaptation' is also a term in marketing to describe 'the process and practice of adapting otherwise standard products and services to meet the needs of varying customer types, either individually or customer groupings'.[32] In Classical Hollywood – and beyond – to adapt Shakespeare is to commodify his works, to exploit unique selling points of previous adaptations and to ultimately prove that film is the new Shakespeare.

Notes

1. These illustrations can be viewed at http://lantern.mediahist.org/catalog/mov picwor432movi_0578 (*Moving Picture World*) and http://archive.org/stream/ motionpictureher17ounse#page/n485/mode/2up (*Motion Picture Herald*).
2. Christine Geraghty, *Now a Major Motion Picture: Film Adaptations of Literature and Drama* (Lanham, Rowman & Littlefield, 2007).

3. 'Adaptation as Exploitation' *Literature/Film Quarterly* 45.2 (2017), https://lfq .salisbury.edu/_issues/first/adaptation_as_exploitation.html (accessed 3 December 2018).

4. Allardyce Nicoll, 'Shakespeare and the cinema', *Theatre and Film* (London, George G. Harrap, 1936), 1–37.

5. *Shakespeare Films in the Making: Vision, Production and Reception* (Cambridge, Cambridge University Press, 2007), 5.

6. André Bazin, 'Adaptation, or the cinema as digest' (1948), in James Naremore. ed., *Film Adaptation* (London, Athlone, 2000), 19–17.

7. Douglas Lanier, '"Retail'd to posterity": Shakespeare and marketing', www .academia.edu/12170687/Marketing_Shakespeare (accessed 29 December 2018).

8. Emma French *Selling Shakespeare to Hollywood: The Marketing of Filmed Shakespeare Adaptations from 1989 into the New Millennium* (Hatfield, University of Hertfordshire Press, 2006), 1.

9. Deborah Cartmell, 'Marketing Shakespeare films: from tragedy to biopic', in Dominic Shellard and Siobhan Keenan, eds., *Shakespeare's Cultural Capital* (Basingstoke, Palgrave Macmillan, 2016), 57–76.

10. E. S. Turner, *The Shocking History of Advertising* (Harmondsworth, Penguin, 1952), 209.

11. Robert Stam, 'Introduction: the theory and practice of adaptation', in Robert Stam and Alessandra Raengo, eds., *Literature and Film: A Guide to the Theory and Practice of Film Adaptation* (Oxford and Malden, Blackwell, 2003), 1–52, 28.

12. Kenneth S. Rothwell, *Shakespeare on Screen: A Century of Film and Television* (Cambridge, Cambridge University Press, 1999), 28.

13. See Deborah Cartmell, *Adaptations in the Sound Era: 1929–37* (New York, Bloomsbury, 2015).

14. *Photoplay*, December 1929, 148. Fan magazines and trade journals are available through the Media History Digital Archive, https://archive.org/details/ mediahistory.

15. *Photoplay*, December 1935, 67.

16. Ibid., September 1936, 98.

17. *Romeo and Juliet* Pressbook, 1936.

18. Stam, 'Introduction', 3.

19. Ibid., 4.

20. Jennifer Barnes, *Shakespearean Star: Laurence Olivier and National Cinema* (Cambridge, Cambridge University Press, 2017), 80.

21. Robert F. Willson Jr., *Shakespeare in Hollywood, 1929–1956* (Madison, Fairleigh Dickinson University Press, 2000), 131.

22. Peter Manso, *Brando* (London, Orion, 1994), 325.

23. '"JULIUS CAESAR" in "SHOWMANSHIP"', Pressbook, 1954, 7.

24. Kenneth L. Geist, *Pictures will Talk: The Life and Films of Joseph L. Mankiewicz* (New York: Da Capo, 1978), 226. The budget is recorded as $1.7 million by Manso, *Brando*, 320.

25. 'THE PERENNIAL APPEAL OF "JULIUS CAESAR"', Pressbook, 1953.

26. Manso, *Brando*, 322.

27. Ibid., 325.

28. 'JULIUS CAESAR, SHAKESPEARE'S POWERFUL DRAMA OF A DICTATOR'S FALL, BROUGHT TO SCREEN WITH ALL-STAR CAST', Pressbook, 1954.
29. Manso, *Brando*, 335.
30. Rothwell, *Shakespeare on Screen*, 48.
31. Gary R. Bortolotti and Linda Hutcheon, 'On the origin of adaptations: rethinking fidelity discourse and "success" – biologically', *New Literary History* 38.3 (2007), 443–58.
32. Charles Doyle, *Oxford Dictionary of Marketing* (Oxford, Oxford University Press, 2003).

3

PETER HOLLAND

Shakespeare 'Live'

Livecast, live from, simulcast, alternative content, cinecast, cinemacast, streamed transmission, outside broadcast, digital broadcast cinema, event cinema, Theatrofilm. It seems that almost every scholar considering the phenomenon of the distribution of theatre performances beyond the theatre where the performance is taking place wants to use a different name for it. As Martin Barker described the sudden growth of such relays in the last decade, it is 'a success story with no name'.[1] Barker, having considered the term 'alternative content' as a 'rather roundabout "what it isn't" industry label', settled on 'livecast', a choice shared by Alison Stone.[2] A different choice might be needed when the focus of attention is a defined segment of the category that 'livecast' will not properly cover: Michael D. Friedman chose 'cinemacast' because he is examining 'these artefacts as broadcasts to cinemas', and is not limiting himself 'to a consideration of "live" or simultaneously shown versions of these performances'.[3]

The range of terms available points not only to the newness of both the event and the critical investigation of it but also to a taxonomic insecurity concerning precisely what is occurring. Take an example. On 12 October 2016 the Royal Shakespeare Company films a production of *King Lear* at that evening's performance and streams it to cinemas so that some audiences are watching it at virtually the same moment as those who are inside the Royal Shakespeare Theatre at Stratford-upon-Avon. But other audiences in other cinemas are soon watching it on a time delay, for the 'movie theatres' receiving the broadcasts on the east coast of the USA do not show them beginning at 2.30 p.m. The same cinema that showed the production at the same time as the performance may also choose to have an 'encore presentation' on a different day, using a hard drive either sent to the venue or with the files downloaded at the venue. The RSC releases the same streamed event on DVD soon after, using Opus Arte as their distributor, labelling it 'Live from Stratford-upon-Avon' and

40

adding some of the kinds of extra features that we expect on DVDs: a Director's Commentary (as a conversation between Gregory Doran and the Assistant Director Anna Girvan), cast gallery, interview with Antony Sher who played Lear, and a special feature, 'Dressed for the Stage: Creating Costumes for King Lear'.

I used the phrase 'same streamed event' but the DVD is not exactly the same as the simulcast: there is, for instance, no intermission, neither in extent (i.e. a fifteen-minute pause which may have been filled simply with a shot of the auditorium emptying or refilling or by conversations and comment with a host) nor by, say, inserting an intertitle reading 'Interval' of the kind used in long feature films. Not having seen the cinema broadcast I have no idea what happened during that time and I can only identify where the interval occurred because the Director's Commentary mentions it. The object, often assumed to be the same, proves to have undergone unmarked transformation. In the same way, Stephen Purcell's two viewings of the 2010 Donmar Warehouse King Lear were different: the first, the live broadcast, had an interruption of the visual feed, a disembodied announcement stopping the performance and then, once the fault had been resolved, the scene (4.6) was restarted, while the second, viewed in the National Theatre's archive, revealed that the technical fault and the first version of the scene had been edited out. The effect was to change the response of the theatre audience, for, having laughed at the first version, the spectators at the Donmar were silent as they watched the second.[4]

What I am beginning to outline is a set of distinctions created among the various forms of distribution and then transformed within the forms of consumption. Erin Sullivan, for a piece on the RSC's Richard II in the same cluster of reviews of 'Live Cinema Relays', watched the performance in Stratford-upon-Avon on successive days, first in the theatre and then in the town's cinema.[5] It is not only that the live experience in the theatre and the simultaneous or disjunct experience in the cinema are different forms of watching but also that, in Purcell's example, the experience in a cinema in Southampton and in the NT Archive are affected by the differences in the object. Those differences are also affected by the conditions of viewing: though Purcell does not need to comment on it, watching on a cinema screen with a large audience is very different from the solitary scholar viewing a monitor in an archive. As the conditions of spectatorship vary so too do the modes of perception: solitary scholarly watching of the archive copy with pen and paper to hand cannot be the same as the communality in the darkened cinema where the production can no more be paused and restarted than can the theatre event itself. Purcell's modes of twice-viewing were also necessitated by one way in which the *NT Live* broadcasts differ from those of the RSC, Shakespeare's Globe or the Shakespeare Festival in Stratford, Ontario – and indeed from the Metropolitan Opera in New York: where the others, even, after an initial reluctance, the Met, release performances on DVD, the National Theatre has to date steadfastly refused to do so, making its liveness a part of an ongoing ephemerality that produces alignment with, though not necessarily similarity to, live theatre.

One way of exploring this complex mess is to go back to the earliest example of the transfer of a complete theatre performance for viewing by cinema audiences, one that uniquely has a correct and unarguable descriptor: Theatrofilm. Of course, some of the earliest examples of filmed Shakespeare began from theatre performances, from the extracts from Beerbohm Tree's *King John* in 1899 through Benson's *Richard III* in 1911 and beyond. Along a parallel track, John Wyver has traced the history of nearly fifty British television adaptations of specific theatre productions.[6] But the key early example analogous to the current wave of transfers of productions to cinema screens came in 1964.

As part of the celebration of the 400th anniversary of Shakespeare's birth, Sir John Gielgud directed Richard Burton in a production of *Hamlet* at the Lunt-Fontanne Theatre on Broadway. Working with Warner Brothers and using a new system proudly dubbed Electronovision, an early version of videotaping, Bill Colleran directed the filming for the producer Bill Sargent, using seven cameras, taping three performances on 30 June and 1 July, towards the end of the run, and then editing the tapes beyond what had been done during the filming to produce a version that was then transferred to film for distribution.[7] The showings in close to 1,000 cinemas across the USA were tightly restricted to four, two per day on consecutive days in September 1964, by which time the Broadway performances had ended. The prints were all intended to be destroyed immediately thereafter. One was given to Burton and that was subsequently restored and released on DVD. 'Theatrofilm', as the experiment was named, was hyped to potential audiences but also to exhibitors. Buchanan quotes extensively from the marketing advice, full of emphatic caps: '"HAMLET" is a FIRST … [G]ear your thinking to terms of PRESTIGE, IMPORTANCE and STATUS … "HAMLET" and Richard Burton are BIG NEWS'.[8] Exhibitors were encouraged to transform their movie theatres with fresh flowers and to ensure that the washrooms were 'clean and freshly stocked – very important'.[9] Given the contemporary slang term for a cinema was a 'fleapit', the move was clearly about making them resemble the high(er)-cultural forms of theatres, enabling the community of spectators to recognise the experience as separate from and of greater cultural worth than the usual act of watching at these movie theatres.

Burton fronted a trailer, telling the audience:

> This has never happened before. The immediacy, the sense of *being there*, is unlike any experience you have ever known. This is the theatre of the future, taking shape before your eyes today and you will be there, part of this historic first.[10]

As the voice-over asserted, 'For the first time in history you'll see a live Broadway hit in your own motion picture theatre'.

The experience of a simulacrum of liveness has become a central issue in consideration of those broadcast over the last decade but the ambiguity was already present for Theatrofilm. Burton's interviewer, in another promotional piece, asserts that the audience at the screenings will 'enjoy the play live but not quite live'.[11] Burton claimed that the performances do not change for the camera:

> It is peculiarly unique ... because none of the actors make any concession to this new process; in other words we don't tone it down to seem like film actors or play it up because the cameras are perhaps a little further away than they would be in a movie studio or a television studio. It's played exactly as is and the result will certainly be unique, possibly extraordinary and possibly epoch-making.[12]

Accident and error are the markers of a guarantee of liveness and audiences connive at the possibility of their presence, even though the publicity here occluded the three recordings in the interests of the frisson of liveness. Burton claims, entirely inaccurately, that

> It will be exactly as they shot it in the theatre. There's no cheating of any kind, no trick shots on the top of somebody's head or anything like that. It is actually what you do see in the theatre.

The trick shot allusion is, I take it, to Olivier's film of *Hamlet* (1948) with its famous shot of the back of Hamlet's head at the start of 'To be or not to be'. But there is a slippage here between the fact that the film will be 'as they shot it in the theatre' and the apparent reassurance that '[I]t is actually what you do see in the theatre'. Yes, the result is made up of takes that are 'as they shot it', without any trickery in the processing of the materials beyond the selection that editing during and after filming involves. But no, it is not what a spectator would have seen, both because of the editing together of multiple performances but also because of the camera positions.

The positioning used now normally includes at the least the mobility of cameras along tracks. The camera plot for the 2014 *Coriolanus* 'cinemacast' that Friedman studied was based on five cameras, four of them on tracks behind the two rows of seats on three sides of the stage and one a TowerCam, 'rigged from above', as Tim van Someren, the cinemacast's director, defines it, that, in Friedman's summary, 'can move up and down a telescoping column, as well as pan, tilt, zoom and focus remotely'.[13] Few of the shots using the TowerCam are angles accessible to any member of the audience and, since the tracks for the other four are behind the rows of seats, nor are their positions those of any 'live' spectator. In the infographic Buchanan reproduces for a nine-camera Electronovision set-up, two more than used for *Hamlet*, six are shown in positions that are effectively theatre seats, one is behind the seats at audience right, and two are upstage angled across the performance space. That is analogous to the camera placings used for *Hamlet*: mostly in the stalls, one in the circle giving a high-angle wide-shot and one in the wings on audience left. The latter two are used fairly rarely, with the one in the wings solely as a way of catching Burton's face when he faces away from the audience and towards the wings, giving the film audience a chance to see something no seat in the theatre made possible.

As Philip Auslander argued, early television deliberately sought to replicate theatre:

> [t]he multiple-camera set-up enables the television image to recreate the perceptual continuity of the theatre. Switching from camera to camera allows the television director to replicate the effect of the theatre spectator's wandering eye.[14]

This aim was particularly strong at the point at which all television was being broadcast live, a phenomenon that is often now forgotten: repeats of early television drama necessitated the actors repeating the performance, making it more like theatre and hence more like livecasts than like Theatrofilm.

The filming of live performance on early television created its own grammar of shot selection. Once the language of camera positions and editing has been established audiences tend to notice the choices only when the conventions are disrupted, when the director or editor deliberately seeks – or accidentally manages – to make the viewer aware of such decisions. When, for instance, Peter Brook in his *King Lear* film (1971) chooses to place the camera so that half an actor's face is in shot and half is beyond the frame or when he edits the scene of Lear's reunion with Cordelia so that there is no establishing shot of the room and the physical location of the characters in relation to each other until Lear's recognition has taken place, we know that these choices create meaning. At other times, camera movement can belie the claim of liveness that purports to define the event. There is no shot in the Burton *Hamlet* that is not from the live broadcast. But, while the film of the English Shakespeare Company's *Richard II*, directed by Michael Bogdanov (1990), is supposedly 'Recorded live at the Grand Theatre, Swansea', Bogdanov acknowledges that some scenes were shot in the afternoons, not during the evening's performance in front of a theatre audience.

Bogdanov's treatment of 1.4 or, as he labels it, 'the Dinner Table Scene', would seem to be part of one afternoon's work. He had intended this to be shot from a crane but there 'was not enough room to operate it on stage and it was expensive'.[15] The scene opens with a close-up of a candelabra, moving back to show men at a table, drinking port, smoking cigars. The camera moves from the view over Aumerle's left shoulder, round the table (catching sight of other diners), to a point looking over Richard's right shoulder down at Aumerle, and then moving back round to end with the same shot of the candles that had begun the scene. One shot is all the scene needed and the result is powerfully effective. But at no point does it define where the audience is in relation to the table; the actors speak across the table and they are placed all round it, without the usual convention of one side being clearly towards the audience, with mutes seated with their backs towards the house, or with the table set on a diagonal. As good as it is, the shot/scene shows a disconnect from the liveness elsewhere, not only through the polish of the camera-work but also through the non-live, non-theatricalised intimacy and privacy of the performances. The actors speak in the knowledge of the closeness of the camera and boom-mike, not trying to fill the large spaces of the Grand Theatre, Swansea. It is a gem of a scene but one set in a context of messiness that is part of this version of live recording and the direct result of trying to film the productions of both history tetralogies in a single week.

By comparison with the frenetic chaos such a schedule produced, the current broadcasts are prepared with an almost obsessive care over a substantial period of time. John Wyver, who acts as Screen Producer for the RSC's 'Live from Stratford-upon-Avon' series, has detailed each step in the process.[16] The series began with *Richard II*, recorded and live-streamed on 13 November 2013. David Tennant, who played the King, has such an enormous fan-base from his days as Doctor Who that the cinemas were packed. It seems a deliberately symbolic act that the very first shot of a series that will finally and quickly include all Shakespeare's plays should be one that would fit Burton's notion of a 'trick shot'. The first image is a strong, perhaps even startling, overhead shot, looking straight down at a woman, hunched down beside a draped coffin, her arm stretched out over it, clearly in grief, before the camera moves back and down, we hear the sound of feet, and people start to come into shot, taking up formal positions behind and beside the coffin, while projections on to the curtains of thin chains behind them create the image of a grand medieval interior but which the foreground revealed as a thrust stage with audience members either side of it, the shot lasting a long 80 seconds, with no dialogue, only the sound of three angelic women's voices, accompanied by a solo trumpet, the singers seen in the gallery, before finally cutting to a medium shot of the two old men, one either side of the coffin, one in tears, grief-stricken, the other patting the mourning woman's arm comfortingly.

Though for Gregory Doran, the production's director, the quality of the filming lies precisely in the fact of its invisibility ('what I think is excellent about the camera-work is that it never draws attention to itself'),[17] I cannot see this opening shot as *not* drawing attention to itself. Everything about it makes one notice it: its length, the opening position directly over the stage, and its virtuosic use of the Moviebird forty-four crane which was placed in the stalls and necessitated the removing of a number of seats. Looking straight down at the grieving immobile Duchess of Gloucester beside her husband's coffin is impossible in the theatre. On the other hand, it is striking, thrilling, a shot that vividly engages our attention. Over-used it could become a cliché: the trailer for the March 2015 relay of the Manchester Royal Exchange production of *Hamlet* that starred Maxine Peake as Hamlet has no fewer than five overhead shots from five different scenes in the course of the 90-second piece.[18] The opening shot in *Richard II* is echoed at the end of the performance, just as the closed coffin of Thomas of Woodstock meta-morphoses into the open coffin containing Richard dragged in by Aumerle. This final shot lasts 110 seconds, moving very slowly from long shot in on Bolingbroke before it angles up to see Richard's ghost in the gallery, catching sight of him in a way that the theatre audience, which can see the actor moving into position, usually does not manage.

Above all, the crane made possible a powerful and intimate close-up in 3.3 at Flint Castle. At the core of the scene – indeed, one could argue, at the core of the entire production – was the moment where Richard looked at the weeping Aumerle, consoled him by stroking his head, saw in Aumerle's eyes the love that Richard had never seen or felt before (I summarise here Doran's own analysis) and, as the camera cut to an even tighter close-up, lent towards him and kissed him. This was, for Wyver, 'very different from anything you could achieve in the theatre, wherever you were sitting, and that underlined the kind of grandeur ... but also the pathos and the desperate sadness of the scene' and Gregory Doran willingly assented: 'Nobody in the audience got that shot. Nobody got that closeness'.[19] I agree, of course, that no audience member could be that close to this potent emotional moment but, nonetheless, every member of the audience was, in a sense, straining towards that close-up, focusing their own gaze as tightly on the move as the camera did.

Though the crane continues to be used in the filming of the RSC's productions, there are, by my count, strikingly fewer 'bravura moments', as Erin Sullivan has called them.[20] In Doran's *King Lear*, the sudden cut to a high-angle shot of Lear on 'All the stored vengeances of heaven fall / On her ingrateful top!' (2.2.335–6) is all the more marked for offering a rare heaven's eye view of the fulminating Lear. But sometimes the bravura lies in restraint. The long conversation of Lear and the Fool in 1.5, a scene dubbed by Doran 'The bus-stop scene', is shot in two versions of a tight shot, one from each side as it were, with the only exception being a long shot of the two from the bottom lip of the stage that then slowly zooms in on them. Moving precisely in its simplicity and with the editing mirroring something of the stillness of the characters here, the shot-choices and editing support the downplayed desperation, leaving us unable to intervene on this painfully growing awareness of Lear that he 'did her wrong'.

Of course, it is of the very nature of the filming of live theatre that certain film conventions become impossible or at the very least impracticable. As Barker noted, dialogue is 'largely ... shown by means of two-shots, as against over-the-shoulder shot-and-reverse (the norm for much film and television)'.[21] Barker ascribes this choice to a hypothesised requirement that 'cameras must not obtrude for the present audience' but that seems to me to be mistaken. Characters in plays by and large do not face each other squarely when talking to each other, for they also need to connect to the theatre audience. Distances between actors on stage are also nothing like those of, say, realist television drama. On the largely bare stage for contemporary Shakespeare performance, angles and distances are, then, such as to make shot-and-reverse itself seem odd, disconnecting the actors from the stage space and the relationship with the audience for which the production has been created and which the live broadcast needs to represent.

The balance in the camera positions for any scene relies on a tension between the extent of the stage space and the mobility of the actors. At times this can produce a predictable dullness about the camera-work. Des McAnuff's 2011 version of *The Tempest* for the Stratford Shakespeare Festival in Ontario, starring Christopher Plummer (dir. for television by Shelagh O'Brien) always shifts from close-up to medium shot as soon as the actor speaking starts to move. In the same way, Robin Lough, who has directed the majority of the livecasts for the RSC, the National Theatre and Shakespeare's Globe, shot Polly Findlay's RSC production of *The Merchant of Venice* (2015) with an almost unremitting focus on the speaking actor shot from waist up. Inevitably, the cinema audience wants to see the speaker in Shakespeare; it would not be satisfied with a reaction shot that left the character speaking as off-screen presence. This problematises the filming of long speeches, but indeed almost any speech longer than a couple of lines necessitates a continuous focus on the speaker that can be boring. Theatre audiences can choose to look away; cinema audiences are assumed to prefer that the camera does not look away.

Obviously, the physical structure of the auditorium makes or refuses to make particular options practicable. This has been most marked at Shakespeare's Globe, not least in the decision to create their filmed productions out of tapings of more than one performance, thereby obviating the risk of helicopters hovering noisily and disruptively overhead or sudden downpours and the other incidental and uncontrollable aspects that are part of the Globe experience. But as crucial a part of that experience is the sustained awareness of the physical structure itself, consequent both on the shared light between audience and stage and the elaborate ornamentation of the stage itself, something that makes it impossible not to see it. The multiple takes and editing recall the techniques of Theatrofilm but the Globe has also allowed for cinema screenings only at a substantial time-gap from the original production. The resultant film is also released on DVD and available through the Globe Player that allows one-time rental streaming or long-term purchase of productions over the last few years and including the cycle of productions from around the world that formed the Globe to Globe festival season in 2012.

As Erin Sullivan comments on one example of the Globe filming, they had adopted 'a filming style that's not dissimilar to the theatre's typical approach to playing: clear, measured, technically spare, simple but hopefully not simplistic'.[22] There are, though, two characteristics that are also dominant. The first is the heavy emphasis on a wide-shot of the full width of the stage structure, making the nature of that space repeatedly and emphatically visible in ways that are never as true of RSC or NT Live filming. That also involves shots across the yard, showing and sharing the crowd of spectators, the visible presence of the community of audience that, while occasionally present in the other filming spaces, is never as central to playgoing as in the Globe. The second is the problem of voice. Of course actors at the Royal Shakespeare Theatre are

48

projecting into a large auditorium but that never involves the volume that is necessary at the Globe (hence the experiment with the actors wearing microphones to amplify their voices during the 2016 and 2017 seasons).[23] The result can make the viewer of the filmed event hear the actors as shouting, creating a proxemic disjunction from the other character to whom they are speaking.

My emphasis here on camera positions and shot-choices echoes the work of other scholars and has been a primary feature of critical study of these broadcasts. In itself, the filming of theatre has provoked our awareness of these areas of filmmaking to an extent completely without parallel in the extensive library of critical work on Shakespeare on film where even passing references to camera-work are still remarkably rare. 'Live from' films, in the interconnection of two forms of spectatorship (in theatre and cinema), provoke the consciousness of the screen director's choices within the physical space of the theatre and in the processes of live-editing. Spectatorship itself becomes foregrounded as the act of watching shifts from our freedom, albeit from the limited point of view of the purchased seat, to the control mechanisms of the remediation to film.

Alone among the different companies' filming methods, the NT Live broadcasts, the first regular transmissions of theatre performances, maintain something of their liveness. Yes, they have from the start had 'encore' performances, allowing repeats and time-shifting. Yes, certain performances (Benedict Cumberbatch as Hamlet in Lyndsey Turner's production at the Barbican Theatre and Cumberbatch again, alternating Monster and Frankenstein with Jonny Lee Miller in Danny Boyle's production of *Frankenstein*) return some years later. But there is a commitment to the versions not being available on DVD and therefore being evanescent as well as always to be seen within the context of cinema audiences – and also therefore necessitating for researchers a trip to the NT archives. The act of watching is then always communal, always within the context of an audience watching another audience watching the production.

But two other characteristics of the NT Live format have been significant. The first is the strong emphasis on the audience in the pre-show sequence so that, as we settle into our seats in the cinema, we watch the playgoers settle into their seats in the theatre. The supposed, though often false, simultaneity of the event, encouraging us to analyse the demographics of the audience or to people-watch, is underscored. By comparison, the RSC's *Merchant of Venice* focuses on the audience only as they leave, with the credits rolling over a shot of the rapidly emptying auditorium. Expectation, that buzz of anticipation that is so exhilarating a part of live performance and which is never as strong in the cinema, is, then, usually made visible and emphatic. The second is the framing of the event by Emma Freud, whose management describes her as 'the public face of the National Theatre'.[24] As Sullivan notes, 'this sometimes heavy-handed framing is rather like being forced to read the programme before the performance begins'.[25] Others have been more irritated: as a columnist in *The Guardian* fulminated, 'The next shock was finding that I had come to see *Coriolanus* starring Emma Freud … the appearance of Ms Freud on screen, whipping us into a frenzy about what we were about to see, was at best superfluous … and at worst obstructive'.[26] Freud's introductions and interval conversations show that NT Live has, in this, copied the Met Opera livecasts, often fronted by Renée Fleming. Quite how to understand the cultural anxiety of transmitting theatre or opera to cinema audiences that this framing manifests is a vexed issue. I would want to compare it with the fresh flowers recommended for exhibitors of Theatrofilm. It marks the division of the cinema audience from the usual live theatre audience, the former now seen as needing assistance, information, encouragement and access to celebrities (the presenter herself and those members of cast and creative team she interviews).

We are at the start of understanding the phenomenon of these transmissions but one aspect needs a final emphasis: the peculiar dominance of Shakespeare within this programming. NT Live did not start with Shakespeare but with Racine's *Phèdre* starring Helen Mirren before moving on to *All's Well That Ends Well*, deliberately chosen as an unfamiliar Shakespeare play and without any star names in the cast. Since then, as well as including all of the National Theatre's Shakespeare productions, NT Live's broadcasts of productions from other theatres have been dominated by Shakespeare: for example, the Turner-Cumberbatch *Hamlet* (2015) from the Barbican, the Grandage-Jacobi *King Lear* (2010) and Rourke-Hiddleston *Coriolanus* (2014) both from the Donmar Warehouse, and Hytner's *Julius Caesar* from the Bridge Theatre (2018). Add to that the fact that only other UK companies undertaking such transmissions (Shakespeare's Globe, the RSC and the Kenneth Branagh Theatre Company) all only broadcast Shakespeare productions – no trace from the RSC of, say, Webster or Jonson – and the absolute supremacy of Shakespeare is overwhelming. Whatever else Theatrofilm began and livecast, cinemacast and the other terms continue, it is plainly confirmation of the cultural capital invested in Shakespeare, whether on screens or live.

Notes

1. Martin Barker, *Live to Your Local Cinema* (Basingstoke, Macmillan, 2013), 1.
2. Barker, 10–11; Alison Stone, 'Not making a movie: the livecasting of Shakespeare stage productions by the Royal National Theatre and the Royal Shakespeare Company', *Shakespeare Bulletin* 34.3 (2016), 627–43.

3. Michael D. Friedman, 'The Shakespeare cinemacast: Coriolanus', *Shakespeare Quarterly*, 457–80, 457 n.1.
4. Stephen Purcell, '*King Lear* performed by the Donmar Warehouse', *Shakespeare Bulletin*, 32.2 (2014), 264–6, 266.
5. Erin Sullivan, '*Richard II* performed by the Royal Shakespeare Company', *Shakespeare Bulletin*, 32.2 (2014), 272–5.
6. John Wyver, *Screening the Royal Shakespeare Company. A Critical History* (London, Bloomsbury/Arden Shakespeare, 2019).
7. By far the best account of the process is by Judith Buchanan in '"Look here, upon this picture": Theatrofilm, the Wooster Group *Hamlet* and the film industry', in Gordon McMullan and Zoe Watts, eds., *Shakespeare in Ten Acts* (London, British Library, 2016), 197–214, esp. 200–3. See also Laurie E. Osborne, 'Speculations on Shakespearean cinematic liveness', *Shakespeare Bulletin*, 24.3 (2006), 49–65, esp. 51–2.
8. Buchanan, 'Look here, upon this picture', 200–1.
9. Ibid., 202.
10. My transcription from the trailer on the DVD.
11. My transcription from the interview on the DVD.
12. Ibid.
13. Friedman, 'The Shakespeare cinemacast', 465, especially figure 4.
14. Philip Auslander, *Liveness* (London, Methuen, 1999), 19.
15. Michael Bogdanov and Michael Pennington, *The English Shakespeare Company: The Story of 'The Wars of the Roses' 1986–1989* (London, Nick Hern Books, 1990), 229.
16. See Wyver, '*Screening the Royal Shakespeare Company*', ch. 6, 'Now-ness: 2000–18'.
17. Gregory Doran in Gregory Doran and John Wyver, 'Director's commentary', on *Richard II* (DVD, London, 2014).
18. See 'Maxine Peake as Hamlet', www.youtube.com/watch?v=q4xVwVwGvPc (accessed 2 February 2018).
19. Doran and Wyver, 'Director's commentary'.
20. Erin Sullivan, '"The forms of things unknown": Shakespeare and the rise of the live broadcast', *Shakespeare Bulletin*, 35.4 (2017), 627–62, esp. 648–55.
21. Barker, *Live to Your Local Cinema*, 13.
22. Sullivan, 'The forms of things unknown', 641.
23. Actors in broadcasts from the National Theatre also wear microphones, often awkwardly visible when the costume or wig will not adequately conceal them, but these are for sound recording for the broadcast, not a permanent feature of the production.
24. 'Emma Freud', COBH, http://cobj.co.uk/client/emma-freud (accessed 8 April 2020).
25. Sullivan, 'The forms of things unknown', 635.
26. See Ryan Gilbey, '*Coriolanus* at the Natoinal Theatre Live: cut the chat and get on with the show', *Guardian* 31 January 2014, www.theguardian.com/stage/2014/jan/31/coriolanus-national-theatre-live (accessed 6 February 2018).

4

MARK THORNTON BURNETT

Shakespearean Cinemas/Global Directions

Once pushed to the sidelines of scholarly enquiry, world cinema is increasingly seen as central to the field of Shakespeare on film. As a wealth of examples begin to be appreciated, so do new methodological approaches present themselves. In this chapter, I consider several directions through the field while acknowledging that no one interpretive method can do justice to the variety of filmic engagements with Shakespeare across the globe. What this chapter suggests, instead, is that different approaches have different utilities and that combining a spectrum of modes of understanding illuminates a corpus of material that only now is being critically integrated. Inside the discipline of Shakespeare and film studies, the world Shakespeare film has traditionally featured only in terms of a small sample of figures; one methodological approach, therefore, has been predominantly auteur-based.[1] This chapter begins with the auteur approach while recognising that it needs to be supplemented. Accordingly, I suggest here additional strategies which privilege regional perspectives, time-bound moments of production and reception, the woman practitioner, and the place of particular plays in the adaptive process. Using examples throughout, I hope both to contribute to the evolving screen canon while making visible the methodological challenges and joys necessarily entailed in any encounter with world Shakespeare.

World Shakespeare films have conventionally been illustrated through discussion of Russian and Japanese auteurs, Grigori Kozintsev and Akira Kurosawa. In his pairing of films, *Gamlet/Hamlet* (1964) and *Korol' Lir/ King Lear* (1971), Kozintsev distinctively draws upon recognisably bleak and northern environs, with Estonian locations discovering the players as in thrall to larger, inhuman forces and profoundly implicated in their worlds. That this has a political complexion is clear from the wide-shot processions of peasants that haunt *Korol' Lir* and the presence in *Gamlet* of communist-style busts of Claudius. As John Collick notes, this is a cinema primarily interested in the relation between 'populist themes' and the 'corrupting processes of absolute power'.[2] Across the two films, the effects of an unrelenting system upon the individual take on an elemental dimension. *Korol' Lir* is cut through with raging fires and scenes of carnage, while the costs of inhabiting a hostile landscape are graphically realised in the silhouettes of lonely figures toiling up a hillside or the spectacle of Lear (Yuri Yarvet) emerging from parched grasses nibbling on a wizened vegetable. *Gamlet* is cast in the same mould, with Hamlet (Innokenti Smoktunovski) frequently lensed against the oppressive castle's walls, which are studded with forbidding faces. For Ophelia (Anastasiya Vertinskaya), a sense of incarceration is powerfully suggested in shots of her stifling black ruff and of a parrot in a cage: she is hemmed in by custom and convention. Yet this is not to deny both films' efforts to endorse something more ameliorative. *Gamlet* concludes with a funeral procession in which the titular protagonist is taken out of the castle towards the sea, suggesting release. It is on a rocky beach that Hamlet delivers an affirmatively angled 'To be, or not to be' soliloquy, and it is over the ocean that we witness a seagull rising upwards, the sign of Ophelia's departing spirit. Similarly, in *Korol' Lir*, the recurrence of the motif of water in scenes centred on the care of Lear hints at compassion and even resistance, these associations being reinforced in the transformative smiles of Cordelia (Valentina Shendrikova) and the flute playing of the Fool (Oleg Dahl) that continues in the midst of devastation. Symbol, place and tonal detail belong with a rich *montage* that hinges on a dynamic conception of social interrelations.

If Kozintsev's films take place in semi-mythical northern landscapes, Kurosawa's unfold in intensely localised environments. His *Throne of Blood* (1957), an adaptation of *Macbeth*, and *Ran* (1985), an adaptation of *King Lear*, take codes and conventions from Japanese history and tradition: in this regard, it is notable that *Ran* bases itself on the *jidai geki*, meaning 'period drama', and that *Throne of Blood* exploits its connections to the *ge-koku-jo*, the narrative of a retainer who dispatches his superior only to assume his power. Above all, it is in the use of stylised modes culled from Noh theatre that *Throne of Blood* and *Ran* reveal a local purchase; when these come into conflict with realist action sequences, suggestive cinematic effects follow.[3] For example, because they are consequent upon the destruction of his troops, in the more theatrically oriented scenes in the rocky wastes devoted to Hidetora/Lear's (Tatsuya Nakadai) madness in *Ran*, the wild and colourful appearance of the protagonist appears inseparable from a mask or persona.

Likewise, when Asaji/Lady Macbeth (Isuzu Yamada), who, for much of *Throne of Blood*, is marked by a Noh-like stillness and poise, breaks with formality and is seen frantically washing, it is the conjunction of different representational idioms that impresses. Via such processes of cultural reorientation, Shakespeare emerges as a continually evolving repository of meaning. Transposition and reinvention – because they take place in languages other than English – direct attention back to the valences of the Shakespearean word. Hence, *Ran*'s reworking of Cordelia into the figure of Saburô (Daisuke Ryû), the brusque-speaking youngest son who challenges his father, prompts us to reflect on his precursor's relative lack of language. Similarly, *Throne of Blood*'s detailing of horses running wild presses us to recall the conjuration in *Macbeth* of horses that 'flung out, / Contending 'gainst obedience'.[4] The same might be said for *The Bad Sleep Well* (1960), Kurosawa's less well-known dystopian adaptation of *Hamlet*, which is set in modern-day Tokyo and utilises *film noir* to examine corporate corruption. The film echoes the play's rhetorical expressions of madness in the embittered scowl of Nishi/Hamlet (Toshirô Mifune), struggling with familial obligations. The compelling character of all three films resides precisely in Shakespearean conjurations and in a productive meshing between thematic suggestion and visual experience.

A more recent entrant into the Shakespeare and world cinema auteur category is Indian director Vishal Bhardwaj, whose trilogy of Shakespearean adaptations has garnered international acclaim. *Maqbool* (2004), or *Macbeth*, innovatively transposes the action of the play by taking Mumbai as its location and subject, substituting for royalty the citizens of the city's underworld, mobster Abbaji/Duncan (Pankaj Kapur) and Maqbool/Macbeth (Irfan Khan), his henchman. Other inventive interpolations include the sequence centred on a visit to a *dargah* (the shrine of a *sufi* saint). As the song of the *qawwals* or singers gathers pace, it becomes self-evident that the address to the godhead simultaneously illuminates the developing intimacy between Maqbool/Macbeth and Nimmi/Lady Macbeth (Tabu), mistress to Abbaji/Duncan: so is the 'Bollywood' convention of the pilgrimage enlisted to highlight spiritual-sexual friction. In *Omkara* (2006), or *Othello*, creativity is at work in the ways in which Omkara (Ajay Devgan), a *bahu bali* or political enforcer in Uttar Pradesh, is presented as, in the words of an objector, a 'damned half-caste', the offspring of a 'bloody slave girl'. Refracting political discussion about India's systems of classification, the identification forms part of the fabric of the film, being affirmed in light-dark cinematography (Dolly/Desdemona [Kareena Kapoor] is distinguished by her fair complexion) and references

54

to Krishna, the 'Dark Lord' of the Indian epics. Constructions of racial divisions are read through other classic stories in such a way as to point up the film's contemporary sensitivities. In a more controversial transposition, *Haider* (2014) shifts the action of *Hamlet* to Kashmir in the 1990s, situating itself in a contested regional space marked by an ongoing history of insurgency. Innovative is the trajectory traced by Haider/Hamlet (Shahid Kapoor) himself: first glimpsed in a green bomber jacket, he is later seen in chequered Kashmiri *pheran*, the garment of choice for Kashmiri separatist leaders, suggesting a radical alteration to how he envisages his *dharma* or duty in relation to his political allegiances. Haider/Hamlet's 'To be, or not to be' dilemma – whether to join the forces of resistance or to submit to subordination – is at the core of the film, and it is only at the close, when he walks away from the blood-strewn, snowy cemetery, that an alternative scenario is suggested.

In such modifications, rewritings and amplifications, the auteur status of Bhardwaj is made abundantly manifest. Yet Bhardwaj's *oeuvre*, like that of Kozintsev and Kurosawa before him, could be differently inflected and assessed. For example, his films might equally well be approached inside a regional perspective: certainly, in India, as recent studies attest, the plethora of film adaptations of Shakespeare, across many Indian languages, is finally gaining overdue recognition.[5] A regional approach is facilitative in several ways. Dudley Andrew notes that the concept of a 'regional cinema' nicely demonstrates how films inhabit local and global or 'glocal' spheres of interaction, and his argument seems particularly applicable to two Asian adaptations, *Go!* (dir. Yukisada Isao, 2001), from Japan, and *Jarum Halus* (dir. Mark Tan, 2008), from Malaysia.[6] Both films centre on conflicted relations between nations and cultures and illustrate how Shakespeare, in Asia, can be marshalled interrogatively to ventilate issues around race, identity and history. An adaptation of *Romeo and Juliet* concerned with unstable and occluded constituencies, *Go!* (dir. Yukisada Isao, 2001) centres on the plight of the *zainichi*, as represented in Sugihara/Romeo (Yôsuke Kubozuka), those individuals of Korean descent who fled the Japanese occupation of Korea and who can be marginalised in present-day Japanese society. So it is that the school gates in the film, the basketball court and even Sakurai/Juliet (Kou Shibasaki) herself operate as ciphers of antipathy, reinforcing the concern of *Go!* with the legacies of the past. The film opens with an on-screen quotation – 'What's in a name? That which we call a rose / By any other word would smell as sweet' (2.1.85–6) – but replaces it quickly with Sugihara/Romeo's embittered voiceover: 'Race, homeland, nation, unification ... makes me sick', he states. The litany of terms, it is implied, constitutes Sugihara/Romeo's translation of Juliet's question from a vexed Korean-Japanese point of view. Even when Sugihara/Romeo does reveal himself, it is to a hostile reception: 'Pop told me ... Don't go out with Koreans ... blood of ... Koreans ... is dirty', Sakurai/Juliet protests. For all it may be discounted, then, nomenclature, as in *Romeo and Juliet*, is seen to function in insidiously adversarial ways. Yet, as its title and dynamic *mise-en-scène* make clear, the film is ultimately concerned with embracing a better society. At the end, Sugihara/Romeo and Sakurai/Juliet leap over the school gates in a shared confrontation with barriers. The simultaneous exclamation – 'What am I? ... I'm me!' – discovers Sugihara/Romeo rejecting the *zainichi* label and claiming his own mode of selfhood. And, via the concluding detail of snow falling on 'Christmas Eve', *Go!* symbolically incorporates into its Japanese vision western paradigms of new beginnings and, notably, the implied reparation of colonial injustice.

With *Go!*, therefore, personal emancipation can be celebrated inside national-cultural histories and tensions, and this involves both a rejection of patriarchal prejudice and an affirmation of self that is not constrained by political praxes. The opposite scenario is developed in *Jarum Halus*, a Malaysian adaptation which, set in contemporary Kuala Lumpur, centres on the Chinese Daniel/Othello (Christien New) as the central figure of alterity. A successful executive at 'Eco-Tech', Daniel/Othello shows authority, confidence and skill, as illustrated in his leading colleagues through 'the new electronic system' and his key role in welcoming the company's German partners. He is as vital to 'Eco-Tech' operations as the 'Valiant Othello' (1.3.48) is to maintaining Venetian supremacy. Adding to the sense of Daniel/Othello's meritocratic rise is the wonderfully sewn handkerchief – the title, *Jarum Halus*, refers to needlework – gifted to Mona/Desdemona (Juliana Ibrahim) as a token of his love. Informing Mona/Desdemona that the handkerchief is the work of his mother, Daniel/Othello explains, 'different pieces of fabric became one masterpiece ... I look at my life like this', his use of a tailoring analogy suggesting his successful integration into Malay society. But *Jarum Halus* gradually reveals that Daniel/Othello is actually adrift in a system that, historically, has been geared, as Jacqueline Lo writes, to protect 'Malay political and cultural supremacy' against 'non-Malay interests'.[7] Repeated shots of the signature buildings of Kuala Lumpur – the Petronas Twin Towers (headquarters of the global energy company), the Kuala Lumpur Tower (a communications hub from which phases of the moon are observed in preparation for Ramadan) and the UMNO skyscraper (the leading political party and promulgator of pro-Malay policies) – suggest adversarial forces of religion, government and globalisation as well as reinforcing Daniel/Othello's status as 'outsider'. Betrayed by Iskander/ Iago (Razif Hashim), who has played upon Daniel/Othello's doubts about his own identity, the protagonist murders Mona/Desdemona, asking, in Cantonese, 'Please wait for me a little longer. I'm coming to find you'. Invoking a Buddhist concept of the passage between worlds, Daniel/ Othello finally articulates himself as 'alien' and 'other'. The integrated utopia longed for in the handkerchief is affirmed only in Daniel/Othello's fantasy of the afterlife.

Neither *Go!* nor *Jarum Halus* attracted sustained attention in Japan or Malaysia, nor have these examples of Asian Shakespeare impacted on the field of Shakespeare and film studies. This is despite the fact that, as Alexa Alice Joubin notes, the 'first decade of the new millennium was for Asian cinematic Shakespeares as the 1990s had been for Anglophone Shakespeare on film'.[8] Joubin is reflecting here on big-budget martial arts Shakespeare films such as *The Banquet* (dir. Xiaogang Feng, 2006), a Chinese adaptation of *Hamlet*, but her comment reminds us of the need methodologically to recognise not only regional perspectives but also production and reception contexts as part of the warp and weft of the meanings of world cinema. Two films – *Hamile: The Tongo 'Hamlet'* (dir. Terry Bishop, 1965), from Ghana, and *Shakespeare Must Die* (dir. Ing K., 2012), from Thailand – suggest the validity of attending to a particular understanding of place *and* momentum. *Hamile* owes its genesis to a stage production of *Hamlet* at the University of Ghana, Legon, which was later made as a feature film by the Ghana Film Industry Corporation, a state-of-the-art production facility backed by Kwame Nkrumah, president of the newly independent Ghana, as part of a programme of artistic and cultural development. Not surprisingly, then, the film is preoccupied with a thematics of place, this showing itself in the dialogue (references to cities such as 'Timbuktu' [England] and 'Sokoto' [Vienna], geographically north of Ghana, suggest a will to situate Ghana at the imaginative centre of a networked African universe) and in the set, a specially built compound constructed to include arches, towers, individual chambers and steps – a type of amphitheatre in the round. In keeping with the film's ethos, the characters wear *kente* textiles, a traditional form of Ghanaian dress that was popularised by Nkrumah and came to function as a signifier of the nation's newly liberated status. To quote Joe de Graft, the director of the stage production, the film concatenated the pride and exuberance of Ghana in the early 1960s: 'there was an outburst of enthusiasm for our own way of doing things', he states.[9]

Shakespeare Must Die also taps into the *zeitgeist*, although in radically contrasting fashion. The film comprises two *Macbeth* narratives –

a theatrical production of *Macbeth* and a second *Macbeth* unfolding in the external world – which, in a tumultuous denouement, merge as one. Via the trajectory of Macbeth, the film constructs Thaksin Shinawatra (the controversial politician who served as Prime Minister of Thailand from 2001 to 2006) as morally and institutionally corrupt, offering up a critical vision bolstered by a representational allegiance between Thai theatre and radical comment. In this way, the film both springs from, and makes an ideological intervention in, its own political milieu. Telling, therefore, is the figuration of Mekhdeth/Macbeth (Pissarn Pattanapeeradej) as the 'butcher' of theatrical tradition – terror-racked, wild-eyed, oily, self-satisfied and cowardly. Referencing the volatility of its circumstances of making, *Shakespeare Must Die* privileges flashes of red (indexing the street clashes between rival political groupings, the 'Red Shirts' and the 'Yellow Shirts', that rocked the country between 2008 and 2010) and positions the witches against documentary footage of a ruined, post-agitation Bangkok. The film's most visceral and violent summoning of history occurs when the production's director is taken away by a gang of red-scarfed thugs who subject him to an extended lynching. As a representative of 'Shakespeare', the director 'must die'. Here, the film harks back to the Thammasat University Massacre. On 5 October 1976, students staged a satirical play which, judged to con-stitute an act of *lèse majesté* because of a supposed hanging scene, provoked a furious response: armed groups supported by the military entered the university and 300 students were subsequently killed. *Shakespeare Must Die*, then, rehearses histories past and present as part of its make-up, representing both an intervention in current politics and a species of trauma cinema that endeavours to make up for derelic-tions of memory through re-visitation and re-enactment.

Any approach to Shakespeare and world cinema that privileges the moment of production and reception will bring into play a range of histories. That is, how particular examples have been received and sub-sequently distributed must be an interpretive concern; in particular, reflecting on why some films (such as *Hamile* and *Shakespeare Must Die*) disappear from view after an initial showing or indeed non-showing can be helpful in understanding the contingencies and arbitrariness with which a canon evolves. In *Hamile*, the rebellion of Laertu/Laertes (Kofi Yirenkyi) is envisaged as a dangerous uprising (a grassroots political movement) from below – in the savannah, villagers emerge from and disappear into the trees – and, in February 1966, just five months after the film was released, President Nkrumah himself was overthrown by the police and military. *Hamile* was, along with other films produced by the

Ghana Film Industry Corporation, confiscated as an example of work that fed the president's personality cult, and no further screenings in Ghana were authorised. Echoing its own internal narrative, *Shakespeare Must Die* was in turn censored – screenings in Thailand were prohibited – by the Thai Film Censorship Board.[10] The narrative was officially perceived as fomenting discontent and jeopardising national security. Despite appeals and public protests, the ban continues. Both *Hamile*, which for many years was thought lost and survives only in a unique Library of Congress copy, and *Shakespeare Must Die*, which subsequent to the ban has only been seen at film festivals outside Thailand, are entries in Shakespeare and world cinema which bear witness to the effect of specific fields of reception or, rather, non-reception – praxes of censorship that dictate their relative invisibility on the critical scene.

Shakespeare Must Die is additionally distinctive in that it is helmed by Ing K., a female director. Included in the soundtrack to *Shakespeare Must Die* are extracts from the Rimsky-Korsakov symphonic suite, *Scheherazade*, based on *The Arabian Nights*, in which a sultan's new wife avoids execution by entertaining her husband with stories. Aligning herself with a woman who reverses a death sentence, Ing K. reflects self-consciously through the score on her own status as a female artist. Certainly, the few world Shakespeare films directed by women demand an approach that attends to a nexus of gender, creativity and directorial emphasis. *As Alegres Comadres* (dir. Leila Hipólito, 2003), a Brazilian adaptation of *The Merry Wives of Windsor*, and *El Triunfo/The Triumph* (dir. Mireia Ros, 2006), a Spanish adaptation of *Hamlet*, answer to this imperative. *As Alegres Comadres* is set in the nineteenth century and is filmed in the town of Tiradentes in the Brazilian state of Minas Gerais. Responsive both to the British heritage film and a utopian tendency in recent Brazilian cinema, it applies a palette of bright, primary colours, invests in wide-screen shots of blue skies, and invokes numerous temporal referents (such as the Maria Fumaça steam train) to declare its affiliations with a nostalgically infused vision of the national past. *El Triunfo/The Triumph* is also historically angled. Unfolding in the Barcelona neighbourhood of *El Ravel* in the 1980s, and prioritising a world that is eclipsed in shots of dark-lit narrow alleyways and puddled gutters, the film centres on Gandhi/Claudius (Juan Diego), a local crime boss and ex-legionnaire, and his memories of the wars in Spanish Morocco. The Hamlet figure, Nen (Antonio Fernández Montoya), a young *rumba catalana* singer, aspires to escape and make his mark in music: the 'triumph' in the title refers to his ambitions for a better life.

These films bear comparison in the ways in which they prioritise women's roles and perspectives. Doing so, they point up intersecting forces of gender, nation and agency. In *As Alegres Comadres*, Ana Lima/Anne Page (Talita Castro) is realised as a cipher for a variety of independent behaviours, suggesting how she functions as a test case for the possibility of non-conformity. Hence, in scenes of love-making with Franco/Fenton (Daniel Del Sarto), she demonstrates self-determination, rejecting parentally chosen suitors. Tellingly, these scenes unfold externally, rather than domestically, affirming the ways in which, as Julianne Pidduck notes, the transgression by the seemingly 'passive woman' of the 'threshold' in the heritage film endorses a 'desiring female gaze'.[11] Moreover, individual will is stamped with national associations. Thus, the appearance of Ana Lima/Anne Page in blue in the masque, flanked by characters in green and yellow, situates her as a metaphor for national unity: yellow, green and blue are the Brazilian flag's dominant colours. (Even before the masque, Ana Lima/Anne Page tries on green and yellow costumes, the idea being that national colours are implicated in her own destiny.) Consistently occupying the centre of the frame, Ana Lima/Anne Page expresses a free-wheeling spirit that is synonymous with the Brazil of modernity. By contrast, in *El Triunfo/The Triumph*, Barcelona is presented as a world divided along national and racial lines. Via scenes involving gang mayhem, the film captures the post-EU tensions of the metropolis, highlighting forces of immigration, and accompanying instabilities, that run counter to Spanish/European policy. In particular, as part of its vision of a Spain caught between the old and the new, *El Triunfo/The Triumph* accentuates the role of Ahmed/Fortinbras (Ahmed Krim), the new kingpin who supplants Gandhi/Claudius' rule. Adapting the film from a *Hamlet*-inspired novel by Francisco Casavella, Ros reflects, in interview, 'I did try to introduce a woman's point of view ... changing the method of narration, inventing new situations, writing some of the songs, and playing up the emotive rather than the physical'.[12] Certainly, Ros' gendered imprint is seen multiply – in a screenplay that departs from the novel, for instance, and in the foregrounding of Chata/Gertrude (Ángela Molina) as a woman buffeted between conflicting local, familial and romantic demands. As screenwriter, she introduces site-specific vernacular spins on Shakespearean language and, as composer, mediates the prose of the novel via the score.

Specifically, in providing the film with Catalan-language music, Ros speaks for a resurgence of Catalan cinema spearheaded by women practitioners and a growing attention to secessionist initiatives. In this film of remembering a former Barcelona, Ros flags the forces at play in the post-

Franco shift to democracy; in the same moment, her adaptation of *Hamlet* illuminates the multiple roles she is obliged to undertake as a creative – as woman, Catalonian and Shakespearean interpreter.

Clearly, Ing K., Hipólito and Ros all find in *The Merry Wives of Windsor*, *Macbeth* and *Hamlet* energies and applications that meet their distinctive ambitions and instincts. This invites us to consider the place of particular plays in the adaptive process. What continuities and discontinuities emerge when we take into consideration play-specific trajectories of interpretation? As earlier parts of this chapter have indicated, *Macbeth* is a well-visited port of call for politically responsive world filmmakers, and here one might suggest that *Throne of Blood* and *Shakespeare Must Die* allegorise, through *Macbeth*, narratives of a political rise and fall that prove immediate and resonant in Japanese and Thai contexts. Equally clear is the frequency with which *Romeo and Juliet* is returned to: *Go!* is but one example of a host of adaptations that envision the Shakespearean narrative of 'star-crossed lovers' in relation to deterritorialisation, urbanisation, demographic shifts, generational conflict and local realignments of gender and race. *Romeo and Juliet* partners with societies caught on the cusp of transition, arguably because the play itself is concerned with a coming of age. Yet it is *Hamlet* to which world filmmakers gravitate with a particular urgency: across all of the world's film industries, adapting *Hamlet* gives access to an eloquence not always permitted to practitioners as speaking subjects and, in conditions of seeming impossibility, allows for the possibility of representation. Cinematic *Hamlet* adaptations matter globally because pertinent conversations cannot always be held publicly, and the play is often mediated in the belief that the word and image can serve an interventionist, transformative purpose. The *Hamlet* story, transferred to the screen, enables social and political critique, to the extent that play can appear more barbed and weaponised that previously conceived.

Two examples – the first German and the second Slovakian – illustrate the multiple attractions of the play to world filmmakers. *Der Rest ist Schweigen/The Rest is Silence* (dir. Helmut Käutner, 1959) is set in the Ruhrgebiet, the industrial heartland of West Germany, and revolves around the identity crisis of John H. Claudius (Hardy Krüger) who returns home after twenty years in exile as Harvard University academic. John/ Hamlet is a philosophy professor with research specialisms in Heidegger and Sartre, a plot update consonant with his involvement in existentialism. The film is distinctive in the ways it gradually unveils Johannes Claudius/ Old Hamlet as having been pushed by his scheming brother into allowing his steelworks empire to manufacture armaments for the Nazi cause, becoming, in his son's estimation, a 'mass murderer'. The film is

structurally arranged so as to highlight a pervasive collective guilt, with
rebuffs and forgetfulness continually forestalling John/Hamlet in his mission to reveal the hidden narratives that shaped his family's involvement.
So it is that the sins of the father are visited on the son, with John/Hamlet's
psychologically vulnerable and dissatisfied state being linked to a traumatic
sense of complicity. In this connection, the reverberations of the film's title
multiply. In particular, 'silence' conjures both those things that are unmen-
tionable and 'cover-ups', extending the play's concerns. There is an echo of
this Shakespearean meaning in the opening credits. As the title comes into
view, splashes of crimson – in what is a monochrome palette – wash over
the lettering, suggesting victimisation, accountability and violence.
Beginning with the words of the play's end, *Der Rest ist Schweigen* con-
templates worlds after defeat and what is entailed in speaking to and about
repressed histories.

Der Rest ist Schweigen invites comparison with the later Slovakian
Hamlet adaptation, *Cigán/Gypsy* (dir. Martin Šulík, 2011), in that this
film, too, is concerned with accountability, legacies and effects. In the
wake of the collapse of communist systems and state socialism, *Cigán*
situates the action of *Hamlet* in a Roma shantytown in Richnava, Eastern
Slovakia, investing in scenes of desperation and disentitlement. Looming
large as a thematic is the fate overtaking traditional communities in the
late twentieth and early twentieth centuries, with *Cigán* charting the
residues of a post-communist moment and identifying material need as
the agent that shapes the lives of the most marginalised of Central and
East European populations. So it is that Adam/Hamlet (Jan Mizigar)
inhabits a shantytown on a scarred hillside; the 'goodly frame, the
earth' (2.2.289) appears a 'sterile promontory' (2.2.290), unforgiving
and inimical. In particular, the film uncovers systems of racism that are
shadowed in expressions of emasculation and processes of economic
humiliation. Forced to leave school and take on the breadwinner role
to help his mother, Adam/Hamlet is consistently rebuffed in his efforts at
improvement – subject to police brutality or ostracised from casual
employment. Throughout, the protagonist faces rejection, either from
the ethnomusicologists/players, who promise an engineering scholarship
and then fail to deliver, or from Julka/Ophelia (Martina Kotlarova) who
is sold to a 'Czech guy', blighting Adam/Hamlet's romantic aspirations.
When Adam/Hamlet stabs Žigo/Claudius (Miroslav Gulyas) to death,
there is no sense of an alteration in his circumstances. In the closing
tableau, Adam/Hamlet, waiting at a bus stop, is still caught in a cycle of
need, still bound for nowhere. The snow falls, with key Hamletian

questions about how to be and how to act finding no reply in an evocative but despairingly open-ended tableau.

To encounter Shakespeare in world cinema manifestations is to encounter a myriad of possibilities for understanding the plays and the ways in which the dramatist's work is engaged with through adaptation. It is to begin to appreciate some of many uses to which the plays are put and to be sensitive to the local and global significances of Shakespearean authority. This chapter has suggested a series of directions through Shakespeare and world cinema: the routes taken often overlap, but in that overlapping is a necessary attentiveness to the powerful work of adaptation. World Shakespeare films invite a different conception of Shakespeare, one that highlights the ongoing ways in which cinema generates new stories in order to resolve old histories or, alternatively, generates new stories in order to countenance histories still in the making.

Notes

1. The 'auteur' is generally understood as an individual artist possessed of a distinctive vision and credited with significant works across a career.
2. John Collick, *Shakespeare, Cinema and Society* (Manchester and New York, Manchester University Press, 1989), 129, 141.
3. Noh is a traditional Japanese musical-theatrical form characterised by stylised gestures and dance movements, masks and a declamatory delivery of dialogue.
4. William Shakespeare, *The Norton Shakespeare*, ed. Stephen Greeenblatt, Walter Cohen, Jean E. Howard and Katharine Eisaman Maus (New York, Norton, 1997), 2.4.16–17. All further references to Shakespeare's plays are to this edition and appear in the text.
5. Poonam Trivedi and Paromita Chavravarti, eds., *Shakespeare and Indian Cinemas: 'Local Habitations'* (London and New York, Routledge, 2018).
6. Dudley Andrew, 'Islands in the sea of cinema', in Kevin Rockett and John Hill, eds., *National Cinemas and World Cinema* (Dublin, Four Courts, 2006), 15.
7. Jacqueline Lo, *Staging Nation: English Language Theatre in Malaysia and Singapore* (Hong Kong, Hong Kong University Press, 2004), 15.
8. Alexa Alice Joubin, *Chinese Shakespeares: Two Centuries of Cultural Exchange* (New York, Columbia University Press, 2009), 12.
9. Joe de Graft, 'Interview', in Bernth Lindfors, ed., *Africa Talks Back: Interviews with Anglophone African Writers* (Trenton and Asmara, Africa World Press, 2002), 77.
10. See 'Press release', www.Shakespearemustdie.com.
11. Julianne Pidduck, *Contemporary Costume Film* (London, BFI, 2004), 26.
12. Interviews between Mireia Ros and Mark Thornton Burnett (1 and 8 December 2017).

PART II

Genres and Plays

5

RAMONA WRAY

The Comedies

This chapter argues that, across periods and media, Shakespeare's comedies on screen constitute a significant body of work that cross-fertilises and interrelates. Adopting innovative templates for re-imagining Shakespeare's 'green world' and Mediterranean settings, screen comedies have found unlikely homes in blighted riverscapes, Oxbridge quadrangles and Californian suburbs. Scriptwriters have pursued imaginative routes through the distinctive syntax of the comedies, and there has been considerable experiment here in terms of updating Shakespeare's language. Comedy is the screen genre where radical constructions of gender and sexuality are often expressed, filmmakers recognising in Shakespeare's comedies opportunities to explore the relationship between agency, voice and embodiment. The comedies on screen function to anticipate many of the themes and concerns energising recent criticism, and in this there is often a pronounced self-consciousness. Harking back to earlier screen experiments, the most recent Shakespearean comedies contemplate their own artifice and showcase strategies of revision dependent on a dense intertextuality. From carnivalesque constructions of the Renaissance to cult constructions of the American high school, Shakespeare's comedies on screen have helped to redefine the relationship between the dramatist and televisual/cinematic art.

A Midsummer Night's Dream is very often the filmmaker's comedy of choice, but there is also a strong tradition of adapting *As You Like It*, *Love's Labour's Lost*, *Much Ado About Nothing* and *The Taming of the Shrew*. Many of the earliest screen outings confront what is representationally involved in imagining the 'green world' – that 'staged realm of escape, recreation and clarification' which is the 'locus of the encounter' in Shakespearean comedy.[1] In *As You Like It* (dir. Paul Czinner, 1936), the country is envisioned as a retreat made up of majestic trees, sylvan glades and thatched cottages. By contrast, the court, lensed in dreamy long shots, is a shimmering, ethereal concoction adorned with water features, carved stonework and distant vistas. But the film simultaneously points up (through the development of key properties) how these seemingly distinctive locations are interlinked. If, at the start, fences separate Orlando (Laurence Olivier) and Oliver (John Laurie), and gates keep the populace at bay during the wrestling match, by the close these features are means of connection, the final scene revealing country swains and court officials moving through now open gates in a massed gesture of accord. Very different in conception is the later British independent feature *As You Like It* (dir. Christine Edzard, 1992). The film's aesthetics have little to do with the play's situation but are influenced by contemporary screen outings, such as Oliver Stone's *Wall Street* (1987). Accordingly, the adaptation unfolds in a grimy metropolis amid the world of finance (the corporate court is distinguished by plate glass, chandeliers, mirrors and see-through doors). Rosalind (Emma Croft) is transported not to a pastoral Arden but to an urban waste scarred by polythene tents and camp fires on the banks of the Thames. This is a dystopian parable, then, and anti-pastoral motifs are purposefully political. Images of the blighted water-side constitute a critique of Thatcher's Britain and spell out a narrative of national decline. Uniquely, the adaptation offers a downbeat conclusion. Decorative details of wasteland plastic (as clothes and curtains) in the final scenes suggest worlds which remain at odds with each other; yellowish lighting implies a sickly and polluted atmosphere; and repeated two-shots (shots in which the frame is occupied by two persons only) of couples talking together over the credits point up a divisive process and individuals who have not yet been integrated. A very different but still bold imaginative transposition is at work in *As You Like It* (dir. Kenneth Branagh, 2006). Set in a 'dream' of Japan, at the moment when the nation 'opened up for trade with the West', the film trades in signifiers such as a cross-dressed *kabuki* performer, a temple, cherry blossom, silk screens and raked gardens. Crucially, the film transmogrifies the court and country dialectic by emphasising the interpenetration of east and west. Dominating the production is Rosalind (Bryce Dallas Howard) who, brown peaked cap and rustic jerkin notwithstanding, is discovered as at home in the Japanese pastoral. Bringing to mind the journey to a 'place of escape' traditionally associated with the Shakespearean comedy, the coiling, walkway of reeds reveals a Rosalind anxious to learn from new cultural experiences.[2] The journey leads to Rosalind's donning of a *kimono* for her wedding and to a moment of *communitas* that affirms an instructive interaction between cultures: the camera's panning over mixed character groupings ratifies the meeting between east and west (costumes are traditionally European and Japanese) and makes a virtue of difference. Across all three examples, filmmakers adopt increasingly innovative templates for mediating the court/country contrast underpinning *As You Like It*, and, as they do so, the pursuit of new horizons is given strikingly visual and kinetic emphasis.

With adaptations that do not face the challenge of representing the 'green world', the need for bold imaginative transpositions is not as acute. Earlier productions of *The Taming of the Shrew* tended to point up an ornate Renaissance landscape. The earliest 'sound' adaptation, *The Taming of the Shrew* (dir. Sam Taylor, 1929), situates Petruchio (Douglas Fairbanks) and Katharina (Mary Pickford) amidst a grand environment filled with arched colonnades, twisting streets, decorated columns and ornate cathedrals, a sumptuous concoction of sixteenth-century suggestiveness. This is one of the first film adaptations that playfully delays Katharina's entrance. (A pronounced sense of a capricious, uncontrollable disposition is created as furniture is thrown from a room, doors slam and nervous servants rush up and down stairs.) The film's noisy domestic business works to dramatise the play's conflictual dynamics, while the positioning of Katharina's bedroom in the *mise-en-scène* – at the top of the magisterial staircase – suggests a space to be conquered by the athletic, roistering Petruchio. Indeed, Katharina is consistently shown against interiors such as rich wall hangings and patterned friezes: to win the 'shrew' means enjoying the property and wealth with which she is associated. Franco Zeffirelli's later film adaptation of *The Taming of the Shrew* (1967) also provides much to savour in its construction of a Renaissance 'Padua'. The camera's gaze settles on Petruchio's sensually appealing castle, undulating alleyways with quaint cobbles and brickwork, abundant greenery and laden orange-trees. Bathed in a surreal light, the setting blurs the boundaries between theatrical and filmic realms, enlisting an ideal of the Renaissance culled from play and painterly traditions and fired by those ideas of popular festivity and inversion associated particularly with the comedies. During the opening cathedral service, the soberly dressed undergraduates suddenly tear off their dun attire to reveal colourful carnival costumes beneath, vertiginous camerawork reinforcing how the solemn mass cedes place to jubilant misrule. Against such polarities the drama of Katharina (Elizabeth Taylor) and Petruchio (Richard Burton) plays out, their private battles finding a correlative in the holiday disorder beyond. In both the Taylor and the Zeffirelli adaptations, we are encouraged to spot parallels with 'real-life' couples – Pickford and Fairbanks, caught in a foundering marriage, and Burton and Taylor, known in the tabloids of the time as the 'Battling Burtons'. The process accords with what Douglas M. Lanier identifies as a filmic tendency to treat the play not as a tale of male dominance but as one of 'two strong-willed lovers forging a romantic *modus vivendi*'.[3] Zeffirelli in particular makes much of the celebrity status of his Katharina; in typically operatic fashion, her spectacularly dressed body eclipses all else in the extravagant frame. These are productions, then, that trade on a rich mix of celebrity, masculine bravado, bodily splendour and aesthetically arresting expressions of the 'Renaissance', animating and invigorating the Shakespearean comic narrative in the process.

Zeffirelli's influence on how Shakespearean comedy continues to be translated on screen is apprehended both in what have become conventions in comedic characterisation (Richard Burton's rough, ready and sexualised Petruchio prepares the way for Damian Lewis' similarly imagined Benedict in the 'Shakespeare Re-Told' 2005 *Much Ado About Nothing*) and in the popularising tendencies that have been furthered by later filmmakers. In common with Zeffirelli, for instance, Branagh casts internationally renowned names in his Shakespeare films and prioritises a shooting style premised on accessibility, vigour and pace. Above all, Branagh popularises Shakespeare's comedies on screen by threading through his interpretations the celebratory impulse traditionally seen as central to Shakespearean comedy, the move to 'harmony and reconciliation' that articulates a collective 'wish-fulfilment'.[4] In Branagh's *As You Like It*, for example, the spectacle of rain falling gently on a lush parkland decorated with prayer flags suggests reconciliation is accompanied by a general blessing and benediction. Similarly, in *Much Ado About Nothing* (dir. Kenneth Branagh, 1993), a festive momentum is maintained through what Mark Thornton Burnett terms 'structural splittings', scenes being cut across by other scenes, the effect of which is to accelerate movement.[5] As part of his heritage-influenced re-imagining, Branagh makes of the masque a set-piece. In this flame-lit, nocturnal episode, animated by laughter, applause, screams and fire-eaters, the camera focuses on intimate groups framed by dancers and the chapel beyond, a reminder of the nuptial narratives on which the action hinges. With its strategic alternation between close-ups and establishing shots of mask-wearing celebrants, the sequence translates Leonato's cue – 'The revellers are entering' (2.1.70) – into a wonderfully theatrical moment. In keeping with its buoyant outlook and sun-soaked Tuscan setting, *Much Ado About Nothing* culminates in a choric rendition of 'Hey Nonny Nonny'. The lushly orchestrated score and spectacle of couples twirling happily – affirmed by the craning camera's dizzying shot – argue forcefully for the value of a joyous, communal initiative. But achieving the communion and consensus demanded by festivity can also mean that the 'melancholy ... complications', as Gary Waller terms them, of some Shakespearean comedies need to be excised.[6] If the conclusion of *Love's Labour's Lost* unconventionally defers sexual consummation (as registered in its unprecedented, unresolved ending), Branagh's 2000 adaptation of the play makes up for what is deemed lacking. So, following upon a breakneck run-through of World War II via fictive interpolations and stock footage, *Love's Labour's Lost* ultimately presents viewers with a montage of D-Day in which the celebrations surrounding the now reunited couples function as a response to Shakespearean generic anomalousness. In this moment, Branagh rewrites Shakespeare to bring the comedies into line with linear narratives of cinematic romance.

Although Branagh's *As You Like It* follows the template of his earlier films in concluding with a confetti-strewn assembly of ebullient dancers, it is not a typical cinema release. *As You Like It* was funded by HBO essentially as a work for television, an indication both of contemporary screen developments and of the increasing kudos of television as a vehicle for the transmission of Shakespearean comedy. Television, of course, has long been attracted to Shakespeare, but rarely with such a comedic focus as in 'Shakespeare Re-Told', BBC's 2005 series of play adaptations, three out of four of which (*A Midsummer Night's Dream*, *Much Ado About Nothing* and *The Taming of the Shrew*) are comedies. Finding inspiration in commercially successful youth-oriented adaptations of *As You Like It*, *The Taming of the Shrew* (*Ten Things I Hate About You* [dir. Gil Junger, 1999]), and *Twelfth Night* (*She's the Man* [dir. Andy Fickman, 2006]), the 'Shakespeare Re-Told' season largely jettisons the Shakespearean language, replacing it with modern vernacular. Jennifer Hulbert, Kevin J. Wetmore Jr and Robert L. York suggest that 'teen Shakespeare' emerges from the 'popularization of Shakespeare in ... mass media' and a more general dismantlement of 'perceptions of the "classical"'.[7] And the same can be said for 'Shakespeare Re-Told': these adaptations extract symbolic capital from a purposeful debunking of Shakespeare which takes place in the same moment as an affirmation that comedies are relevant to, and resonate with, an alternative demographic. In their use or rather non-use of Shakespearean language, the 'Shakespeare Re-Told' comedies go much further than earlier screen outings. While an earlier strategy might have been to add to and approximate (the credit line in the 1929 *The Taming of the Shrew*, for example, specifies 'William Shakespeare with additional dialogue by Samuel Taylor', and several quasi-Shakespearean lines are interpolated), the general rule, following Zeffirelli, is for directors ruthlessly to amputate and truncate text, replacing it instead with physical and visual business. Yet a more complex linguistic negotiation is taking place in 'Shakespeare Re-Told'. In *Much Ado About Nothing*, for example, Benedict's rationalisation of his change of heart and his decision to broadcast his feelings ('There'll be some fun at my expense, of course ... [But] love is just one of those things a man grows into ... like jazz or olives') brings the anterior text explicitly and playfully to mind ('I may chance to have some odd quirks and remnants of wit broken upon me ... but doth not appetite alter? A man loves the meat in his youth that he cannot endure in his age' [2.3.223–7]). Via such substitutions, the adaptation both comically flirts with and gestures to its precursor. Encouraging identification of the 'original', it issues reminders of Shakespeare in the interests of advertising and excusing its own translating procedures. The strategy is not dissimilar to those adaptations set in an American high school. In *Ten Things I Hate About You*, for example, Shakespeare is referenced in the recommendation of the teacher ('Shakespeare knew his shit'), while his language is echoed in Kat/Katharina's (Julia Styles) vernacular retelling of Sonnet 141 ('I hate the way you talk to me'), a set-piece moment that emphasises her creative centrality and self-consciously indexes the film's distinctive title.

Shakespeare-in-the-high-school films overtly subscribe to youth identifiers – schoolkid pranks, teenage romance, homework, parties and objecting parents (whose roles are correspondingly amplified). In contradistinction, finding contemporary inspiration in popular television drama such as *Cold Feet* and *This Life*, 'Shakespeare Re-Told' primarily anatomises the 'thirty-something' experience, mediated in terms of careers and lifestyle. Filmed with hand-held camera and subscribing to a realist shooting style, the 'Shakespeare Re-Told' *Much Ado About Nothing* fills out the backstory implicit in Shakespeare's play via a retrospective inset – dated three years previously – in which Benedict is shown ditching Beatrice (Sarah Parish) via text. Now paired as co-anchors on a daytime television show (as Leonard [Martin Jarvis], the programme controller, puts it, 'the frisson is what the public wants to see'), they bitch and squabble as the adaptation homes in on the realities of later life romance. Similarly, the 'Shakespeare Re-Told' *The Taming of the Shrew* concentrates much more exclusively on thirty-something singletons, Petruchio (Rufus Sewell) and Katherine (Shirley Henderson). Initially, the two appear an unlikely match. The hasty marriage is explained in the light of career, media and gender pressures; if Katherine were to marry, it is suggested, she would become the prime candidate for the party leadership because her married status would attract the favourable voter response not allowed the single woman. Referencing professional lives and work-life balance, and replacing the tensions of the Shakespearean family with friends and work colleagues, 'Shakespeare Re-Told' finds comic mileage in focusing erotic energy on a mature couple, with the features of the rest of the Shakespearean play shrinking back accordingly.

The emphasis in 'Shakespeare Re-Told' on the gendered and often sexist nature of the contemporary workplace recalls the ways in which patriarchal rule has been interrogated in recent critical work. Certainly, criticism's tendency has been to note the ways in which the plays foreground eloquent and self-determined women players, to the extent that the comedies as a whole have come to represent sites for a 'radical renegotiation' of the 'sex-gender system'.[8] In this connection, screen adaptations of the comedies have proved predictive, a stress on the position of women and the construction of gender being self-evident from the earliest adaptations. In *The Taming of the Shrew* (1929), Katharina's garb – a feathered black hat, a whip, high-heeled boots and earrings – announces her resistance to the normative, and this is reinforced via shots of her appearing ill-at-ease in more conservative attire (such as the white wedding dress). Other adaptations mediate gendered concerns through realisations of the inhibiting nature of the woman's milieu. Zeffirelli's *The Taming of the Shrew* is typical: repeatedly focusing in glorious close-up on Taylor's famous violet eyes, the camera establishes how Katharina's efforts at visual independence are socially limited. After her marriage is announced, for example, Katharina is discovered struggling to see through a tiny stained-glass porthole above a door, and the fact that she is forced to climb up to locate it, and the jumble of colours that the window casts on her face, point to a form of domestic imprisonment. In an extension to the idea, Branagh's *Much Ado About Nothing* gives voice to the freedoms Kate is looking for, showing a woman in command of her social and cultural domain. Before the opening credits, Beatrice's (Emma Thompson) solitary voiceover rendition of 'Hey Nonny Nonny' is experienced in a moment of revision: a woman authorises a process of textual and ideological appropriation. What has been termed Beatrice's 'iconoclastic voice', moreover, is given a verbal *and* material form, particularly when we see her recital from a book enrapturing her picnic party – in this adaptation, at least, female authority is achieved.[9]

As well as centralising the female characters, critical work on Shakespeare's comedies has highlighted the 'blurring of sexual difference ... [characters] who are desired as both man and woman' and the ideological freight of acts of cross-dressing.[10] Again, an understanding of gendered identities as alternately emancipating and destabilising informs the earliest screen examples. Czinner's 1936 *As You Like It* shows a heroine whose clothes release expressions of desire. Playing Rosalind, Elisabeth Bergner, sporting puffed sleeves and a cloak, jumps, laughs, skips, cajoles and provokes. As Shakespeare's cross-dressed heroine holds her arms aloft, hugs trees and offers instruction, it is clear that her swapping genders has proved enabling. Trevor Nunn's *Twelfth Night* (1996), which deploys a heritage model (featuring a nineteenth-century ancestral pile and turn-of-the-century costumes) to bespeak a high Victorian moment, pushes further the playful dimensions of gender change. The ship-board prologue figures Viola (Imogen Stubbs) and Sebastian (Stephen Mackintosh) as entertainers in a concert party. Initially, the twins are repre-sented in oriental attire as women from a harem, yet, after the voices separate into soprano and baritone, and the veils are torn aside to reveal mutually worn moustaches, gendered affiliations are thrown into disarray. The accompany-ing song – a version of 'O mistress mine, where are you roaming?' (2.3.37–51) – appears as a reflection on the predicament of gender. Because the film foregrounds the idea of masquerade, male and female roles are matters of enactment, and transvestism is seen as a form of liberation. Spinning on cross-dressing, the 'Shakespeare Re-Told' *The Taming of the Shrew* discovers a morning-suited Petruchio who breaks down, confessing, 'I can't do it ... not dressed like this ... There's something she needs to know about me'. A quick cut reveals a modern-day coming out – the inebriated Petruchio arriving at church dressed in a leather skirt, fishnet stockings and high heels. The updating of a Shakespearean convention works multiply, nodding to the play's Induction while putting into contemporary parlance debates around trans-gender identity. The switch is facilitative, complicating the play's repre-sentation of Petruchio (in 3.2) as a 'mean-apparelled ... eyesore'.

As the *Four Weddings and a Funeral*-style wedding in *The Taming of the Shrew* confirms, the 'Shakespeare Re-Told' season trades on a series of very English settings – country piles, the west country, London, the Houses of Parliament, and, in the case of *A Midsummer Night's Dream*, a Butlins-style leisure complex. In contrast is the film adaptation, *Much Ado About Nothing* (dir. Josh Whedon, 2012), which also draws on discourses about thirty-something romance but which lends the formula a specifically American feel. Making of the plot an extended weekend house party, and elaborating a twenty-first century commentary on commitment-phobic men and romantically disappointed women, Whedon exploits the associa-tions of a Santa Monica setting with sharp shots of polished limousines, steaming jacuzzi tubs and glimpses of palatial residences. (Filming took place in the director's own home, and the black-and-white palette affirms the work's art-house credentials.) Even if the film brings Messina to mind in exterior glimpses of intricately organised gardens and isolated Italianate architectural details, this is a resolutely southern Californian Shakespeare, full of sunny natural light, slick clothing and casual culture. Suiting the conceit, *Much Ado About Nothing* registers a sense of a professionally intimate and socially assured community in the high-end party-carnival mode, complete with acrobats, cocktails, bespoke cup-cakes and designer phones. The last are crucial props via which plots are hatched, criminals

74

filmed, conversations overheard and news received. The emphasis on the phone rather than the report encapsulates how technology is increasingly privileged as a newly credible way to translate Shakespeare's situational comedy. Similarly facilitated by technological advancement is the 'Shakespeare Re-Told' *Much Ado About Nothing* in which a CCTV system and a television studio are the plausible – and hugely entertaining sites – for Petruchio's eavesdropping and gulling. In Whedon's film, surveillance and architecture also go together, as in the frequent enlistment of windows and mirrors: characters hide behind them or look into them, highlighting motifs of spectatorship, looking and scrutiny. Such properties are integral to the mobile filming method, as the camera floats effortlessly through interlocking spaces, eavesdropping on events from a balustrade, spying on intrigues in the making.

Whedon is typical of the ways in which screen adaptations follow Renaissance theatrical practice in their predilection for casting well-known comedians in key comic roles. In his *Much Ado About Nothing*, Nathan Fillion plays Dogberry, and, in common with other members of the cast, had previously participated in a number of Whedon's television productions (*Firefly* and *Buffy the Vampire Slayer*). Similarly, standing in for Shakespeare's clowns Richard Tarlton, Wil Kemp and Robert Armin are the likes of Michael Keaton (Dogberry in Branagh's *Much Ado About Nothing*) and Griff Rhys Jones (Touchstone in Edzard's *As You Like It*). Making Shakespeare accessible is a priority for the comic actor, and, in a film such as Branagh's *Much Ado About Nothing*, Dogberry's painfully enunciated delivery, complete with comic pauses, of a line such as 'Write down "Master Gentleman Conrad"', bespeaks that film's commitment to delivering on the language's comic potential. The same can be said for Whedon's *Much Ado About Nothing* in which many familiar expressions are gloriously revisited. These range from Beatrice's injunction to 'follow the leader', which results in a conga, to Benedict's promise that he will 'draw' his 'wit' (he produces a gun). Several lines, traditionally cut, are reintroduced, including Claudio's 'I'll hold my mind, were she an Ethiope' (5.1.38), included to reflect pejoratively on the character's insensitivity. The moment suggests that an unsayable and unacceptable moment in Shakespearean comedy can now be revisited, albeit in a context which is explicitly and rightly condemnatory.

Linguistic experiment aside, much of the meaning of Whedon's *Much Ado About Nothing* is communicated via music. The film's soundtrack, with an emphasis on percussion, strings and keyboards, makes itself felt most obviously in two songs, 'Heavily' and 'Sigh No More', which, combining male and female vocals in the delivery of Shakespearean lyric, suggest the male-female conflicts at the heart of the play while also establishing overlapping notes of sadness, yearning and amatory excitement. In doing multiple duty, the soundtrack to the film follows in the footsteps of those screen comedies which have lent heavily on non-diegetic scores both to establish mood (alternating electronic flutes and strangulated oboes in Edzard's *As You Like* It accentuate the film's sombre undertow) and to assist in characterisation (the 'Shakespeare Re-Told' *Much Ado About Nothing* opens with the Tom Jones song, 'Love is like candy on a shelf, / You want to taste and help yourself', which points up a distinctive stress on the self-absorbed, career-minded lovers). In its most sustained application, as Branagh's *Love's Labour's Lost* exemplifies, music is fully – diegetically – integrated, explicitly substituting for language. Reworking the play as a Hollywood musical, and gesturing to other Shakespearean adaptations conceived originally as stage musicals, Branagh situates the action of the play in the 1930s, privileging an 'Oxbridge' setting with a library, quadrangle, riverside and garden. Predominantly, the tone is reflective – the sense that that this idyllic moment is about to pass is reflected in musical numbers such as Jerome Kern's 'The Way You Look Tonight' and newsreels that contemplate the imminence of war. The lyrical wit of songs from the 1930s and 1940s is entirely at home in an adaptation geared towards approximating comic wit. So, when Berowne (Kenneth Branagh), contemplating love's elemental power, concludes, 'And when love speaks, the voice of all the gods / Make heaven drowsy with the harmony' (4.3.320–1), the film slips into a joint performance of Irving Berlin's 'Cheek to Cheek', with its celestial refrain, 'Heaven, I'm in Heaven'. In this sense, *Love's Labour's Lost* directs attention to its own adaptive procedures, highlighting the challenges of finding correlatives for comedy, the gains of situating the play in a new generic medium, and the intertextual ramifications of privileging song over text.

The intertextuality that *Love's Labour's Lost* summons via music is enriching in that it draws on associations between comedy and the 'metadramatic self-consciousness' of the Shakespearean stage – the ways in which 'stage realism' can become not so much a 'limitation' but, instead, a 'strength, an opportunity to suggest multiple layers of meaning'.[11] On screen, the specific manifestation of the metatheatrical (the meta-filmic or the meta-cinematic) works in additionally generative fashion. Engaging here is the epilogue to Czinner's *As You Like It*: self-consciously headed 'Epilogue', the sequence reveals Rosalind, through trick photography, alternating in her costume, one moment in a wedding dress, one moment in rustic garb. The switching and swapping evoke both the character's divided history and point up the playfulness the film, through the actress, has made available.

In the Taylor adaptation of *The Taming of the Shrew*, Katharina/Pickford turns slyly to camera to wink after the seemingly 'straight' rendition of the wifely obedience speech. This knowing gesture introduces an ironic discrepancy, a rupture to the codes of the genre, and a suggestion of audience-character collusion. At the close of Nunn's *Twelfth Night*, there is a variation on the manoeuvre, with Feste (Ben Kingsley) leaving the stately home in an autumnal mist and proceeding to a cliff overlooking the ocean to deliver, direct to camera, the last line of his song, 'And we'll strive to please you every day'. Both the repetition of 'every day', and the purposeful breaking of the fourth wall, affirm the continuing work of Shakespearean reinvention. An extended concluding sequence in Branagh's *As You Like It* goes even further, confronting and exposing the materiality of filmmaking. Rosalind delivers her epilogue as she traverses a modern car park thronged by assistants, technicians and camera crew – the production personnel make visible the back-stage work on which the adaptation depends. Multiple kinds of dissolution are brought to bear on the sequence, with glimpses of a curtain and a stylised painting of the happy couples intimating the dismantlement of the film's world. In this transition from one order to another, the director flags up what is involved in the creative process. *As You Like It* is the only one of Branagh's Shakespeare films in which he does not appear, except in audio cameo as the director exclaiming 'And cut!'. The delicious blur here between practice and product brings into play the histories of the comedies on screen. It demonstrates the extent to which Shakespearean comedy thrives in screen media and the ways in which screen media have in turn have made Shakespearean comedy their own. In this winningly comedic moment, the power of the play – and the filmmaker – is applauded at the same time as the possibilities of the art form are celebrated.

Notes

1. Lisa Hopkins, 'Comedies of the green world: *A Midsummer Night's Dream, As You Like It*, and *Twelfth Night*', in Heather Hirschfeld, ed., *The Oxford Handbook of Shakespearean Comedy* (Oxford, Oxford University Press, 2018), 520–36 (520).
2. François Laroque, 'Shakespeare's festive comedies', in Richard Dutton and Jean E. Howard, eds., *A Companion to Shakespeare's Works: The Comedies* (Oxford, Blackwell, 2003), 23–46 (29).
3. Douglas M. Lanier, 'Shakespearean comedy on screen', in Hirschfeld, ed., *Handbook*, 470–86 (481).
4. Gary Waller, 'Much joy, some terror: reading Shakespeare's comedies today', in Gary Waller, ed., *Shakespeare's Comedies* (London and New York, Longman, 1991), 1–28 (10).

5. Mark Thornton Burnett, '"We are the makers of manners": the Branagh phenomenon', in Richard Burt, ed., *Shakespeare after Mass Media* (New York, Palgrave, 2002), 83–106 (88).
6. Waller, 'Much joy', 9.
7. Jennifer Hulbert, Kevin J. Wetmore Jr and Robert L. York, *Shakespeare and Youth Culture* (New York, Palgrave, 2006), 61–2.
8. Phyllis Rackin, 'Shakespeare's cross-dressing comedies', in Dutton and Howard, eds., *Companion*, 114–46 (121).
9. Jean E. Howard, *The Stage and Social Struggle in Early Modern England* (London and New York, Routledge, 1994), 68.
10. Waller, 'Much joy', 13.
11. William C. Carroll, 'Romantic comedies', in Stanley Wells and Lena Cowen Orlin, eds., *Shakespeare: An Oxford Guide* (Oxford, Oxford University Press, 2003), 175–92 (180).

6

PETER KIRWAN

The Environments of Tragedy on Screen: *Hamlet, King Lear, Macbeth*

– Everything the light touches is our kingdom.
– What about that shadowy place?
– That's beyond our borders. You must never go there.

In an iconic scene of Roger Allers and Rob Minkoff's Disney retelling of *Hamlet*, *The Lion King* (1994), Mufasa and Simba stand atop Pride Rock and survey their lands. The borders of the kingdom are clearly delineated, a necessity for a kingdom whose success and prosperity depends on the careful balance of the 'circle of life'. The violation of the borders of that world brings with it tragedy and a disruption of the natural world, resulting in the green plains being scorched with fire and the ecosystem of the animated world nearly destroyed.

For plays written for the bare stage of the Elizabethan theatre, *Hamlet*, *King Lear* and *Macbeth* have provided fertile ground for filmmakers to explore the complex environments, both natural and man-made, that shape events. Indeed, the most acclaimed films are those that break most decisively with the theatrical limitations of fixed sets and establish fresh filmic environments, as Russell Jackson argues:

> The responsibility of creating a tragic universe has been accepted by some films of *Hamlet*, *Macbeth*, and *King Lear* ... [Olivier, Welles and Brook] make distinctive and forceful interpretative statements, an environment in which existential anxieties and criminal excesses will flourish.[1]

Recurring throughout the extensive screen heritage of these plays is an investment in the kinds of environment that incite and catalyse tragic action. While this might be an inevitable consequence of the tendency towards environmental naturalism in screen adaptation, there are political implications. *Hamlet*, *Lear* and *Macbeth* are all concerned with monarchs and the fate of nations, and the large scale of the cinema screen invites directors to link the protagonists of tragedy to the broader 'circle of life' of the worlds

79

they inhabit, tracing the interconnections between individual, environment and society. Chris Lukinbeal argues that filmic space 'emphasizes landscape and cinema as a cultural production, a space that is mediated by power relations', and in this chapter I consider the ramifications of this across environments from the open to the urban to the psychological.[2]

Open Spaces

The Lion King restages *Hamlet* against a vast (animated) landscape, the pride of lions a speck within a broader functioning world. Turning Hamlet into a cub focuses the attention on the Hamlet-figure's need to understand where he fits within a broader society. It is revealing, in this sense, that the Ghost's 'Remember *me*' of Shakespeare (1.5.91) is twisted here to the Ghost of Mufasa telling Simba 'Remember who *you* are' (my emphases). As well as reframing the tragedy to the standard 'believe in yourself' message of Disney films, the choice locates value and worth in the understanding of one's own function within a larger world.

The vastness of open spaces is a recurrent trend in cinematic adaptations of the tragedies, especially when such vastness can be used to depict human conflict as small, even insignificant, within it. This is the case with Akira Kurosawa's take on *King Lear*, *Ran* (1985), which begins and ends by framing its protagonists against imposing mountainous landscapes, and which stages a debate between the Fool figure, Kyoami, who complains that the gods are punishing them, and the Kent figure, Tango, who tells him that the gods are disinterested rather than cruel. The smallness of humanity within the landscape is also endemic to the Western, a genre that adaptors of *King Lear* are repeatedly drawn to, in films such as *Broken Lance* (1954), *A Thousand Acres* (1997) and *King of Texas* (2002). Connecting all of these films is an insistence on the experience of living in the natural world, a world under threat whether from the ravages of fire and war or the industrialisation of the railroad. The fate of the protagonists is inextricably linked to that of the landscape.

Macbeth has most frequently been adapted for screen in versions that emphasise the claustrophobia and internal spaces of the play, refiguring Scotland as a state of mind; as Courtney Lehmann argues, 'Scotland has historically been invoked on film as a place that is, in point of fact, anywhere *but* Scotland'.[3] However, the two most high-profile cinematic adaptations of the play trade heavily on their location settings, externalising Macbeth's psyche and the power struggles of the play in their landscapes. Roman Polanski's 1971 film, financed by Playboy, remains as controversial as its director, expelled by the Academy in 2018 following forty years of exile from the USA for rape of a minor. *Macbeth* was made in the immediate aftermath of the murder of his wife Sharon Tate and their unborn child, and the violent film's legacy and influence are inseparable from the traumas inflicted and suffered by its director. Justin Kurzel's 2015 film, the director's second feature, is similarly violent but with an emphasis on the aestheticisation of violence where Polanski's film is mundane in the ugly practicality of its bloodshed. External locations provide the backdrop for the medievalist fantasies of these period-set productions: much of Polanski's film was shot in Northumbria and Snowdonia, while Kurzel made spectacular use of the Isle of Skye; both chose the iconic Bamburgh Castle as the exterior of Dunsinane.

The built locations of Polanski's film (as in Orson Welles's *Macbeth*, discussed by Emma Smith in Chapter 14) provide only temporary and partial respite from the elements, with winds blowing shutters and stable doors open, and the rain constantly beating down. Polanski's aesthetic is medievalist, indulging in a richly realised mise-en-scène of everyday castle life. The mundanity of the world is part of what makes its violence so horrific, particularly when Lady Macduff is surprised while bathing her young son. The murderers are seen approaching on horseback from some distance, their unstoppable advance drawing attention to the vulnerability of Macduff's home, which is set ablaze in a sequence that not only desecrates but destroys the domestic space.

But while horrors await indoors, the exterior spaces attempt to conjure a mythic connection between the supernatural and the landscape. The film opens with the witches (crone, mother, maiden) in isolation on a bleak, seemingly endless beach that, following a rising of mist, becomes the muddy battleground of the Thane of Cawdor's defeat. The witches are defiantly humdrum, seen going about domestic chores and dragging tools and ingredients. Yet they are at home among the exposed elements that rain down on Macbeth and Banquo (and, in the film's coda, on a returning Donalbain), and the blurred edges between interior and exterior space allow the influence of these rainy meetings into the castles.

Kurzel's *Macbeth* is even more rooted in its landscapes. Michael Fassbender's Macbeth first appears on a battlefield emerging from a knee-high fog, as if himself one of the mountainous peaks rising above the clouds. This iconic image is the first of many in a film that is so invested in static shots and slow motion that it is almost better read as a series of still photographs in which actors barely move while intoning the lines. While the film is aurally monotonous, its carefully composed visuals seek to situate Macbeth's journey as an arc in relation to the landscape.

The opening images see the Macbeths burying their dead child. They ritually place coins on the corpse's eyes, a treatment Macbeth also accords to a young victim of the battle, returning the boy to the earth even as he and the other living soldiers themselves sleep in hollowed-out divots that evoke graves. Unlike Polanski's film, which clearly distinguishes the spaces of Macbeth and the witches, here Macbeth is at home on the heath as they are. For the first half of the film Macbeth moves continuously left in the space of the frame, gradually detaching him from the natural world. Macbeth's 'castle' is little more than a series of huts and tents, and Macbeth murders Duncan in a tent with only canvas separating them from the stars. But at Dunsinane, the endpoint of his journey, Macbeth is hemmed in by vaulted ceilings. Low angles frame Macbeth against a repressive physical structure, stressing his entrapment.

But as the film passes its halfway point, Kurzel returns to the outdoors. Lady Macduff and her children are pursued through the woods rather than attacked in their own home, and Macbeth has them burnt at the stake outside Dunsinane, in front of a watching populace. The smoke of the executions drifts across the screen as the camera pans right to capture the inferno from a distance, and at this moment the direction of both the camera and Macbeth reverses. Macbeth marches right, back into the outdoor space, to face Malcolm's army – who have not only hewn down branches but set Birnam Wood alight. Macbeth and Macduff's showdown takes place against an apocalyptic backdrop as Scotland burns to a crisp; and as the two men slump in mutual defeat, Malcolm and his troops march past towards Dunsinane, ignoring the combatants who have returned to the earth.

These films produce landscape as empathetic to shifts in power relations, especially in the apocalypse that accompanies Macbeth's defeat in Kurzel's film. Kurosawa's films take a similar tack. In his *Macbeth*, *Throne of Blood* – whose Japanese title is closer to *Castle of the Spider's Web* – the titular castle appears from thick fog, showing the transient nature of human activity against a vast, unchanging landscape. Shot on the slopes of Mount Fuji, *Throne of Blood* is built on a bed of volcanic ash and smoke. The constant mist almost overwhelms Washizu and Miki (Macbeth and Banquo) as they flee their encounter with the spirit in Cobweb Forest; and, at the end of the film, Washizu (pierced by dozens of arrows as his men turn against him) falls face first back into the ankle-level mist, moments before the castle itself fades again out of existence. *Ran*, like Kurzel's *Macbeth*, enacts the power shifts of the play as an apocalypse on the landscape. The bright greens of the valley at the start of the film are transformed through war to burnt blacks and browns, the valley becoming a nuclear wasteland. In both of Kurosawa's films the landscape endures longer than those who inhabit it, though not without scars.

The Russian director Grigori Kozintsev places emphasis on the landscape as a space of transformation and a space that is itself transformed. Courtney Lehmann sees this as inflected by the death of Stalin in 1953. 'For three decades, Stalin had baited his own people with visions of the "promised end", which in the end, led only to the "image of that horror": the grotesque spectacle of their own suffering – for nothing'.[4] The opening of *Korol' Lir* (1970) follows directly from the spectacle Stalin bequeathed to his people. The film begins with a slow procession of hundreds of impoverished and disabled serfs moving through a barren landscape, littered with boulders. As one, they come to a halt before the horizon-spanning walls of a fortress seen from an extreme low angle to emphasise the barrier that they pose; on the other side, the castle is full of lavishly dressed nobles. Kozintsev's humanist impulse makes visible those who will be affected by those within; their silent expectation the voiceless protest of a betrayed underclass. The vast spaces of *Lir* exaggerate the littleness of Lear (Yuri Yarvet) himself, and during his madness he returns to the peasants, becoming socialised rather than separated: just one more disenfranchised human against the 'desert inferno'.[5] Later, a tracking shot follows his stretcher through the faceless armies recruited on his behalf. At other times the landscape seems overwhelmingly oppressive, as when Gloucester and Edgar cross a seemingly endless flat plain, captured from an extreme high angle. Gloucester suddenly buckles to his knees, dying. His hands reach out and touch Edgar's face, tracing the shape of his skull in a sudden burst of recognition, and Edgar kisses his father's hands before they go limp. The isolation of the two figures in the emptiness is a visual representation of Gloucester's inability to see his surroundings, making this final moment of connection all the more powerful.

The Interplay of Space in Kozintsev's *Hamlet*

What Lukinbeal refers to as the transformation of place into space, in which the specific and architectural is reframed as spectacle and metaphor, is perhaps best illustrated by a close study of Kozintsev's magisterial *Gamlet* (1964).[6] The film begins with crashing waves, Elsinore seen only as a dark shadow on their surface, indelibly linking the shifting waters with the castle. As Lehmann argues,

> much like living in the shadow of Stalin, whose subjects could only speculate as to how far the invisible hand of the State might stretch, in *Gamlet*, the castle architecture never appears in its entirety, emerging only in fragments that terrorize the imagination with thoughts of the enormity of the whole.[7]

Gamlet develops a careful interplay between the landscapes and the built environment of Elsinore, which constantly encroaches on the world outside it. The sheer scale of the landscapes is evident as Innokenti Smoktunovski's Hamlet first appears, his horse galloping under a vast cloudy sky. The castle is an imposing fortress, whose heavy drawbridges and thick walls suggest a relative stability. Even the very solid Ghost, when it appears, is iconic, shot from an extreme low angle, dressed in full armour with cape billowing in the wind. The solidity of the Ghost contrasts markedly with the thick clouds and sea spray against which it is silhouetted by the low angle; Hamlet, meanwhile, is framed against the stormy sea as he listens to the Ghost's words. The sublime Ghost contrasts with the development of the world within the castle which, as in Polanski's *Macbeth*, is richly realised and populated with activity. The difference is the scale of the castle: when the scene moves away from the crowded state rooms, individuals such as Claudius and Polonius seem tiny within the cavernous rooms, and Gertrude is swallowed up the enormous bed on which she receives the news of Hamlet's distraction.

The Ghost's visit returns Hamlet to the sublime. Polonius discovers him lounging on a rock, and after listening to the Player King's speech he descends to the violent waves and sheer rocks. He speaks 'To be or not to be' in voiceover as he walks away from the camera towards a large rock with sea spray crashing behind it, clearly evoking Caspar David Friedrich's painting 'Wanderer over the Sea of Fog'. The waves provide an almost constant background score, and Hamlet keeps dragging people outside of the solid walls of the castle and down towards those waves, including arranging for the Players to perform by the shoreline. A long transitional sequence sees Claudius walking through his immaculate halls, descending from the safe confines of the castle and finally arriving in the exposed environs of the Players' performance space. Claudius's distempered march back to the castle pulls the court, including Hamlet, back inside, and in the scenes following 'The Mousetrap' the film becomes claustrophobic; Claudius's soliloquy (uninterrupted by Hamlet) is delivered to a mirror, the camera pulling in closely on his reflection, and Hamlet's violent struggle with his mother in her large but shadowy bedroom is interrupted when he spies a Ghost who, this time, remains hidden from the viewer.

The film repeatedly turns space into metaphor, especially as Hamlet leaves the castle and pauses to watch Fortinbras's army seemingly emerging directly from the waves that have been crashing against Elsinore's walls. Left behind, Ophelia wanders the castle in mourning black and veil, her women chasing her to try and keep her clothes from falling off. She makes her way to the battlements where her voice blends with the sound of the waves as she casts off her clothes. In an editorial coup, her body is subsequently revealed floating beneath the surface of a river as rain begins to fall; and then a sequence of cuts follows a bird flying left to right over the sea, circling round as it reaches Hamlet, who is standing on the shore. Hamlet begins his slow walk back along a river, meets Horatio, and finally arrives at the seaside grave at the same time as Ophelia's funeral procession. The linking of Hamlet and Ophelia through filmic montage and physical waterways transcends place and finds emotional resonance between the separated protagonists.

At the film's conclusion, the dying Hamlet walks dazedly through an open door into the air, and leans against a rock to murmur 'The rest is silence', leaving the sound of waves to be overtaken by the sound of Fortinbras's arriving army. Everyone gathers next to the sea, and as his body is returned to the castle, the camera returns to the shadow of the castle on the waves. The final interplay of architectural shadow and wild landscape, implying an uncertain future for Elsinore is a fitting final image for a film whose spaces reflect the shifting power relations of the play.

Urban Space

Mark Shiel and Tony Fitzmaurice treat cinema 'primarily as a spatial system ... [that] gives it a special potential to illuminate the lived spaces of the city and urban societies, allowing for a full synthetic understanding of cinematic theme, form, and industry in the context of global capitalism'.[8] This potential has especially been recognised by directors of the tragedies interested in the contemporary. One of the most high-profile, and most explicitly connected to global capitalism, is Michael Almereyda's 2000 *Hamlet*, which retains Shakespeare's text but transfers the action to the glass towers of the Denmark Corporation in contemporary New York, in a film which associates Hamlet's discontent with the malaise of youth in a mediatised world. In the transition to contemporary worlds, the move to the city takes the interplay between built and natural environments into the streets. The city allows directors to develop sprawling, interconnected communities in which the protagonists of *Hamlet*, *Lear* and *Macbeth* are forced into closer proximity with one another, and where actions have immediate impacts.

Vishal Bhardwaj draws on the tropes of the gangster genre to locate *Macbeth* and *Hamlet* among, respectively, the seedy criminal underbelly of the city (*Maqbool*, 2003) and the urban battlegrounds of the conflict in Kashmir (*Haider*, 2014). Life in these cities is mobile and unsheltered, both exposing and anonymous, as when Haider (Bhardwaj's Hamlet-figure), hides out in a video shop or turns up in a market square to rally the people in the name of freedom. The city paradoxically makes it possible to both conceal one's own identity, but also impossible to escape it.

The transposition to cities changes the stakes of the conflict from nations to institutions, kings to leaders. The world of corrupt business and mob rule is especially popular, from Joseph L. Mankiewicz's *House of Strangers* (1949), a noir-inflected take on *Lear* in which Lear becomes an Italian immigrant banker, to the Italian-American Mafiosi film *Men of Respect* (1990), which resituates *Macbeth* in the offices and restaurants of the New York Mob, to the bloody *Macbeth* of Geoffrey Wright, set in the violent underworld of Melbourne. One of the best realised is Don Boyd's *My Kingdom* (2001), which translates *Lear* to contemporary Liverpool. The Irish immigrant gangster Sandeman (Richard Harris) watches as his wife Mandy is gunned down in the street next to him. The subsequent rupture in the family turns on youngest daughter Jo's refusal to inherit responsibility for the family business. Her elder sisters, meanwhile, take control of city spaces hitherto run by Sandeman, including football clubs, brothels and nightclubs, which form the city's hidden hierarchies, cordoned off from the outside world by red ropes and guarded doors. Sandeman is forced out of these protected spaces into the public spaces of the city, accompanied by his biracial grandson. The two outcasts fish in the Mersey, Sandeman finding some momentary peace as the immigrant is battered by the Irish Sea winds.

Much of *My Kingdom* is seen through the eyes of Aidan Gillen's Barry, a local detective and loose analogue for Edmund, assigned to investigate Mandy's murder. Taking exception to Quick, an out-of-town customs officer pursuing the Sandemans, Barry confronts him against the backdrop of the Mersey.

> You come over here to Liverpool from Manchester with your movies and photos and set up shop, tellin' us, warnin' me about people I grew up with. These people are just trying to survive like the rest of us ... This city is a dead end for them – no work, no future.

The compromised Barry sees the Sandemans as representative of a city fending for itself against outsiders, especially in the wake of the Thatcher government's abandonment of Merseyside, and he ultimately aligns himself with the sisters he has known since childhood. Quick, conversely, sees Sandeman as the cancer ravaging Liverpool. Yet Quick's apparently clearer view is undermined when he is blinded and left to stumble across railway tracks into the path of an oncoming train. Meanwhile, when Sandeman's grandson is drowned in the river, Sandeman finds the boy washed up on the rocks, an indictment of the city's treatment of outsiders that has only grown more poignant in the wake of images of refugees washed up on English beaches. In a twist on Shakespeare, Sandeman and Jo survive, but Sandeman is last seen walking down a causeway towards the Mersey shore, marginalised from Liverpool, which remains standing even as its inhabitants are consumed.

Consumption is also central to the versions of *Macbeth* that select restaurants as their primary settings. Billy Morrisette's *Scotland, PA.* (2001) follows Joe McBeth as he and his wife plot to take over a fast-food diner. As with *My Kingdom*, an out-of-town policeman, Lieutenant McDuff, is assigned to look into local goings-on. Mark Thornton Burnett notes that the film's 'Scotland' is a town 'founded by seventeenth-century émigrés fleeting religious persecution'.[9] This deliberately self-conscious connection to *Macbeth* foregrounds precisely the distinction from Shakespeare's play, tying in with Lehmann's observation that 'the idea of "Scotland" operates as a powerful metonymy for a place that is everywhere and nowhere in particular'.[10]

On the small screen, the BBC's 2005 *Shakespeare Re-Told: Macbeth* casts James McAvoy as Joe Macbeth, head chef of a three-Michelin-star restaurant whose celebrity owner, Duncan Docherty, takes credit for the food. Here, the witches are binmen whose insight comes from their intimate knowledge of the people whose rubbish they dispose of. While the wise-cracking witches serve an overtly comic function, they are connected to a broader thematic interest in waste. Macbeth lectures his kitchen boys on 'respect' as he butchers a pig's head, the camera capturing the deconstruction of the animal into neat strips that waste nothing. But as soon as Duncan's blood is spilt, Macbeth slips into the very wastage – smashing bottles and spilling milk, throwing food at dissatisfied diners, and seeing excess blood everywhere – that he characterises as lacking respect, and that creates the need for the binmen who haunt him. The Macbeths begin as paragons of order, with Joe managing the immaculate kitchen and Keeley Hawes's Ella running front-of-house, but the wastage and disorder become outward manifestations of their inner turmoil, Ella smearing lipstick across her face in a final act of waste before falling from the restaurant's roof. Within the urban environment, as in *My Kingdom*, corruption and waste cannot be concealed.

The claustrophobia of the working-class urban environment is best realised in Penny Woolcock's television film *Macbeth on the Estate* (1997), which opens on

> what looked like an urban battlefield – Sarajevo, perhaps ... By the time the opening camera pan had finished its sweep across the horizon, taking in grey tower blocks sticking up like amputated limbs in the distant background, spectators were aware that this urban landscape wasn't Bosnia. It was Birmingham. And it was now.[11]

Woolcock, primarily a documentary-maker, worked with professional and amateur actors within the deprived Ladywood Estate, offering a fascinating distillation of *Macbeth* into an extremely delimited environment made up of narrow corridors, working men's clubs and the balconies of high-rise flats. The televisual documentary style renders the desperate circumstances of this film's inhabitants, and their inability to escape, profoundly moving. Carol Rutter focuses on Susan Vidler's Lady Macbeth who seeks protection in her own home.

> As she escapes further into the interior of her home, moving from the front door up her stairs towards her bedroom, she hesitates on the landing in front of a closed door – and opens it. Behind that door is a blue room, a nursery, preserved like a shrine, meticulously ordered.[12]

The absent presence of the Macbeths' dead child haunts the film as thoroughly as the small children who act as the witches, and serves as a reminder of the solidity of memories in a world where community ties and the constraints of poverty and class prevent escape. The transposition of 'Out damned spot' to the act of obsessive hoovering, attempting to create order in constrained circumstances, is telling in this respect, as is the sudden fantastical dislocation of Macbeth's sofa to a forest glade at the moment he is shot, allowing him for a fraction of a second the illusion of freedom. The enclosed environments of *Macbeth on the Estate* are as psychological as they are architectural.

Inner Space

Ethan Hawke's Hamlet in Almereyda's film is, himself, a filmmaker. His personal art, a series of collage-style films, represents his attempt to control and shape the conflicting narratives of a mediatised world. Katherine Rowe argues that

> For Almereyda's Hamlet, the personal video *is* the technology of interiority among a variety of modern media … All but one of Hamlet's soliloquies are framed as video sequences that he has composed. As he dies, we see his life flash back in the same grainy black-and-white collage.[13]

Maurice Hindle finds that the approach admits the viewer to 'Hamlet's painful consciousness' in a way that contrasts with the 'scheming corporate power' of Claudius.[14] The idea that Hamlet's art offers a form of direct access to Hamlet's mind sets up a complex series of paradoxes around what Rowe calls the 'technology of interiority'; Hamlet's self-expression manifests as a collage of the expressions of others, and the space of his mind is displaced onto the video screen. Yet this is part of a long history of attempts to realise interior space through the primarily visual language of film.

Laurence Olivier's *Hamlet* (1948) has long been read for its Freudian associations. Russell Jackson quotes Roger Furse on Olivier's vision of 'a dream-like, cavernous place as the setting for a drama which is centred in the shadowy regions of the hero's mind'.[15] This film and Welles's *Othello*, 'represent the most intimate of relationships between their protagonists' state of mind and the surroundings created for them to move through, supported by cinematographic techniques that reinforce the sense of our being privy to their vision and experience of the world'.[16] In this sense, it is possible to see Elsinore itself as a 'technology of interiority' that renders Hamlet's psyche concrete. The clearest rendition of this is at the conclusion of the nunnery scene. Ophelia is left sobbing on the stairs as Polonius and Claudius leave. In a bravura montage, the camera traces the spiral concrete stairs of the castle upwards away from her, the camera spinning and the strings of the orchestra increasingly frenetic until the camera hits the skies, then pans back down over the crashing sea to reveal the back of Hamlet's head; the camera enters his head to another orchestral swell, revealing waves superimposed over an image of his head as the audience hears 'To be or not to be'. Olivier's camerawork renders the castle of Elsinore a spatial metaphor of Hamlet's inner turmoil. Maurice Hindle notes that the scene is 'relocated from its textual position *before* the nunnery scene, which has the effect of suggesting that the agonised debate on suicide is caused by his troubled relationship with Ophelia'.[17] The connection is reinforced architecturally through the spiralling stairwell and intrusive camera that cinematically situates Ophelia's existence in Hamlet's skull.

The tendency of stage-to-screen productions of *Hamlet*, *Lear* and *Macbeth*, working on a lower budget for television and derived from more sparsely designed theatrical productions, is also to focus interior space, turning the lack of exterior locations into interpretive metaphor. Gregory Doran's 2009 screen version of his RSC production of *Hamlet* retains the blocking of the stage production but uses CCTV cameras to enhance the production's interest in surveillance, all the while closing in more closely on David Tennant's prince. Doran's and Rupert Goold's respective adaptations of their productions of *Macbeth* for the RSC (2001) and Chichester Festival (2010) utilise narrow corridors and basement settings, creating a bunker mindset for the play that shows off Antony Sher and Patrick Stewart's psychologically inflected performances to great effect. But perhaps the most extreme example is the recording of Trevor Nunn's celebrated *Macbeth* in 1979, directed for television by

Philip Casson. With the actors shot against stark black backgrounds, the film strands its characters in undefined space, with the primary reference point the camera itself. As well as capturing extraordinary live moments such as Judi Dench's unearthly howl during the sleepwalking scene, the stripping away of all environment places the focus entirely on internal, psychological conflict.

The logical conclusion of the subordination of space to interiority, finally, perhaps comes in Kit Monkman's 2018 film of *Macbeth*, which shot its actors against green screen and then built a CGI environment around the actors in post-production. The environment is a cross-sectional doll's house, from which the camera pulls back to reveal action happening simultaneously in adjoining 'rooms'. All of the action is contained within this structure, and the structure itself is unfinished, with sketches of invisible walls and stair-wells leaving the edges of the space undefined. The clear separation from a 'real' world – especially at the end, when the structure is revealed to be an enormous sphere – creates a metaphorical filmic space in which characters are juxtaposed according to thematic and psychological distance rather than geographical principles. The film emphasises connections of cause and consequence; in one disturbing sequence, the camera pans down from Macbeth to reveal the murder of Lady Macduff happening in a room below, connecting victim and murderer. Alison Findlay and Ramona Wray highlight the 'unsettlingly compressed and compacted' nature of time in the film, but this compression is inseparable from the spatial compression that disrupts linear narrative to create an experiential simultaneity, exchanging the epic landscapes of Kurzel and Polanski for a more paranoid and fluid visualisation of violence and guilt.[18]

The meta-cinematically constructed nature of Monkman's film makes explicit the role of 'power relations and the mediation of meaning' in the creation of cinematic landscapes.[19] Without a physical set, the actors relied on theatrical-style blocking to position themselves in relation to one another, and as Macbeth withdrew from company in the second half of the film, heading towards the battlements and featureless sky at the top of the sphere, his isolation was both from other bodies and from space. The approach of the borders of the film's world by tragic protagonists at the end of the films is a recurring feature, from Sandeman approaching the Mersey to Fassbender's Macbeth facing the scorched heath, from Smoktunovski's Hamlet yearning for the sea to Vidler's Lady Macbeth imprisoned by the walls of the nursery. Space and body work together, and the tragic fall is finally rendered as a confrontation between the two, the protagonist destroyed by or with the environment that they have shaped.

Notes

1. Russell Jackson, *Shakespeare and the English Speaking Cinema* (Oxford, Oxford University Press, 2014), 33.
2. Chris Lukinbeal, 'Cinematic landscapes', *Journal of Cultural Geography*, 23.1 (2005), 3–22 (4).
3. Courtney Lehmann, 'Out damned Scot: dislocating Macbeth in transnational film and media culture', in Richard Burt and Lynda E. Boose, eds., *Shakespeare the Movie II* (New York, Routledge, 2003), 231–51 (232).
4. Courtney Lehmann, 'Grigorii Kozintsev' in Mark Thornton Burnett, ed., *Great Shakespeareans: Welles, Kurosawa, Kozintsev, Zeffirelli* (London, Bloomsbury, 2013), 92–140 (101).
5. Lehmann, 'Grigorii Kozintsev', 136.
6. Lukinbeal, 'Cinematic landscapes', 15.
7. Lehmann, 'Grigorii Kozintsev', 103.
8. Mark Shiel, 'Cinema and the city in history and theory', in Mark Shiel and Tony Fitzmaurice, eds., *Cinema and the City: Film and Urban Societies in a Global Context* (Oxford, Blackwell, 2001), 1–18 (6).
9. Mark Thornton Burnett, 'Figuring the global/historical in filmic Shakespearean tragedy', in Diana E. Henderson, ed., *A Concise Companion to Shakespeare on Screen* (Malden and Oxford, Blackwell, 2006), 133–54 (149).
10. Lehmann, 'Out damned Scott', 232.
11. Carol Chillington Rutter, *Shakespeare and Child's Play* (Abingdon, Routledge, 2007), 179–80.
12. Ibid., 184.
13. Katherine Rowe, '"Remember me": technologies of memory in Michael Almereyda's *Hamlet*', in Richard Burt and Lynda E. Boose, eds., *Shakespeare the Movie II* (London and New York, Routledge, 2003), 37–55 (46).
14. Maurice Hindle, *Shakespeare on Film*, 2nd ed. (London, Palgrave Macmillan, 2015), 220.
15. Jackson, *Shakespeare and the English Speaking Cinema*, 41.
16. Ibid., 43.
17. Hindle, *Shakespeare on Film*, 212.
18. Alison Findlay and Ramona Wray, 'A review of *Macbeth* (dir. Kit Monkman, 2017)', *British Shakespeare Association*, 30 June 2017. www.britishshakespeare.ws/bsa-news/a-review-of-macbeth-dir-kit-monkman-2017/ (accessed 15 January 2018).
19. Lukinbeal, 'Cinematic landscapes', 14.

7

VICTORIA BLADEN

Two Tragedies of Love: *Romeo and Juliet* and *Othello*

In the last 15 years, over 30,000 men, women and children have been
killed in the name of Honour ... Killing innocent love is not Honourable.
It is an act of cowardice and a crime against humanity.

Postscript to *Dhadak* 2018, India, dir. Shashank Khaitan

Love collides with violent conflict in Shakespeare's *Romeo and Juliet* and
Othello. Desire and death are inextricably linked, as Shakespeare's language evocatively plays out, creating a range of challenges and opportunities for filmmakers and their visions of the plays. In both works, the
blocking agents to love magnify the passions yet raise the stakes, rendering
the lovers' bonds fatal in divided worlds. Key to the plays are questions of
identity, and the borders between Shakespeare's lovers have been interpreted in the twenty-first century in profoundly political ways, resonating
with inter-racial, caste and ethnic conflict, honour killings, domestic violence and discourses of sexual politics and gender identity. Adaptations of
the love tragedies form a central vein of Shakespearean screen history, and
the plays have been imagined and remediated in a wide range of contexts
and spaces. This chapter seeks to survey the landscape of *Romeo and
Juliet* and *Othello* on screen; while not exhaustive, it illustrates the
scope and range of possibilities the plays have offered to filmmakers
from various cultures.

Romeo and Juliet

Romeo and Juliet is arguably one of Shakespeare's most transmutable
works in terms of global cross-cultural reach.[1] Early adaptations include
the first silent short directed by J. Stuart Blackton (1908, USA), and the
lost silent film directed by Francis X. Bushman and John W. Noble
(1916). The first full-length production, directed by George Cukor in
1936 for MGM, featured Leslie Howard and Norma Shearer as mid-
dle-aged lovers, too old for rash decisions, and constituted a lavish star-

92

vehicle for Shearer, whose husband Irving Thalberg was the film's producer.[2] During the Second World War, a Mexican comedy version, *Romeo y Julieta* (1943), directed by Miguel M. Delgado, referenced Cukor's version and starred Cantinflas, a prominent Mexican comedian. In the post-war period, Renato Castellani's adaptation (1954) utilised neo-realism and drew on the artistic legacy of Italy in creating its aesthetics. The Russian production *Romeo i Dzhulyetta* (1955), directed by Lev Arnshtam and Leonid Lavrovsky, was a filmed version of Sergei Prokofiev's ballet of *Romeo and Juliet*, choreographed by Lavrovsky.

Two landmark productions of the 1960s were *West Side Story* (1961) and Franco Zeffirelli's *Romeo and Juliet* (1968). The former, directed by Robert Wise and Jerome Robbins, adapted the 1957 Broadway musical, which transposed the interfamilial conflict of the Montagues and Capulets to the Jets and Sharks, New York street gangs.[3] A remake is in the pipeline, directed by Stephen Spielberg, with the script by Tony Kushner, the Pulitzer prize-winning dramatist of *Angels in America* (1993).[4] Zeffirelli's *Romeo and Juliet* became one of the best-loved adaptations in the play's history. Eschewing big-name actors, he cast unknown, beautiful teenagers, Leonard Whiting and Olivia Hussey, in the title roles.[5] Laurence Olivier voices the prologue and epilogue. Zeffirelli presented an Italian Renaissance aesthetic, evoking the sophisticated yet potentially violent urban spaces of fifteenth-century Italy, and many of the scenes were filmed on location near Rome and around Tuscany. The film was also in dialogue with its historical moment of production; created during an era of social unrest and protest, Romeo and Juliet are 'flower power' protagonists and their deaths resonate with the rebellion of 1960s youth against the strictures of the older generation. Zeffirelli claimed that he wanted the film 'to be a young people's *Romeo and Juliet*', and his aim to appeal to the new generation reflected his admiration for Bernstein's *West Side Story*.[6] Zeffirelli's adaptation was highly successful at the box office, as well as critically acclaimed, a 'masterpiece of intricately choreographed music, poetry, and photography', as Kenneth S. Rothwell aptly describes it,[7] and it has remained a touchstone for subsequent directors.

A decade later came Alvin Rakoff's TV adaptation for the BBC (1978). Zeffirelli's film was a hard act to follow, despite echoing its costume choices of multi-coloured tights and striking cod-pieces. The production presented a less sexy pair in Patrick Ryecart as Romeo, at twenty-six struggling to make it up the vine to the balcony, and Rebecca Saire as an innocent and earnest Juliet. The young Alan Rickman plays a seething and dangerous Tybalt, and the fight choreography is convincing. The aesthetic again was Italian Renaissance and the harmonious arches and architectural features of the sets, as well as the cloister garden, invoke Renaissance paintings.

Romeo and Juliet has always migrated beyond the Anglophone world.[8] *Qayamat Se Qayamat Tak* (1988), directed by Mansoor Khan, is set in modern Delhi where the continued practice of arranged marriages and patriarchal control of the female body generate the obstacles for the lovers. In the play, the hatred between the families is unexplained, but this adaptation begins with an interlude that explains the basis of the interfamilial hostility. An unmarried woman Madhumanthi (from the 'Montague' family) falls pregnant but her boyfriend Ratan (from the 'Capulet' clan) is trapped between her and his impending arranged marriage. Madhumanthi commits suicide and her brother Dhanraj Singh appears at the wedding with her body, shooting the groom in revenge. After Dhanraj's release from jail, his son Raj/Romeo (Aamir Khan) falls in love with Rashmi/Juliet (Juhi Chawla), from the Capulets, kickstarting the familiar narrative.

Baz Luhrmann's *Romeo + Juliet* (1996) remains one of the most popular and successful adaptations, striking in its bold, postmodernist aesthetic.[9] Its strategies of visual excess and hyperbole invite the spectator to enter into the high-octane world of lovers and fights, while its playful literalisation of language and punning maintain a metafictional stance, highly self-aware in its process of adapting Shakespeare. In Luhrmann's vision, the societal warfare is between corporations; it is the vicious competition of the modern city and a globalised economy that threaten love. Any Christian messages of love and compassion are reduced to kitsch crosses that flood the imagery. Water is also a key component of Luhrmann's aesthetic, facilitating the idea of the lovers in a suspended womb-like, death space outside of the ordinary flux and violence of their society. Water features in the iconic balcony scene, where floating in the pool becomes an analogy of the celestial spaces the lovers create through their metaphors. This temporary space of transcendence is repeated at the end, a post-death space outside of time.

Song, as the vehicle for expressing emotion and inner thoughts, has proved a significant dimension in many of the *Romeo and Juliet* adaptations. In *West Side Story*, each of the original musical numbers marks key stages in the narrative. In Luhrmann's, the soundtrack, drawn from a range of contemporary pop songs, had a successful independent life as a soundtrack album, tied to the youth-focused style of the film. In *Qayamat*, the conventions of Bollywood govern the narrative's structure whereby songs, often coinciding with dream sequences, create pauses in the narrative, places and spaces where the lovers can be briefly suspended in temporary bliss before continuing on the relentless drive towards death.

94

Less well-known adaptations from the late twentieth-century also include *Romeo.Juliet* (1990), directed by Armando Acosta (USA), which used a feral cat cast with the cats' voices dubbed by prominent actors, and the spin-off *Tromeo and Juliet* (1996), directed by Lloyd Kaufman, a punk adaptation where parting, rather than being 'such sweet sorrow', instead 'totally sucks'. The play has also been the subject of a number of animations, including István Kató Kiszly's *Romeo and Juliet* (1931, Hungarian) and *Shakespeare: The Animated Tales* (dir. Efin Gambour 1996). Gonzo's animation series *Romeo x Juliet* (2007), an appropriation rather than an adaptation, imagines Verona as a floating city supported by the tree of life, Escalus.[10] *Gnomeo and Juliet* (2011), directed by Kelly Asbury, relocates the Capulet/Montague conflict to the garden with an Elton John soundtrack and heavy doses of Shakespeare puns.

When *Romeo and Juliet* moves into queer adaptation, the barriers of familial conflict transpose into discourses on gay prejudice. *Private Romeo* (2012), directed by Alan Brown, is set in a US military school where most of the staff and students are away on an assignment, leaving a small number of cadets and junior supervising officers. The orders are to carry on as usual and part of this is a class on *Romeo and Juliet*. The boundaries of the play-within-a-film expand and blur with ordinary life in the eerie and mostly-deserted spaces of the school. Consistent with the genre of the mirror film, the Shakespearean scenes, including the language, spill over and become part of the frame narrative. Love blossoms between the protagonists playing the leads, Sam Singleton, the Romeo figure (Seth Numrich) and Glenn Mangan, Juliet (Matt Doyle). In a rare happy ending, Juliet's kiss revives Romeo (Figure 7.1) and the film ends with Juliet singing to the camera. Brown has reflected how Shakespeare provided a vehicle for articulating the suffering from anti-gay prejudice and bullying.[11] The happy ending not only resists the Shakespearean tragic genre; it also constitutes a political resistance to the tendency in film to kill off the gay characters.[12]

In 2013, three very different adaptations were released. *Romeo & Juliet* directed by Carlo Carlei, with a script written by Julian Fellowes, echoed Zeffirelli's in using a traditional Italian Renaissance setting. It imagined Romeo (Douglas Booth) as a young sculptor, suggesting Michelangelo. The script drew in part from Shakespeare's dialogue, while adding freely to the lines, thus raising the question of the boundary between Shakespeare and 'Not Shakespeare'.[13] Poignant moments include when Romeo hears of Juliet's (Hailee Steinfeld) supposed death, and a low angle camera sets his head against the stars of a Renaissance fresco. It evokes the

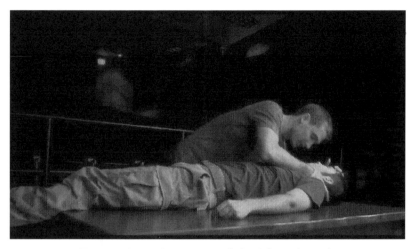

Figure 7.1 *Private Romeo* (2012): finding Juliet in the tomb.

Figure 7.2 *Dhadak* (2018): the anti-balcony scene at the conclusion.

language of the play, picking up the idea of the star-crossed lovers. Although visually beautiful, chemistry was lacking between the leads, and the impoverished quasi-Shakespearean dialogue deflated the energy of the tragedy. Shakespeare's play invites us to feel the passion of the young lovers, yet also to see their tragic impetuousness and immaturity. Successful adaptations enable us to share in both perspectives, as with Zeffirelli's and Luhrmann's. Where the love between the two central protagonists is unconvincing, as in Carlei's, we remain distanced and the idea of passionate love prepared to risk all is an abstract, rather than a lived experience.

Two thousand and thirteen saw the release of another Bollywood adaptation, *Goliyon Ki Rasleela Ram-Leela*, directed by Sanjay Leela Bhansali. The warring clans are located in a village renowned for the manufacture and sale of arms, an apt context for a contemporary *Romeo and Juliet*. The leads are not nubile teenagers but mature, muscular lovers, and Ram (Ranveer Sigh)/Romeo, deals in porn movies and stolen cars. The tragic ending differs from the play in that the lovers agree to commit suicide together by shooting each other, appropriate for a film whose title translates as 'a play of bullets'.

Also in 2013, *Romeo and Juliet* extended, perhaps inevitably, into the zombie genre with *Warm Bodies* (2013), directed by Jonathan Levine. In the aftermath of the zombie apocalypse what separates the lovers is the line between life and death, or does it? The tagline for the film is 'He's still dead but he's getting warmer'. Zombie R (Nicholas Hoult) is lonely, spending his days shuffling along with the other zombies on the dead side of the dividing wall until things look up when he meets living girl Julie (Teresa Palmer). Although Romeo eating the brains of her (now ex)-boyfriend Perry (Dave Franco) is an initial obstacle to the relationship, eventually love blossoms, triggering a process of re-humanisation not only in R but in his other zombie mates. In a surprise happy ending, the lovers end up together and alive (mostly); and after the humans and the good zombies team up to defeat the Bonies, zombies too far gone in the decomposition process, even the dividing wall, which resonates with the US/Mexican border, comes down. The key word 'exhume', with its dual meaning of dig up and revive, becomes a reflection on the need for contemporary humanity to reconnect with itself and renew its perspectives on others.

Ophelia (2018), directed by Claire McCarthy, which retells *Hamlet* from the perspective of Ophelia (Daisy Ridley), enters into intertextual dialogues with *Romeo and Juliet*. It appropriates the fake-death-using-poison motif whereby Ophelia fakes her own death to escape a forced marriage. A menacing Claudius (Clive Owen) recognises the threat that this rebellious Ophelia poses and insists on her marrying, unaware that Ophelia and Hamlet have already secretly married (again, tapping into *Romeo and Juliet*). The apothecary figure is transposed to Gertrude's sister (Naomi Watts, who also plays Gertrude), a cunning woman who hides in the forest and had an earlier relationship with Claudius.

Dhadak (2018), written and directed by Shashank Khaitan, is arguably one of the most devastating of recent *Romeo and Juliet* adaptations. Shakespeare has had a rich screen afterlife in Asian cinematic culture and *Romeo and Juliet* has been used as a lens to confront a range of contemporary problems.[14] *Dhadak*, where caste differences generate the interfamilial conflict, highlights the ongoing tragedy of honour killings. At first, the film appears to explore the potential of an afterlife for Madhukar/Romeo (Ishaan Khattar) and Parthavi/Juliet (Janhvi Kapoor). What if they escaped and began a new life, even had a child? The film lulls the audience into the temptation of hoping for a happy ending. However, the Capulets do not forget and forgive, and at the climax, Romeo and the child are murdered, thrown from a balcony, their bodies landing in front of Juliet. In this anti-balcony scene (Figure 7.2), the director again undercuts the mirage of emotional autonomy for many young lovers in restrictive cultures. The film ends with the numbing statistic quoted in the epigraph to this chapter.

Othello

Othello explores the fatal consequences of love crossing the boundaries of race, as constructed by early modern discourses of difference, and the equally lethal constructions of women that facilitate Iago's machinations and Othello's misperceptions. Othello, although a respected military leader, is linked with the zones of otherness that haunt the Eurocentric conceptual map. A gifted storyteller, Othello retells the narratives linked with the peripheral spaces he has travelled through, yet as an other himself, he is vulnerable to these same narratives. Ultimately, the lovers are too fragile for the racial and misogynist discourses that construct monsters of racial and female others, retold by another powerful story-teller, Iago.

How have filmmakers responded to this play about entrapment by narrative?[15] There were several short, black-and-white *Othello*s produced in the silent era, directed by: William V. Ranous (1908, USA, Vitagraph); Franz Porten (1908, Germany); Mario Caserini and Gaston Velle (*Otello*, Italy, 1906), based on Giuseppe Verdi's opera; Ugo Falena (Italy 1909); and Arrigo Frusta (*Othello the Moor*, Italy 1914). August Blom directed *Desdemona* (*For Aabent Tæppe*, Denmark 1911/12), an early mirror film, and a full-length black-and-white adaptation was directed by Dimitri Buchowetski in 1922 (Germany) with Emil Jannings, in black make up, in the title role.[16] Early television versions in Britain comprised: an abridged production directed by George More O'Ferrall (1937), with Anthony Quayle as Cassio; another production directed by O'Ferrall (1950), starring André

Morell as Othello; and the BBC production directed by Tony Richardson (1955) with the earliest recorded screen performance of a black actor playing Othello – Gordon Heath.[17]

During the Second World War, there was a condensed black-and-white film (45 mins) directed by David MacKane (UK, 1946). The first of the notable adaptations of the play, directed by Orson Welles, was released in 1952. It begins with the tragic aftermath, framing the whole story in effect as a flashback while Iago (Micheál MacLiammóir) hangs in a cage dangling above the street, awaiting his fate. The production was characterised by striking camera work and dramatic chiaroscuro effects. Welles explored the play's theme of monstrosity through the camera's ominous framing of Othello, and with some intriguing elements as part of the *mise-en-scène*, such as when a demonic sculptural element leers in the background when Othello is reeling from Iago's poison.[18] Welles also explored the theme of entrapment with evocative shots of Desdemona (Suzanne Cloutier) in a labyrinthine space, enmeshed amidst columns like prey for the Minotaur. Following soon after Welles's, the production directed by Sergei Yutkevich (USSR, 1955), with Sergei Bondarchuk in the lead, was unique among the *Othello* films in including interpolated scenes of Othello's past as a slave; after he suffers the effects of Iago's (Andrei Popov) poison, Othello returns to the hull of a ship, his mental torture thus linking to his past.

In *All Night Long* (1962), directed by Basil Dearden, *Othello* was transposed to the 1960s London jazz scene, changing the tragic ending to comedy. Stuart Burge's adaptation (1965) was developed from John Dexter's 1964 National Theatre production with a blacked-up Laurence Olivier in the lead and Maggie Smith as Desdemona. Olivier's performance has generally attracted negative criticism for its 'histrionic' acting and racial stereotyping.[19] At the same time, Peter Holland has argued for a reconsideration of the performance, arguing that it may be the closest a contemporary audience can get to 'the ambiguities and problematics of early modern representations and constructions of Othello'.[20]

In the 1980s, Jonathan Miller directed *Othello* for the BBC (1981), with Anthony Hopkins in the lead role. Janet Suzman's *Othello* (1988) tapped into racial politics in casting a black actor, John Kani, at a time that South Africa was still under apartheid. In 1994, the *Othello* as part of *Shakespeare: The Animated Tales* was aired, directed by Nikolay Serebryakov with screenplay by Leon Garfield and the lead voiced by black English actor Colin McFarlane. In Oliver Parker's 1995 production, with Laurence Fishburne in the lead, Kenneth Branagh as Iago and Irène Jacob as Desdemona. Fishburne presents a striking and exotic

99

Othello, his evocative pearl earring foreshadowing the play's reference to 'the base Indian' who 'threw a pearl away/ Richer than all his tribe' (5.2.356–7). There is a long history of vexed racial casting issues surrounding *Othello*. While Ira Aldridge was the first black actor to play Othello on stage in the nineteenth century, and Heath the first on screen, it was not until Parker's production that the role was played by an African American actor in a general-release film.[21]

In the *Othello* screen history, Shakespearean adaptation has intersected with real-life tragedy. The Parker film coincided with the O. J. Simpson trial, the narrative of which became eerily *Othello*-like.[22] Then Tim Blake Nelson's *O* (2001), set in a high-school, coincided with a real-life school shooting, and its release had to be delayed. The 2001 adaptation directed by Geoffrey Sax, from a screenplay by Andrew Davies, is set in London in the context of race riots arising from the death of a black man, Billy Coates, in custody. John Othello (Eamonn Walker) is a senior police officer undermined by Ben Jago (Christopher Eccleston), who makes the viewer complicit through his offsides direct to the camera. Moreover, in a bleak ending, Jago remains unpunished and in fact is promoted.

Filmmakers have responded to the geopolitics of *Othello* in various ways.[23] Parker and Miller feature maps, globes and navigational instruments. Yutkevich's globe captivates Desdemona, as Othello's tales have done. Suzman's set included a large Renaissance-style map as backdrop. Many of the adaptations invoke the idea of the monstrous through grotesque decoration in the background, subtly linking Othello and Desdemona with hybridity and the subhuman. In Sax's adaptation, John Othello is positioned before atlas figures in a key scene of unravelling, the aesthetic tapping into the histories of black slavery.[24] Suzman has John Kani visually replace the grotesque decoration on the map, ideologically revealing Othello's 'monstrosity'.[25]

Othello has proved capable of moving beyond the bounds of racial politics to explore other areas of violence. In the Mexican film *Huapango* (2004), directed by Ivan Lipkies, Otilio (Alejandro Tommasi) is white.[26] The film thus shifts its focus to gender violence, particularly in the macho and patriarchal Latino culture. Women are framed within the dangerous Virgin/whore paradigm; Santiago/Iago's (Manuel Landeta) secret shrine to Julia/ Desdemona (Lisset Salazar), reveals his lethal obsession, and after Otilio kills Julia, he decorates her corpse like a saint. In *Souli* (2004, France, Madagascar), directed by Alexander Abela, Carlos (Eduardo Noriega), the Cassio character, is a Spanish student looking for a lost sacred African story; he searches for the renowned Senegalese poet and storyteller Souli (Makena Diop), the Othello figure.[27] Souli, now a recluse and working as a fisherman, lives with a young French woman, Mona (Jeanne Antebi), the Desdemona figure. A French trader Yann/Iago (Aurélien Recoing), resentful that Mona has left him for Souli, manipulates Carlos to divide the lovers. The aesthetics of the film, with its emphasis on natural elements, and the soundtrack have similarities with Abela's earlier *Makibefo* (1999), a *Macbeth* adaptation.

Omkara (2006), directed by Vishal Bhardwaj, who directed the earlier Shakespearean adaptation *Maqbool* (2003), relocates *Othello* to India and transposes its inter-racial divide to one of caste.[28] Omkara (Ajay Devgn) heads a crime gang and supports a local politician; subsequently, he rises to become a contender in the state elections. Ishwar 'Langda' Tyagi (Saif Ali Khan), the Iago figure, is resentful of being overlooked when Omkara promotes Kesu Firangi (Vivek Oberoi), the Cassio figure. A kamarbandh, an ornate waistband that invokes suggestions of a chastity belt and female bondage, replaces the iconic handkerchief as the damning and illusory evidence against Dolly Mishra (Kareena Kapoor). Othello's outsider position is transposed here to Omkara's status as the illegitimate child of a high caste Brahmin father and lower caste mother. Langda's nickname translates as 'limp' in Hindi, and subtly references Othello's comment at the end of the play where he looks in vain for Iago's cloven hoof as a sign of monstrosity. The motif of the swing creates foreshadowing, suggesting a pendulum and Othello's wavering mind; it culminates in the swinging day bed where Desdemona's corpse swings above that of Othello's in the tragic aftermath.

Another haunting adaptation in the last decade has been *Otelo Burning* (2011), directed by Sara Blecher, where the play is transposed to a South Africa on the cusp of a post-apartheid world (Nelson Mandela is released during the events of the narrative). However, violence is ever-present.[29] Located within the surf culture of Lamontville, a township south of Durban, the narrative centres on Otelo Buthelezi (Jafta Mamabolo), an expert surfer, who is betrayed by his friend Mandla Modise (Sihle Xaba), leading to the death of Otelo's twelve-year-old brother Ntwe (Tshepang Mohlomi), murdered by gang members who wrongly believe he is an informer. Otelo's girlfriend Dezi (Nolwazi Shange) is raped by Mandla, tapping into the gendered violence at the heart of *Othello*. However, Otelo does not kill Dezi; instead, he shoots Mandla at a surfing competition, and then essentially suicides by heading out into the waves for a final, fatal surf. The film centres on the intertwined relationships of the black characters, so that when the viewer sees white South Africans as spectators at a surf competition, the white world appears as one of alien outsiders. The intra-black violence is the product of the country's long history of racial violence and Blecher reflected on how Shakespeare provided a relevant vehicle for the story: 'We layered Othello's story into it so it becomes a story of betrayal and greed. We wanted to make a story about what's going on in South Africa now, but how do you do that? With a historic story'.[30]

Othello adaptations have used a variety of techniques for conveying motifs of entrapment. Aesthetics include various bars, cages, shadows creating effects of enclosure, and lighting effects. Nelson uses gym equipment to visually encage Odin (Mekhi Phifer) and Hugo (Josh Hartnett). *Otelo Burning* has shots through metal patterned doors and the fencing around the pool. Similarly, visual imagery conveys Desdemona's entrapment and the films have explored imagery of bars and cages to convey discourses of female oppression, including the iconic bed, the space of sex and death. In Lipkie's *Huapango* at the tragic climax, Julia climbs darkened stairs where Otilio waits in the bedroom like a monster in its lair. Other imagery in relation to Desdemona invokes the lethal Virgin/whore binary, as in Welles, *Huapango*, and the motif of the spiral staircase in *O* that embodies the marvellous/monstrous paradigm relevant to constructions of race and gender that entrap Odin, the school's star basketball player, and Desi Brable (Julia Stiles), his beautiful A-crowd girlfriend.[31]

While filmmakers have explored the aesthetics of black and white in resonating with the core theme of race, another prominent vein of imagery has been water, tapping into the imaginative spaces of maps that inform the play, and Othello's description of Desdemona as 'false as water' (5.2.143). Parker's Iago plays with chess pieces that symbolise his manipulation of the other characters, and when he drops the white queen and black king in the well, as if they were voodoo dolls, the imagery anticipates the deaths and sea burial of Othello and Desdemona. Sax's adaptation presents John Othello's haunting fantasies in reflections in the water, recreating Venice in London; and in *Otelo Burning*, the narrative begins and ends with the sea, linking the prophecy of Ntwe's death with Otelo's death in the surf.

In an era of globalised Shakespeare, the love tragedies have been drawn on in a wide variety of cultural contexts to highlight contemporary problems of violence generated by discourses that frame humans as property. In *Romeo and Juliet*, the children are not only the property of their parents, to be used as items of exchange in the marriage economy; they are also expected to be heirs of their parents' hate. In *Othello*, violence results from the construction of racial or gendered others as monsters, and the framing of the female body as unreliable property, susceptible of escaping beyond masculine control. As this brief survey has illustrated, the love tragedies provide a wide range of possibilities for exploring these darker aspects of human nature.

Notes

1. On *Romeo and Juliet* on screen start with: Courtney Lehmann, *Romeo and Juliet: The Relationship between Text and Film* (London, Methuen, 2010); Russell Jackson, *Shakespeare Films in the Making* (Cambridge, Cambridge University Press, 2007), ch. 3; Mark Thornton Burnett, *Shakespeare and World Cinema* (Cambridge, Cambridge University Press, 2013), ch. 6. A future volume on *Shakespeare on Screen: Romeo and Juliet* is planned as part of the Cambridge University Press *Shakespeare on Screen* series.
2. On the 1936 MGM and 1954 Castellani productions, see Jackson, ch. 3 and Patricia Tatspaugh, 'The tragedies of love on film', in Russell Jackson, ed., *The Cambridge Companion to Shakespeare on Film*, 2nd ed. (Cambridge, Cambridge University Press, 2007), 141–64.
3. See Courtney Lehmann, *Romeo and Juliet*, 103–33.
4. Zoah Hedges-Stock, 'Steven Spielberg to remake *West Side Story* – but will it clash with the new Indiana Jones film?' *Daily Telegraph*, 29 January 2018; '*West Side Story*: high school student cast as Maria in Spielberg remake', *BBC News*, 15 January 2019, www.telegraph.co.uk/films/2018/01/29/steven-spielberg-remake-west-side-story-latino-cast/ and www.bbc.com/news/world-us-canada-46875067 (both accessed 26 April 2019).
5. Jackson, ch. 3; Lehmann, *Romeo and Juliet*, 134–66; Kenneth S. Rothwell, *A History of Shakespeare on Screen: a Century of Film and Television* 2nd ed. (Cambridge, Cambridge University Press, 2004), 126–31.
6. Anon., 'A new *Romeo and Juliet*', *Look*, 31 (1967), 55; Rothwell, *A History of Shakespeare on Screen*, 128.
7. Ibid., 126.
8. Rosa M. García-Periago, 'In search of a happy ending: the afterlife of *Romeo and Juliet* on the Asian screen', *Journal of the Spanish Association of Anglo-American Studies*, 38.1 (June 2016), 185–200; Rafik Darragi, 'The perfect, impossible love: three Egyptian film adaptations of *Romeo and Juliet*', *Critical Survey*, 28.3 (2016), 175–80.
9. Lehmann, *Romeo and Juliet*, 167–206; Peter Donaldson, '"In fair Verona": media, spectacle and performance in *William Shakespeare's Romeo + Juliet*', in Richard Burt, ed., *Shakespeare After Mass Media* (Basingstoke, Palgrave, 2002), 59–82.
10. Jim Casey, 'Hyperomeo and Juliet: postmodern adaptation and Shakespeare', in Christy Desmet, Natalie Loper and Jim Casey, eds., *Shakespeare/Not Shakespeare* (Basingstoke, Palgrave Macmillan, 2017), ch. 4; Yukari Yoshihara, 'Tacky "Shakespeares" in Japan', *Multicultural Shakespeare: Translation, Appropriation and Performance, The Journal of University of Lodz*, 10.25, 83–97.
11. Information from the film's web site: www.privateromeothemovie.com/about/.
12. Peter Debruge, 'Film industry shouldn't be so quick to pat itself on the back', *Variety*, 328.15 (2015), 98–9.
13. On this issue, see Desmet, Loper and Casey, eds., *Shakespeare/Not Shakespeare*.
14. For example, see Courtney Lehmann, '"An elan of the soul"? Counter-cinema and Deepa Mehta's *Water*', *Shakespeare Bulletin*, 34.3 (2016), 43–50. Also see

the Indonesian adaptation *Romeo Juliet*, directed by Andibachtiar Yusuf, which highlights the deadly violence between supporters of rival soccer teams.

15. See Sarah Hatchuel and Nathalie Vienne-Guerrin, eds., *Shakespeare on Screen: Othello* (Cambridge, Cambridge University Press, 2015) and Anthony Davies, '"An extravagant and wheeling stranger of here and everywhere." Characterising *Othello* on film: exploring seven film adaptations', *Shakespeare in Southern Africa*, 23 (2011), 11–19.

16. Sarah Hatchuel and Nathalie Vienne-Guerrin, 'Introduction: ensnared in *Othello* on screen', *in Shakespeare on Screen: Othello* (Cambridge, Cambridge University Press, 2015), 5.

17. BFI Screenonline, www.screenonline.org.uk/tv/id/566380/index.html (accessed 26 April 2019).

18. Victoria Bladen, '*Othello* on screen: monsters, marvellous space and the power of the tale', in Hatchuel and Vienne-Guerrin, eds., *Shakespeare on Screen: Othello*, 26 and 30.

19. Hatchuel and Vienne-Guerrin, 'Introduction', 5. Russell Jackson, *Shakespeare and the English-Speaking Cinema* (Oxford, Oxford University Press, 2014), 103.

20. Peter Holland, 'Rethinking blackness: the case of Olivier's *Othello*', in Hatchuel and Vienne-Guerrin, eds., *Shakespeare on Screen:* Othello, ch. 3.

21. Hatchuel and Vienne-Guerrin, 'Introduction', 2–7.

22. Ibid., 11.

23. Bladen, '*Othello* on screen', ch. 2.

24. Ibid., 29.

25. Ibid., 28.

26. Aimara da Cunha Resende, '*Othello* in Latin America: *Otelo de Oliveira* and *Huapango*' in *Shakespeare on Screen:* Othello, ch. 8.

27. Anne-Marie Costantini-Cornède, 'African kings: *Makibefo* (1999) and *Souli* (2004), Alexander Abela's transcultural and experimental screen Shakespeare', *Shakespeare en devenir*, 12 (2017), http://shakespeare.edel.univ-poitiers.fr/index.php?id=1126; Burnett, *Shakespeare and World Cinema*, ch. 1.

28. Florence Cabaret, 'Indianizing *Othello*: Vishal Bhardwaj's *Omkara*' in Hatchuel and Vienne-Guerrin, eds., *Shakespeare on Screen: Othello*, ch. 7.

29. Chris Thurman, 'Editorial', *Shakespeare in Southern Africa*, 25 (2013), iii–v; and Glen Thompson, '*Otelo Burning* and Zulu surfing histories', *Journal of African Cultural Studies*, 26.3 (2014), 324–40.

30. Roger Young, 'Zulu surf films' (an interview with Sara Blecher) *Mahala* (20 July 2011), www.mahala.co.za/culture/zulu-surf-films/ (accessed 26 April 2019).

31. Bladen, '*Othello* on screen', 35.

8

KINGA FÖLDVÁRY

'Sad Stories of the Death of Kings': *The Hollow Crown* and the Shakespearean History Play on Screen

Looking back at the history of the moving image, we may notice a curiously uneven attention to adaptations of Shakespeare's histories. The genre boasts a number of firsts: the first Shakespeare play recorded, even if only partially, on screen was *King John,* advertising Herbert Beerbohm Tree's production in 1899, and the first feature film based on a Shakespearean play was James Keane's 1912 *Richard III,* starring Frederick Warde. A few of the plays have inspired award-winning films by the greatest actor-directors of the twentieth century, notably *Henry V* by Laurence Olivier (1944) and Kenneth Branagh (1989), *Richard III* by Olivier (1955), the *Henry IV* plays by Orson Welles in his *Chimes at Midnight* (1965); others have been popularised by star-studded casts, as in Richard Loncraine's *Richard III* (1995). Some of the plays, however, have been completely absent from the silver screen, although adapted for television, since the chronological inter-connectedness of their source material lent them easily to serialisation. The best-known of these history cycles were made under the aegis of the BBC: *An Age of Kings* (1960), produced by Peter Dews, and John Barton and Peter Hall's *The Wars of the Roses* (1965), based on the Royal Shakespeare Company's 1964 productions. Since the mid-1960s, a number of televised theatre performances have followed suit, among them Michael Bogdanov's and Michael Pennington's *The Wars of the Roses,* a recording of the English Shakespeare Company's 1987 History Cycle made in 1989 and published on video in 1990.[1] The single complete series which included all of the history plays was of course the BBC *Shakespeare Collection,* created by Cedric Messina and originally broadcast in the UK between 1979 and 1985. In spite of its predominantly theatrical visuality, the series' significance is undoubted, if for no other reason than because it includes the single full-length adaptation of both *King John* and *Henry VIII.* The four parts of the first tetralogy (*Henry VI, Parts 1–3,* and *Richard III*) in particular, directed by Jane Howell in a stylised, playground-style setting, are ranked among the best of the whole enterprise.

As if attempting to make up for lost time, the twenty-first century has returned to the genre with a vengeance in the form of *The Hollow Crown*, a two-season television series, produced by Sam Mendes and broadcast on BBC2 in 2012 and 2016. Although the choice of plays may seem surprising at first, one thing is clear: in this day and age, it is precisely television that appears best situated for a revival of the history play. One reason why television may be the most appropriate medium for this venture lies partly in today's convergence culture; it is no longer the silver screen of the cinema, but the larger and larger television screens, or the smaller and smaller screens of computers and handheld devices that vie for viewers' attention with the Internet, streaming services, video games and social media platforms. The creators of *The Hollow Crown* series are fully aware of the significance of television audiences, many of whom are first-time viewers of Shakespeare histories. Ben Power, the adaptor of the text, explains his excitement over this opportunity to convert viewers to the classics: 'It's wonderful that these films reach a larger audience than is possible in the theatre. We wanted to use contemporary film-making techniques to show that Shakespeare can be engaging, dynamic and cinematic.'[2]

At the same time, the series does not deny its strong roots in the world of the theatre, not only in the form of a stellar cast of senior and novice Shakespeare actors, but also in its centralisation of the Shakespearean language, even if this emphasis on the text at times (particularly in the final episode of the second series, *Richard III*) results in a somewhat hybrid product. Nonetheless, *The Hollow Crown* also exemplifies a number of the central controversies surrounding contemporary Shakespeare adaptation, including political agendas, screen and stage traditions of acting and textual interpretation, together with the changing awareness of the viewing public of Shakespeare as a (high or pop) cultural phenomenon. In a way, *The Hollow Crown* simply returns to a previously tried and trusted format – but the changed contemporary mediascape gives added vigour to the television series, the signature format of the twenty-first century.

How does then the Shakespearean history play fare when its admittedly anachronistic situatedness in an increasingly distant past comes into contact with the realistic visual representation characteristic of historical television? *The Hollow Crown* creators had no easy task: some of the history plays are ranked as the least popular ones in the whole Shakespearean canon, and the rest have already been immortalised by the great actor-directors of the twentieth century. To counter these iconic productions, the new series relies on the current popularity of television as a medium, and emphasises the potential of the sequential nature of the histories, even if '[t]here is no evidence that Shakespeare's own public ever saw the English history plays in sequence'.[3] Yet neither does *The Hollow Crown* deny the plays' power as star vehicles, or the power of a stellar cast, easier to assemble for a television project than to sign on for a long theatrical run, to increase viewing numbers. Nonetheless, I also believe that the resulting product is characterised by a number of complexities, both in its attitude to the Shakespearean source material, and in the way it attempts to find a commercially viable but artistically uncompromising position between the performative traditions of stage and screen.

The most noticeable and most often debated example of this slight hybridity is the series' controversial attitude to ethnic diversity in casting, particularly in *Henry V* and in the second series. By virtue of its international distribution (together with legal and illegal streaming and downloading typical of contemporary popular visual culture consumption), the films compete for attention on the same screens that accommodate a vast array of popular television series, from *The Tudors* through *Vikings* to *Game of Thrones*, characterised by an almost hyperreal visual historicity. The links between episodes also change the interpretive network surrounding individual plays, markedly contrasting this type of reading with a traditional cinematic interpretation.

In the Service of Ideology

As Rosemary Gaby notes, 'British productions of Shakespeare's history plays have often been associated with occasions of national significance',[4] most blatantly in the case of *Henry V*, commonly appropriated in the service of various agendas, linked to historical circumstance and political ideology.[5] But if Laurence Olivier's *Henry V*, produced in 1944 in aid of the war effort, must be read against the context of World War II; if Kenneth Branagh's 1989 version of the same play can be seen as a reference to 'post-Falklands'[6] British history, or as the actor-director's personal journey from a Northern Irish working-class background to the pantheon of English Shakespeare theatre; then what is the interpretive backdrop to be observed in relation to *The Hollow Crown*?

The immediate socio-historical moment of the films' creation provides a convincing answer, but may not be able to tell the story in its entirety. The first series of *The Hollow Crown*, comprising the plays of the second tetralogy (*Richard II*, dir. Rupert Goold; *Henry IV, Parts 1 and 2*, dir.

Richard Eyre; *Henry V*, dir. Thea Sharrock) was broadcast during the summer of 2012, as part of the Cultural Olympiad, a programme series produced in celebration of the London Olympic Games and the Queen's Diamond Jubilee. As a result of a generally positive critical response, including several award nominations and wins, among them BAFTAs for Ben Whishaw and Simon Russell Beale, the production was given the green light for another season of three films (*Henry VI, Parts 1 and 2*, *Richard III*, all three directed by Dominic Cooke), called *The Hollow Crown: The Wars of the* Roses, which aired in early 2016. This second cycle was presented amidst much Shakespearean celebration, in the year of the 400th anniversary of his death, with the worldwide Shakespeare industry in full swing since the 450th birth anniversary festivities in 2014. No other special occasion or historic significance is mentioned either in the publicity materials or the DVD extras, apart from the fact that the production team was hoping to use the momentum gained in the first season to popularise an even lesser known group of plays. Yet, with the advantage of historical hindsight, one can hardly fail to wonder how the broadcast of the second cycle, dominated by a haunting sense of an internally divided kingdom, ruled by manipulative and monstrous monarchs, just preceded the Brexit referendum, when British identity and the country's relationship to Europe was at its most uncertain. As Víctor Huertas Martín notes in his review, '[a]t a time in which the British nation faces one of its greatest historical crises, *The Wars of the Roses* appears as a more than appropriate topic'.[7] Another topical connection was noticeable in the USA, where the second series was screened in December 2016, right after the election of Donald Trump as president, as Alison Keene notes:

> this second series of the *Hollow Crown* ends in a much darker and more uncertain place than Tom Hiddleston's rousing St. Crispin's Day speech in 2012's *Henry V*. And yet, in 2016 it also feels far more fitting that instead of 'We few, we happy few, we band of brothers,' we have 'now is the winter of our discontent.'[8]

As if to reflect this controversial topicality, both celebratory and mournful, the journey of the project has not been completely without obstacles. Series showrunner Sam Mendes, for all his national and international renown both as an Oscar-winning director and producer of Hollywood films and British theatre productions, could not secure the financial backing of BBC Worldwide, and had to turn elsewhere for support. At the end of the day, the series were produced, although nominally for the BBC, with joint backing from Neal Street

Productions, Carnival/NBC-Universal and Thirteen. As Dan Leberg sums up the complex arrangement: '[t]he fundamental condition of *The Hollow Crown*'s multinational production partnership, wherein NBC-Universal is the primary investor, is that BBC2 retains distribution rights within Great Britain, and NBC-Universal retains all international distribution rights, including DVD and digital download sales'.[9] The irony is that it was precisely the financial viability of selling Shakespeare on television that was called into doubt by the BBC, even though the choice of Shakespeare as the single most appropriate author for the celebratory year seems to have come from the Corporation itself. Nonetheless, the hesitance clearly reflects the controversial position of televisual Shakespeare, placed at the crossroads of popular and high culture, practised out of necessity and a sense of mission, since the charter of the BBC includes its obligation to provide 'high-quality … output and services which inform, educate and entertain',[10] while also investing taxpayers' money in a financially responsible manner.

The Serial Context

The decision to produce the histories in a sequential format was there from the inception of the project; when BBC Worldwide withdrew the financial backing they had promised, and offered funding only for *Richard II*, Mendes refused to accept this compromise.[11] The significance of this decision, I believe, points beyond the grandeur of the directorial vision, as the presentation of the four plays as a television series has implications for the interpretation of the individual episodes and the group as a whole. The two seasons of *The Hollow Crown* also offer the perfect example of the blurring boundaries between 'series' and 'serials': while the first four episodes could be better characterised as a series since they preserve the structural independence of the Shakespearean source dramas, the second group, the three episodes broadcast in 2016, present the chaotic period of the Wars of the Roses as a continuous story, that is, like a serial, in which the original textual units, particularly of the three *Henry VI* plays, have all but dissolved. To further complicate terminology, *The Hollow Crown* also resembles a 'mini-series', a classic staple of televised adaptations, which is in fact a short serial. In popular use, however, 'series' appears to be taking over in reference to all types of sequential broadcasts, therefore this chapter also employs this term in this inclusive, general meaning.

The most obvious advantage of the format is naturally its familiarity to viewers, also noted by *The Guardian*'s critic, Mark Lawson:

the linked sequence of [the four films] tell a sequential story, with recurring characters and so have a structural similarity with the four-part family drama, a staple of TV fiction. In this sense, *The Hollow Crown* can be seen as a relative of *The Tudors*, though with significantly better dialogue.[12]

Placing the dramas in a sequence also has the – perhaps unwanted, at times even uncomfortable – effect of a stronger focus on the historical precedents, which are sometimes blatantly suppressed in Olivier's *Henry V*, or even in Branagh's version of the same. As a result, while we would find it hard to imagine Olivier's Henry as a rambunctious Prince Hal, it is equally hard to forget Tom Hiddleston's image as the young prince, which will continue to remind both the newly minted king and the audience of *The Hollow Crown Henry V* of the journey he (and his house of Lancaster) had to take to secure the crown. But this backstory may precisely be what necessitates the heavier (and oft-criticised) cuts in *Henry V*: to allow Hiddleston's young king to grow into his role as a mighty war hero, the series needs to suppress the shady justification for the French campaign, which is so emphatic in Branagh's film. The scenes that show the French as ridiculous and therefore worthless enemies, as in Olivier's version, are equally absent; in the 1944 film, it is the Dauphin's character who shoulders most of the blame for the bloodshed, and the French king is presented as senile, although generally benevolent – since the French were allies in World War II, it would have been unwise to show them all as sworn enemies of the English nation. In *The Hollow Crown*, all of these uncertainties regarding the French campaign are silenced for the sake of the serial cohesion, and the same serial connection allowed the condensation of the *Henry VI* plays into two episodes, cutting away Jack Cade and other subplots. The remaining narrative can find its focus much earlier on the rise of Richard III to power – particularly since the face of this Richard, Benedict Cumberbatch, was the long-awaited sight for sore eyes for a significant portion of the viewing public. *The Hollow Crown* also exemplifies the workings of contemporary television series in terms of authorship, as Ramona Wray convincingly argues, showing ways in which 'one auteur's invention can cross-fertilise with another's, generating diverse engagements inside a larger televisual experience', in a 'newer model that is transforming an appreciation of Shakespeare for the modern viewer'.[13]

Apart from the serial structure reinforcing plot cohesion, stylistically the series often relies on popular visual culture, using either the actors' popular roles, or the evocation of a number of commercial genres to streamline storytelling. Such genres include the war film and action film, particularly in the case of Tom Hiddleston, whose past career as an action hero in various Hollywood blockbusters reinforces the warrior attitudes of his Prince Hal and even more his depiction of Henry V. The interplay between Shakespearean roles and non-Shakespearean characters is also remarked by the actor himself when he claims in an interview that Shakespeare led him to superheroes and therefore he finds the transition back to Shakespeare natural and welcome.[14] The costume designers of both seasons mention football games as an influence on battle scenes, acknowledging the power of the familiar visual vocabulary in the representation of the antagonism between opposing social groups.[15] Nigel Egerton, costume designer for the second series, explains the need for colour coding to distinguish between the two sides in battle scenes with reference to the two Manchester football teams: 'it's a way of separating the sides visually. ... It's a United versus City type affair.'[16]

One may lament the way such attitudes bear witness to a dumbing down of Shakespearean material, but the reality of television is that programmes do not exist in isolation, even less so than theatre or cinema productions. As watching television is still the most popular leisure time activity both in the UK and in the USA,[17] it is inevitable that programme choices are often made with a view to the options competing for viewers' attention on the same household screen. It is also telling that a number of reviews, both commercial and scholarly, make references to popular film and television, likening *The Hollow Crown* to the popular HBO television series *Game of Thrones*[18] (in a rather telling error, one reviewer keeps referring to the series as *The Hollow Throne*),[19] others identifying actors based on their previous roles in the *Harry Potter* franchise,[20] the Marvel Cinematic Universe, *Downton Abbey* or the *Sherlock* series.[21]

Colour-blind Casting in *The Hollow Crown*

Yet, for all the media-conscious visual and structural elements of the series, in one crucial aspect *The Hollow Crown* falls back more on a theatrical than a televisual model, and I believe this mixed model resulted in the single most controversial feature, antagonising otherwise generally satisfied viewers: the employment of actors of colour. In the first season, we find three non-white actors in a cast of over 100; in *Richard II*, the Bishop of Carlisle is played by Lucian Msamati, while Lord Ross is played by Peter de Jersey and in *Henry V*, we can find Paterson Joseph in the role of York (no actor of colour appears in the *Henry IV* films). As it appears from viewer comments, what most people found at odds with their general perception of the series as a whole was the historical inaccuracy of employing any coloured actor to play medieval English nobility. While acknowledging the artistic achievement of all three actors, many commenters criticise the BBC's all-too-eager sense of political correctness, which does not have anything to do with the plays' representation of British society, then or now. Not to mention the fact that the Duke of York, played by Paterson Joseph in the *Henry V* episode, is historically the same person as the Duke of Aumerle, played by the very white Tom Hughes in *Richard II* (son of Edmund, first Duke of York, played by David Suchet), therefore such uneven colour-blind casting disrupts the internal cohesion of the series as a whole. Such casting clearly works against the otherwise marked attempts at historical accuracy, emphasised via location shooting, convincing costume and prop design, even the never-before-seen realism of the scoliotic back of Richard III in the final episode.

The problematic element of casting a single actor of colour in a whole film – even if in such a positive and enlarged role as that of the Duke of York in *Henry V* – is that it emphasises colour and therefore race into a meaningful marker (Figure 8.1). As L. Monique Pittman argues, this distinction transforms York 'from an example of responsive multicultural television practice into the expendable "black best friend" of the film', embodying even 'the magical negro stereotype, the black man who nurtures white masculinity and then willingly departs the scene once his healing power has worked its magic'.[22] In *The Wars of the Roses*, the role of Queen Margaret, played by Sophie Okonedo, a black British actress, is even more controversial.

Figure 8.1 *The Hollow Crown: Henry V* (2012): 'We happy few . . .' – Paterson Joseph (Duke of York), Tom Hiddleston (King Henry) and Richard Clothier (Earl of Salisbury).

Okonedo excels in her portrayal of Margaret and her dynamism is one of the driving forces of the whole season, as Serena Davies claims in her review for *The Telegraph*: 'Okonedo got the role of her life as Margaret, and grabbed it, nails outstretched, uniting the three films as she blazed through them, leaving scorched earth behind her.'[23] Yet by being practically the single actor of colour in all three episodes of the second season, her Otherness – characterised by sexual promiscuity, manipulative plotting, her vengeful nature and an association with the supernatural through her curses in *Richard III* – is defined predominantly in racial terms. As a result, her excellent performance must by necessity acquire a darker, racial interpretation, all the more noticeably in the context of the Brexit referendum, at a time when British identity was being redefined as anti-European.

Both Joseph and Okonedo are thus objects – even victims – of such tokenistic casting that 'appears symptomatic of a British multicultural policy that still requires further reflection and reform',[24] according to Pittman. In general, the kind of colour-blindness that characterises *The Hollow Crown* seems to me a rather cautious, or even cowardly solution, neither opting for a visually plausible historicity – even if such solutions are often based on equally prejudiced ignorance: Ruth Morse points out the paradox of accepting Jewish actors, but refusing black ones, both being equally ahistorical.[25] What I find even more troubling is the way *The Hollow Crown* employs coloured actors only for roles that are in some indirect way associated with treachery and betrayal. The Bishop of Carlisle is publicly punished in *Richard II*, but even the title of the great and loyal Duke of York will pass on to his nephew, Richard, Duke of York, who goes back on his oath of loyalty and turns against Henry VI, and by this betrayal effectively starts the Wars of the Roses. As a result, the colour-blind casting in the whole series may be counter-productive, reinforcing the most conservative racial stereotypes by implying how people of colour cannot be trusted – or at least confusing the series' position in terms of its media context, making it appear a hybrid of theatre and film. In the realistic medium of the television, going against the grain of audience expectations can easily determine the fate of a new work. As H. R. Coursen remarks: 'One reason why documentaries work well on television is that they do not ask us to "suspend our disbelief"'.[26] Even if these expectations are unrealistic – Shakespeare wrote fiction, after all, and even historical documentaries are by nature fictional, since they need to employ contemporary actors, reconstructions of events and characters – by invoking the atmosphere of documentary realism with the general visual feel of the locations, even small inaccuracies may end up causing outrage among dedicated viewers.

Icons of Power: The Chessboard and the Crown

Dedicated viewers are in fact a key to the appreciation of film in the age of digital media: audiences used to adjusting their viewing experience to their own liking are ready to offer attention to visual detail that characterises only the discerning viewer or the fan of popular culture. On-demand television, DVD box sets, streaming and downloading all allow a closer look at the screen, repetition and rewinding, which helps the enthusiast to focus on the visual icons that *The Hollow Crown* abounds in. Apart from the different colour palettes used for various courts and factions, the heritage epic feel enhanced by the location shooting (mentioned by most cast members as a strong influence on their own engagement with the plots), a number of iconic elements add to the plot in an unspoken, but visually impressive manner. In the second season, the game of chess played by the Earl of Warwick and the Duke of York keeps reminding us that politics is a power play, where strategy and an ability to hide one's intention are of the utmost importance. This game will gain even more significance in *Richard III*, where Richard is constantly seen with his chessboard, in fact, from the first scene of the play to the last, but he never shares the board with anyone, thus refusing to acknowledge anyone as his equal (Figure 8.2). The obsessive nature of his power play will also find expression in the way the pieces are sometimes thrown on the ground, or the repetitive noise coming from his compulsive tapping on the board. The film ends with two short scenes appended after the coronation of Richmond as Henry VII; the camera takes us down to

Figure 8.2 *The Hollow Crown: Richard III* (2016): Icons of Power – Benedict Cumberbatch (Richard III).

Richard's dungeon, now empty save for a single fallen figure of a chess piece – a king – lying on the ground. Then it cuts immediately to the battlefield, scattered with corpses, where Queen Margaret observes a pile of bodies being thrown into a mass grave, in a final tableau of 'of graves, of worms, and epitaphs' (*Richard II*, 3.2.141) – the magnified image of physical destruction mirroring the diminutive symbol of the monarch's fall. This ending may also be seen as a respectful nod towards Jane Howell, whose *Richard III* in the BBC Shakespeare series (1983) ends with a pile of corpses, with Margaret sitting on top, cradling Richard's dead body, her deranged laughter the only sound competing with the howl of the wind in the final moments of the film.

At the heart of *The Hollow Crown*, however, is a single icon, implied already in the title of the series: the crown. In the same way as the crown is both a physical object and a symbol, and its hollowness is also interpretable in various ways, Richard II's words from the first episode haunt the whole series, questioning our understanding of the nature of monarchy, power, divine right and human ambition. Yet nothing expresses this connection running through all seven episodes more eloquently than the visual and physical variations on the theme of the crown itself. Nearly all kings are seen wearing a variety of crowns throughout their reign, fitting the crown jewels to the ceremonial or military occasion. In coronation scenes, nearly all of them wear a closed crown complete with arches and velvet cap. The exception is Tom Hiddleston's Henry V, who is crowned with the simple open crown we have come to know as his father's crown, decorated with oak leaves and crosses. This is already a much less elaborate design than the one worn by Richard II even on everyday occasions, bedecked with precious stones, as fitting the effeminate but aesthetically refined monarch. Henry IV's crown has no coloured stones, but after the coronation, his son exchanges this for an even simpler design, with only crosses and fleurs-de-lis on the golden circle. The simple concave – in fact, hollow – design of the crosses is in line with the more masculine tone characteristic of Henry V's reign in the series, and this is the crown his son, Henry VI is seen wearing most of the time. Yet, for all his naturally puritanical attitude, the young and long-haired Henry VI cuts a weak and effeminate figure, on whose head the hollowness of the crown is painfully visible. Richard III wears again another open crown, one with a noticeable velvet padding inside its circle, which emphasises, even exaggerates the discrepancy between the size of the symbolic jewel and the head it adorns, as if it were a spectacularly unfitting body natural that has come to represent the body politic in his person.

Thus out of the many significant actions the crowns are exposed to by their wearers (Ramona Wray provides a careful reading of a number of

instances from the first season), Sam Mendes and his team create an
overarching motif that tells

> sad stories of the death of kings:
> How some have been depos'd, some slain in war,
> Some haunted by the ghosts they have deposed,
> Some poisoned by their wives, some sleeping killed,
> All murdered. For within the hollow crown
> That rounds the mortal temples of a king
> Keeps Death his court. (*Richard II*, 3.2.152–8)

Earlier in this chapter I have referred to the claim that film adaptations
of Shakespearean histories are always presented at moments of national
significance, and now I am forced to wonder how such a visually spectacular but extremely grim portrayal of one of the most violent periods of
English history may be seen as representative in the contemporary mediascape. In the near prophetic words of *The Telegraph*'s critic, Jasper
Rees: 'People will talk of these films' timeliness as the UK rips itself apart
over the referendum. But for all the fretting over Englishness, *The
Hollow Crown* is finally a study of paternity and kingship.'[27] And one
has to agree: royal it is in every sense of the word, since *The Hollow
Crown* is also a treasure-trove of several generations of Shakespearean
talent, their collaboration made only possible by the medium of television, while it also offers a beautiful tableau of the architectural heritage
of the British Isles. But beyond this roll call of greatness, the series also
showcases a number of competing adaptational strategies, examples for
the cross-fertilisation between theatre, cinema and television, beside
exemplifying a number of critical debates, from the representation of
female, non-English or non-British voices and accents, colour-blind or
colour-conscious casting, set against the demands of historical realism
expected from the contemporary screen – in brief: the reality of British
television Shakespeare today.

Notes

1. David Fuller, 'The Bogdanov version: the English Shakespeare Company *Wars of the Roses*', *Literature/Film Quarterly*, 33.2 (2005), 118–41 (118).
2. 'The Hollow Crown – The Wars of the Roses press pack', *BBC Media Centre*, 3 May 2016, www.bbc.co.uk/mediacentre/mediapacks/warsoftheroses (accessed 31 December 2018).
3. Lois Potter, 'The second tetralogy: performance as interpretation', in Richard Dutton and Jean E. Howard, eds., *A Companion to Shakespeare's Works, Vol. II, The Histories* (Oxford, Blackwell, 2003), 287–307 (288).

4. Rosemary Gaby, '"The days that we have seen": history and regret in *Henry IV, Parts One* and *Two*, *The Hollow Crown* (2012)', in R. S. White, Mark Houlahan, Katrina O'Loughlin, eds., *Shakespeare and Emotions: Inheritances, Enactments, Legacies* (Basingstoke, Palgrave Macmillan, 2015), 231–39 (231).

5. See, for example, Peter S. Donaldson, 'Taking on Shakespeare: Kenneth Branagh's *Henry V*', *Shakespeare Quarterly*, 42.1 (Spring 1991), 60–71; Graham Holderness, '"What ish my nation?" Shakespeare and national identities', *Textual Practice*, 5.1 (1991), 74–93; Robert F. Willson, Jr., 'War and reflection on war: the Olivier and Branagh films of *Henry V*', *Shakespeare Bulletin*, 9.3 (Summer 1991), 27–29, to mention but a few of the early scholarly reflections on the two films.

6. Holderness, 'What ish my nation?', 84.

7. Víctor Huertas Martín, 'Review of Dominic Cooke, dir., *The Hollow Crown: The Wars of the Roses*. (BBC, 2016)', *Sederi* 27 (2017), 231–37 (231).

8. Alison Keene, '"*The Hollow Crown*: the Wars of the Roses" Review: Benedict Cumberbatch is exceptional', *Collider*, 9 December 2016, http://collider.com/the-hollow-crown-the-wars-of-the-roses-review-benedict-cumerbatch/ (accessed 1 January 2019).

9. Dan Leberg, '*The Hollow Crown*: quality television and colonial performances', *Reception: Texts, Readers, Audiences, History*, 10 (2018), 27–49 (33).

10. Department for Digital, Culture, Media and Sport, 'Royal Charter for the Continuance of the British Broadcasting Corporation', *Gov.uk*, 15 December 2016, https://assets.publishing.service.gov.uk/government/uploads/system/uploads/attachment_data/file/577829/57964_CM_9365_Charter_Accessible.pdf (accessed 1 January 2019).

11. Maggie Brown, 'Sam Mendes: BBC Worldwide rejected "Hollow Crown" Shakespeare films', *The Guardian*, 2 July 2012, www.theguardian.com/media/2012/jul/02/sam-mendes-bbc-worldwide-shakespeare (accessed 1 January 2019).

12. Mark Lawson, '*The Hollow Crown*: as good as TV Shakespeare can get?', *The Guardian*, 29 June 2012, www.theguardian.com/tv-and-radio/tvandradioblog/2012/jun/29/the-hollow-crown-shakespeare-bbc2 (accessed 1 January 2019).

13. Ramona Wray, 'The Shakespearean auteur and the televisual medium', *Shakespeare Bulletin*, 34.3 (Fall 2016), 469–85 (483).

14. 'It's a privilege to be back ... Shakespeare makes me feel more alive, says *Thor* star Tom Hiddleston', *Evening Standard*, 18 December 2013.

15. Eliza Kessler, 'Henry IV and Henry V: Q&A with the costume designer', *BBC TV blog*, 5 July 2012, www.bbc.co.uk/blogs/legacy/tv/2012/07/henry-iv-v-shakespeare.shtml (accessed 1 January 2019).

16. 'The Hollow Crown – The Wars of the Roses press pack', *BBC Media Centre*, 3 May 2016, www.bbc.co.uk/mediacentre/mediapacks/warsoftheroses (accessed 31 December 2018).

17. Cf. Ofcom, 'Media nations: UK 2018', 18 July 2018, www.ofcom.org.uk/__data/assets/pdf_file/0014/116006/media-nations-2018-uk.pdf (accessed 1 January 2019); Bureau of Labor Statistics, US Department of Labor, 'American time use survey – 2017 results', 28 June 2018, www.bls.gov/news.release/atus.nro.htm (accessed 1 January 2019).

18. For example, Leberg, '*The Hollow Crown*: quality television and colonial performances', 30.

19. David Livingstone, 'Silenced voices: a reactionary streamlined *Henry V* in *The Hollow Crown*', *Multicultural Shakespeare: Translation, Appropriation and Performance*, 12 (27), (2015), 87–100 (90, 91 and 93).

20. Ruth Morse, '*The Hollow Crown*: Shakespeare, the BBC, and the 2012 London Olympics', *Linguaculture* 1 (2014), 7–20.

21. For example, L. Monique Pittman, 'Shakespeare and the cultural olympiad: contesting gender and the British nation in the BBC's *The Hollow Crown*', *Borrowers and Lenders*, 9.2 (Spring 2016), 25, n. 8.

22. L. Monique Pittman, 'Colour-conscious casting and multicultural Britain in the BBC *Henry V* (2012): historicizing adaptation in an age of digital placelessness', *Adaptation*, 10.2 (2017), 176–91 (184).

23. Serena Davies, 'A chilling end to *The Hollow Crown*, series two, review', *The Telegraph*, 21 May 2016, www.telegraph.co.uk/tv/2016/05/21/a-chilling-end-to-the-hollow-crown-series-two-review/ (accessed 1 January 2019).

24. Pittman, 'Colour-conscious casting', 185.

25. Morse, '*The Hollow Crown*', 11.

26. Herbert R. Coursen, *Watching Shakespeare on Television* (Cranbury NJ and London: Associated University Presses, 1993), 20.

27. Jasper Rees, 'Cumberbatch outrageously steals every scene in *The Hollow Crown* – first look review', *The Telegraph*, 30 March 2016, www.telegraph.co.uk/tv/2016/03/30/the-hollow-crown-henry-vi–first-look-review/ (accessed 1 January 2019).

9

PETER J. SMITH

The Roman Plays on Film

Until the millennium there were few significant cinematic versions of
Shakespeare's Roman plays.[1] The most prominent exception is Joseph
Mankiewicz's canonical *Julius Caesar* (1953), which has attracted large
amounts of critical attention.[2] On the small screen, with the exception of
the, by now rather dated, BBC Shakespeare, the pickings are even more
slender.[3] While there has been talk for some time about a Roman equivalent
of the history plays' *The Hollow Crown*, nothing has appeared to date.[4]
Since 1999 two major films of Roman plays have been released which
I consider here in some detail.[5]

Julie Taymor's *Titus* has been around the longest and so it has
amassed a reasonable critical commentary, but Ralph Fiennes's
Coriolanus has not yet generated the sustained scholarly attention that
it deserves. Both of these films challenge the formulaic representation of
Rome as comprising sombre senates, sandals and togas over hairy legs.
This hackneyed portrayal is radically updated by Taymor and Fiennes,
whose films speak to the recent conflicts in the Balkans, Bosnia and the
former Yugoslavia. Jennifer Flaherty emphasises what she considers to
be the films' shared sense of the reciprocation of classical and modern,
and the manner in which they fold ancient and contemporary hostilities
into each other, in order to deploy the Roman plays in the cause of
pacific commentary: 'Both films suggest that violence and war are part
of a continuous human condition – and that Shakespeare's early modern
construction of Rome can be equally applied to antiquity or the
present.'[6] In this way, these films offer a coherent as well as
a politically engaged post-millennial aesthetic and a hardy refutation of
the pseudo-Roman-ness of both Mankiewicz (on the big screen) and the
BBC series (on the small one).

Coriolanus

In an interview published in 2012, Ralph Fiennes describes how, in anticipation of his directorial debut, he sought the guidance of one of theatre's most experienced practitioners:

> I actually talked briefly to Peter Brook before we shot this, and I was able to ask his advice. When Brook made his film of *King Lear* [in 1971], he felt that the cinema does not tolerate anything that's overtly theatrical. It has to be naturalistic. That is what I tried for in *Coriolanus*, and so, if it is naturalistic, then the audience relaxes.[7]

In his voice-over commentary to the DVD version of the film, he emphasises how this spoken naturalism is at odds with theatrical conventionality: 'One of the things I felt in this was that the speaking of verse should be as naturalistic as possible. The scary word in all this is "theatre". I mean cinema and theatre are arguably miles apart and yet they're also extremely close.'[8]

When Fiennes played Coriolanus on stage at the Gainsborough Film Studios in 2000 (dir. Jonathan Kent for the Almeida), his performance was anything but naturalistic. My own response was critical of his overt theatricality, mainly to do with an exaggerated projection: 'His first furious entrance in which he mocks the citizens' cowardice was conducted at top volume and this left him hardly anywhere to go in subsequent scenes. A mere increase of volume on such an already high level was hardly noticeable and, very quickly, his performance became unnuanced.'[9] Similarly, Susannah Clapp's verdict highlighted this histrionic tendency: 'a lot of the verse can't be heard. A lot of it is bellowed'.[10]

Reprising the role for the cinema, a decade later, Fiennes was determined to, in the words of Gary Crowdus, 'eliminate from the film any trace of theatricality, especially the declamatory style of verse speaking ... in favour of a more *naturalistic*, conversational style'.[11] Fiennes relied upon the experience of two Shakespearean veterans in his casting of the roles of Volumnia and Menenius: 'When you have actors like Vanessa Redgrave and Brian Cox speaking the lines, it sounds completely natural.'[12]

Fiennes's aspiration to stress cinematic naturalism, is perhaps his film's most conspicuous achievement. With its lumpy hand-held camera sequences (Barry Ackroyd, the director of photography, has a background in documentaries), its rolling television news (with real-life news anchor, Jon Snow), its war-torn situation, snatched conversations and its employment of factual settings, such as the Serbian parliament chamber in Belgrade, as well as its inclusion of authentic news footage of the war which led to the break-up of Yugoslavia, this is a film characterised by a 'dangerous documentary-style realism'.[13] Robert Ormsby suggests that 'Fiennes's main concern is to allow the viewer clearly to follow the unfolding combat narrative while experiencing the disorientation of battle.'[14]

This realism is partly to do with psychological verisimilitude and partly to do with setting. In terms of character, Fiennes explains, of the protagonist: 'I think you can get closer to Coriolanus on film than you can on stage. ... whereas on stage, you just can't get in, film is often about getting into the eyes.'[15] At several seminal points the camera dwells on the facial expressions of key characters in a way that hints at the complexities of their psychobiographies. On stage, of course, the closest we get to this is the soliloquy. In film this sense of an inner consciousness is often achieved by the close-up. Examples of this are plentiful throughout the film but notable here is the instance when an embarrassed Coriolanus waits in a corridor outside the Senate meeting, his anxiety clear from his eyes and his pained attempt to avoid the enquiring look of the cleaner (Bora Nenić) pushing his trolley. Later, arriving in Antium, the camera closes in on Coriolanus' eyes as he squints at a boy riding by on a horse. The tight close-up recalls the eyes of Clint Eastwood in *The Good the Bad and the Ugly* (dir. Sergio Leone in 1968). Katherine Duncan-Jones draws attention to Fiennes's 'piercing blue eyes, increasingly alienating and nihilistic'.[16] Subtle facial expression is part of the cinematic vocabulary unavailable (except in the most melodramatic of cases) to the theatre performer: 'Always for me the film was very much about faces. Every face, every moment of a face carries an expression, is a history, is a life, even for a fleeting moment.'[17]

Fiennes's ambition to make the film naturalistic is also reliant on its setting. The film's locale is not the classical majesty of Rome but the grimy remains of war-damaged Belgrade. A caption near the beginning distances us from the stoic nobility of ancient Rome: this is not the eternal city but 'A Place Calling Itself Rome'. This is the title of John Osborne's adaptation of Shakespeare's *Coriolanus* (1973). While Fiennes's film uses Shakespeare's language, Osborne's stage directions for the rioting citizens sound very much as they appear in Fiennes's film: '*a cross section* MOB *of* STUDENTS, FIXERS, PUSHERS, POLICEMEN, UNIDENTIFIABLE PUBLIC, *obvious* TRADE UNIONISTS [and, exactly as in Fiennes's film] *Roman troops can be in flak jackets and helmets*'.[18] The effect of this slippery (mis)identification is to challenge our sense of classical gallantry, stoicism and endurance. Fiennes insists on the film's geographical *dis*-location: 'It could be Chechnya. It could be Afghanistan. It could be recent history in Latin America. It could be Israel and Palestine.'[19] He acknowledges the influence here of Baz Luhrmann's *Romeo + Juliet* (1996): 'What I did take from that film was, particularly, his complete creation of a world that I couldn't tell you where it was but I knew it was somewhere today and I believed it, whether it was Mexico or Miami or something.'[20]

This is not a place of historically underwritten nobility but a recognisable world struggling to be born, a world torn by the ravages of modern warfare, identical to the cityscapes of the Balkan conflicts we saw every night on our television screens throughout the 1990s. As Martius and his infantry take Corioles, we see the shattered citizenry sitting on doorsteps or in the dilapidated ruins of bombed-out houses. At one point, Aufidius (played by Gerard Butler) stumbles across a car containing the corpses of a slaughtered family. A small child lies in the dirt by the open passenger door; there is nothing heroic about this urban fighting. The contrast between the cyborg-like warrior in body armour (with hints of Jacob Epstein's terrifying sculpture, *The Rock Drill*, 1913 and Paul Verhoeven's film *RoboCop*, 1988) and walkie-talkie helmet and brandishing an automatic rifle, smeared with dirt and blood, and the crisp uniforms with gold swags and chests full of medals, underlines the dependence of ceremonial politics upon the carnage of guerrilla warfare. The trappings of civilisation are inseparable from the barbarism that supports them. Fiennes's protagonists are the opposite of classical heroes; rather they personify the brutality of superpowers intent on military supremacy: 'Rome is what I call a power state in this film. It's suggestive of Russia or the US or China.'[21]

Coriolanus, in deference to his mother's wishes, appears at a television studio in order to mollify the people. Menenius and Cominius (John Kani) struggle to keep Coriolanus on the rails but, when he is accused of 'treason' (3.1.165–6) by the tribunes (James Nesbitt and Paul Jesson), he explodes with 'You common cry of curs ... ' (3.3.124). Ranting and spitting like a wild animal, Fiennes allows Coriolanus' fury full throttle. The crowd are silent, fearful, and Coriolanus exits with the calm declaration, 'There is a world elsewhere' (3.3.139).

The alternative is the Volscian stronghold of Antium. This section of the film was shot in the Bay of Kotor, Montenegro, on the Adriatic coast. With its families eating at outdoor cafés, the town is sunny, friendly and welcoming. Coriolanus watches, tucked behind a wall, as Aufidius jokes and slaps the backs of the city's inhabitants with a demeanour that contrasts with his own frosty speechifying, earlier, in the Roman market place. But the nerve-centre of the Volscian army is quite different from the ceremonial display of the Roman Senate. Aufidius and his commanders meet in a series of low-ceilinged cellars – a sequestered hide-out in which we previously witnessed a captured Roman shot in the head by Aufidius himself. It is a dimly lit secret location, heavy with shadows, at which the sudden appearance of Coriolanus causes panic and the immediate bristling of several firearms.

Offering his enemy his service or his life, Coriolanus bares his neck for Aufidius' knife. With his blade pressed to his enemy's throat, Aufidius speaks of his intensely erotic adoration: 'Thou noble thing, more dances my rapt heart / Than when I first my wedded mistress saw / Bestride my threshold' (4.5.117–19). 'That speech', Fiennes remarks, 'is the key acknowledgement of his romantic, erotic enthusiasm for Coriolanus.'[22] We next see a naked Coriolanus having his head shaved by an old woman. Aufidius takes over the ritual of this shaving. John Garrison notes how 'the scene is one of simultaneous purification, initiation, and erotic submission' and he points out that Coriolanus shifts his gaze from 'Aufidius's face to his crotch'.[23] For Fiennes the sexual undertones of the sequence are ineluctable; it is characterised by a 'gentle homoerotic undertone ... [Aufidius has] been dreaming about Coriolanus and he's obsessed with him. It's unquestionably there'.[24] For John Logan, responsible for the shooting script, this sexual interest is a development of the erotic energies of the protagonists' initial encounter: 'The first confrontation between the hated rivals – Coriolanus and Aufidius – is long, violent and very purposefully homoerotic.'[25] He goes on to describe their combat as 'something like a Francis Bacon painting: two men merged and grappling in something that is partly a hideous death struggle and partly great sex'.

The world of Aufidius' soldiers is exclusively masculine and, with shaved heads like Coriolanus, they are an undifferentiated mass of seething, drunken, sweating testosterone. Aufidius' alienation from his own army is figured in the way that he retains his tousled hair and full dark beard. His troops are now emulating the shaven inhumaneness of Coriolanus, and Aufidius registers the threat of his former enemy's growing influence over them: 'He watered his new plants with dews of flattery, / Seducing so my friends' (5.5.22–3). In their night-time, drink- and drug-fuelled running amok, dancing and shearing one another's heads, they resemble the madmen of Francis Ford Coppola's *Apocalypse Now* (1979). Ormsby suggests that Coriolanus has 'exchanged the Rome of electronically regurgitated ceremonies for a world elsewhere of primal masculine rites more suited to the brutal spirit he displayed in battle'.[26]

Fittingly, a barber's chair, gilded with gold spray-paint, becomes the parodic throne (Figure 9.1) in which Coriolanus slumps arrogantly to receive first Menenius and subsequently his family. Cominius' lines are given to Titus Lartius (Dragan Mićanović): 'he does sit in gold, his eye / Red as 'twould burn Rome' (5.1.63–4). Menenius, repulsed by his former protégé, makes his way, in despair, to a grim canal path and opens a vein with a pocket knife. For

Figure 9.1 *Coriolanus* (2011): Caius Martius (Ralph Fiennes) enthroned in the gold barber's chair.

Katherine Duncan-Jones, 'Menenius's slow, lonely death . . . is one of the film's most imaginative additions. It is all the more moving for the old man's deployment of a tiny pen-knife with which he slits his left wrist.'[27] Peter Holland, however, finds that this sequence 'unsatisfyingly transmute[s] the play's drive. [Menenius' interpolated suicide contradicts] Shakespeare's decision that only Coriolanus should die in the play . . . fracturing a crucial marker of Martius' separation from the rest of the cast'.[28]

With Menenius dead, Volumnia is Rome's last hope. As she and Jessica Chastain's Virgilia arrive at the derelict factory that forms the Volsci army base, they are wolf-whistled and catcalled. They face Coriolanus and kneel to him. Fiennes's account of the making of the exchange is worth citing. Note how, yet again, he stresses the importance of naturalism:

> I suggested she [Redgrave] kneel about six feet away, and she tried that, but then she said, 'No, I think I need to be closer to you.' She came really close and put her hands on my knees. With that physical proximity, it became very intimate. Then, when she began to speak, she spoke to me gently, very directly, privately. . . . But she did this intensely naturalistic thing, which just unlocked it.[29]

Earlier in the film, as Volumnia dresses Coriolanus' fresh wounds, Virgilia puts her head round the bathroom door. Met with the indifference of mother and son, and excluded from their intimacy, Virgilia quietly withdraws and makes her way to the bedroom of the sleeping Young Martius (Harry Fenn). She tidies his military toys and kneels down beside him breathing in his breath (recalling, though not actually uttering, the beautifully intimate description from Shakespeare's narrative poem): 'Comes breath perfumed, that breedeth love by smelling' (*Venus and Adonis*, line 444). These two parallel scenes

(Volumnia tending to her offspring, Virgilia tending to hers), taking place at the same time, underline the importance of the maternal forces which seek to protect but which ultimately destroy, a power which will cost Coriolanus his life: 'O mother, mother! / What have you done?' (5.3.183–4).

The fate of Coriolanus is sealed and, in keeping with the anti-heroic status of the film, it takes place on a bare road, in a kind of no-man's land, near an abandoned petrol station. Aufidius and his henchmen have been waiting for Coriolanus and set the warrior in a rage with the use of the trigger word, 'traitor' (5.6.85) and the demeaning 'boy' (103). 'Let him die for't' (120), mutters Aufidius (in the play this line is spoken by the conspirators) and, following a violent struggle between Coriolanus and half a dozen of Aufidius' men slashing knives, Aufidius approaches Coriolanus to finish him off personally with the same knife we saw him hold earlier to his enemy's throat.

The homoeroticism of the previous violence is here too. The script's directions read: 'Aufidius steps to [Coriolanus]. Takes his neck. Pulls him onto the knife. Driving it into him. Cradling his head like a lover'.[30] Garrison's description of the moment notes how Aufidius 'tenderly grasps the back of Coriolanus's head – as if about to impart a kiss rather than to deliver a killing blow'.[31] Having stabbed him, Aufidius gently lays the body onto the road. For Fiennes, this is the erotic climax: 'The end of the film is the closest there is to a homoerotic expression, and I wanted to show it through the murder, the closeness of the death and the way Aufidius holds Coriolanus, the way the knife, which is the opening image of the film, finally penetrates Coriolanus.'[32]

The play's coda, in which Aufidius expresses his regret, is cut, and the film's closing image is of Coriolanus' corpse being unceremoniously dumped onto the metal sheeting of a flat-bed truck, 'Like a sack of potatoes. Sprawled ungainly in death. No ritual or ceremony. No honour. Snap to black.'[33] His twisted limbs and bloodied torso suggest a crumpled parody of his military, political and familial authority. As the credits roll, a mournful singer (Lisa Zane) keens Mikis Theodorakis's *Sta Pervolia* in Greek, the very language of classical tragedy. Boika Sokolova explains: it is 'a plea to Death to release a soldier for a night, to allow him to embrace his mother'.[34]

Titus

In the closing sequence of Julie Taymor's *Titus*, Young Lucius (Osheen Jones) rescues the baby of Tamora and Aaron (Jessica Lange and Harry Lennix) from a cage and carries him in slow motion out of the Colosseum into a bleak but open landscape that has water, which means there's possibility for fruition, of cleansing, of forgiveness. It's also a movement towards the sunrise, which is the next generation or the next one hundred years or the next millennium [the film was released in 1999].[35]

In spite of Taymor's utopian prognosis, it is not easy to make the case for any lasting benignity. As is well known, *Titus Andronicus* is a blood bath, involving severed heads, hands and a tongue, as well as cannibalism and a vicious rape. The play begins with the hewing of Alarbus' 'limbs till they be clean consumed' (1.1.129) and, in the film, we see Titus' sons enter with a dish containing his 'entrails [with which they] feed the sacrificing fire' (144). Clara Escoda Agustí suggests that the film's ubiquitous brutality is too intense to be quenched by its upbeat ending: 'this sense of violence being overpowering is certainly a feeling *Titus*'s audiences must leave the cinema with'.[36]

Taymor explained the importance of Young Lucius to her conception: 'I was intrigued with this idea of the child's experience of violence ... and the opportunity to have this child be the eyes for the audience.'[37] While Young Lucius is hardly in Shakespeare's play, he becomes almost ubiquitous in Taymor's film and just as he completes *Titus*, so he is seen in its opening sequence. Wearing a paper bag with eye-holes torn into it, he sits at a 1960s kitchen table eating sausages, drinking milk and playing with military toys – a combat helicopter, a Roman centurion, crawling marines, a robot, toy soldiers. As he simulates their fighting his meal disintegrates into carnage with lashings of tomato ketchup serving as blood, and a jet fighter crashing into a slice of cake. Carol Chillington Rutter suggests that 'This adult-free zone shows the continuity between consumption, violence and play.'[38] However, Elsie Walker reads this not as a moment of escape from the influence of adulthood but rather as an anticipation of its subsequent brutality: 'From the beginning of the film Taymor is concerned with the ways children are initiated into ongoing legacies of violence.'[39]

The fighting becomes increasingly intense and the ambient noise – the child's simulation of explosions and gunfire, traffic, human voices and *Pop Goes the Weasel* from a television set – all the more frenetic. The table-top battle becomes mysteriously real and the shaken kitchen cabinets shed glasses and crockery. The window is blown in by a bomb blast, forcing Young Lucius under the table from whence he is grabbed by a steampunk Clown (Dario D'Ambrosi) who carries him, to the whistles of falling bombs, down a staircase to emerge in a huge coliseum: 'the archetypal theater of cruelty, where violence as entertainment reached its apex'.[40] As the child is held aloft, a ghostly cheer greets him and he looks back to see the entrance to his apartment as a burning theatre set.[41]

In its slippage from one world to the next – 1960s kitchen, steampunk dystopia, Roman Colosseum (and later), 1930s Fascism (Rome's EUR district), the Roman Forum (complete with a giant hand reminiscent of Shelley's 'Ozymandias' which adumbrates Titus' and Lavinia's severed hands) and cobbled streets, terracotta interiors, forests and pastoral gardens – Dante Ferretti's design juxtaposes and frequently superimposes widely separate historical periods. Titus (Anthony Hopkins) is in classical Roman armour and long cape while his brother Marcus (Colm Feore) wears a shirt with an Edwardian round collar and tie; Chiron (Jonathan Rhys Meyers) shows off an extravagant silver lamé suit that would not look out of place in *Star Trek*, while Alan Cumming as Saturninus in glossy lipstick, eyeshadow and a floppy asymmetric hair-do, is a cross between 1980s New Romanticism and Hitler. Lange's Tamora wears a gold *Wonder Woman* breastplate sculpted to reveal the contours of her breasts (and prompting Saturninus' lascivious comment 'A goodly lady' (1.1.261), pronounced with all the camp suggestiveness of the famous British comedian, Frankie Howerd) while Lavinia (Laura Fraser) portrays a delicate Audrey Hepburnesque impishness and Givenchy grace.

The anachronistic aesthetic looks back to Terry Gilliam's *Brazil* (1985) and ultimately Fritz Lang's futurist *Metropolis* (1927). Saturninus sits on a vast metal throne surmounted by the head of a snarling, steel she-wolf (Figure 9.2) and Chiron and Demetrius (Matthew Rhys) party in a subterranean torture chamber, at one end of which is an enormous turbine sticking through the wall. Later the Clown reappears in a motorised tuk tuk while Titus' army pour into the coliseum in strange tank-like vehicles, horse-drawn chariots and motorbikes in a mash-up of *Ben-Hur* (dir. William

Figure 9.2 *Titus* (1999): Saturninus (Alan Cumming) and the 'wolf's head' throne.

127

Wyler, 1959) and *The Wild One* (dir. László Benedek, 1953). As he sits on the steps of the Mussolini-era Palazzo della Civiltà Italiana, a newspaper blows into Young Lucius, reminding us of the fatal disappearance of Robert De Niro's Harry Tuttle in *Brazil*. A frenetic orgy takes place in what looks like Rome's Pantheon (with the addition of a large pool), the hole in the ceiling allowing an entry point for the shower of Titus' arrows. In its multiple settings, spread across several centuries, *Titus* insists on the pervasive omni-presence of violence: as Taymor's commentary puts it, 'the film represents the last 2000 years of man's inhumanity to man'.[42] Just as Fiennes's location 'could be Chechnya [or] Afghanistan [or] Latin America', so the opening directions of Taymor's screenplay read, 'We could be in Brooklyn or Sarajevo.'[43]

But there is also a ludic quality to this multiple layering of different places, times, references and echoes. Indeed, one of the most allusively dense and intriguing examples of this is in the appalling reimagining of Lavinia's rape, the third (and most fearsome) of the film's five 'Penny Arcade Nightmare' sequences which, as Taymor puts it, 'depict, in abstract collages, fragments of memory, the unfathomable layers of a violent event, the metamorphic flux of the human, animal and the divine'.[44] We have already witnessed the aftermath of the crime itself when Chiron and Demetrius leave the maimed Lavinia stranded on a tree stump in the middle of a mudscape. Later in the film, as Lavinia writes her rapists' names in the dirt, she re-lives the attack in a sequence of terrible intensity: 'when a woman has to testify at a rape trial she is re-experiencing the rape', explains Taymor.[45] Marcus demonstrates how she may, holding the top of Titus' stave in her mouth and steering it with her arms, inscribe the names of her attackers in the dust. He offers the penile tip to her mouth but she baulks at it and tucks it between neck and shoulder. To loud rock music, and in a wash of blue light, Lavinia is imaged with a doe's head and forefeet standing on a classical column as two tigers lunge at her. In this way the sequence picks up the language of Shakespeare's play but also figures the helplessness of Lavinia confronted by the male tigers of Chiron and Demetrius.[46]

The two sequences – the attacks, real and recalled – roll together into a complicated amalgam a number of allusions to other texts, theatre productions, films and sculptures. Lavinia's twigged hands are cruelly reminiscent of Bernini's *Daphne and Apollo* (*c.* 1623) as well as Tim Burton's cinematic fantasy, *Edward Scissorhands* (1991). The reimagining sees Lavinia in a white billowing skirt, which she attempts to hold down against an updraft in an allusion to Marilyn Monroe in *The Seven Year Itch* (dir. Billy Wilder, 1955). Taymor commented: 'The famous image ...

128

seemed an apt modern iconic parallel to add to this scene of humiliation and rape. I was interested in exploiting our store of not only classical, but also contemporary myths.'[47] Monroe's sexually charged persona is juxtaposed, in Lavinia, with the regal modesty of Grace Kelly whom Taymor, in a rather sinister way, describes as wearing 'little black gloves and a full bell skirt, daddy's little girl all ready for defilement'.[48]

Chasing Young Lucius over a field, leading into the above sequence, Lavinia is costumed in a long red dress with extended sleeves, dropping away from her wrists and reaching almost to the ground. The costume echoes the red ribbons worn by Vivien Leigh, standing in for blood, in Peter Brook's iconic theatre production of 1955. Ultimately, of course, underlying this confluence of references is the subliminal allusion to the classical Venus de Milo.

Taymor's is an inherently allusive and self-conscious style, one that thrives on a hybridity between old and new, serious and playful, canonical and popular. Perhaps the most wryly facetious example of this is Tamora's disguise as Revenge. She wears a fan of carving knives in a parody of a showgirl's ostrich-feather headdress but which also alludes to the spiked crown of the Statue of Liberty. The irony of Liberty's diadem comprising the murderous weapon that does for so many of *Titus'* characters, is both sardonic and ingenious.

The film's climax is its third violent banquet (which echoes the earlier ones of the opening kitchen table and that involving the murder of the fly). Six Goths sit opposite six Romans while Tamora and Saturninus occupy the heads of a long table. Titus, in full chef's whites and assisted by Young Lucius, dishes up large slices of pie. As the guests dig in, Lavinia, veiled, enters modestly and sidles up to her father so that she has her back against his chest. Following the discussion about Virginius slaying his own daughter (to prevent her being raped), Titus snaps Lavinia's neck and gently lays her to the floor. He names her rapists, Chiron and Demetrius, at the same time as he reveals their whereabouts: 'Why, there they are, both baked in this pie, / Whereof their mother daintily hath fed, / Eating the flesh that she herself hath bred' (5.3.59–61). As Tamora inserts her fingers into her mouth in order to gag, Titus thrusts his knife into her neck.

The play's chain-reaction of murders follows in rapid sequence: Saturninus, mounting the table tears, with his teeth, a candle from a candelabrum to reveal the third of three sharp prongs. These he rams into Titus' chest. Lucius snatches Saturninus by his collar and belt and drags him down the full length of the table, plates and cutlery flying in the mayhem. He dumps Saturninus back in his chair and, grabbing a large serving spoon, shoves this down the emperor's throat. The action suddenly freezes as Saturninus tumbles back from the table. Lucius' airborne spit and a goblet of spilled wine are suspended mid-air. As the film unfreezes, the spit lands with a thud and Lucius shoots Saturninus in the head.

The gunshot moves us instantly to the interior of the Colosseum, the dining room carnage precisely reconstructed as a murderous theatrical performance. A densely packed crowd of spectators is faded in to occupy the seating around the action and while Marcus addresses them via a microphone, 'You sad-faced men, people and sons of Rome ... ' (5.3.66), his sobering rhetoric is accompanied by the Clown casting clear plastic sheets over the various corpses. Lucius gestures towards Aaron's caged baby, held aloft by the Clown in an echo of the display of Young Lucius at the film's opening. Aaron, his arms lashed to a horizontal pole, is lowered into a hole, glancing directly at the viewer as he laments any good deed he might have done. Lucius announces the degrading disposal of Tamora's corpse – 'throw her forth to beasts and birds of [for the text's "to"] prey' (196).

Young Lucius gingerly opens the lid of the cage and, as he takes the baby to his chest, the cries of many babies mingle with the caws of birds, the sounds of new birth and carrion scavengers forming a discordance which is then overlaid with the tolling of bells in clear defiance of Lucius' earlier decree: 'No mournful bell shall ring her burial' (197). The baby's tiny face looks back over Young Lucius' shoulder as he walks slowly from the Colosseum into a new dawn, the movie freezing as the rising sun breaks the horizon. This closing sequence has aroused fierce disagreement among the film's commentators. For Peter S. Donaldson, 'nothing in the action of the film or in Shakespeare's play suggests that the territory outside the walls is safe. This is where Tamora's body will be thrown to be eaten by dogs and birds.'[49] Jim Welsh and John Tibbetts argue, by contrast, that Young Lucius' 'final exit out of the Coliseum towards the dawning of a new day with evil Aaron's baby in arms symbolically is a journey towards redemption' and Jonathan Bate is even more blithely cheerful: 'the movie ends on an uplifting note with a closing image of singular beauty, evoking a new dawn'.[50] Striking in its preservation of ambiguity here is Taymor's own uncertain description, hedged with hesitancy: 'The boy keeps moving towards the exit, towards the *promise* of a daylight as if redemption were a *possibility*.'[51]

Conclusion

For Shakespeare's first audiences, classical Rome provided an unassailable object lesson in the achievements of civilisation (*civitas*). With its pioneering developments in architecture, road building, sanitation, education, military discipline and mercantile efficiency, Rome offered a model of progress to which the early modern aspired. Its colonial supremacy was testament to the city-state's political efficiencies as well as the ruthlessness of its ambition. In literary terms the eroticism of Ovid, the rhetoric of Cicero and the epic vision of Virgil, not to mention the theatre of Plautus and Seneca, demonstrated the kinds of edification fitting such an urbane culture.

But by Shakespeare's lifetime, Rome had become the epicentre of Catholic corruption, tainted by its association with Papal authority and a religion which – to the Protestant mind – harboured dangerous insurgency and an aggressive enmity. There is little evidence that Shakespeare partook in the extreme forms of Reformation zeal that characterised some of his contemporaries but Rome, for him as for them, was less a physical location than a contradictory set of ideas: ancient and modern, pioneering and bloated, innovative and complacent, pacific and brutal. Shakespeare's Roman plays offered their original audiences a sustained but unresolved series of ambiguities; in the cases of *Titus Andronicus* and *Coriolanus*, heroism, loyalty, courage and influence as well as superciliousness, nepotism, corruption and violence.

By avoiding any specific locality, geographically or temporally, both Taymor and Fiennes ensure that it is this Shakespearean idea of Rome which both hosts and inflects their analyses of human conduct. Taymor's Roman vision is of a 'wilderness of tigers' (3.1.53), nasty, brutish and internecine, but it is not one without humour, intelligence and a density of allusion which self-consciously improvises around Shakespeare's play in the context of contemporary culture. As for Fiennes's *Coriolanus*, it too clearly demonstrates less the specific location or mechanisms of a particular struggle (between Romans and Goths) and more the dynamics of conflict itself, maternal, familial, tribal and national. In these uncompromising ways, both films lay bare the continuing relevance to the twenty-first century of 400-year old plays about 2000-year old stories.

Notes

1. Graham Holderness and Christopher McCullough, 'Shakespeare on the screen: a selective filmography', in Anthony Davies and Stanley Wells, eds., *Shakespeare and the Moving Image: The Plays on Film and Television* (Cambridge, Cambridge University Press, 1994), 18–49.
2. Of the thirteen essays in Sarah Hatchuel and Nathalie Vienne-Guerrin, eds., *Shakespeare on Screen: The Roman Plays* (Mont-Saint-Aignan, Publications des Universités de Rouen et du Havre, 2009), no fewer than seven are concerned with Mankiewicz's film.

3. The BBC Shakespeare broadcast the Roman Plays as follows: *Julius Caesar*, 1979; *Antony and Cleopatra*, 1981; *Cymbeline*, 1982 and *Coriolanus*, 1984. *The Spread of the Eagle* – a nine-part adaptation of *Coriolanus, Julius Caesar* and *Antony and Cleopatra* – aired on the BBC in 1963.
4. Ben Dowell, 'BBC looks to follow *Hollow Crown* films with Shakespeare's Roman plays'. *Radio Times*, 16 May 2016, www.radiotimes.com/news/2016-05-16/bbc-looks-to-follow-hollow-crown-films-with-shakespeares-roman-plays/ (accessed 23 December 2018).
5. Vittorio and Paolo Taviani's 2012 arthouse film, *Caesar Must Die* (*Cesare deve morire*), set in the high security Rebibbia Prison in Rome, follows the inmates as they rehearse and stage Shakespeare's play. The shared location of prison and play prompts a meditation on the overlap between real-life betrayal, murder and violence and its theatrical representation.
6. Jennifer Flaherty, 'Filming Shakespeare's Rome: the "preposterous contemporary" eternal city', *Interdisciplinary Literary Studies: A Journal of Criticism and Theory*, 17 (2015), 228–40 (237).
7. Gary Crowdus, Richard Porton and Ralph Fiennes, 'Shakespeare's perennial political thriller: an interview with Ralph Fiennes', *Cinéaste*, 37 (2012), 18–23 (22).
8. Ralph Fiennes, voice-over commentary to DVD of *Coriolanus*.
9. Peter J. Smith, 'Review of *Coriolanus*', *Cahiers Élisabethains*, 58 (2000), 95–6 (95).
10. Susannah Clapp, 'A soldier to cry on', *Observer*, 18 June 2000.
11. Crowdus, Porton and Fiennes, 19 (my emphasis).
12. John Logan, *Coriolanus, Screenplay* (New York, New Market Press, 2011), 117.
13. Philip French, *Guardian*, 22 January 2012.
14. Robert Ormsby, *Coriolanus: Shakespeare in Performance* (Manchester, Manchester University Press, 2014), 227.
15. Ralph Fiennes, 'The question of *Coriolanus*', in Susannah Carson, ed., *Living with Shakespeare* (New York, Vintage Books, 2013), 220–7 (221).
16. Katherine Duncan-Jones, 'Shakespeare in bits and pieces', *Times Literary Supplement*, 5677 (20 January 2012), 17.
17. Fiennes, DVD commentary.
18. John Osborne, *A Place Calling Itself Rome* (London, Faber, 1973), 13–14.
19. Jen Vineyard, 'Ralph Fiennes teases Blofeld role in new Bond film *Skyfall*; talks Shakespearean adaptation of *Coriolanus*', *Indiewire*, 7 November 2011.
20. Kevin Polowy, 'Q&A: Ralph Fiennes on his Bard badass *Coriolanus*', www.mtv.com/news/2808659/ralph-fiennes-interview-coriolanus (accessed 23 December 2018).
21. Cath Clarke, 'Interview: Ralph Fiennes on *Coriolanus*', *Time Out London*, 10 December 2012.
22. Fiennes in Carson, *Living with Shakespeare*, 223.
23. John Garrison, 'Queer desire and self-erasure in *Coriolanus* (2011)', *Literature/Film Quarterly*, 42 (2014), 427–32 (433 and 432).
24. Quoted by Vineyard, 'Ralph Fiennes teases Blofeld role'.
25. Logan, *Coriolanus, Screenplay*, 107.
26. Ormsby, *Coriolanus: Shakespeare in Performance*, 237.
27. Duncan-Jones, 'Shakespeare in bits and pieces', 17.
28. *Coriolanus*, edited by Peter Holland (London, Bloomsbury, 2013), 140.
29. Crowdus, Porton and Fiennes, 'Shakespeare's perennial political thriller', 23.

30. Logan, *Coriolanus, Screenplay*, 103.
31. Garrison, 'Queer desire and self-erasure', 434.
32. Fiennes in Carson, *Living with Shakespeare*, 223.
33. Logan, *Coriolanus, Screenplay*, 104.
34. Boika Sokolova, 'An anatomy of collapse: Ralph Fiennes' film *Coriolanus* (2011)', in Panka Dániel, Pikli Natália and Veronika Ruttkay, eds., *Built Upon His Rock: Writings in Honour of Péter Dávidházi* (Budapest, Kiadta az Elte Btk, Angol-Amerikai Intezet, 2018), 350–8 (358).
35. Maria De Luca, Mary Lindroth and Julie Taymor, 'Mayhem, madness, method: an interview with Julie Taymor', *Cinéaste*, 25 (2000), 28–31 (29).
36. Clara Escoda Agustí, '*Titus* (1999): framing violence and activating responsibility', *Atlantis*, 28 (2006), 57–70 (65).
37. De Luca, Lindroth and Taymor, 'Mayhem, madness, method', 28.
38. Carol Chillington Rutter, 'Looking like a child – or – *Titus*: the comedy', *Shakespeare Survey 56* (2003), 1–26 (11).
39. Elsie Walker, 'Julie Taymor's *Titus* (1999), ten years on' in Hatchuel and Vienne-Guerrin, eds., *Shakespeare on Screen: The Roman Plays*, 23–65 (57).
40. Eileen Blumenthal, *Julie Taymor: Playing with Fire: Theatre, Opera, Film* (New York, Harry N. Abrams, 1999), 220.
41. Taymor writes, 'We shot the opening and closing scenes for the film in the winter of 1998. Two months later, with the war in Kosovo, this would have been impossible. The irony of shooting these scenes in the Balkans [in Pula, Croatia] lay heavily on all of us.' Julie Taymor, *Titus: The Illustrated Screenplay* (New York, Newmarket Press, 2000), 182.
42. Julie Taymor, voice-over commentary to DVD of *Titus*.
43. Taymor, *Titus: Screenplay*, 19.
44. Ibid., 183.
45. De Luca, Lindroth and Taymor, 'Mayhem, madness, method', 30.
46. Menenius tells Sicinius that 'There is no more mercy in him [Coriolanus] than there is milk in a male tiger' (*Coriolanus*, 5.4.29).
47. Quoted in Blumenthal, *Julie Taymor: Playing With Fire, Theatre, Opera, Film* 188.
48. Taymor, *Titus: Screenplay*, 181.
49. Peter S. Donaldson, 'Game space / tragic space: Julie Taymor's *Titus*', in *A Companion to Shakespeare and Performance*, edited by Barbara Hodgdon and W. B. Worthen (Oxford, Blackwell, 2005), 457–77 (474).
50. Jim Welsh and John Tibbetts, '"To sup with horrors": Julie Taymor's Senecan feast', *Literature/Film Quarterly*, 28 (2000), 155–6 (156); Jonathan Bate, 'Introduction' in Taymor, *Titus: Screenplay*, 8–13 (13).
51. *Titus: Screenplay*, 185 (my emphases).

IO

ANTHONY GUY PATRICIA

Screening Shakespearean Fantasy and Romance in *A Midsummer Night's Dream* and *The Tempest*

With one third of its interrelated triumvirate of plots grounded in the world of faerie, a world that Shakespeare's conception of was principally inspired by Ovidian myth and legend as well as the lore of England's Warwickshire, *A Midsummer Night's Dream* is probably the most fantasy-like play Shakespeare ever wrote.[1] But therein lies its central production challenge: How do you make the faerie world of the play sufficiently wonderous without stretching credulity to the breaking point? This chapter considers four screen productions of the play, by directors Max Reinhardt and William Dieterle (1935), Peter Hall (1968), Adrian Noble (1996) and Michael Hoffman (1999).

The opening stage direction of Act 2, scene 1 of the First Quarto (Q1) of *A Midsummer Night's Dream* sets out the basics in a single, blunt line: 'Enter a Fairy at one door and Robin Goodfellow at another', and then the two characters begin to speak.[2] Beyond these minimal cues, though, readers must imagine all of the particulars for themselves. Editions of Shakespeare's plays may indicate that the scene takes place in a wood or a forest. Filmmakers, on the other hand, must convey this information visually in a way that captivates viewers and lulls them into believing what they see taking place in that wood or forest on screen is 'real'. The experience of watching Reinhardt and Dieterle's introduction to the faerie world is rather akin to watching a cinematic version of a child's picture book brought to life. It begins with an establishing shot of a painted backdrop of a bucolic night-time landscape. The night sky is filled with the twinkling stars of the Milky Way, and above all, in the left corner, floats a full moon that, on the left side, gleams, and on the right, resolves itself into dark grey as one's eyes travel its circumference.

After a few moments of focus on the tableau described above, the scene suddenly shifts to one of real pines and firs standing sentinel in a real forest as opposed to a painted one. Then, once again, the scene switches and, from their vantage point on the forest floor, viewers see that the trees

134

before their eyes are now younger, thinner, denser, and surrounded by a mass of ferns and brush. Here the leaves and vines and such glitter in a way that is impossible in an ordinary forest. What follows then is a series of five shots of typical forest life. The cumulative effect of all this is one of qualified verisimilitude. From it we know that this forest is a mixture of the make-believe and the real; it is not entirely one or the other. Both are essential to its proper functioning.

As such, we are not jolted by implausibility when the camera then directs our attention to a patch of the forest ground piled with thick sheaves of leaves, from under which a shirtless boy-like figure (Mickey Rooney as Puck) with blond hair and incipient satyr's horns on his head emerges. He stretches, wipes the sleep out of his eyes, gazes at the moon-filled sky, then begins screaming like a banshee while pounding his fists on a nearby tree trunk. Thus he wakes all of the other creatures in the forest.

A significant part of the mass awakening Puck initiates is the appearance of a heavy, milky-white mist that quickly covers the forest floor. As the majestic tones of Mendelssohn play on the soundtrack, the mist transforms into a bevy of female ballet dancers, all dressed identically in shimmery leotards and skullcaps. Given the fantastical nature of this place – it is a place where anything can happen – it makes perfect sense when the dancers that appeared out of the mist are revealed to be the fairies that comprise Titania's (Anita Louise) train of followers. The same can be said about the male dancers that make up Oberon's (Victor Jory) fairy cohort, all of whom are dressed in black and whose costumes are complete with wings that make them seem very much like enormous bats – appropriate garb for vaguely menacing figures in service to the Fairy King who threaten the Fairy Queen and her acolytes. Oberon's costume is very similar to that of his followers: black and batlike. What makes him stand out is the crown he wears, which consists of a circle of six-inch high leafless tree branches, indicating he, as king of it, is part and parcel of the forest faerie world.

A unicorn, an orchestra made up entirely of bald gnomes as instrument players, and a young child dressed all in silver as a miniature Indian rajah: these are three other fantastical elements that add to the 'reality' of Reinhardt and Dieterle's representation of the wood outside Athens. Reinhardt and Dieterle show Bottom's (James Cagney) transformation into an ass. When Bottom goes off stage during the amateur actors' rehearsal in the faerie wood, Puck follows him. Bottom remains unaware of Puck's presence behind him; and Puck blows a handful of seemingly invisible forest detritus in Bottom's direction – making him itch. As he is scratching, the head morphs from that of a man into that of an ass.

A series of blurred shots shows Bottom's mouth lengthening into the muzzle of an ass complete with enormous buck teeth; his face becoming hairier and hairier; and his ears rising higher and higher from the sides of his head.

Peter Hall's depiction of the faerie world is quite unlike that of Reinhardt and Dieterle. All of the scenes involving the fairies – and the interiors – were shot on location at Compton Verney in Warwickshire as opposed to a soundstage.[3] This results in a palace wood that is, by default, utterly naturalistic – if not hyper-naturalistic; it is a real rather than fantastical place in which dreamlike things happen. Thus Hall, too, in his own way, has created a faerie *mise-en-scène* that allows its make-believe elements a high degree of plausibility. We can have no doubt that it *is* a place where fairies are at war because of the conflict between their king and queen; it *is* a place where a man can be partially transformed into an ass; and it *is* a place where human lovers come to escape the fate that the court has in store for them were they to remain there.

When the action shifts from Athens to the forest Hall, unlike Reinhardt and Dieterle, spends comparatively little time on establishing shots. In fact, a single shot – that lasts for just over two seconds – of a silhouetted owl hooting from its perch among bare tree branches against a dark grey sky suffices as the transition marker between the two places. Then the camera focuses viewers' attention on a young female fairy child who suddenly appears running through an overly backlit forest and tossing glitter hither and thither into the air until she plops down into a puddle and awakens Puck (Ian Holm) with the resulting splashes of water. After realising what has happened and who or what it is that is in front of him, Puck begins his interrogation: 'How now, spirit, whither wander you?' (2.1.1), and the ensuing dialogue makes it clear that all is not well in the faerie world.

Once it is established in time and space, a number of other fantasy elements complement Hall's naturalistic depiction of the wood, three of which will be touched on here. First, the majority of the fairies in Titania's and Oberon's respective trains are portrayed by young male and female children with long hair and otherwise androgynous features. They also have a tendency to appear something like Dickensian street urchins trans-planted to the forest outside Athens: they are often dirty and grubby, rather than clean, polished fairies. This only adds to the verisimilitude of the wood. Second, all of Hall's fairies, including Titania and Oberon and Puck, have green skin, indicating just how much a part of the fabric of the forest they are. Furthermore, reflecting the period in which Hall's film was made, near full nudity like this for the adult fairies, especially Titania, some of whose body parts are barely covered – is *de rigueur*. And third, at the age of thirty-six, Ian Holm's Puck is not a child as he was in Reinhardt and Dieterle's *A Midsummer Night's Dream*. Even so, he is no less mischievous and no less fun, despite an odd habit of sticking his tongue out as far as possible and hissing like a snake at various times throughout the film. In addition, to mark Puck's exits and entrances, Hall uses jump cuts to make it seem as if he simply appears and vanishes: one millisecond he is there, the next he is not. These entrances and exits are accompanied by special sound effects, such as a 'swoosh' or a 'sharp plucking of a string', emphasising aurally their impossible suddenness.

Hall's directorial choices endow his representation of the wood with a high degree of plausibility. Interestingly, though, Bottom's metamorphosis – one of, if not the – most fantasy-like aspects of the play, is handled with more fidelity to the play's text than in Reinhardt and Dieterle's treatment of the material. In this case, viewers do not see the physical change. When the actor returns to the rehearsal at Peter Quince's (Sebastian Shaw) summons, he is bearing a fully-realised ass's head.

Adrian Noble's film, which derives from his 1994 stage production for the RSC, uses the conceit of the entire play being a fantastical dream.[4] It opens with a shot of the stars in space, then the camera descends through a thick layer of fluffy blue-white clouds, and finally enters the open window of nice, middle-class house. The camera pans around the room, which is chock full of well-beloved toys – including a puppet theatre – until it focuses on a young boy of about nine or ten years of age sleeping in his bed. Curled up in the boy's arms is a copy of *A Midsummer Night's Dream* illustrated by Arthur Rackham.[5] Within seconds, the boy is, presumably, sleepwalking, through a series of colourful hallways and doors until he finds himself looking through an oversize keyhole, watching and listening to Theseus (Alex Jennings) and Hippolyta (Lindsay Duncan) in a large, ornate dining room discussing their imminent nuptials. When Egeus (Alfred Burke) bursts in, he walks right past the boy who makes his way into the room as well, and sits under the table observing his elders arguing and debating about Hermia and Lysander's fate.

Noble's representation of the transition from the 'real' world of the Athenian court and its artisans is as fantastical and dreamlike in its own way as the transitions of Reinhardt and Dieterle and Hall. As the actors are leaving the meeting place in which they considered their initial plans for performing before the duke and duchess, they are caught in a heavy rainstorm. Peter Quince's (John Kane) umbrella is wrenched out of his hand and taken up high into the sky by the wind. As it moves ever higher, it changes colour from black to green, then, as it begins to descend, a floating Puck (Barry Lynch; a young man, not a boy) – dressed in bright yellow overalls sans shirt, socks and shoes – latches onto it. After looking around a bit, Puck's gaze alights on a spirit and he inquires, 'Whither wander you?' As she responds, the shot widens and viewers see the spirit is, like Puck, perched on another green umbrella hanging in the sky and is dressed in a feathery pink bodysuit with a matching hairpiece. They are surrounded by dozens upon dozens of oversized yellow light bulbs hanging from strings substituting for trees.

Obviously, Noble's forest was constructed on a soundstage. Yet, like the forests of Reinhardt and Dieterle and Hall, it, too, is a fantastical place where anything can happen, and at the same time a place where the make-believe and the real combine to enchant in a unique way. Noble does not shy away from using special effects in the faerie wood when warranted. For example, when Puck is explaining to the spirit why Oberon is upset with Titania, he pinches a raindrop from the corner of his umbrella and blows it into the air. The raindrop expands and becomes a screen in which the dreaming boy appears, complete with a turban on his head, as the changeling the Fairy King and Queen are arguing so vehemently over. In keeping with this motif, Titania and her train of fairies arrive in the lighted forest on expanding bubbles the dreaming boy has blown into existence from a plastic wand over and into the toy puppet theatre seen earlier in his bedroom. All of the fairies sport feathery costumes in bright pastel colours, with bodysuits for the females, leggings for the males, and both with matching feathery head coverings. Oberon (Alex Jennings, who also plays Theseus) and Titania (Lindsay Duncan, who also plays Hippolyta) are dressed more regally, but their long hair is styled into feathery-like tresses complemented by matching leaves. These are the figures of fantasy as dreamt into being by an imaginative young boy.

The actors begin to rehearse their play in the lighted wood right underneath the bower of the Fairy Queen, which is an enormous, pink, inverted umbrella. When Bottom (Desmond Barrit), following his script, goes off stage to see about a noise he has heard, Puck, unnoticed, climbs onto his back and thus goes with him. Then, in the tradition of Hall, Noble does not show Bottom's metamorphosis as it happens. First, when Bottom returns on his cue, audiences see the horrified expressions of Flute (Mark Letheren) and Peter Quince before being presented with Bottom with an ass's head. This Bottom does not wear a corresponding muzzle, but is made up with a long, patchy-thin white beard, oversized buck teeth, large, hairy, floppy ears, and a pair of motorcycle goggles. Viewers see Bottom with an ass's head at the same time as his fellow actors who flee in terror.

The fact that all of this is an elaborately constructed fantasy – successful in large part because of Noble's fully-realised faerie world *mise-en-scène* – is made clear when Oberon releases Titania from her enchantment and she wakes, as startled as any human would be waking from such strange dreams, and proclaims: 'My Oberon, what visions have I seen! / Methought I was enamoured of an ass' (4.1.75–6). When he points out to her that, yes, she really was in love with an ass-headed man, a revolted Titania is moved to declare: 'O, how mine eyes do loathe his visage now!' (4.1.78). Thus Noble – and Shakespeare – return us to 'reality'.

Michael Hoffman's *A Midsummer Night's Dream* premiered in the last year of the twentieth century.[6] Nevertheless, he chose to set his production at the end of the nineteenth. In the main, this decision affected the *mise-en-scène* of the Athenian court and its artisans more than anything else. It is most apparent in the characters' costumes – high-necked, floor-length dresses for women; dapper suits, all buttoned up tight, for the men; and hats for all – as well as the fact that the then newfangled invention of the bicycle is a recurring motif throughout the film. The *mise-en-scène* of Hoffman's faerie world is quite different; arguably, it is a more conventional representation of a fantastical place. It is also as fully-realised a place in space and time as the faerie woods of the directors who brought *A Midsummer Night's Dream* to the screen before him.

Hoffman introduces the fairies even before the film's action proper begins. Each of the title cards that flash across the screen is preceded and/or accompanied by the flittering appearance of anywhere from one to half-a-dozen animated fairies; they look like orbs of golden light spinning as the music including Mendelssohn as well as selections from Italian operas, plays on the soundtrack. In relatively short order, the scene switches to 'Monte Athena', a Tuscan estate where the servants are in a welter of preparation for a celebration: the wedding of Theseus and Hippolyta. In the kitchens, two anthropomorphic fairies, one male, one female; unseen by anyone other than Hoffman's viewers, yet dressed in proper, lower-class Victorian style; are filling a brown sack with plate and silverware that, along with the horn of a phonograph, end up in a rather large cart that they push and pull by hand while several of their animated cohort circle in the air around them.

Like Reinhardt and Dieterle, Hall, and Noble, Hoffman provides his viewers with a transition between the 'real' world of Monte Athena and the faerie world that begins with the despondent Helena (Calista Flockhart). As she is walking her bicycle up one of the hilly streets of the city in an intense thunderstorm, she pauses and says, 'I will go tell him [Demetrius] of fair Hermia's flight. / Then to the wood will he tomorrow night / Pursue her' (1.1.246–8). In the very next shot, Helena is lying in wait outside the gates of Monte Athena; when Demetrius (Christian Bale) races past her on his bicycle, she chases after him on hers. As the camera follows them, it picks up a couple of animated fairies, who are soon joined by a couple of satyr-like fairies, all of whom head into a cave presided over by a forbidding-looking stone face. Inside, it turns out to be something of a faerie bar or nightclub, a scene of bacchanalian excess. Over all of this, another manly, rather than boyish, Puck (Stanley Tucci) keeps watch. It is here that Puck meets the spirit and wonders wither she wanders.

Hoffman's faerie wood was meticulously crafted on a soundstage at Cinecittà Studios in Rome, thus sharing a heritage with the forest of Reinhardt and Dieterle.[7] When the Fairy King (Rupert Everett) and Fairy Queen (Michelle Pfeiffer) meet, the fairy world shakes and trembles to the point where both of their trains fear for their well-being if not their lives until Titania brings the tumult to a halt, and she and Oberon proceed to argue over the changeling boy. In addition to being inhabited by fairies with glittery skin, this forest is also populated by Janus figures, a Medusa, and a turtle that Puck rides on top of as if it were a horse. It is a make-believe/real place where anything can happen.

Bottom's metamorphosis is shown by Hoffman, following in the footsteps of Reinhardt and Dieterle and Hall. When Bottom steps out of rehearsal and walks off to see about a noise, and to practise his lines, he is far enough away from his fellow actors that they cannot observe what happens to him; but Hoffman's audience is able to watch. While pacing, he turns around and sees a top hat on a tree stump and a walking stick with a donkey's head for a handle nearby. These were not there before and Bottom is intrigued by them. He walks over and fits the top hat on his head and simultaneously takes the walking stick in his left hand. From behind, Puck appears and blows gold fairy dust onto Bottom's neck. Bottom itches, but he otherwise remains completely unaware of Puck's presence.

Puck blows another handful of fairy dust onto the tree stump and it transforms into a shimmering reflective surface. The hammy Bottom admires himself – with the top hat and walking stick – for several moments before the scene switches back to the actors' rehearsal and Bottom is summoned to take his place again by Peter Quince (Roger Rees). Bottom is then seen from behind as he walks back into the practice run saying, 'If I were fair, Thisbe ... ' (3.1.99) while simultaneously removing the top hat from his head. The camera shifts perspective so that we see Flute (Sam Rockwell) who, taking one look at Bottom, starts screaming in fear. The shot cuts again so that the audience can see Bottom from the front, and he is utterly transformed: he has no muzzle, nor does he have oversized buck teeth, but his ears are as long as a donkey's, and his hair and beard have grown out in an especially scraggy manner. In short, he now has the head of an ass when, only moments before, he had the head of a man. This fantastical metamorphosis makes perfect sense taking place as it does within Hoffman's enchanted faerie wood. As has been the case throughout Hoffman's film, what comes after Bottom's becoming an ass-headed creature follows Shakespeare's play text.

The fairies of *A Midsummer Night's Dream* are kin to Ariel, the airy spirit under Prospero's command in *The Tempest*. *The Tempest* presents filmmakers with challenges of verisimilitude similar to those of *A Midsummer Night's Dream*. Between radical appropriations like Fred Wilcox's *Forbidden Planet* (1956), Paul Mazursky's *Tempest* (1982) and Peter Greenaway's *Prospero's Books* (1991); and more or less traditional adaptations like Derek Jarman's *The Tempest* (1979), Rodney Bennett's *The Tempest* (1980) for the BBC, and Julie Taymor's *The Tempest* (2010), screen directors have met the demands of this Shakespearean romance with their individual creative aplomb. Examination of the films by Jarman and Taymor suggests the scope the play affords for filmmakers.

Jarman's film begins with Prospero (Heathcote Williams) fitfully dreaming of a ship at sea caught in a powerful storm. Upon waking and dressing, he strides purposefully into his study – a place fit for an incomparable sorcerer like himself filled with a desk, candles, books, paper, writing utensils, bottles of wine, and alchemical, astrological and philosophical symbols peppering the décor. He calls out for Ariel (Karl Johnson): 'Come away, servant, come; I am ready now. / Approach, my Ariel, come!' (1.2.188–9). Prospero's voice rises as he repeats himself summoning Ariel until the final word he speaks, 'Come!', issues from him as an angry imperative. At the same time, Prospero seems apprehensive, as if he has some doubts about the power he has over the airy spirit.

Then a knob in the study door turns and rattles of its own accord; the chandelier above tinkles as if a sudden wind has moved through it; a terrified spider scrambles for safety underneath a magnifying glass; and, on the desk, a glass tumbler with dark amber liquid in it falls over, spilling its contents. And Ariel's disembodied voice is heard telling

Prospero that he has come 'To answer thy best pleasure. Be't to fly, / To swim, to dive into the fire, to ride / On the curled clouds' (1.2.191–3). But all Prospero wants to know is if Ariel has 'performed to point the tempest that I bade thee?' (1.2.195). Ariel assures Prospero he has, 'To every article' (1.2.196), and as he speaks these words, thunder booms, lightning flashes, and with a jump cut in the film, the spirit appears where he was not before: leaning against a wall behind Prospero. This is as fantastical a representation of Ariel as any of the screen treatments of the fairies in the productions of A Midsummer Night's Dream explored above; it is at once eerie, enigmatic and believable.

Jarman's Ariel is tall, thin to the point of being emaciated, clad in belted white overalls complete with matching white gloves and, despite a full head of thick, dark brown hair, the skin of his face and neck are shot in such high light that the skin of his face and neck is unnaturally white; almost luminescent, in fact. Though perhaps not as transparent as we might expect an airy spirit to be, this Ariel is definitely a figure of fantasy. A short while later, Ariel appears all of a sudden in a mirror placed on a fireplace mantel overlooking Miranda's bedroom as he explains how the ship in Prospero's dream, and its human passengers – Prospero's enemies – made it to safe harbour.

One of the more shocking scenes involving Ariel in Jarman's film begins with him looking into a mirror and repeating the phrase, 'Let me remember thee what thou hast promised / Which is not yet performed me' (1.2.244–5); it is as if he is working up the courage to actually say the words to his master – an entirely human thing to do. Finally, he wakes Prospero and confronts him about the fact that Prospero has not fulfilled his promise to give him his liberty. Prospero's response is to remind Ariel of the story of how Prospero freed him from his bondage to the witch Sycorax. As Prospero narrates it, Jarman includes a sequence of images depicting Sycroax as a grotesque, naked woman with her son, Caliban, equally naked, nursing at her breast, and Ariel – also naked and looking very human rather than like a spirit – at the end of a heavy chain-leash controlled by Sycorax. The point could not be any clearer: Prospero really did liberate Ariel from such disgusting foulness. Chastened, Ariel promises to do whatever Prospero asks of him or out-right orders him to do.

Made thirty years after Jarman's, with a far larger budget and using the very latest in special effects technology, Taymor's The Tempest is a Shakespeare film of and for the twenty-first century.[8] Though not the first production on stage or screen to do so, Taymor's Prospero is changed to Prospera and played by Helen Mirren, who brings a strong matriarchal gravitas to the character. Taymor's camera also directs a great deal of attention to the volcanic rock that is a dominant feature of the Hawaiian location: Prospera's island is by turns lush and desolate; welcoming and forbidding; familiar and strange.

Following the text of Shakespeare's play fairly closely, the film opens with the storm at sea engulfing the ship from Naples in its tumultuous grip. Audiences, along with Miranda (Felicity Jones), watch the vessel struggle mightily from the clifftop shore. As discordant rock music plays, Miranda starts to run while the ship is beset on all sides by overwhelming waves. The film then cuts to a shot of Prospera on a promontory, wearing a cloak made of material that seems to mimic the island's rocky structure, holding a large staff over her head. And she is screaming at the top of her lungs as if her very life force is spilling out of her. That she is the cause of the storm and the ship's travails in the sea is thus made perfectly clear; her power is that great.

Later, in their cell in a large cave on the island, there is a pool of water that Prospera makes her way to once she has put Miranda to sleep after telling her about their true history. Kneeling next to the pool, Prospera summons Ariel. Immediately the water begins to ripple, and then the camera takes viewers deep within its depths until Ariel appears and hails Prospera as he twists and turns and rises to the surface of the pool with an ostentatious splash. Not unlike Jarman's, Taymor's Ariel is tall and wiry with white, luminescent skin and a shock of thick brown hair on his head. At Prospera's request, the airy spirit recounts the part he played in his mistress's storm (1.2.196–207). The speech is complemented with intercut images allowing audiences to see Ariel using his fingers to set fire to the ship's hull, rigging and sails; splitting himself into multiple Ariels to wreak even more havoc; making himself large enough to cradle the ship in the palms of his hands; and, finally, flicking a finger at the ship, now completely in flames, causing it to explode.

Ariel seems to very much enjoy telling Prospera of the efforts he practised on the king's ship, but his mood changes instantly and dramatically when she tells him there is more work for them to do. Out of the water of the pool now, crouched at Prospera's feet and grasping at her legs, he, almost cowering, says: 'Is there more toil? Since thou dost give me pains, / Let me remember thee what thou has promised, / Which is not yet performed me' (1.2.243–4). After she disdainfully asks what 'is't thou canst demand?' (246), Ariel rears up to his full height and shouts: 'My liberty'. He is revealed to be completely naked – though with his genitals strategically concealed – and, through expert use of special effects, he is entirely transparent.

143

Prospera upbraids Ariel for his moody ungratefulness. Taymor's depiction of this exchange – in which Prospera reminds Ariel of his previous servitude to the witch Sycorax – follows Shakespeare closely. However, unlike in Jarman's treatment of this part of the play, Sycorax and Caliban are absent. Instead, Taymor shows a grove of thick transparent trees appearing in the background behind Prospera and Ariel, as well as Ariel being imprisoned by Sycorax in the trunk of one of the cloven pines, where he was to remain for twelve long years, suffering unconscionably until Prospera arrived on the island and, hearing his plaintive cries and pitiable moans, freed him from his barbaric bondage. The recounting of this story leaves Ariel twisted and prostrate on the ground until, realising his error in attempting to defy Prospera, he is re-energised by her promise to free him within two days – if he continues to do as she commands in that time period.

Taymor uses special effects in the scenes involving Ariel and Alonso, the King of Naples, Gonzalo, his councillor and the would-be murderers Antonio (Prospera's usurping brother) and Sebastian (Alonso's brother). When the four men come upon the mirage feast Ariel and Prospera have made manifest, it vanishes as soon as they reach out to touch the food. And then Ariel appears to them as an enormous winged demon of a creature who castigates them as the 'three men of sin' (3.3.53) who dared to 'supplant good Prosper[a]' (70) as Duke of Milan – and deserve to pay the price for such a foul deed. Fittingly, when Ariel departs, Antonio and Sebastian are so maddened they believe Ariel has left behind a flock of dark birdlike creatures that do nothing but torment them; yet audiences can clearly see Antonio and Sebastian striking at the empty air with their swords.

One part of Taymor's *The Tempest* that Jarman did not include in his film involves Prospera asking Ariel for a report on how 'fares the king and's followers?' after they have endured the torment of Ariel's winged demon. Ariel tells her in a soft voice, 'Your charm so strongly works 'em / That if you beheld them, your affections / Would become tender' (5.1.18–19). Prospera is astonished to hear this and asks Ariel if he really believes what he just said. And Ariel claims that 'Mine would ... were I human' (20). This is an incredibly poignant moment, one that particularly marks *The Tempest* as a romance rather than a comedy or a tragedy. It resonates all the more when, not long thereafter, Ariel leaves Prospera, having earned his freedom, never to return to her side again.

In both *A Midsummer Night's Dream* and *The Tempest*, Shakespeare presented audiences with the words his audiences needed to believe in things like faeries, human metamorphosis into the non- or only partly human, airy spirits, the magical and the improbable. As I hope I have demonstrated above, all of the filmmakers who have adapted or appropriated these plays into screen productions dealt with those aspects of Shakespeare's plays with all due seriousness. In so doing, they crafted wholly believable visual worlds of fantasy and romance that complement Shakespeare's textual versions.

Notes

1. See M. W. Latham, *The Elizabethan Fairies* (New York, Columbia University Press, 1930); Jonathan Bate, *Shakespeare and Ovid* (Oxford, Oxford University Press, 1994); and A. B. Taylor, *Shakespeare's Ovid* (Cambridge, Cambridge University Press, 2000).
2. See, for example, 'Facsimile viewer: *A Midsummer Night's Dream*, Quarto 1 (British Library)', Internet Shakespeare Editions, accessed 6 May 2019, http://internetshakespeare.uvic.ca/Library/facsimile/book/BL_Q1_MND/13/?zoom=500.
3. Kenneth S. Rothwell, *A History of Shakespeare on Screen: A Century of Film and Television*, 2nd ed. (Cambridge, Cambridge University Press, 2004), 140.
4. See the discussion of Noble's film and the stage production from which it derives in Gary Jay Williams, *Our Moonlight Revels: A Midsummer Night's Dream in the Theatre* (Iowa City, University of Iowa Press, 1997), 255-7.
5. See William Shakespeare, *A Midsummer Night's Dream*, illustrations by Arthur Rackham (London, William Heinemann, 1908).
6. See Michael Hoffman, *William Shakespeare's A Midsummer Night's Dream* (New York, HarperCollins, 1999).
7. Rothwell, *A History of Shakespeare on Screen*, 253.
8. See Julie Taymor, *The Tempest* (New York, Harry N. Abrams, 2010).

PART III

Critical Issues

11

RUSSELL JACKSON

Questions of Racism: *The Merchant of Venice* and *Othello*

> As social threats rise, cultural norms shift, and group polarization turns extreme, we are being subjected to ever more brazen displays of dehumanization – magnifying our worse impulses. We cannot afford to let them flourish.
>
> Jennifer Eberhardt, *Biased. The New Science of Race and Inequality*, 2019[1]

This chapter considers the treatment of ethnic and cultural identity in adaptations of two plays in which they are an integral element, *The Merchant of Venice* and *Othello*. Complex characterisation is in danger of being short-circuited by unconscious bias, those 'worse impulses' of the kind analysed in Eberhardt's study of the social mechanisms of prejudice, pulling audiences back to racial stereotypes, dehumanising Shylock and Othello despite the efforts of filmmakers to counter such assumptions. In *The Merchant of Venice* anti-Semitism and its consequences in recent and current politics unavoidably complicate a play whose romantic elements are already made uneasy by issues of patriarchal control and materialism. In *Othello* the challenges of representing 'the Moor' himself are not simply resolved by casting an actor of colour in the role.[2] Productions also have to deal with the manner in which agency is wrested from the titular hero by a villain who can seem to have taken charge of way the audience perceives the action. This is especially disturbing in a play that Ania Loomba aptly describes as 'both a fantasy of interracial love and social tolerance, and a nightmare of racial hatred and male violence'.[3]

'Race' has wider implications in Shakespeare's works, and its political ramifications extend beyond the plays on which this chapter focuses. The postcolonial aspects of *The Tempest* – Prospero's usurpation of the island, paralleling his own expulsion from his dukedom, and the characterisation of Caliban as a 'savage and deformed slave' – are emphasised

149

in Julie Taymor's film (2011) to a greater extent than in those directed by
Peter Greenaway (1991) and Derek Jarman (1980). In Taymor's film,
when Caliban (Djimon Homisou) confronts Prospera (Helen Mirren)
with 'This island's mine, by Sycorax my mother / Which thou tak'st
from me' (1.1.333–4), she turns her head away, as if unable or unwilling
to answer directly, and the physical and verbal eloquence of this African
male, exotic but in no way 'deformed' (the description in the 1623
Folio's list of characters) make him a force to be reckoned with. There
is a suggestion that in this case the stigmatised 'Other' on the island may
in fact be the 'Better'. Nevertheless, in this play the issue of ethnic or
'racial' identity is not as strongly emphasised as in *The Merchant of
Venice* and *Othello*, where the language of modern racism is heard and
the characters and action come near to the embodiment of persistent
prejudices. Iago's racist language is shared by Roderigo and, to a lesser
extent, Desdemona's father Brabantio: as Michael Neill observes, 'One of
the terrifying things about *Othello* is that its racial poisons seem so
casually concocted, as if racism were something that Iago, drawing in
his improvisational way on a gallimaufry of quite unsystematic prejudices and superstitions, made up as he went along.'[4] The same can be
said of the characters (notably Antonio and his friends) whose anti-
Semitism is such a prominent feature of *The Merchant of Venice*. Does
Portia share this attitude, and if so, do the play's romance and comedy
qualify its effect?

The Merchant of Venice: Renaissance, Victorian and Modern

The television version based on Jonathan Miller's 1970 National Theatre
production, with Laurence Olivier as Shylock, and Michael Radford's
2004 film, with Al Pacino, differ markedly in their choice of setting.
Miller, himself Jewish, insisted that the anti-Semitism in the play was
'just that awful anti-Semitism of businessmen', and he did not want to
'treat it as racial anti-Semitism, although that had come to the fore in
Europe by the nineteenth century'.[5] The prejudices of Miller's late nineteenth-century Venetians, in their world of suave mercantile negotiations
and elegant café society, are uncomfortably close to those of our own
world, while Radford, at pains to emphasise that anti-Semitism was rife
in Renaissance Venice – though not shared by all its citizens – provides his
audience with a means of escape. In the opening scenes a Jew is thrown
into the Grand Canal by a mob and Antonio is even seen to spit on
Shylock's gabardine. This is followed by a sequence that summarises the
conflicts: shots of Hebrew texts being burned; Antonio being blessed in

church by the priest who encouraged the mob; courtesans flaunting their flesh in public; Jews in the synagogue, with Jessica in the women's gallery; and Lorenzo making a clandestine visit to the Ghetto, where he sees Jessica emerging with her father from the synagogue and – setting up that 'love interest' for the film – dropping a handkerchief for her suitor to pick up. The television version of Trevor Nunn's 1999 National Theatre production, set in the 1930s, suggests even more forcefully than Miller's the political consequences of the attitude of its least sympathetic characters, Salerio, Salanio and Gratiano. Like his 1989 *Othello*, Nunn's *Merchant* benefits from its origins in a studio theatre, with a basic set that accommodates, as in the theatrical version, the Venetian café society, the darker confines of Shylock's house and Portia's modish salon at Belmont.

In his analysis of Miller's theatre production, James C. Bulman notes the impact of Olivier's Shylock in what one reviewer described as 'a period ... increasingly conscious of its insistent minorities, wary of its silent majorities, and nervous of bloody conflict between the two', making this version seem like 'the play Shakespeare ought to have written'.[6] Shylock, with his carefully constructed gravity of demeanour and suavity of speech, seems at first to be a candidate for inclusion in the commercial if not social circle of Antonio and his associates. Although references to his being literally spat upon by Antonio seem out of place – and he has no 'Jewish gabardine' – this Shylock is treated with undisguised contempt by the gentiles. The sense of his otherness is repeatedly underlined not only by their behaviour, but also by the slightly over-deliberate enunciation of his speech and by such incidental business as his touching the *mezuzah* on his doorpost as he enters and leaves his house. The merchants of Miller's Venice constitute a 'tribe' (as Bulman observes) whose 'badge' of civility Shylock embraces, but 'only by dodging and circling one another do they betray their deeper antagonisms'.[7] Miller cuts Shylock's aside: 'I hate him for he is a Christian; / But more for that in low simplicity / He lends out money gratis, and brings down / The rate of usance here with us in Venice' (1.3.38–41). As well as being appropriate to the version's naturalistic televisual mode, here its removal is appropriate to the social situation of the moment. In Radford's film, with its insistence on the Renaissance context, the situation is different, and the same cut seems rather to be made to maintain the Jew's credentials as an object of sympathy. In Nunn's production, Henry Goodman's Shylock, his prayer shawl visible under his conservative suit and his yarmulke worn under his fedora, is (in Charles Edelman's phrase) 'friendly towards Bassanio, but wary of Antonio in the first scene'.[8]

Here the medium is not so strictly confined by conventions of screen naturalism, and the aside is spoken with a degree of irony.

As the grounds for his vindictiveness increase, Olivier's Shylock assumes more outward signs of his faith: after Jessica's desertion he is seen at home in his shirt sleeves and wearing the yarmulke previously hidden by his top hat, and when he tells Tubal he will 'have the heart' of Antonio 'if he forfeit' (3.2.115) he is putting on his prayer shawl. The photograph of Leah, which he kisses when he mentions the 'turquoise' she gave him, helps to establish an emotional life that exists alongside the less sympathetic concern to guard his wealth. In the scene of arbitration over the bond, when Gratiano and Bassanio declare that they would willingly sacrifice their wives to save Antonio, this Shylock is serious rather than dramatic in his exclamation 'These be the Christian husbands!' and his reflection that he would rather Jessica had married 'any of the stock of Barabbas' than a Christian (4.1.292–4). (Radford omits the reference to husbands, keeping the emphasis on the loss of Jessica.) Staged as a hearing in chambers rather than, as in Radford's film, a public spectacle, Miller's scene pits Shylock against the members of the club he can never join. On hearing the penalties enacted against an alien who 'attempts [to] seek the life of any citizen' (347–8) he collapses in what seems to be an incipient stroke. After his slow exit, supported by his secretaries, an anguished cry is heard. In the theatre, as on screen, this was a chilling disruption of any relaxation or celebration on the part of the Christians. Radford has the legal process conducted before the Doge, and attended by two factions: a crowd of Christian Venetians, noisily partisan, and a group of Jews in their distinctive red caps. Tubal, who in the play appears only in one scene (3.1) as Shylock's trusted friend, with news from Genoa, is useful in establishing the distinction between Shylock and his coreligionists. In Radford's film the latter (who include Tubal) are anxious but undemonstrative, and clearly disapprove of Shylock's behaviour: at the end of the film, the doors of the synagogue will be shut against him. Nunn's Tubal, who has entered the court alone, and is the only Jew present apart from Shylock, leaves pointedly when his friend prepares to carry out the 'sentence' on Antonio.

Miller's Antonio (Anthony Nicholls) is suavely contemptuous, with no compunction in insulting Shylock: his warning that 'the devil can cite Scripture for his purpose' (1.3.98) is spoken without regard to whether or not he is overheard. Bassanio has a moment of apprehension when his friend insists on Shylock becoming a Christian as condition of the waiving of the death penalty, but shows no degree of sympathy for the Jew. Radford is at pains to associate anti-Semitic behaviour with the libertinism of Bassanio and his friends – we see Shylock at dinner with them, clearly discomfited by their behaviour and the presence of the courtesans they entertain. This is the scene Shakespeare did not write. Nunn creates it by having Shylock join Bassanio in the nightclub where Antonio and his friends were discovered in the opening scene. The floorshow is in full swing, and it features Young Gobbo making his debut as a stand-up, with lines from 2.2 giving a comic account of his life with the Jew.

So far as Morocco and Portia's reaction to him are concerned, Miller makes the suitor a dark-skinned, eloquent figure in a Westernised dress uniform – possibly educated at a French military academy – and Radford's prince is a genial leader in white robes with a warlike retinue to whom many of his reflections are addressed. After his departure Lynn Collins, relieved but also amused, does not speak 'Let all of his complexion choose me so' (2.7.79). Derbhle Crotty, in Nunn's production, encounters Chu Omambala's elegant Morocco, 'a dashing prince' who has Portia 'desperately hoping he would choose the right casket, and becoming tearful when he [does] not'.[9] The line is spoken, but as if to conceal her feelings from her entourage of maids.

Miller's Portia (Joan Plowright) speaks it to Nerissa as a private joke, but the casual racism is unambiguous. Her conduct towards Shylock in the hearing before the Duke is uncompromising – Miller was anxious to remove any sentimentality from her speech on 'the quality of mercy' (4.1.181–202), which comes from her impatience that an important concept has not been grasped.[10] This Portia has ignored Jessica when she arrived in Belmont with Lorenzo, and in the final scene she has difficulty remembering her name. Miller also ends with a moment that encapsulates the play's unresolved quality and juxtaposes Shylock's daughter and her father's adversary. Jessica is in the foreground reading her deed of gift, Antonio a little way behind her with the letter that tells him his fortunes have been restored. He gestures as if reaching out to her, but this goes unheeded. As the screen fades to black the *Kaddish* is heard. Radford, working with a radically cut text, manages to give Portia a moment with Jessica in the final scene, but the latter's remorse is evident: she fingers the 'turquoise' when news arrives of her father's defeat. In the film's final moments she looks out across the lagoon, watching a hunter spear fish with a bow and arrow. Meanwhile Antonio, left alone in the villa, gazes out of the window, presumably at the same scene, though we are not given a point-of-view shot to establish this.

Of the three Shylocks, Henry Goodman's, informed by the actor's own background, is the most intensely wedded to his Jewishness, witnessed by the prayer shawl beneath his well-cut suit jacket and the yarmulke underneath his elegant fedora. At home this Shylock inhabits a world of religious observance and familial devotion: he and his daughter converse briefly in Yiddish, and before he leaves to dine with the Christians, he turns away for a moment of prayer and remembrance before a photograph of his dead wife Leah that sits, flanked by two candles with a prayer book on the table in front of it. The value Goodman's Shylock places on his family combines tenderness with severity – after slapping Jessica on the cheek he holds her close as they sing in Hebrew the traditional prayer *Eshet Chayil*, 'A Woman of Virtue'.[11] His daughter's flight to the Christians is an emotional as well as economic and cultural betrayal. By the final scene Jessica seems to have acquired some of the fashionable ease (and dress sense) of Belmont, but the news from Venice shakes her, and the play ends with her in the foreground, singing *Eshet Chayil* once again, a moment that cuts short the exultation of the Christians behind her. Like Miller's off-screen *Kaddish*, this returns the focus to the daughter and her feelings towards her father.

Othello: Who Tells the Story?

In one respect *Othello* may seem less problematic than *The Merchant of Venice*, in that none of the sympathetic characters – with the exception of Desdemona's aggrieved father – uses racist language. Nevertheless, the representation of Othello himself presents a difficulty. Up to the late 1960s most stage, film and television productions offered white actors in varying degrees of skin colouring to represent the correspondingly varied definitions of a 'Moor'. In three notable screen versions, Othello is *very* black. Emil Jannings, in Dmitri Buchowetski's 1922 film, Orson Welles in his own 1952 adaptation, and Laurence Olivier in Stuart Burge's film of John Dexter's 1964 National Theatre production, all adopt more or less elaborate makeup, with Olivier's the most notoriously studied in physicality and voice as well as skin tones. More significant than the physical impersonation by a white actor, itself no longer acceptable, is the extent to which even a black actor's performance may seem to endorse the notion that a black male is likely to be violent in his jealousy. Moreover, the play's catastrophe includes an act of appalling domestic violence that can seem to endorse deep-seated racist myths of miscegenation and its consequences. As Thomas Cartelli and Katherine Rowe demonstrate, the 'erotically charged objectification of the black male body' can work to 'strengthen the already dramatically privileged point of view of Iago, or more correctly, the dramatic function the character Iago fulfills'.[12] In the cinema, showing is invariably preferred to telling: seeing may result in believing, so that illustrating Iago's allegations and Othello's delusions can seem to endorse Iago's ownership of the film's specular economy.

In his 1952 film Welles's personal performance dominates in eloquence and physicality, and his makeup is as much an element of the film's expressionistic techniques as a signifier of race. The visual vocabulary of light and dark is announced from the very first sequence. Blackness in the imagery, like the recurrence of bars, gratings and eccentric camera angles, emblematises psychological and spiritual confusion and, ultimately, destruction. From the first shot, in which his face emerges from darkness as he lies on his funeral bier, Othello's black features are part of this pattern, and in tenebrously lit scenes and shots, with his person confined physically, he is effectively imprisoned by Iago's strategies and the film's mirroring of them.

On film Olivier's performance, by all accounts powerful in the theatre, is distanced as much by its superabundance of nuance as by the elaborate makeup. It is difficult to be convinced that the figure on the screen is any other than Olivier, giving a virtuoso rendition of a great text. Some elements of the performance – such as Othello's almost insolent nonchalance in the first act, or the tenderness with which he speaks to Desdemona before his mind has been poisoned – are strikingly effective. Others, notably the transports of anger and grief, are questionable. Describing rehearsals for the stage production, Kenneth Tynan noted that in 4.2, when 'the superman runs amok', the actor 'resorts to shrill and wailing head notes that savour slightly of self-indulgence'. He concludes that 'it is Othello, not Olivier who is indulging himself emotionally', but asks 'will the audience know the difference?'[13] In the film, Olivier's Othello suffers by the comparison with the Iago of Frank Finlay, favoured by the intimacy afforded by the camera. Here, as in some other screen versions, Othello's mastery of his own narrative, especially in his last moments – 'Soft you, a word or two before you go' (5.2.347) – is in danger of being usurped by Iago.

A similar imbalance between the leading actors occurs in Oliver Parker's 1995 *Othello*, the first mainstream cinema version with a black actor in the title role. Barbara Hodgdon characterises Laurence Fishburne's Moor as 'a powerfully controlled, self possessed figure, radiating a quiet, reserved dignity from a magnificent physical presence' in a 'possession of the role' contrasting with both Olivier's Othello and, problematically within the film, Kenneth Branagh's 'reptilian' Iago.[14] Similarly, Fishburne's vocal delivery, as Hodgdon points out, couples 'soft African-American sound to vaguely "foreign" intonation patterns', and stands out not only from the speech of the British cast members, including Branagh, but also from that of the Italian actors who play the Duke and Brabantio and, more significantly, Irène Jacob as Desdemona. The predominant effect is that Othello is (as Michael Anderegg suggests) 'strong without being dangerous' and 'hurt but insufficiently angry'.[15] Nevertheless, the restraint makes his eruptions of violence all the more shocking, especially as they contrast with the lyrical eroticism of the scenes showing the couple's wedding night and those that illustrate his erotic imaginings of her coupling with Cassio. It is here that the film's specular economy is closest to upholding the racist fantasy of the sexualised black male.

In his dual capacities as actor and director Welles overshadows his Desdemona (Suzanne Cloutier). The most effective female voice is that of Emila (Fay Compton), who lives in a world of common sense detached from the prurient fantasies of Iago (Micheál MacLiammóir) and the romantic enthusiasm of her mistress – and, for that matter, Othello. In Burge's film Joyce Redman's Emilia has a moment of tenderness for her husband at the end of scene when she gives the handkerchief to Frank Finlay's Iago: especially significant, given the actor's theory that Iago's 'loathing of Othello's sexuality and his alienation from Emilia' are the consequence of his having been 'impotent for years'.[16] In Parker's film Jacob's Desdemona, tenderly amorous and excited by the new and exotic milieu she has entered, is complemented by a keenly observant and pragmatic Emilia (Anna Patrick), but the most impressive performer of the role on screen is Zoë Wanamaker in the 1989 television version of Trevor Nunn's RSC production. Here the camera consistently catches her watching her husband (Ian McKellen), aware of the hidden depths behind his bonhomie and moving gradually to a sympathetic alliance with Desdemona. Imogen Stubbs is a feisty Desdemona, unrestrained in her affection but unprepared for the effects of her husband's jealousy. Emilia, though, sees trouble coming from the moment they arrive in Cyprus. Subtleties of relationships and nuances of behaviour and language are effectively carried over from the cast's experience of a studio theatre production whose intimacy complemented the television medium. The vocal and physical authority of Othello, played by the black opera singer Willard White, contrast effectively with the nervous linguistic and behavioural detail of McKellen's Iago, a 'born' non-commissioned officer. There is no question here of the fetishising of Othello's black male body. Arguably, issues of race are subordinated to other concerns, identified by Virginia Mason Vaughan as 'the search for meaning in human relationships, the struggle to find trust and intimacy in a world of appearances, the fragility of human bonds'.[17]

Othello Transposed: Tim Blake Nelson's *O* and Geoffrey Sax's *Othello*

Release of *O*, directed by Tim Blake Nelson, was scheduled for April 1999, but was held back for two years on account of the murder on 20 April of twelve students and a teacher at a high school in Columbine, Colorado.[18] Both *O* and the British 2001 television film *Othello*, directed by Geoffrey Sax from a script by Andrew Davies, address the racial politics of their respective societies, but to different effect.[19] 'O' is the nickname of Odin James (Mekhi Pfifer), the only African American student in an almost exclusively 'white' prep school, brought in to raise the basketball team's standing. His prowess has earned him respect in the school, and the love of Desi (Julia Styles), the Dean's daughter. The coach's son Hugo (Josh Hartnett) is angered by his father's award of the 'Most Valued Player' title to Odin and his public declaration that he loves him as if he were his son. When Odin identifies Mike Cassio as his right-hand man on court, Hugo plots his revenge. Sexual jealousy and race-derived anxieties on the part of Odin will be his weapons.

Hugo makes use of his own girlfriend Emily and the hapless (and unattractive) Roger, the film's equivalent of Roderigo, who is to kill Mike. In the catastrophe, Hugo shoots and kills both Mike and Roger (who has bungled the attempted murder). Odin strangles Desi and, when she reveals his machinations, Hugo shoots Emily. Confronted by the truth, Odin takes Hugo's gun and pursues him through the dorm. Facing his tormentor, he turns the gun on himself. The film ends with Hugo under arrest: as he is taken away we hear a soliloquy in voice-over, reflecting on his desire to 'soar like a hawk'. The visual image of a black hawk – the team's mascot – figures in the opening and concluding sequences, a metaphor adopted by Hugo for his own ambition. Its contrast with the whiteness of the doves kept in a cupola at the top of the school's spiral staircase is a correlative for the Odin/Desi relationship as well as for Hugo's desires, first heard in voice-over in the opening sequence and repeated at the end: 'a hawk is no good around normal birds. He can't fit in . . . one of these days everyone's going to pay attention to me'. By speaking as prologue and epilogue, Hugo lays claim to the story. This is no mere 'teen movie': high school, as Hodgdon points out, is represented as 'a crisis culture where adolescents define their relations to the world through performances of maturity, a microcosm of a larger culture that idolises sports heroes and is shot through with violence'.[20] In this context, Hugo's chagrin at being passed over by his father the coach has a familial and generational dimension not present in Iago, and his malignity can be identified – like that of Finlay's Iago – in terms of popular post-Freudian psychology.

Odin is haunted not by his real background, but the racist version of it. In an early scene Desi teases Odin that he can use the word 'nigger' while it is forbidden to her, and her father (as Hugo knows) is prompt to believe the black student is a sexual predator. Crucially, the stigmatising word is also heard in hip-hop lyrics on the soundtrack and surfaces again in dialogue towards the end in the mouths of Hugo and (damagingly) Mike. Hugo tells Odin 'They [Desi and Mike] call you the nigger man'; and Odin insists before his death that he did not come from a stereotypical 'poor black' background of drugs and crime, and should not be remembered as 'the nigger that lost it back in high school'.

In Sax's film John Othello (Eamonn Walker) a black officer in London's Metropolitan Police, is promoted to the rank of Commissioner (the commander of the force) over the head of his friend and mentor Ben Jago (Christopher Eccleston). Othello has faced down an angry mob after the killing of a black suspect in a drugs raid, and his elevation meets the Met's need for a positive message. The Commissioner has been forced to resign when he is recorded making racist comments immediately after delivering a speech calling for greater diversity in appointments. Jago destroys Othello's career and his marriage to Dessie (Keeley Hawes), a white woman from a privileged background, causes the death of the couple, and succeeds to the extent of replacing Othello as Commissioner. Sax's *Othello* is a direct commentary on the controversy over 'institutional racism' in the force, exacerbated by the failure to investigate fully the murder of a black teenager in 1993 and the subsequent cover-up.[21] In *O* the pace of editing varies, encompassing the excitement of the basketball matches, brisker 'ordinary life' passages, slower elegiac sequences, more deliberate dialogue scenes (such as those corresponding to the 'temptation' of Othello by Iago) and the elegiac opening and closing shots of doves. Sax achieves the urgency of news reporting. As Kenneth Rothwell observes, 'rapid editing pushes the narrative forward at a fast-forward pace', while 'acrobatic camera work reinforces the movie's Iago-centredness with numerous tight close-ups of Jago, branding him as a sneaky, insinuating treacherous villain'.[22]

Even more decisively than other versions, Sax tilts the narrative towards its Iago figure, with his frequent smiles of complicity to the viewer and a racist rant, shown in a long tracking shot through the corridors of the Met's headquarters that, as none of his colleagues takes any notice, can only represent his fantasy. When he reaches the street he engages the camera with a speech that reinforces his wooing of the viewer. Although his governing motive would seem to be ambition, emphatically expressed in the final shot of him posing for a photograph in his official regalia as Commissioner, other statements suggest a more complex psyche. 'Who knows what makes us do things?' he asks, and in a voice-over during the final shot he challenges us and reiterates his opening words: 'It was about love, that what you've got to understand. Don't talk to me about race, don't talk to me about politics.' As the camera moves to a close-up, he turns to face it: 'It was love – simple as that.' In *O*, other filmic devices consistently give us Hugo's point of view or place him in relation to other characters so as to imply it, but Ben Jago's to-camera speeches and his racist rant take the film beyond the screen realism that confines Hartnett's Hugo to voice-over mode.

Nelson and Sax both address racial prejudice and its social consequences to powerful effect, using the matrix offered by the play with a directness not achieved in most screen versions. (A notable but frustratingly elusive exception is Liz White's 1980 production, filmed with an all-black cast and crew but never commercially released: Peter Donaldson describes it as 'an Othello in which the historical experience of black Americans plays a central role.')[23] In *O*, ingrained prejudice wells up alarmingly at moments in a story dominated by Hugo's envy and his gnawing desire to 'soar'. Sax focuses on an insidious political aspect of prejudice: its availability as a means to an end. No other version of the play has concluded its narrative with the Iago figure in a position of power, or this aggressive command of the medium itself. Perhaps the closest parallel is the erotic fulfilment achieved by Branagh's wounded Iago in Parker's *Othello*, when, bidden to look on the 'tragic loading of this bed' he crawls onto it as if to assert his possession of his victims and the achievement of the greater part of his task. With their vivid depictions of sexual aggression, domestic violence, racial antipathy and psychological manipulation, all the screen versions of *Othello* share an ability to disturb and shock with a play that is never easy viewing. To add to the discomfort, Iago can sometimes seem in control of the viewers' experience, soliciting their complicity with 'brazen displays of dehumanisation' of the kind identified by Eberhardt.

Notes

1. Jennifer Eberhardt, *Biased. The New Science of Race and Inequality* (London, Heinemann, 2019), 152.
2. On casting, see Celia R. Daileader, 'Casting black actors: beyond Othellophilia', in Catherin M. S. Alexander and Stanley Wells, eds., *Shakespeare and Race* (Cambridge University Press, 2000), 177–202; and Ayanna Thompson, *Passing Strange. Shakespeare, Race and Contemporary America* (Oxford, Oxford University Press, 2011).
3. Ania Loomba, *Shakespeare, Race, and Colonialism* (Oxford, Oxford University Press, 2002), 91.

4. Michael Neill, '"Unproper beds": race, adultery and the hideous in *Othello*', in *Putting History to the Question. Power Politics and Society in English Renaissance Drama* (New York, Columbia University Press, 2000), 237–68 (249).

5. 'Work in progress: a dialogue with Jonathan Miller', in Michael Romain, *A Profile of Jonathan Miller* (Cambridge, Cambridge University Press, 1992), 21–94 (42). See also Jonathan Miller, *Subsequent Performances* (London, Faber and Faber, 1986), 104–8.

6. James C. Bulman, *Shakespeare in Performance. The Merchant of Venice* (Manchester, Manchester University Press, 1991) 99, quoting Benedict Nightingale, *New Statesman*, 8 May 1970.

7. Bulman, 81.

8. Charles Edelman, ed., *Shakespeare in Production: The Merchant of Venice* (Cambridge, Cambridge University Press, 2002), 84.

9. Ibid., 85.

10. Miller, *Subsequent Performances*, 107.

11. Edelman, *Shakespeare in Production*, 84 identifies the song and gives a translation in an appendix.

12. Thomas Cartelli and Katherine Rowe, *New Wave Shakespeare on Screen* (London, Polity Press, 2007), 122. On Olivier's performance as Othello see also Stephen Buhler, *Shakespeare in the Cinema. Ocular Proof* (New York, SUNY Press, 2002), 40–1.

13. Kenneth Tynan, ed., *Othello. The National Theatre Production* (London, Hart-Davis, 1966), 10.

14. Barbara Hodgdon, 'Race-ing *Othello*, re-engendering white-out, II', in Richard Burt and Lynda E. Boose, eds., *Shakespeare the Movie, II: Popularizing the Plays on Film, TV, Video, and DVD* (London and New York, Routledge, 2003), 89–104 (90).

15. Michael Anderegg, *Cinematic Shakespeare* (Lanham, Rowman and Littlefield, 2004), 136.

16. Tynan, *Othello*, 8.

17. Virginia Mason Vaughan, *Othello, a Contextual History* (Cambridge, Cambridge University Press, 1994), 218.

18. Hodgdon, 'Race-ing *Othello*', 99–100 summarises the background.

19. Sax's *Othello*, a co-production of London Weekend Television (LWT), the Canadian Broadcasting Corporation and WGBH Boston, is available at www.youtube.com/watch?v=cIcCE3s_rFc (accessed 9 June 2019).

20. Hodgdon, 'Race-ing *Othello*', 99.

21. On the production's topicality see Peter J. Smith, '"Institutionally racist:" Sax's *Othello* and tethered presentism', Sarah Hatchuel and Nathalie Vienne-Guerrin, *Shakespeare on Screen: Othello* (Cambridge, Cambridge University Press, 2015), 76–91.

22. Kenneth S. Rothwell, *A History of Shakespeare on Screen. A Century of Film and Television*, 2nd ed. (Cambridge, Cambridge University Press, 2004), 260–1.

23. Peter S. Donaldson, '"Haply for I am black": Liz White's *Othello*', in *Shakespearean Films/Shakespearean Directors* (Boston, Unwin Hyman, 1990), 127–44 (127). Filming took place between 1962 and 1966: a copy is accessible by prior arrangement in the Performing Arts Division of New York Public Library.

12

COURTNEY LEHMANN

'A Wail in the Silence': Feminism, Sexuality and Final Meanings in *King Lear* Films by Grigori Kozintsev, Peter Brook and Akira Kurosawa

Referring to *King Lear*, Kate McLuskie argues that the 'action of the play, the organisation of its point of view and the theatrical dynamic of its central scenes all depend upon an audience accepting an equation between "human nature" and "male power".[1] Even the spectacle of Cordelia's martyrdom is precisely that – a spectacle – not only of an uninhabitable concept of ideal 'womanhood', but also, as McLuskie persuasively argues, of 'patriarchy restored'.[2] Silent and obedient, Cordelia is in many ways the perfect Renaissance woman. But as Shakespeare's play implies, she is ultimately too good for this world, dying in the service of the plot. Indeed, Carol Chillington Rutter contends that the most important scene Cordelia plays occurs in 5.3, when she is a corpse in Lear's arms, for it is over her dead body that the play's conflicts are resolved. In Rutter's subtle formulation: 'Looking at the body as a sign loaded with "story", we discover ... that the body that plays dead works at the margin: it comes in at the end; it collects up final meanings'.[3] At the other end of the spectrum are the play's only other female characters, Goneril and Regan, who rebel against the established order by waging war and pursuing their sexual desires. And what better 'final meaning' is there to reap from their dead bodies than a cautionary tale about women whose pursuit of economic, geopolitical and sexual autonomy leads headlong into anarchy? All too conveniently, Goneril and Regan play the demons to Cordelia's saint. These rigid binaries – and the impossible subject positions they impose on women – are the inventions of patriarchy, and of misogyny in particular. Only one of the films explored here challenges this debilitating construction of sex and gender.

Few would dispute that there are three truly pioneering versions of *King Lear* on film: Grigori Kozintsev's *Korol' Lir* (1970), Peter Brook's *King Lear* (1971) and Akira Kurosawa's *Ran* (1985). These adaptations not only represent the best versions of *King Lear* ever made but also rank among the most important Shakespeare films of all time. Despite their separation across time, space and culture, the directors shared notes and visited each other at various points in their filmmaking careers, and their versions of *Lear* reflect both their affinities and differences. Financed by and produced within the former USSR, Kozintsev's adaptation of *King Lear* is unabashedly epic. Filmed through predominantly medium and long shots, *Korol' Lir* features thousands of extras, along with burning landscapes, runaway livestock and a soundtrack by Dmitri Shostakovich. By contrast, Brook's *Lear*, shot in the bleak, wintry, and windswept landscapes of northern Jutland, is sparse, abstract and decidedly self-conscious in its camera work, becoming a veritable study in cinematic alienation effects. *Ran*, which does not retain any of Shakespeare's language but freely adapts its plot and poetics, is similar to Kozintsev's film in its cinematic grandeur, employing a cast of thousands, exploiting the special effects born of natural landscapes, and featuring scenes with no less than two hundred horses – not to mention stunning Technicolor, which sharply contrasts with Brook's and Kozintsev's black-and-white adaptations. Ironically, despite the fact that Kurosawa converts Lear's daughters to Hidetora's sons in *Ran*, the director only began to truly appreciate Shakespeare's play through the lens of Goneril and Regan. Explaining that at first, he did not understand 'the ferocity of [Lear's] daughters' response to Lear's feeble attempts to shed his royal power', he soon realised 'that his power must rest upon a lifetime of bloodthirsty savagery'.[4] Indeed, what warrants Goneril and Regan's 'ferocity' in response to their father's bequests? What might Shakespeare's play look like from the perspective of his daughters?

To adapt *King Lear*, as Jane Smiley argued in the process of writing her own *Lear* spinoff *A Thousand Acres*, is to assume 'the courage to fall into total darkness'.[5] Kozintsev himself struggled with this psychological abyss, noting in his film journal, *The Space of Tragedy*, that '*Lear* was not a film on which I was working but a life which had entered my own from which it was too late to escape.'[6] In Shakespeare's play, it is Cordelia and, to a lesser extent, Edgar, Kent and ostensibly Lear himself, who embrace this 'fall into total darkness' – into the nihilism of the 'nothing' that 'comes from nothing' (1.1.90), in Lear's obscene pun. Indeed, as a woman, Cordelia is the site of negation – of the 'nothing' that invokes the legal status of women in Renaissance England while also underscoring the obsession with female sexuality that prevails in Lear's prurient tirades and the Fool's unrelenting innuendos. Building on what is mere suggestion in Shakespeare's play, Smiley's novel is narrated from the perspective of

Ginny (Goneril) who, along with Rose (Regan), are sexually abused by their father Larry Lear, while the Cordelia character, Caroline, is spared. Apropos of this ontological trauma, Rutter's observation that, in the tragedies, 'Shakespeare habitually uses the woman's body to proxy the crisis of masculine self-representation that is the play's narrative focus',[7] is borne out with a vengeance in *King Lear* – and largely reinforced by its screen history. Hence, throughout this broader analysis of Shakespeare's play on film, I will also focus on the ways in which both the real and representational violence that is endemic to patriarchy is displaced onto the bodies of women – a symptom, in Rutter's words, of a 'crisis in masculine self-representation' that seeks to recuperate its own, self-affirming 'final meanings' by inscribing them in the folds of wounded female flesh.

More Sinned Against than Sinning?

Despite corresponding throughout their respective, simultaneous films of *Lear*, Kozintsev's and Brook's films are wildly different. *Korol' Lir* begins with a tight shot of partially exposed toes jutting out from under make-shift burlap shoes, which trudge through a barren, dust-strewn landscape as a reed instrument intones a mournful cry. When the camera pulls back to reveal ever increasing numbers of hunched and hobbled masses, we recognise the signs of a war-ravaged human and natural geography. Sweeping shots of the steep wasteland that the refugees traverse beyond the fortress walls point to a monarch who has indeed 'ta'en / Too little care of this' (3.4.32–3). Heard before he is seen, Yuri Yarvet's Lear enters the picture in the form of off-screen laughter, as the jingle of the Fool's bell foretells the king's opening appearance in his throne room in a mask – a prop which, Kozintsev observes, 'is a special theme in the art of our times'.[8] Peering between the burnt out eye-holes of a mop head, the king chortles as he hands the prop back to the Fool and, suddenly serious, proceeds toward the fire. Once seated there, the king unfurls a corner of his robe to reveal the Fool tucked underneath; with genuine affection, Lear pats him on the head – a moment of tenderness that poses marked contrast to the king's ensuing treatment of Cordelia and Kent. After yanking Cordelia by the arm while violently rebuking her, the king berates Kent – humiliating him until, as an exclamation point, he spits on him. Underscoring Lear's precipitous descent into madness, Kozintsev, rather than moving directly from the conclusion of this scene into Edmund's soliloquy on bastardy, interpolates a scene that shows the dread but diminutive sovereign maniacally racing up an exterior staircase leading to the castle's massive battlements which, with torches blazing, invest the entire scene with an apocalyptic aura. When Shostakovich's score ceases, Lear continues his tantrum; as his body twitches in rage, the king excoriates his uncomprehending subjects below by shouting the non-sequitur:

> The barbar[ian] . . .
> That makes his generation messes
> To gorge his appetite, shall to my bosom
> Be as well . . . relieved
> As thou my sometime daughter! (adapted from 1.1.117–21)

Wresting these lines from their context in Scene 1 and converting them into a stand-alone speech, Kozintsev highlights the extremity of Lear's response to Cordelia's perceived rejection. Perhaps by virtue of the language barrier that Yarvet was forced to navigate as a native of Estonia, there is a restless and at times reckless energy that pervades his performance, adding dramatic depth to his portrait of the fragile and failing king.

Brook's film begins intentionally less dramatically. As the credits roll, the camera pans back and forth among a group of noblemen, who stand motionless and expressionless outside the fortress. The cinematic frame cuts them off at a strange angle, just above the shoulders, so that the viewer – unable to see the extension of their bodies or the ground that supports them – experiences an unsettling sense of dislocation. When the scene shifts to a crude throne room, the face of Paul Scofield's intimidating Lear is lit from below against the near-total darkness of the cave-like dwelling. The resulting chiaroscuro effect leads to the perception that the king's head is unmoored from his body, even floating – a tableau that is evocative of the horror film genre. These alienation effects afford the only segue into the film-proper, which begins with Lear's third line: 'Know that we have divided / In three our kingdom' (1.1.36–37). Unlike the frail appearance of Yarvet's Lear, Scofield's monarch wears a massive cloak made of thick black animal fur that makes him appear massive and simian-like as he ambles, hunched and seething, about his throne in the wake of Cordelia's unexpected reply – or is it rebellion? Indeed, whereas Yarvet depicts a king who is well on his way to madness, Scofield portrays a towering and terrifying autocrat, and a figure whose daughters have much greater reason to fear.

In his book on theatre, *The Empty Space*, Brook suggests that the misogynistic reception of Lear's daughters is not signalled by anything in the play itself at the beginning of the action. Citing Goneril's speech professing that she loves her father 'more than words can wield the matter'

(1.1.55), Brook argues that there is no reason *not* to take Goneril at her word. 'In fact', he continues, 'if Goneril in her first appearance does not play a "monster", but merely what her given words suggest, then all the balance of the play changes – and in the subsequent scenes her villainy and Lear's martyrdom are neither as crude nor as simplified as they might appear'.[9] In Brook's adaptation, Goneril utters her lines in an affectionless, matter-of-fact manner and appears neither smug nor scheming upon the revelation of her third of the inheritance. Rather, she looks withdrawn and numb, forming words with her mouth that she chews on awkwardly, without uttering them out loud. This visual crux is precisely the sort of 'speaking silence' that feminist critics have seized upon in their revisionist interpretations of *King Lear*, arguing that female silence can be construed as subversive – a point to which I will return by way of conclusion. Regan is initially even more guarded than her sister; approaching the throne, slowly and deliberately, she has an incredulous look in her eye, as if she doubts the veracity of his words and the sincerity of his generosity. Unlike the otherworldly beauty of Cordelia in Kozintsev's adaptation, in Brook's film, Cordelia is plain; there is nothing to distinguish her visually from her sisters except for her younger age. Significantly, both directors employ a distinct cinematic grammar in their representations of Cordelia; whereas Kozintsev reserves the film's only close-ups for his angelic vision of her, Brook highlights Cordelia's vulnerability by repeatedly framing her with her back to the camera while facing Lear – a specular economy that pinions her between his obscene gaze and the audience's inescapable voyeurism.

Rather than making Lear a tragic hero as Kozintsev does, Brook reads Shakespeare's play as a masculinist narrative that appeals, in Kate McLuksie's words, to the 'transcendent values of love and filial piety and which affords no rights to the powerless within it'.[10] This feminist awareness is encoded in the camera's treatment of Goneril, when Lear – unexpectedly – reserves the full flush of his rage for her. A series of establishing shots show Lear's retinue in various stages of passing out within the fortress, drunken and grazing on scraps left over from a night of heavy feasting. Brook leaves little doubt that these are '[m]en so disordered, so debauched and bold, / That this our court, infected with their manners, / Shows like a riotous inn' (1.4.221–3). Following a flash cut to an uncomfortably tight shot of Goneril's disapproving, owl-like gaze, she proceeds to upbraid her father and his men, until Lear dashes his crop to the ground and, hunched and shaking his head in fury like a lion unfurling its mane, he proceeds to upend the massive banqueting table with a primal roar. Based on the off-screen sound of women screaming, it is unclear whether the ensuing scene of pillage will also involve the plunder of rape. But after Lear's boorish henchmen have completely destroyed the banqueting room and it is clear that he intends no further harm, he fumes: 'Detested kite, thou liest. / My train are men of choice and rarest parts ... ' (1.4.241–2). Lear's hyperbolic statement is clearly belied by the optics of the savage scene that the king has just created, and reinforced when he proceeds to curse Goneril's womb. Visibly fighting back tears, Irene Worth's Goneril squares her jaw and resists rising to the bait of her father's rage, withholding any response that might 'legitimat[e] his wrath'.[11] Throughout the real and rhetorical violence featured in this scene, Brook's camera seems to be increasingly in league with Goneril, as frequent reaction shots reveal the steady erosion of her filial bond in the face of her father's barbarism. Her performance, as Rutter contends, 'understands Lear's daughters anew, not as Ugly Sisters but abused children whose father is responsible for inventing the metaphors that turn them, one by one, into monsters'.[12]

A samurai period film representative of the *Jidaigeki* genre, Kurosawa's *Ran* is radically different in its opening gestures.[13] As the opening credits roll, panoramic shots of warriors on horseback overlooking steep ravines and majestic green mountain passes invite the viewer to contemplate the film's exquisite colour palate. There is a luxury to the pacing as well as frequent scenes that are imbued with the haunting stillness of Noh drama – a genre that influenced both Brook's and Kozintsev's interpretations of *King Lear*. Suddenly, a rustling noise breaks the silence and three wild boars stream into focus as they rumble through heavy undergrowth. A shot of the Lear character, the aging patriarch Hidetora, shows him taking aim with his longbow at one unlucky boar, followed by a flash cut to the title card that reads, simply, 'Ran'. The ambiguity implicit in this editing strategy, which implies that the title 'Ran' can apply not only to the hunter but also to the hunted, is raised half-jokingly by Hidetora, when he explains to his sons that they will not eat their kill because, as the title cards read: 'He was a very old animal. His carcass is too tough and foul. Just like me, old Hidetora. Would you eat me?' he asks, unsuspectingly.[14] After Hidetora gives away his authority and castles to Taro and Jiro, Saburo, the Cordelia figure, dishonours him by telling the truth: the Great Lord has been reduced to 'a senile, old fool'. Unable to comprehend his father's shocking transformation and foreseeing the worst, Saburo chastises him for acting out-of-character: 'You have butchered countless people, spilled measureless blood', Saburo reminds him. 'And you showed no mercy nor any pity.' Though Hidetora concedes his power anyway, casting Saburo away in outrage, it is clear that Hidetora has risen to and maintained his stranglehold on power only through 'a lifetime of

166

bloodthirsty savagery', recalling Kurosawa's description. A ruthless incarnation of Shakespeare's senile king, Hidetora is unequivocally the least sympathetic of the Lear figures examined here.

Provocatively, Kathy Howlett views the female characters in *Ran* as agents rather than objects, arguing that the samurai culture depicted in the film is 'challenged by the women who are entrapped within it'.[15] For example, although Kurosawa converts the king's daughters to sons in keeping with the medieval samurai tradition, he invents the character of Lady Kaede, who is married to Hidetora's first-born son Taro, and provides her with a tragic backstory that almost seems to justify her treachery. A conflation of Goneril, Regan, Edmund and Lady Macbeth, Lady Kaede employs extreme economy of expression and gesture, in keeping with the film's stylised Noh dimensions, to explain that she grew up and lived in the First Castle until Hidetora murdered all of her people. 'And now I am back in this castle', she drones. 'How impatiently I have longed for this day.' Looking at an unspecified place on the floor in front of her, she adds, stoically: 'Right there is where my mother took her own life.' The implication is clear; by far the most prevalent war crime, rape would most certainly have preceded the murder of her mother in her besieged home.

But it is not long before Lady Kaede assumes a blatantly evil cast when, newly widowed, she seduces Jiro, the new Great Lord. Forcing him into a prone position, she seizes his sword, licks the battle blood off of his neck, and insists that he supply her with the head of his wife, Lady Sué. A devout Buddhist, Lady Sué is, like Cordelia, a sacrificial figure; she is intercepted and killed when she returns to her war-ravaged keep to retrieve her brother's flute – his only source of joy ever since Hidetora blinded him in his youth. Whereas the noble Lady Sué's death occurs off-screen, Lady Kaede, as a woman who explicitly threatens male power, is subject to a graphic execution. When, at the end of the film, she receives Lady Sué's head with great satisfaction, Lady Kaede exclaims: 'All that I have set out to accomplish I have done.' Suddenly, a jump cut to a white wall doused in a massive splatter of blood informs us that Lady Kaede has been decapitated – in gratuitous, horror film-style. Although it is perhaps admirable that Kurosawa finds a place for women beyond mere concubinage in *Ran*, the decision to subject both Lady Kaede *and* Lady Sué to identical, 'phallic' punishments – death by beheading – underscores the expendability of women, both 'good' and 'bad', in the world that *King Lear* dramatises, a disturbing affirmation of Ania Loomba's claim that 'Agency is often made visible by the violence of the dominant response against its expression ...'.[16]

The Eye of the Storm

The middle of the play, featuring the storm and Lear's revelations on the heath, is rendered uniquely in each film. For Kozintsev, the storm features hurricane-force gales and horizontal rain. An impressive aerial shot captures Yarvet's Lear distractedly wandering a vast expanse of cracked earth, a landscape that suggests the faultlines in the king's sanity. By contrast, Brook represents the storm scene through avant garde camerawork; frames that are either completely black or white externalise Lear's internal confusion and violent mood swings, while rapid intercutting between images drawn from both the play and the king's own phantasmogoric imagination – including a tableau of Goneril approaching Lear with what appears to be an urn – demarcate his unambiguous descent into a more permanent state of psychosis. Although *Ran* also includes a storm, Hidetora's real battle is against the music of Tsurumaru's flute. Evocative of Gloucester, the blind Tsurumaru plays his instrument to entertain Hidetora when the Great Lord stumbles upon his hovel for shelter from the rain. Featuring discordant, high-pitched notes in rapid succession, the panicked rhythms of the flute imitate the sound of a throttled hummingbird, beating its wings in a vain frenzy. Clasping his hands over his ears while staggering backward, Hidetora is 'cut to the brains' (4.5.189) by the incriminating noise, as though he were being attacked by an invisible enemy. Meanwhile, Kyoami, the Fool, seems to revel in Hidetora's pangs of conscience by glaring at his master and compounding Tsurumaru's musical indictment with the sardonic lyric: 'Ding dong the bell that tolls in hell!' Tinged with self-sabotage and punctuated by spasms of tears, the young Kyoami's litanies are more caustic, cruel and, at times, confused in *Ran* than those of his counterparts in other *Lear* adaptations. Feminised by his ambiguous sexuality and social station – and yet indispensable to Hidetora – Kyoami is dependent for his protection and survival on his master, an unlikely *quid pro quo* relationship which, on some level, makes him complicit in Hidetora's treachery.

Although many critics identify Kyoami as a homosexual (*shudo*), his character is better described as gender fluid. Played by the famous Japanese transvestite actor 'Peter', the Fool is coded visually in ways that reinforce his sexual and gender ambiguity. For example, he is cross-dressed, wearing a kimono-style robe along with pants, and his hair is tied in a loose ponytail rather than a tight samurai bun. When prompted to entertain the warriors, Kyoami wags his ponytail from side-to-side in unison with his entire body as he sings in jest about the Great Lord who 'sways like a branch in the wind'. But what Kyoami intones next acquires a sexual connotation: 'First he likes to swing this way, then he likes to swing that way. How the wind blows, nobody knows ...'. This reference to 'swinging both ways' alludes to the fickleness of fate while alluding to Kyoami's non-binary approach to sex and gender as performance – a tribute to the more gender-fluid traditions of Kabuki theatre and male-male samurai romances from the *nanshoku* literary tradition. And although *Ran* can hardly be called a feminist film, in the absence of such a narrative, Kyoami's story serves as a reminder that the future of feminist filmmaking depends upon the recognition of its inter-sectionality with struggles related not only to gender but also to sexual identity, race and class. In the end, playing both the Fool and the foil to Hidetora, Kyoami functions – paradoxically – as the unlikely guarantor of his master's masculinity, as Kathy Howlett brilliantly observes: 'Ironically, Kyoami's sexually ambiguous presence confirms the Great Lord's samurai identity.'[17]

The Space of Tragedy

For Kozintsev, Brook and Kurosawa, the nihilistic core of – and potential catharsis proffered by – the concluding scenes of *King Lear* crystalise in distinctly different tableau. For Kozintsev, the spiritual centre of the play is the reconciliation of Lear and Cordelia. Upon waking to see his youngest child, Yarvet's Lear looks at her tear-stained face and implores her: 'be your tears wet?' In an interpolated gesture, Yarvet gingerly reaches to touch Cordelia's cheek and, pausing to taste the salt, he affirms: 'Yes, faith. I pray, weep not' (4.6.64), a moment that Kozintsev identifies as the crux of the film. The tragic epicentre of Brook's film hinges on the nihilistic treatment of the reunion between Lear and Gloucester. Peppered with horrific jokes about Gloucester's blindness, Lear's 'preaching' is evocative of Artaud's theatre of cruelty. Yet it is not the bitter lucidity of Scofield's words but rather Gloucester's incessant weeping that resonates throughout this scene, literalising the king's melancholy musings that 'we came crying hither ... When we are born, we cry that we are come / To this great stage of fools' (4.5.174; 178–9). Significantly, in *Ran*, Kurosawa assigns these lines to the Fool, who exclaims, in keeping with his brutal cynicism: 'Hell! When man is born, he cries. And when he's cried enough, he dies.'

But the emotional apex of *Ran* is evinced by the death of Saburo. Poised on the back of Saburo's horse, Hidetora, still giddy from their reunion on the battlefield, reassures his youngest son that, with the wars over, 'We'll have long talks, just father to son.' As Hidetora leans for-ward laughing, Saburo is sabotaged and felled by musket fire; collapsing backwards, he absorbs the blow and inadvertently saves his father's life. Through the figure of Saburo, Kurosawa literalises the concept of Cordelia as a martyr. Kozintsev's and Brook's films, by contrast, deconstruct the tenacious fiction – and patriarchal fantasy – of Cordelia's saving grace. Opting, like Shakespeare, not to show her hanging, Kozintsev employs an exquisitely composed shot of a noose blowing in the breeze, framed by an archway with a view of the sea. Brook ups the ante by showing Cordelia's neck snapping via a disturbing jump cut. In both films, Lear's reaction to Cordelia's murder is introduced through a dreadful, off-screen wail, whereas *Ran* goes out with a whimper when, gasping for air, Hidetora whispers: 'Saburo. Saburo!' In all three films, the extremity of the tragedy manifests itself in the failure of the Cordelia character's 'saving love' to save anything at all.[18] Hence the nihilistic exchange between Kent and Edgar, when they speculate whether this is 'the promised end' or the mere 'image of that horror' (5.3.218–9). Indeed, is it possible that the worst is yet to come? *King Lear* leaves us stranded in the throes of this ontological despair.

Feminist Disruptions

If Cordelia, as victim and martyr, and Goneril and Regan, as villains and monsters, prove to be unsatisfying sources of a feminist politics, then what constitutes a feminist interpretation of *King Lear*, and can a male director navigate this challenge? Whereas Kozintsev and Kurosawa cling tenaciously to misogynistic polarities, framing the female characters as all good (Cordelia, Lady Sué) or all bad (Goneril and Regan, Lady Kaede), Brook's vision of the play's three women is more subtle. In the face of Scofield's abusive, alpha-male monarch, Cordelia's silence resonates as a potential rebellion and, perhaps, as a rejection of his insistence on equating quantities of love with stores of capital. Taking exception to the play's suggestion that the only alternative to power that is organised vertically and male is female anarchy, Brook's film seems to value the struggle without reinforcing its misogynistic conclusion. His female characters, including Cordelia, are hardened, dirty and stoic in an unforgiving world; their deaths are difficult and drawn out. More brutal than poisoning, Goneril kills Regan with her bare hands, savagely wrestling her to the ground. In the immediate aftermath, Goneril, suddenly catatonic, rocks herself like a trauma-stricken child until she has the momentum to bash her skull against the cliff face. If there is a 'feminist' message in Brook's film then it lies in the recognition that if life in the Renaissance, as Hobbes asserted, was 'nasty, brutish, and short', then it was even harder for those who lived only as extensions of male property. It is for this reason why, although Brook does not offer an overtly feminist interpretation of *King Lear*, he creates the conditions of its possibility, by leaving room for characters other than Lear to occupy what Kozintsev calls 'the space of tragedy'. And in this 'empty space', as Brook titled his own thoughts on Shakespeare, we may begin to understand the feminist message – in McLuskie's terms – which 'insist[s] that the alternative to the patriarchal family and heterosexual love is not chaos but the possibility of new forms of social organisation and affective relationships'.[19]

The Promised End?

Although critics tend to read the conclusion of Kozintsev's epic film as redemptive – a homage to the people's resilience in the face of historical trauma as the villagers start to rebuild their lives amidst the burning rubble, the film's conclusion is more ambivalent. Preceded by the off-screen crying of the Fool, the final scene shows him sitting on the ground as the litter carrying Lear and Cordelia passes by; his crying ceases only when a soldier kicks him in the ribs and he crumples to the ground. Gathering himself with difficulty, the Fool slowly sits up and begins to play his makeshift woodwind. 'There was no need for an overture', recalls Kozintsev, not even from the great Shostakovich: 'I wanted the sad home-made pipe to sound like a wail in the silence.'[20] Insisting on materialising the worst, Brook's adaptation ends with total silence. Rather than leaving the viewer speculating about 'the image of that horror', Cordelia's body is borne off with the remnant of the noose still around her neck – a directorial decision that forms the visual bookend to Lear's last words in Brook's film: 'And my poor fool is hanged' (5.3.281). As the camera holds steady on eye-level, the king reclines backwards toward death, receding from view until only the tip of his elbow juts into the frame. Through the very end, Brook privileges perspectives that are partial, fleeting, and skewed in a play which, by virtue of its multiple texts alone, frustrates narrative closure.

The conclusion of *Ran* is equally, if not more disturbingly, ambivalent. In the spirit of Gloucester's cynical epiphany that 'As flies to wanton boys are we to th' gods / They kill us for their sport' (4.1.37–8), Kyoami cries, upon Hidetora's death: 'Are there no gods anymore? Is there no Buddha?' After Saburo and Hidetora are carried out on a bier, a long shot reveals the blind Tsurumaru heading for a cliff ledge. When his cane falters at land's end and he lurches forward, the anguished flute sounds he played earlier for Hidetora shriek from an off-screen space. Recoiling backwards, he loses his grip on his prayer scroll, which unfurls on the ground below to reveal an image of the

Buddha. Yet this visual answer to Kyoami's existential question is equivocal at best: have the gods just saved Tsurumaro from falling, or do they mock the absurdity of his predicament? Pulling back to medium distance and then a final signature long shot, the camera freezes on Tsurumaro still facing the cliff as the sun sets. For the blind man who, in the wars, lost his flute – and the sister who was executed in attempting to retrieve it – the shrill, choked spasms of sound seem to tempt him to the ledge, fading, along with the tableau, into a wail in the silence.

Notes

1. Kathleen McLuskie, 'The patriarchal bard: feminist criticism and Shakespeare: *King Lear and Measure for Measure*', in Jonathan Dollimore and Alan Sinfieldm eds., *Political Shakespeare: Essays in Cultural Materialism*, 2nd ed. (Ithaca and New York, Cornell University Press), 88–108 (98).
2. Ibid.
3. Carol Chillington Rutter, 'Body parts or parts for bodies: speculating on Cordelia', in Carol Chillington Rutter, *Enter the Body: Women and Representation on Shakespeare's Stage* (London and New York, Routledge, 2001), 1–26 (2).
4. Quoted in Peter Grilli, 'Kurosawa directs a cinematic "*Lear*"', *New York Times*, 15 December 1985.
5. Jane Smiley, 'Shakespeare in Iceland', in Marianne Novy, ed., *Transforming Shakespeare: Contemporary Women's Re-Visions in Literature and Performance* (New York, Palgrave, 1999), 159–79 (171).
6. Grigori Kozintsev, *King Lear: The Space of Tragedy, The Diary of a Film Director* (Berkeley and Los Angeles, University of California Press, 1977), 131.
7. Rutter, 'Body parts or parts for bodies', 251.
8. Kozintsev, *King Lear*, 8.
9. Peter Brook, *The Empty Space, A Book About the Theatre: Deadly Holy, Rough, Immediate* (New York, Simon and Schuster, 1968), 14.
10. McLuskie, 'The patriarchal bard', 105.
11. Rutter, 'Body parts or parts for bodies', 251.
12. Ibid., 251–2.
13. Most films from the *Jidaigeki* genre take place during the period 1603–1868.
14. All lines cited from *Ran* are quoted directly from the subtitles in the 2014 Lions Gate release of the DVD.
15. Kathy Howlett, *Framing Shakespeare on Film* (Athens, Ohio University Press, 2000), 115.
16. Ania Loomba, 'The colour of patriarchy: critical difference, cultural difference and Renaissance drama', in Kate Chedgzoy, ed., *Shakespeare, Feminism and Gender* (New York: Palgrave, 2001), 235–55 (245).
17. Ibid., 119.
18. McLuskie, 'The patriarchal bard', 99.
19. Ibid., 106.
20. Kozintsev, *King Lear*, 255.

13

PATRICIA LENNOX

Violence, Tragic and Comic, in *Coriolanus* and *The Taming of the Shrew*

The oldest surviving Shakespeare film is a violent moment in a celluloid fragment from 1899. A little over a minute long, it is shorter than an online trailer. Shot at an open-air film studio in London, it recreates for cinema a scene from a stage production: Herbert Beerbohm Tree, as the poisoned monarch in *King John*, squirms in extended, excruciating agony as he dies.[1] This is where violence in Shakespeare on screen begins.

Violence, deeply embedded in the human condition, is equally embedded in Shakespeare's plays whether history, tragedy, comedy or romance. When the definition is broadened with twenty-first century categories, including abuse, prejudice, and harassment, violence can be identified lurking somewhere in every single play. In *Shakespeare and Violence* R. A. Foakes examines this 'wildness that erupts at the heart of civilisation in Shakespeare's plays'. He tracks 'Shakespeare's fascination with the underlying problem of violence' and argues that his plays 'provide an increasingly complex exploration of issues relating to it'.[2]

This chapter uses Foakes's observation as the starting point for exploring some (but not all) screened versions of *The Tragedy of Coriolanus* and *The Taming of the Shrew*. It considers tropes of violence shaped by the circularity of polymorphous cross-pollinations among stage/cinema/television. In *Coriolanus* the presence of an increasingly bloodied Caius Martius Coriolanus on stage reflects the popularity of graphic violence in films from mid-twentieth century onwards. The slapstick violence in early film adaptations of *The Taming of the Shrew* has been transmuted into broad farce on stage and returned to the screen as recorded performance. These were chosen because violence plays an interesting role in them and there are readily available versions representative of decades of screened Shakespeare.

From its inception cinema has had a fascination with violence. Comic violence in hundreds of silent film comedies includes anarchistic attacks on social order, destruction of objects, but also inflicting humiliation. This is satisfying when it brings down the pompous, but pathetic when the victim is Charlie Chaplin's little Tramp or one of Mary Pickford's orphan girls. Even the blameless Man in the Moon has a rocket jabbed into his eye and sheds tears in Georges Méliès' 1902 *A Trip to the Moon*. Early cinema featured acts of cruelty, including executions and battles, in documentaries and fictions. As a story-driven film, the 1903 *The Great Train Robbery,* has a surprisingly high body count: bandits, lawmen and innocent bystanders die dramatically but bloodlessly. Soon, however, blood was on the screen in Shakespeare films. The screen history of *Macbeth,* for example, reflects fluctuations of restraint and bloody excess. One of its earliest, Vitagraph's 1908 *Macbeth*, was censured for its goriness – 'you see the dagger enter and come out and see the blood flow and the wound that's left' making it 'worse than the bloodiest melodrama ever'.[3] *The Real Thing at Last*, James Barrie's 1916 comic film (30 minutes) spoofed the American makers of an imagined *Macbeth* film. In it, Lady Macbeth took buckets of blood to Duncan's chamber and was 'covered in gore' on 'out damned spot'.[4] Later *Macbeth* films, silent and sound, were more restrained until Roman Polanski splashed gore on the screen in 1971, and filmmakers have followed, according to taste and budget.

Shakespeare films generally shape physical violence according to prevailing conventions. How gruesome, how bloody, how graphic? Compare the battle scenes in Shakespeare films and this becomes clear. A classic example is the Battle of Agincourt in Laurence Olivier's 1944 patriotic *Henry V* with its fierce but bloodless clashes and armour flashing in the sun. In contrast, Kenneth Branagh's 1989 film has the grim reality of modern combat films. His Agincourt has mud, blood, sweat and a shot of a severed hand in homage to *All Quiet on the Western Front* (1930). Shakespeare films include scenes that are only desccribed in the plays, offering additional opportunities for screen carnage. This can be as disparate as Rivers stabbed through the mattress in Richard Loncraine's 1995 *Richard III*; soldiers walking under the hanged body of Bardolph in Branagh's *Henry V;* the bloodied 'nest' of Macduff's slaughtered children in Polanski's *Macbeth*, and several scenes in Ralph Fiennes' *Coriolanus*.

Julie Taymor's 1999 film *Titus* put the play's multiple murders, mutilations, amputations, rape and (unwitting) cannibalism on screen in a mix of 'the pain, the scream, the mess of blood, the rags to stop the bleeding', 'Penny Arcade' dream sequences, Fellini-influenced surreal humour, and an ending with 'the promise of daylight as if redemption were a possibility'.[5] The film's negotiation of violence has received extensive critical attention, and will not be discussed further in this chapter. Instead, it seems useful to consider other examples of violence in Shakespeare plays on screen. *Coriolanus* and *The Taming of the Shrew* serve that purpose well: in the former, violence is physical and tragic; in the latter it is comic but unsettling. Together these films put on the screen two major aspects of Shakespeare's 'wild' eruption – blood and laughter.

Coriolanus: 'Boy of Tears' and Blood

Violence (verbal and physical) threads through *The Tragedy of Coriolanus* like arteries in a body. The screen makes highly visible the play's physical violence marked by signifiers of masculinity: bleeding wounds (received or given in battle) and the scars they leave. This section of the chapter considers the presence (quantity and use) of blood and scars in five screened productions: RAI television (1965) directed by Claudio Fino, the version in the *BBC Shakespeare Plays* (1984), Théâtre National Populaire – Villeurbanne (2006), Ralph Fiennes's film (2011) and the Royal Shakespeare Company (2018). As a group they demonstrate the shift in theatrical interpretations of Caius Martius Coriolanus. The nineteenth- to mid-twentieth-century theatre's noble Roman, shown in Thomas Lawrence's painting *John Philip Kemble as Coriolanus*, has become, instead, a battered action-film hero. As cinema became more graphically violent in films like Sergio Leone's *A Fistful of Dollars* (1968), Sam Peckinpah's *Straw Dogs* (1971) and Quentin Tarentino's *Usual Suspects* (1995), so did stage productions of *Coriolanus* – and their marketing. Coriolanus's aristocratic profile became a bloodied face on theatre posters that blurred boundaries between theatre and film advertising.

Caius Martius Coriolanus has become the Shakespeare 'poster boy' for violence. Cinema-influenced advertisements (posters, print ads, trailers) have created an iconic image as recognisable as Richard III's hump or Lear's white beard. When, in 1977, the Royal Shakespeare Company's poster used the blood-streaked face of Coriolanus (Alan Howard) to promote Terry Hand's production, it was clear that they were using 'Hollywood-style sex-and-violence posters to attract young people'.[6] The poster for the RSC's 1994 production had the slogan 'A Natural Born Killer Too', a reference to Oliver Stone's film *Natural Born Killers* (1994). See, for example, on-line images of the RSC *Coriolanus* posters: Ian Hogg (1972); the drawing of an anonymous splayed body (1978); Toby Stephens (1994/1995); Greg Hicks (2002); Sope Dirisu (2017/18); and the National Theatre's for Ian McKellen (1984). The image of the bloodied actor (often bare chested) illustrates newspaper reviews,[7] and dominates live broadcast *Coriolanus* trailers, including the Donmar Warehouse production featuring Tom Hiddleston, the RSC's with Dirisu and Fiennes's film.

Although this promotional material suggests that the play is a spectacle of blood, it is not. Bloodied Martius appears in only a single act. At the end of 1.4 there is the stage direction: 'Enter Martius bleeding, assaulted by the enemy'. This blood (his own and that of his victims) is the result of his single-handed attack on the city of Corioles. It remains and is commented on in scenes 1.5, 6, 8, 9 and is followed by stage directions at the beginning of 1.9: 'Enter Martius, bloody'. Later Martius is remembered as 'a thing of blood' (2.2.109). His conflation with blood begins earlier when his mother proudly imagines 'his bloody brow' that 'more becomes a man / Than gilt his trophy' and equates Martius's imagined wound with 'Hector's forehead when it spit forth blood / At Grecian sword contemning' (1.3.36, 41–42, 44). Afterwards Martius's twenty-seven scars are used as proof of valour, like medals engraved on the body. Although further violence is constantly threatened, it is not realised on stage until the play's final scene.

Considering the promotional materials' emphasis on violent images, the question is: How much blood is shown – and how is it integrated into the play? The 1965 Italian television production by RAI has no blood, though the chiaroscuro shadows on the actor's face when he emerges from Corioles suggest its presence. Broadcast from the television studio in black and white this traditionally staged production is notable for its intelligent performances. The sets are relatively bare, but with multiple spaces; the costumes are a familiar combination of sculpture-inspired antique Roman dress and 1950s Italian cinema sword and sandal epics. Blood might simply have been considered unnecessary, or been omitted because the national network was discreet about televised violence, or as an economic use of time in a live broadcast, or even to protect the costumes. The production succeeds without it.

The RAI broadcast marks a turning point, after which the blood flowed from the screen's Italian spaghetti westerns into productions of *Coriolanus*. Stage blood continues to drench actors playing Martius and in quantities that keep pace with increasingly graphic cinema and television violence. Recently, between entering and exiting Corioles, Tom Hiddleston stood in a wading pool backstage while blood was poured over him. The trailer shows the result seen on stage.[8] The RSC's 2017 production used over two pints of stage blood for each performance, half of it dumped on Sope Dirisi during Act 1. Throughout the RSC DVD's commentary, a conversation between director Angus Jackson and sound designer

Carolyn Downing, there are observations about connections with 'tough guy' television series, like *The Wire*, and action films. When the very bloodied Dirisi exits Corioles, holding the city's heavy metal gate above his head, his costume is 'like Sylvester Stallone in action hero blockbuster *The Expendables*'.[9] The play's opportunities for action are seized by Jackson, and are fierce. The murderous intensity of the fight between Martius and Aufidius (equally bloody and identically dressed) is powerful. It moves all around the stage and is like an illegal no-holds barred fight match. The death of Martius is equally disturbing. Aufidius, now in a suit and tie, calmly removes his jacket, grabs Martius and floors him, then kills him by methodically pumping his elbow against Martius's windpipe. It is a long thirty seconds. However, strong as the images of violence are in this production, they are not integrated with the rest of the play.

In contrast, versions for stage (available on DVD), television and film by directors Christian Schiaretti, Elijah Moshinsky and Ralph Fiennes have successfully integrated violence throughout. Schiaretti's Théâtre National Populaire production starts silently with ruffians viciously attacking a prosperous young man. His beaten and stripped body is left lying on stage, slash wounds visible on his back. There is no blood in the incident. Instead, deep red arterial blood is reserved solely for Martius (Wladimir Yordanoff). The exceptions are Aufidius and Volumnia, but only when Martius stains them. Between 1.4 and 1.9, as Martius becomes increasingly bloodied an unexpected side of this arrogant, patrician emerges – he is intoxicated by blood. It liberates him. At first, when Martius emerges alone from Corioles, a thick layer of it covers his face. In contrast, there is merely a streak on his metal breastplate, and none on his velvet doublet – this sumptuously dressed production has mid-seventeenth-century style dress, with elegant ruffs, rich fabrics and decoration. He refuses to wash the blood off. Masked with it, arrogance gone, he is elated, struts, even does a little jumping dance step. Later he returns even bloodier, nearly naked, doublet and breastplate gone, his thin shirt soaked with wide bands of blood around the waist and on the sleeves. His frenzied combination of gore and glee sets him even further apart from the still immaculately dressed troops and commanders.

The battles are a series of ritual movements. When soldiers lift huge silk flags they reveal the bloodied Martius and a spotless Aufidius facing each other. Their confrontation moves quickly from the civility of a classic duel to chaos, fighting with bare knuckles, grappling, rolling on the ground. Both men end up covered with blood, which in this production marks affinities. There is no further blood visible until 5.3 when they sit beside each other, wearing identically blood-stained shirts (though not the ones from Act 1). When Martius kneels and embraces his mother, the wet blood stains her grey penitential smock. The death of Martius is unusual. Aufidius starts to confront him, but Martius is killed by Volscian soldiers. They stab him repeatedly and block Aufidius's attempts to stop the attack. When they abandon the corpse, he embraces it. During his closing lines, he fights back tears. He, too, has become a 'boy of tears'.

In the *BBC Shakespeare Plays*' *Coriolanus*, the director, Elijah Moshinsky, challenges 1980s television conventions by eroticising the fight between Martius (Alan Howard) and Aufidius (Mike Gwilym). Moshinsky envisioned it as 'a gladiatorial combat between two big, big men' and told the fight director Malcolm Ransom, 'I want it violently erotic or erotically violent', capturing the men's love/hate relationship that runs through the play.[10] Alan Howard's sneering Martius enters Corioles alone on horseback, a cape wrapped over his armour. (Except for Etruscan armour all costumes were Jacobean in shape but without decoration.) He returns still sneering but exhausted, armour gone, shirt drenched in blood, sword covered with gore. Moshinsky favoured editing with quick cuts, so immediately after Martius re-enters Corioles with armoured soldiers in the classic Roman 'turtle' formation, the battle is revealed as chaos. Nearly naked fighters grapple, slash out, and die against a background of smoke and fire. The sequence throbs with masculine physicality; blood is the sexual lubricant. The scene builds, with a throbbing rhythm like Ravel's *Bolero,* towards Martius and Aufidius's confrontation: 'a carefully choreographed stripping off of weapons and Jacobean clothes till the two are locked, nearly naked, in an almost loving, sado-masochistic conflict'.[11] The camera stays so close that it sometimes goes out of focus. The peaceful scene that follows has a post-coital mood: Martius on a bed while his wounds are dressed.

The erotic charge in Act 1's confrontation culminates in Act 5 where Moshinsky directs Martius's death as sexual climax. When the attack on Martius begins, he wins the struggle with Aufidius for the dagger; then forces Aufidius to stab him – over and over. There are eight blows and each time Martius cries out, 'die, die'. Aufidius echoes him seven times.[12] As with their earlier battle, the camera stays close. It concentrates on the faces and upper bodies, never shows the weapon or blood; the screen shifts in and out of focus in rhythm with the men's cries.

When *Coriolanus* was finally filmed for cinema, directed by Ralph Fiennes, in 2011 and released in 2012, its marketing image was familiar: the bloodied face of Caius Martius Coriolanus (Fiennes). The DVD package promises 'bloodied, brutal and brilliant'. This time the marketing message (action film, tough, masculine, gritty) is accurate and deeply embedded in the film. Fiennes, in collaboration with screenwriter John Logan, delivers *Coriolanus*'s promised violence in a film that is also an intelligent conversation with Shakespeare's play. There is rarely a moment in the film's 123 minutes where violence is absent from the conversation. The civil and military violence that rumbles underneath the play takes over the screen. Battles and civilian protests are shown as they happen or are reported on television and laptops. Filmed in Bosnia, much of this resembles familiar news footage.

Martius enters Corioles in a seventeen-minute sequence. After an explosive device wipes out his soldiers, he walks alone into a bombed out building (his Corioles). The camera follows, filming from his point of view, shows him keyed up (alert to danger), fierce (shoots a man), compassionate (spares a woman weeping by a corpse), humane (accepts a drink of water) and brave (successfully struggles with an attacker who wounds him). When, twenty-two minutes into the film Martius and Aufidius meet, both are drenched in gore. Their combat is brutal, personal, follows the familiar pattern: weapons laid aside in favour of close physical contact. Logan wanted it to look like a Francis Bacon painting; Fiennes wanted to show their 'obsessive intent' by fighting with 'messy intensity'.[13]

An unexpected element is the parity the film gives Aufidius (Gerard Butler). Much of the marketing material includes a double portrait of him with Martius. Fiennes, with shaved head, steely blue eyes, and set jaw of a professional soldier, contrasts with Butler's bearded guerrilla freedom fighter. Added scenes that flesh out Aufidius's character, making him more humane, include angry frustration seeing bodies of civilian victims and easy-going sociability with villagers in Antium. Fiennes's exemplary director's commentary includes an eloquent description of Martius's death, on a lonely road, with only Aufidius and a few Volscian soldiers present. He wanted an 'almost erotic death image', with the death blow struck in 'the embrace of two heroes out of mythology'.[14] Martius's body is dumped unceremoniously, but only after Aufidius has cradled it with tenderness, a final tribute to the noble warrior who became a 'boy of tears' weeping into his mother's skirt.

The Taming of the Shrew: Comic Violence is Not an Oxymoron

The Taming of the Shrew can be an uncomfortable play, and comic violence is often used in productions to deflect its problematic domestic politics. The screened versions discussed below offer a sampling of negotiating *Shrew*'s violence (psychological and physical) between 1908 and 2012. These include two mass-market films starring celebrity couples, Mary Pickford/Douglas Fairbanks, directed by Sam Taylor (1929) and Elizabeth Taylor/Richard Burton, directed by Franco Zeffirelli (1967). The *BBC Shakespeare Plays' Shrew* (1980) and the Shakespeare Globe's stage production (2012) are products of hybrid entertainment/educational programmes. Film versions of *Shrew* on-line (as of this writing) include D. W. Griffith (1908), ten minutes of the British and Colonial production company (1923), Ernst Lubitsch's spin-off *Kohlhiesel's Daughters* (1920), and the documentary *Kiss Me, Petruchio* (New York Shakespeare Festival) with Meryl Streep and Raul Julia (1981).[15] In silent films, and in 1929 with sound, *Shrew*'s domestic violence is a gift to slapstick's subversive comedy with scenes including household chaos, fractious wooing and a wrecked dinner. In slapstick no one gets hurts, but people are kicked, tripped, punched, humiliated, their egos deflated; objects are thrown, smashed, dismantled, demolished. Entire rooms are left shattered. Propriety is confronted, order turned to chaos, and social convention disrupted. Filmmakers have added scenes that are only described in the play: the wedding ceremony, the trip to Petruchio's villa, and a bedroom scene based on Petruchio's plans to prevent Kate from sleeping (4.1.169–97).

No matter how a screen version has been cut or rearranged, Katherine and Petruchio are responsible for servants being berated, pummelled, slapped, knocked down, the target of hurled objects, mix-ups, confusion, and chaos. Zeffirelli's Kate's reign of terror has the sound of breaking glass, slammed doors, splintering wood, accompanied by shrieks and growls. In the play's first act, with its impressive number of opportunities for Kate to torment her sister, Taylor's first line is not Shakespeare's. She chases Bianca with scissors, threatening, 'I will mar you so no man will want you'. The first appearance of Mary Pickford's 'silent' Kate is a master class in timing comic violence with sight gags piling up in rapid succession. In sixty-six seconds of mayhem (nineteen increasingly rapid camera shots) friends, servants and family tumble down stairs, escape from the room, tug at both sides of a closed door, dodge shattering crockery, hide in a grandfather clock, are hit with a pillow, are hit with a jug and get a black eye. The dog hides; the cat escapes. A mirror shatters. A painting falls and a head pokes through the torn canvas – one of the oldest gags in silent comedy: Griffith's 1908 Kate repeatedly bangs a painting on a suitor's head until the canvas breaks. Finally, calmly, the camera pans across a wrecked bedroom to Kate, whip in hand, fierce and glowering.

A similar onslaught against servants is repeated at Petruchio's decaying villa. He abuses them with threats, kicks, twisted ear lobes, thrown food. Zeffirelli's Petruchio beats a servant with a roasted chicken. The dinner scene fits perfectly with silent comedy's signature routine: the progressive destruction of material objects. In Ernst Lubitsch's *Kohlhiesel's Daughters* Liesel and Xavier (the Kate and Petruchio figures) sit down for a dinner where he plans to start 'taming' her. A broken soup plate is the first step towards the complete destruction of everything in the room, its contents finally a pile of rubble in the hallway. Again, it is the timing, the quick escalation of unbelievable violence that liberates laughter. Stage versions rarely have the same opportunity as films for destroying things. One of the simplest – and funniest – attacks on an innocent object is Meryl Streep's New York Shakespeare Festival entrance. Her muscle-flexing Kate strides on stage, kicks over a stool, then with great deliberation steps on a flower, crushing it like a cigarette butt.

The wooing is the most physically violent scene in these versions. Encouraged by Sam Taylor to adopt his usual screen persona, Douglas Fairbanks's Petruchio is a replay of his dashing heroes – Zorro, Robin Hood the Black Pirate. Pickford, directed to use 'the old Pickford tricks' hated her performance: a 'spitting kitten' instead 'of being a forceful tiger-cat'.[16] Nevertheless, in the wooing scene she manages to give Petruchio multiple slaps where the play indicates only one, and repeated lashes with her whip. He laughs, takes it lightly, which further frustrates her. This is not the case with Zeffirelli's wooing scene. Burton's Petruchio is a loutish drunk, much stronger than Kate, made larger by the costume and wearing lifts on his shoes.[17] He also laughs all the time, but with mocking coarseness. This wooing scene is, for the most part, not the promised romp, but a long sequence closer to a horror film, with a woman trying desperately to save herself.

The Globe production is broad slapstick, inherited from silent films but inflated and coarsened. It is fast-paced, unsubtle and successful at raising laughs. The wooing scene is a knock down, dragged-out fight between Kate (Samantha Spiro) and Petruchio (Simon Paisley Day). The well-matched opponents are choreographed like professional wrestlers, both giving as much as they receive. When he chases her, she uses it to trap and hit him again. The audience roars with laughter when he throws her over his shoulder, turns round and accidentally hits her head on the column – there are effectively clear sound effects. She is unfazed, and his slightly concerned look gets a second laugh. The audience had been 'prepared' to laugh at absurdities by the Globe's theatrical sleight of hand in staging the 'Induction' scene. Christopher Sly, Shakespeare's drunken tinker, appears as an aggressively drunken member of the audience. He climbs on stage, urinates on a column and falls asleep. Actors dress him in costume and he becomes Petruchio. (This distancing device was introduced at the Young Vic in 1977, and made popular by Michael Bogdanov in his 1978 RSC production.)[18]

In the wedding ceremony added by film directors, Fairbanks's Petruchio is the easy-going swashbuckler, contentedly disrupting propriety. He arrives late, further delays the ceremony while he stands at the altar slowly eating an apple. The gag continues with the embarrassment of a wedding guest handed the gnawed core – a perfect example of silent film comedy's small assaults on dignity, occurring within a much larger assault. Zeffirelli stages the wedding so that Petruchio attacks the ceremony with the unsubtle antics of a *commedia dell'arte* Zanni. This Petruchio is a show-off who marches in, grabs and drinks the holy wine, and really hits the priest.

The films' invented bedroom scenes include Griffith's version where Petruchio throws out blankets, pillows, mattress, bed curtains and bed frame until nothing is left. For Pickford/Fairbanks the scene marks the turning point in Petruchio's attempted taming. She knows his plans and so outsmarts him at every move. She pretends to sleep, to be comfortable with a mattress on the floor and, when he opens a window, to enjoy the gale-force winds that blow in. Still when she shoves him, he pushes back and it escalates into a shoving match that looks like the actors letting loose their actual frustrations. In her memoir Pickford describes 'the strain and tension of those months working with a Douglas who no longer cared apparently about me or my feelings' nor for any aspect of making this film.[19] Ironically, in this film resolution comes about after Kate throws a stool at Petruchio's head. Bandaging the small wound, she realises that she can win by feigning submission.

Jonathan Miller's *The Taming of the Shrew* for the BBC was the first of six plays he produced and directed for the BBC series. Miller was fascinated with what could be achieved on the television screen, as this production, one of his best, demonstrates. It is a non-farcical *Shrew*, interpreted according to Miller's view of Elizabethan/Jacobean values. 'Petruchio's clear headed, confident assault on Kate's temper and temperament' is based on 'sound religious and social views of the time' where hierarchal order (king, husband, father) ensured social order.[20] Kate (Sarah Badel) is not deliberately shrewish and suffers from her behaviour. The result is a *Shrew* that is intelligent, moving, and funny but closer to the verbal style of screwball comedy. There are rare traces of slapstick, two specifically with Kate. Leaving the piazza she pushes over a dwarf who has been taunting her with kissy gestures; at home after leaving a room, she is out of sight, but her leg shoots back through the doorway to kick the maid's bottom. Kate's disordered temperament is established by contrast rather than destruction. Her first encounter with Petruchio (John Cleese) is a battle of wits. When she slaps him, he surprises her by murmuring 'Hm, mm'.[21] He is intrigued, and quietly says, 'I'll cuff you if you strike again.' Miller includes one broad comic detail: Petruchio's wedding hat – an oversized conglomeration of turkey feathers that tickle the bystander. In order for Baptista to talk with him, the old man must stand under the feathers, as under an umbrella. As with the Globe's production with its Grumio (Pearce Quigley) inspired by *Blackadder*'s servant Baldrick, Miller includes far more of the play's master/servant banter and slaps.

Like love, violence in Shakespeare's plays and their screen versions has an infinite variety. The two plays chosen for this chapter reflect not only the changing ways in which violence is portrayed (and sold) on screen, but, with the inclusion of *The Taming of the Shrew*, considers the expanded categories of violence. In *Shakespeare and Violence*, Foakes cites *Coriolanus* as proof that violence is 'inseparable from human aspirations, ideas, and even the desire for peace'.[22] He makes no mention of *Shrew*, even though the same might be said for its situations. It is useful to keep in mind that nearly all the examples of Shakespeare on screen discussed in this volume engage with violence at some point. Sometimes it is subtle, sometimes brutal; it may be present as an underlying threat, or as realised action, or even subverted as Miller does with *Shrew*. In Shakespeare violence is rarely far from the centre of the work. The same is true for cinema, television and the computer screen.

Notes

1. See Judith Buchanan, *Shakespeare on Silent Film: An Excellent Dumb Discourse* (Cambridge, Cambridge University Press, 2009), 57–73.
2. R. A. Foakes, *Shakespeare and Violence* (Cambridge, Cambridge University Press, 2003), 16.
3. *Moving Picture World*, 13 June 1908, quoted in Buchanan, 197.
4. Buchanan, *Shakespeare on Silent Film*, 193.
5. Julie Taymor, *Titus. The Illustrated Screenplay, Adapted from the Play by William Shakespeare* (New York, Newmarket Press, 2000), 185.
6. David Lisch, 'Bard meets pulp fiction' *Independent*, 9 September 1995.
7. For reviews of the 2002 RSC *Coriolanus*, see Benedict Nightingale, *The Times* and Charles Spencer, *Daily Telegraph*, both 28 November 2002; Paul Taylor, *Independent Supplement*, 4 December 2002; and Georgina Brown, *Mail on Sunday*, 26 January 2003.
8. *Coriolanus* trailer, '*Coriolanus* National Theatre Live starring Tom Hiddleston', www.youtube.com/watch?v=bJPL89U2NH0 (accessed 18 June 2019).

9. Gill Sutherland. 'Review: *Coriolanus* Royal Shakespeare Company RSC', *Stratford-upon-Avon Herald*, 3 October 2017.

10. Henry Fenwick, 'The production', *The BBC Television Shakespeare: Coriolanus*. (London, British Broadcasting Corporation, 1984), 24.

11. Fenwick, 'The production', 25.

12. David Daniell describes Howard's similar death as Coriolanus on stage in 1977: he 'flung himself on his own sword in Aufidius' hands. Mortally wounded, he cried "Kill, kill" before falling face down'. *Coriolanus in Europe* (London, Athlone Press, 1980), 41.

13. Ralph Fiennes, director's commentary. DVD *Coriolanus,* dir. Ralph Fiennes.

14. Fiennes, DVD commentary.

15. The 2015 Stratford Ontario Shakespeare Festival's production of *Shrew* with Deborah Hay and Ben Carlson, though not discussed here, is recommended.

16. Mary Pickford, *Sunshine and Shadow* (New York and London, Heinemann, 1956), 311.

17. For Burton on his costumes, see Chris Williams, ed., *The Richard Burton Diaries*, (New Haven, Yale University Press, 2012), 97, 118, 44 (shoes in *Shrew*).

18. Graham Holderness, *Shakespeare in Performance: The Taming of the Shrew* (Manchester, Manchester University Press, 1989), 75–9.

19. Pickford, *Sunshine and Shadow*, 307–12.

20. Jonathan Miller, *Subsequent Performances* (London, Faber and Faber, 1986), 119–22.

21. Ibid., 122.

22. Foakes, *Shakespeare and Violence*, 191.

PART IV

Directors

14

EMMA SMITH

The Shakespeare Films of Orson Welles

The Shakespeareana of Orson Welles (1915–1985) range across media to include radio and gramophone productions, stage realisations, performance-attentive editions for readers, television adaptations, numerous unfinished stage and film projects, and an extensive body of self-conscious commentary, from interviews to documentaries, that reflects on his Shakespearean career. Many of these productions cross-fertilise, as Welles recycles sets, scripts and governing paradigms across stage, screen, audio and publicity. He appeared on American television as King Lear in a production directed by Peter Brook, and one of the projects left unfinished at his death was a cinema adaptation of *The Merchant of Venice*.[1] In this chapter I will focus on his three completed films: *Macbeth* (1948), *Othello* (1952) and *Chimes at Midnight* (1965), with a particular emphasis on the critical and interpretive framework they bring to bear on their plays. While these films share a certain cinematic language with each other and with Welles' canon of non-Shakespearean films, and while they have been expertly interpreted as a collective biography of Welles himself,[2] I am most concerned here with their creative relation to the Shakespeare plays they reimagine, argued through close analysis of selected sequences. Welles' particular cinematic genius translated and transformed the linguistic and thematic qualities of the texts. The result is new film art, and, most importantly for this chapter, visually dynamic Shakespeare criticism.

In the welter of commentary, interviews and reflection on his career, Welles never discussed his wider reading of Shakespearean criticism or the source of his views on Shakespeare's art. There is no further reading listed with the three plays published as *Everybody's Shakespeare* in 1934, unsurprisingly, since their explicit aim was to get young readers to think about the plays theatrically. Nevertheless, one overarching theme emerges from his three Shakespearean films: Welles's abiding sense that Shakespeare's works anthropomorphise the poignant shift from a medieval or communal or pagan past to an individualistic, brutal or pragmatic present. That Shakespeare stood at the threshold of modernity was, for Welles, the source of his perennial applicability. In discussion with Peter Bogdanovich, he noted that Shakespeare 'was very close, you understand, to quite another epoch, and yet he stood in the doorway of our "modern" world. His lyricism, his comic zest, his humanity, came from these ties with the past. The pessimism, of course, is closer to our modern condition.'[3]

This crucial idea of a transitional historical period is repeated frequently in prefaces and interviews. It appears to derive from Johan Huizinga's influential work translated into English in 1924 as *The Waning of the Middle Ages*, in which 'the expiring Middle Ages' was identified with 'a tone of extravagant passion that never appears again', when 'every event, every action, was still embodied in expressive and solemn forms, which raised them to the dignity of a ritual'.[4] That this transition and its tensions were expressed in the noble, sacrificial body of its divided hero further aligned Welles' Shakespeare with nineteenth-century theories of tragedy. Hegel's emphasis on tragic conflict resonates with the arc of Welles' Shakespeare films:

> the true development of the action consists solely in the cancellation of conflicts *as conflicts,* in the reconciliation of the powers animating action which struggled to destroy one another in their mutual conflict. Only in that case does finality lie not in misfortune and suffering but in the satisfaction of the spirit, because only with such a conclusion can the necessity of what happens to the individuals appear as absolute rationality, and only then can our hearts be morally at peace: shattered by the fate of the heroes but reconciled fundamentally.[5]

Welles' three completed Shakespeare films all depict a melancholic resolution of temporal and psychological conflict in the sacrifice of the central protagonist, played, in each case, by Welles himself. Even *Chimes at Midnight*, organised around the ostensibly comic figure of Falstaff (and released in the UK with the title *Falstaff: Chimes at Midnight*), emerges as a mournful tragedy of transition, its belated hero stranded in a wintry landscape representing inhospitable historical change.

Macbeth (1948)

One of Welles' most celebrated theatrical productions was his Haitian *Macbeth*, a Federal Theater Project in 1936–1937. The stage production, with an African American cast, stressed the primitivism of Haitian society.

In many ways the production influenced Welles' 1948 film, although the racial – and racist – dimension of the theatre production was obscured by the depiction of Macbeth's Scotland as the foggily barbaric location of the clash between pagan and Christian religions. Welles' *Macbeth* has often been identified as theatrical in style: the director economised on an epically abbreviated shooting schedule (often claimed as the standard twenty-one days for the studio's films) by blocking and rehearsing the film via a stage production in Salt Lake City in May–June 1947, and its characteristic long takes emphasise the dramatic scene, rather than the cinematic shot, as the primary unit of composition. But there are clear filmic influences too. Michael Anderegg calls *Macbeth* a 'Shakespearean Western', and, certainly, the studio Republic Pictures was best known for this genre, producing more than twenty B-movie Westerns in 1948, the year of *Macbeth*'s release.[6]

But a closer cinematic parallel to Welles' tragedy is actually *film noir*, as a contemporary account of the genre made clear: 'deep shadows, clutching hands, exploding revolvers, sadistic villains and heroines tormented with deeply rooted diseases of the mind flashed across the screen in a panting display of psychoneurosis, unsublimated sex, and murder most foul'.[7] Replace revolvers with daggers, and this is a recognisable account of Welles' psychologically and visually extreme *Macbeth*. *Noir*'s characteristic shadow and low-key lighting, its preference for unbalanced compositions, extreme high-angle shots, claustrophobic framing, and a *mise en scène* 'designed to unsettle, jar and disorient the viewer in correlation with the disorientation felt by the noir heroes', are also keynotes of the Shakespeare film.[8] And the film's juxtaposition of Lady Macbeth and Lady Macduff corresponds to the binary visual and moral archetypes of spider woman and nurturing woman traced in feminist analyses of women's manipulative, sexualised roles in *film noir*.[9] Welles' *Macbeth* thus combines its theatrical genesis and shooting style with a generic transformation that owes everything to contemporary cinematic tastes.

The play's gothic prologue sequence explores these divergent influences. Swirling clouds part to reveal shadowy figures silhouetted on a contorted craggy outcrop, reciting 'double, double, toil and trouble': the camera focuses into their bubbling cauldron as they list their ingredients and plunge their hands into the thick, steaming potion. They produce a clay figurine at the ominous line 'there to meet with Macbeth'. Welles cuts the entirety of Shakespeare's 1.1, thus giving no political explanation for Macbeth's promotion to Thane of Cawdor, nor any larger social context for the protagonist's ethical struggle. Instead, he opens the film proper after the credits, with the gallop of horses' hooves (the Western influence), watched by the strange figures intoning 'by the pricking of my thumbs, something wicked this way comes'. Macbeth and Banquo ride across a desolate studio landscape of blasted trees, backlit by lightning, oppressed by a lowering sky (François Truffaut noted that 'everything is savage in this film whose strength is that it doesn't contain a single shot filmed in natural locations').[10] The camera angles of the ensuing dialogue are unsettling in their disruption of the expected shot-reverse-shot editing that would show the alternating points of view of speakers. We look down on the horsemen from a high angle from behind the weird sisters, but as Macbeth speaks, the camera adopts a low angle looking up from the ground in front of their horses. We see the witches from behind, placing first a chain of office and then a crown on their clay idol. When they respond to Banquo, the shot places them in the left of the frame, looking right, disrupting the spatial continuities established by the previous sequence. Enter Welles' major interpolation into the play, a figure named 'Holy Father', whose entrance is signalled by a cross intruding on the frame from the bottom right. Macbeth follows the vanishing figures into swirling mists, with an extreme low-angle shot framing him, alone, against the turmoil into which the prophecies have forever pitched him. We watch his encounter with the king's messengers from a high angle, as if from the witches' craggy outpost, and they re-emerge to watch him as the captains gallop off together. The final frame of the sequence shows the witches standing on their rock, holding forked sticks that are a visual echo and challenge to the long cross brandished by the Holy Father.

Macbeth, caught between two worlds, has exited left with the forces of Christianity, but his soliloquy drew him right towards the witches. He will increasingly occupy the right hand part of the frame for the rest of the film. 'The main point' of *Macbeth*, Welles discussed with Peter Bogdanovich, 'is the struggle between the old and new religions. I saw the witches as representatives of a Druidical pagan religion suppressed by Christianity.'[11] The spatial cinematography of the encounter reveals that Macbeth is wavering, just as the juxtaposition of high- and low-angle shots alternately diminish his agency and grotesquely emphasise it. This Macbeth is both puppet and agent. That the next scene opens with a close-up of flickering flames before increased light reveals Macbeth dictating to the Holy Father his letter to Lady Macbeth further emphasises his visual association with the iconography of the mysterious witches.

The film's most dazzling expressionist sequence is the series of cuts that capture the play's own nervy splicing of scenes around the murder of Duncan. A high-angle shot shows Macbeth's soliloquy 'If it were done', as Lady Macbeth returns down the stone staircase having delivered a poisoned cup to Duncan's guards. As the couple embrace, a potentially clichéd romantic shot is undermined by ominous heavy shadow. Her face is entirely obscured, and a low-angle shot of the two of them in deep darkness highlighted against the damp wall of the castle indicates that their conspiracy has dwarfed their moral authority. Banquo and Fleance are originally tiny in the background on the castle battlements, and as Banquo moves downstairs in the frame, he is still much smaller than the massy dark silhouette of Macbeth on the right. The visuals ironically undermine the dialogue, revealing the menace behind Macbeth's answer to Banquo's 'who's there?': 'a friend' (2.1.9–10). A brief shot shows Lady Macbeth's shadow falling menacingly across the sleeping Duncan, followed by a sequence in which Macbeth hallucinates a dagger. The combination of low-angle shots against a murky background and some blurred images suggests that we are both inside and outside of Macbeth's point of view. An extreme blurred close-up of his face captures this paradox: we are losing our empathic connection to him as he is losing his mind. A sharply focused, miniature Lady Macbeth in the back of the frame traces the shifting power dynamic of their relationship: alternate shots first establish her in a conventional diminutive position, but at her encouragement 'We'll not fail' (1.7.61), Macbeth moves into the background and she takes up the dominant position.

What is so compelling about this claustrophobic, chiaroscuro sequence is the way editing redraws the dynamic between husband and wife, alternately casting the partners as dominant in a powerful visual correlative of their shifting conversation. Welles' own verdict on the film was that 'our second half worked better, after the first murder. The second half is the study of the decay of a tyrant. Nobody can play the first *and* second half. An actor who can do one can't do the other.' The oppressive shadows and distorted angles that construct the murder of Duncan form the expressionist hinge between these two halves.[12] Here, Macbeth, and *Macbeth*, take an irrevocable step into moral darkness.

Othello (1952)

Welles' *Othello* was famously marked by production problems. In his later documentary for German television, *Filming Othello*, Welles described again, with some pride, the scramble for money, locations and costumes that has left its mark on a finished film 'made on the instalment plan'.[13] For some commentators and reviewers, these contingencies register as handicaps. For example, the necessity of producing a soundtrack almost entirely post-production, including dubbing Welles' own voice onto minor characters, results in problems of synchronisation and audibility (these were somewhat ameliorated by the 1992 restoration and rerelease). On the other hand, these accidents of production are often cited as spurs to particular creative ingenuity: the description of the delayed costumes that prompted the reimagining of Roderigo's murder in a visually arresting Turkish bath scene is proudly retold by Welles in numerous contexts. Production contingencies have become an inseparable part of the myth of the film.

Sometimes the unintended consequences of pragmatic filming decisions are suggestive. The much-discussed problems of sound in the film, together with Welles' dense collage of quotations from different scenes of the play that results in a script not always altogether comprehensible, have the joint effect of minimising language as a primary tool of communication. This boldly cuts through one of Shakespearean film's abiding problems – what to do with all those words. As Anderegg suggests, 'we are forced to pay close attention to the primarily visual clues for the meaning of this verbal structure'.[14] For Jack Jorgens producing his influential taxonomy of filmed Shakespeare in 1977, Welles' *Othello* occupied the highest aesthetic category of 'filmic': Welles quoted this judgement approvingly in *Filming Othello*.[15] We might go further to say that Welles' great contribution to the Shakespeare on film is decisively – if in part by accident – to replace a verbal structure with a visual one. And the film's restless short takes, what André Bazin called the 'extreme fragmentation of the *decoupage*', are thus the cinematographic equivalent of the broken verbal phrases, those 'goats and monkeys' to which Iago brings his formerly eloquent general.[16] Welles' film has little stylistic affinity with the play's lyrical mode – what the mid-century critic G. Wilson Knight famously called 'the Othello music' – and more immediately aligns itself with the disruptive, improvisatory bricolage of Iago.[17]

This juxtaposition of styles is evident in the striking visual and aural threnody of the film's opening. The film opens to black, with a face revealed, upside down, eyes closed. Light enters horizontally, as if curtains were being drawn, against a heavy drum beat. The camera zooms back to show the hands crossed over the body, then swoops down again, behind the bier as it is raised on the shoulders of bearers. A new shot shows the funeral bier darkly silhouetted in the bottom left of the frame against a large bright sky, with a tiny row of soldiers holding spears on the low horizon. The choral music in close harmony rises on the soundtrack. The funeral procession moves into mid-shot, silhouetted against the sky, angled uphill with a party of dark-clad monks behind. The camera shifts to put this scene into the distance, with another religious figure, dressed in pale robes and bearing a cross, leading a second procession in mid-shot. The two processions run in temporary parallel and a close-up shows a gauzy covering over a female body, against the outlines of the other funeral procession also in sight. The two processions seem to converge physically, and an overlayered shot brings them together, the transparent cloth of the female procession shrouding the dark outline of the male procession in a double exposure-effect.

A change in the musical tempo and a flurry of activity cutting across the screen from right to left is immediately disruptive of the ritual solemnity built over the sequence. We see the outline of a man dragged by a rope attached to his neck, and then a rapid sequence of giddy shots, with an unsteady, hand-held pan round the onlookers as if from the point of view of the captive, dragged into a yard filled with people. A high-angle shot shows the crowds gathering around him, held back by soldiers, as he is pushed into a cage. A momentary point-of-view shot shows the bars and his taunting captors, and the funeral procession in dark outline beyond. The cage is hoisted from the battlement walls, but instead of the expected high-angle point-of-view shot we expect, we get an extreme low-angle shot of a solemn onlooker. The sequence cuts between a low-angle shot of onlookers crossing themselves, the cage and the wheeling high-angle shot of the proceedings. The funerals continue on the battlements as the camera drops down the wall to black and thence to the film's playbook-like title. The whole sequence, drawing on the traditions of Eisenstein and European art cinema rather than Hollywood, takes almost five minutes, without a word of the text being spoken.

Marguerite Rippy reads the opening as 'a civilisation in decline, visually conjuring a funeral procession in which monks, heroes and villains move among and through each other like figures on a chessboard, all dwarfed by ominously towering yet insubstantial stick-like crosses that again evoke Welles' *Macbeth*'.[18] In *Filming Othello*, Welles explained: 'the grandeur and simplicity are the Moor's, the dizzying camera movements, the tortured compositions, the grotesque shadows and insane distortions, they are Iago, for he is the agent of chaos'.[19] This reading of the film suggests Iago's complete control over events from the start, when his cinematic language of distortion and fragmentation interrupts the solemn ritual of the protagonists' joint funeral. Just as the play pulls its characters away from Venice to Cyprus, so the film tugs its visual language into splinters and shadows.

Welles' prologue also powerfully conveys the inevitability of the tragedy. Beginning with the end – a favourite narrative technique for Welles, used most famously in *Citizen Kane* (1941) – means the question for the film is how or why, not what. The tragic telos is overdetermined because it has already completed its destructive arc at the point when the film begins: Welles' *Othello* renovates Shakespeare's play by beginning where the drama ended.

Chimes at Midnight (1965)

In taking on the character of Falstaff in *Chimes at Midnight*, Welles entered into an ongoing critical debate that was already at least two centuries old. In his simultaneous, contradictory affection for both Hal and Falstaff, Welles seems to draw on A. C. Bradley's influential essay 'The Rejection of Falstaff' (1902). Bradley proposed that with Falstaff, Shakespeare 'overshot his mark. He created so extraordinary a being, and fixed him so firmly on his intellectual throne, that when he sought to dethrone him he could not.' For Bradley the new king's ultimate 'rejection' of his former companion was a necessary part of his maturation into an 'ideal man of action': the problem was that Falstaff was too large and compelling a personality to play along with this narrative of reformation.[20] In Welles' hands this misalignment takes on tragic colouring, as the entire narrative is structured to catalyse this final incompatibility. Samuel Crowl notes that the film's 'overriding visual and structural emphasis is to signal farewell, to say a long goodbye to Falstaff'.[21] As the director told Juan Cobos and Miguel Rubio in 1966, 'I directed everything, and played everything, with a view of preparing for the last scene. The relationship between Falstaff and the Prince is not a simple comic relationship ... but always a preparation for the end. And as you see the farewell is performed about four times during the movie, foreshadowed four times.' The reason for this stress on the scene of Falstaff's rejection was its symbolic weight: 'the film was not intended as a lament for Falstaff, but for the death of Merrie England ... It is more than Falstaff who is dying. It is the old England, dying and betrayed.'[22] In patching together scenes and lines from three Shakespearean plays, *1* and *2 Henry IV* and *Henry V* (Welles discarded a sequence with Richard II's coffin which would have further extended the historical reach),[23] *Chimes at Midnight* emphasises the teleological reading of Shakespeare's history plays popular in the mid-twentieth century.[24] Here, though, the telos is structured less around Prince Hal's reformation than Falstaff's rejection: like Harold Bloom, Welles sees these plays less as a Henriad than a Falstaffiad.[25]

The film's final sequence is thus its defining moment, by bringing out the pathos and the ambivalence of Falstaff's fall from favour. Welles' direction, and his clever incorporation of lines from *Henry V*, allows for the king's harsh banishment to be mitigated, even as Falstaff's death curtails any possibility of reconciliation. Henry's triumphant entry as king is shot from an alienating distance through an unruly crowd of onlookers and soldiers, and the dense obscuring verticals of spears and banners. The low-angle camera position emphasises the emotional and hierarchical difference between the crowd and the mounted monarch: reverse shots from a high angle suggest his newly elevated position, looking down on his people. The soundtrack of cheers and fanfares, and the continued extreme long shot of the royal procession, shows clearly that our – and Falstaff's – privileged access to Hal and the intimacies of the Boar's Head Tavern are over.

As the procession moves indoors to the austerely perpendicular ecclesiastical architecture associated with John Gielgud's aloof Henry IV, the music becomes more sombre. The procession takes on a religious character, with white-robed priests swinging thuribles led by a mitred bishop. The cut to Falstaff eagerly ushering in Shallow with the confident 'I will make the king do thee grace' (5.5.5–6), makes clear how out of place his cheery self-interest, 'sweating with desire to see him' (24–5), is in this new, chillily ritual world. A shot from Falstaff's point of view follows a distant Henry who is oblivious to onlookers, and the accompanying shot, as the camera tracks Falstaff's attempt to push through the guards, captures his transgressive energies. At his interruption the procession stops, with the king, resplendent in heavy robes and crown and bearing the sceptre, back to the camera. A high-angle shot shows Falstaff kneeling in the foreground, and Henry's unyielding back at the rear of the frame. Henry's slow, deliberate reply to Falstaff's greeting is 'I know thee not old man.' An extreme low-angle shot shows him turning to face Falstaff, distorted by the angles into a tyrant king: 'how ill white hairs become a fool and jester' (47–8). The next few shots allow for a slight softening of this rejection: Henry bids Falstaff to his prayers and his mortality in an eye-level close-up, but when the knight approaches him again, the distance between them is reinstated with an extreme low-angle shot of the king, towering again over the supplicant.

But the shifting emotional dynamic of the scene continues. Henry speaks the words of banishment publicly, and then, in a lowered voice as if privately, the softer version allowing him 'competence of life'. Falstaff watches him shrewdly, a slight smile of understanding on his lips, as Henry turns and leaves. It is as if they understand one another and the exigencies of the public position in which

Henry now finds himself. The procession moves on, leaving Falstaff and Shallow, alone, dwarfed in the shadowy precincts of the cathedral, moving slowly and sparsely after the pomp of the crowds Falstaff's final appearance in the film is in a lighted archway, tiny, in an empty, forbidding castle wall, dwarfed by the impersonal scale of the environment: He turns to look at the camera: 'I shall be sent for soon . . . at night' (87–8), and then continues, leaning heavily on a stick, to move through the opening. After a short sequence of noblemen reviewing events, the young page pushes through the crowd to announce that Falstaff is sick. Bardolph makes clear the compromised cause and effect: 'The King is a good King, but it must be as it may' (*Henry V*, 2.1.120).

The dissolve to a bright outdoor shot with the king and his nobles, amid flags and armed men, declaring the campaign in France, is a jolt to the rhythm of the sequence: Henry is moving onwards; Falstaff is in retreat. But Welles' screenplay repurposes lines in *Henry V* when Henry orders clemency for an arrested man, arguing that it was 'excess of wine that set him on' (2.2.42). By making these about Falstaff, the film endorses the knight's own sense that the king is performing, rather than inhabiting, his newly harsh discipline. But it is too late. The scene cuts to the yard of the Boar's Head Tavern and a large coffin: 'Falstaff is dead.' Mistress Quickly's eulogy is straight, poignant, without the innuendo sometimes found in her account (Welles admitted that the film was less funny than he anticipated, and allowed that perhaps 'some scenes should be much more hilarious');[26] the tavern is quiet and still. Bardolph and Peto wheel the coffin out of the gate into the landscape – watched by Mistress Quickly, with a voice-over narration: 'The new king, even at first appointing, determined to put on him the shape of a new man. This Henry was a captain of such prudence and such policy, that he never enterprised anything before he had forecast the main chances that it might happen. So humane withal, he left no crime unpunished, nor friendship unrewarded. For conclusion, a majesty was he that lived and died a pattern in princehood, a lodestar in honour and famous to the world all way'. Ralph Richardson's clipped tones, a patchwork from Holinshed's *Chronicles*, are ironised by the melancholy movement of the cart bearing Falstaff's coffin away, watched by Mistress Quickly and by the looming cold walls of the castle. The tone of the film's 'sad, still ending', and its sympathies for Falstaff are clear: the final credits run against a loop of soldiers and citizens at Henry's coronation, replaying the ceremony as brute triumphalism now that Falstaff is gone.[27] Welles' claim that Falstaff was a 'good pure man' is, like other of his comments on his work, less complex than the film itself.[28] *Chimes at Midnight* captures not the decline of a heroic individual but instead the inevitability that Falstaff needs must succumb to the processes of history.

Shakespeare on Film: 'You Can't Put a Play on the Screen'

A cameo appearance on television's *I Love Lucy* in 1956 captured Welles' Shakespearean competitiveness. 'I think you're the greatest Shakespearean actor in the whole world', gushes Lucy. 'I think you're better than John Gielgud, I think you're better than Maurice Evans, I think you're better than, than Sir Ralph Richardson.' Welles cut in: 'You left out Laurence Olivier.'[29] The exchange is revealing, but Welles is a significant Shakespearean not as an actor, but as a director. His distinctive gift is to translate verbal into visual poetry, and the techniques by which he achieves this remediation respond to the same close analysis we might usually apply to linguistic shapes and figures. His Shakespeare is not naturalistic but expressionist, externalising personal and social psychologies, and using a distinctively cinematic idiom to disrupt rather than reify notions of character, continuity and location. And although Olivier's Shakespeare films *Henry V* (1944) and *Hamlet* (1948) were much more commercially and critically acclaimed than Welles', they now look like period acting pieces compared with the rangy, edgy poetry of *Macbeth*, *Othello* and *Chimes at Midnight*. Welles' cinematic chutzpah, based on the conviction that 'you can't put a play on the screen. I don't believe in that – I don't think Shakespeare would have believed in it. He would have made a great movie writer', produced three extraordinary critical interpretations of Shakespeare.[30] Like the best interpretations, in criticism as in creative adaptations, these films are selective, partial and sometimes contradictory. Nevertheless, in their bold originality, they decisively unsettle the orders of aesthetic and imaginative priority that still govern analyses of Shakespeare on film. Welles' Shakespeare canon contributes to postmodern theories of adaptation that figure the 'play as process' rather than fixed original.[31] Although Welles always denied that his films were accurate representations of their plays – '*Othello* the movie, I hope, is first and foremost a motion picture'[32] – nevertheless, the value of his films for readers and students of the plays is in their intensely and inventively visual poetry of alienation and decline. All Shakespearean films cut large swathes of the text: only Welles reinstates the plays' densely, lyrically ambiguous language within the syntax of cinema.

Notes

1. On Welles's television performance in *King Lear*, see Simon Callow, *Orson Welles. One Man Band* (London, Jonathan Cape, 2015), 138–41. Scenes and speeches for *The Merchant of Venice* were shot at various times during Welles's peripatetic career: they are referred to in his conversations with

Peter Bogdanovich, and some have been included in documentaries about Welles. See Orson Welles, Peter Bogdanovich and Jonathan Rosenbaum, *This is Orson Welles* (London, HarperCollins, 1993), 23, 30 and 34.

2. See, for example, Peter Conrad, *Orson Welles: the Stories of his Life* (London, Faber, 2003).

3. Welles, Bogdanovich and Rosenbaum, *This is Orson Welles*, 212.

4. Johan Huizinga, *The Waning of the Middle Ages: A Study of the Forms of Life, Thought and Art in France and the Netherlands in the XIVth and XVth Centuries*, translated by F. J. Hopman (London: Edward Arnold, 1924), 28 and 9.

5. G. W. F. Hegel, *Aesthetics: Lectures on Fine Art* (Vol. 2), translated by T. M. Knox (Oxford, Oxford University Press, 1975), 1215.

6. Michael Anderegg, *Orson Welles, Shakespeare, and Popular Culture* (New York, Columbia University Press, 1999), 97.

7. From *Life* magazine in 1947, quoted in Thomas Schatz, *Hollywood Genres* (New York, Random House, 1981), 111.

8. J. A. Place and L. S. Peterson, 'Some visual motifs of film noir', *Film Comment*, 10 (1974), 31.

9. See E. Ann Kaplan, 'Introduction', in E. Ann Kaplan, ed., *Women in Film Noir*, new edition (London, British Film Institute, 1998), 5–8.

10. François Truffaut, in André Bazin, ed., *Orson Welles: A Critical View* (London: Elm Tree Books, 1978), 16.

11. Welles *et al.*, *This is Orson Welles*, 214.

12. Ibid., 216–17.

13. *Filming 'Othello'* dir. Orson Welles (1978), included in the Criterion Collection Blu-ray, 2018.

14. Anderegg, *Orson Welles, Shakespeare, and Popular Culture*, 103.

15. Jack Jorgens, *Shakespeare on Film* (Bloomington and London, Indiana University Press, 1977), 11: a still from *Othello* illustrates the filmic mode.

16. Bazin, *Orson Welles: A Critical View*, 109.

17. G. Wilson Knight, *The Wheel of Fire: Essays in Interpretation of Shakespeare's Sombre Tragedies* (Oxford, Oxford University Press, 1930). On Iago and improvisation, see Stephen Greenblatt's important essay 'The improvisation of power', in his *Renaissance Self-Fashioning: From More to Shakespeare* (Chicago and London, University of Chicago Press, 1980).

18. Marguerite H. Rippy, 'Orson Welles', in Mark Thornton Burnett, Courtney Lehmann, Marguerite H. Rippy and Ramona Wray, eds., *Welles, Kurosawa, Kozintsev, Zeffirelli: Great Shakespeareans Volume XVII* (London, Bloomsbury, 2013), 30.

19. *Filming* Othello (1978).

20. A. C. Bradley, 'The rejection of Falstaff', *Oxford Lectures on Poetry* (London, Macmillan, 1920), 259 and 256.

21. Samuel Crowl, 'The long goodbye: Welles and Falstaff', *Shakespeare Quarterly*, 31 (1980), 373.

22. Juan Cobos and Miguel Rubio, 'Welles and Falstaff', *Sight and Sound*, 35 (1966), 159.

23. Interview with Keith Baxter, in Bridget Gellert Lyons, ed., *Chimes at Midnight* (New Brunswick, Rutgers University Press, 1988), 269.

24. See, for instance, E. M. W. Tillyard, *Shakespeare's History Plays* (London, Chatto and Windus, 1944).
25. Harold Bloom, *The Anatomy of Influence: Literature as a Way of Life* (New Haven, Yale University Press, 2011), 67.
26. Cobos and Rubio, 'Welles and Falstaff', 159.
27. Jorgens, *Shakespeare on Film*, 121.
28. Cobos and Rubio, 'Welles and Falstaff', 159.
29. Quoted by Anderegg, *Orson Welles, Shakespeare, and Popular Culture*, 3.
30. Welles *et al.*, *This is Orson Welles*, 228.
31. M. J. Kidnie, *Shakespeare and the Problem of Adaptation* (London, Routledge, 2009), 5.
32. Quoted in Bazin, *Orson Welles: A Critical View*, 114.

15

ANNE-MARIE COSTANTINI-CORNÈDE

Kurosawa's Shakespeare: Mute Heavens, Merging Worlds or the Metaphors of Cruelty

Akira Kurosawa (1910–1998) is an internationally recognised filmmaker, praised for his technical virtuosity and extensive knowledge of arts.[1] He was a drawer and painter before becoming a screenwriter at the age of thirty, then an assistant director and eventually an independent director as he made his first feature film *Sanshiro Sugata* (1943). He is also a cultural enigma, both regarded as the Japanese artist *per se* eager to promote local culture – films like *Rashomon* (1950) or *Seven Samurai* (1954) contributed to make Japanese art and traditions known to the world – but also a filmmaker strongly influenced by western or Russian art, cinema or literature, Renoir, Ford, Hollywood masters, Eisenstein, Gorky or Dostoevsky, as shown by his versions of *The Idiot* (1951) and *The Lower Depths* (1957). Such cultural coalescence is also due to a general trend to internationalisation. In the 1950s, Mitsuhiro Yoshimoto explains, films could no longer be produced out of the spheres of 'global capital', and national boundaries were necessarily transgressed.[2]

Kurosawa's three Shakespeare films were *Kumonosu-jo/Macbeth* (1957), first translated as *Castle of the Spider's Web*, then *Throne of Blood*; *The Bad Sleep Well/Hamlet* (1960); and *Ran/King Lear* (1985), respectively qualified as period, 'foreign', 'translation and expropriation'[3] films, in any case based-on-Shakespeare ones reflecting the paradox inherent to any trans-cultural adaptation, the internal tension between the model's essential themes restitution and effective contextualisation. Their narratives, freely modelled after the plays' plots, show a reduced number of characters and dialogue rendered in vernacular language, systematically transformed and simplified.

Kumonosu-jo is a *jidai-geki*, historical and samurai film like *Rashomon* and *Seven Samurai*, the latter a model for *The Magnificent Seven* (1960). Both films propelled Kurosawa's cinema on the international scene and Japanese culture along with it. The wish for cultural merging is central to the making of *Throne of Blood*. *Macbeth* (along with *Hamlet*) was Kurosawa's favourite Shakespeare play, a simple story, he said, and one which he wanted to adapt because of the cultural similarities or 'links' between the 'incidents' within the plot and samurai traditions prevailing during *Sengoku-jidai* feudal civil wars (1467–1568), specifically during the *ge-koku-jo* period: the expression means literally 'a retainer murders his lord and deprives him of his power'.[4]

Warui Yatsu Hodo Yoku Nemuru/The Bad Sleep Well, a *mono-gendai*, modern film, is a social satire which depicts the corruption of governmental and corporate contemporary Japan. In doing so, the film also revitalises *Hamlet*'s main tragic themes of revenge in both a personal and collective perspective.

Ran is another *jidai-geki*, samurai, costume film, this time an epic colour fresco drawing both on the painterly and cinematic animated movement to construct a universe of utmost violence. 'Modelling' on *King Lear* consists in a seamless merging-in from the life of real historical figures, Lord Motonari Mori and his three sons during the sixteenth-century *Sengoku-jidai* period, and that of the fictive Lear, with the two stories combined.

Whether set in modern or medieval context, each film achieves a successful cross-cultural coalescence in its own way. Techniques differ in the three films. *Throne of Blood* blends realism and symbolism and constructs its own metaphorical system. *The Bad Sleep Well* operates effective contextual displacements sustained by film noir aesthetics. *Ran*'s samurai epic goes beyond personal fates issues to suggest mankind's doom. How is the coalescence between Japanese contexts and Shakespeare cultural worlds achieved? How are time gaps bridged or (eastern-western) trans-cultural issues handled? How are trans-medial (stage-cinema) aesthetics superimposed?

Kurosawa deemed *Throne of Blood* to be 'experimental'. *Macbeth* was to be adapted first with a view to use real locations and landscapes and set the action in a realistic historical context. Art director Kohei Ezaki, along with Yoshiro Muraki, carefully reconstituted Cobweb Castle after the impressive, wooden sixteenth-century models like Kumamoto fort in Kyushu. Mount Fuji's greyish, ashen slopes were deliberately chosen because of the presence of thick mists, which was also meant to provide for a relevant symbolical visual framework.[5] Noh compositions and techniques were to be used in the *mise en scène*, stylised Noh walking-with-dragging-feet movements used by Asaji or Kaede in *Ran* fit to suggest both characters' rampant, cunning evil. Noh masks were to help actors and serve minimalist characterisation, typifying traits, for instance the Heida warrior mask for Washizu/Macbeth or the *Shakumi* mask of a woman on the verge of madness for Asaji/Lady Macbeth (Isuzu Yamada).

Mazes and Hazes: Mythic Spaces

Unlike the play where the Witches appear from the outset, almost abruptly, with 'When shall we three meet again?' (1.1.1), the Weird Woman's appearance is here postponed. Instead of showing evil, the film suggests its forms and effects by means of an action-commenting chorus and a story-encompassing framing device as two similar shots display the ruins of Cobweb Castle shrouded in thick fog, over which the camera is seen moving slowly, and a chorus heard in voice-over comments on human passions: 'Here was once a mighty fortress where lived a poor warrior / Murdered by ambition / His spirit walking still.' This narrative postponement has the effect of bringing forward main themes and enhancing the moral dimension of evil, incidentally pointing it as essentially human. As James Goodwin suggests, 'the chant reiterates a Buddhist teaching on *mujokan*, the impermanence and brevity of worldly aims'.[6] The local, cultural perspective blends with a wider, humanist vision: the circular pattern drawn by the very reiteration triggers off the metaphorical mechanism suggestive of human tragic flaws and fate in a Kott-like Grand Mechanism image. The plot as such opens with the details of war in a typical *jidai-geki*, period sequence: samurai head of clan, Lord Kuniharu Tsuzuki/Duncan (Takamaru Sasaki) learns about Washizu and Miki's unexpected victory up north against traitors Fujimaki and Inui, then a series of wipe-over effects and cuts reveal Taketoki Washizu (Toshiro Mifune) and Yoshiaki Miki/Banquo (Minoru Chiaki) riding under pouring rain, an element Kurosawa had mastered since *Seven Samurai,* before the warriors enter Cobweb/Birnam Forest.

The Forest expedition is ritualistic. From the outset realism blends with symbolism. This is where the supernatural first manifests itself, the warriors blinded by an unnatural light, a mad laughter heard somewhere, and the place 'full of deceptive appearances between the fair and the foul as it rains and shines',[7] a network of visual and aural effects which deconstruct verisimilitude *effets de réel*[8] and effectively displace the play's images of an elemental heath, 'In thunder, lightning, or in rain' (1.1.2). The protagonists are caught by means of long shots, seemingly relegated in the distance and lost in a hostile environment. As the dark, ominous-looking branches in the foreground obstruct both the warriors' sight and ours, the wooden intricacies stand as a visual equivalent of the web-trap image, which conveys the meaning of physical entrapment and mental alienation. The maze, 'the wood that catches up the invaders as if in a spider's web',[9] is a mindscape, the objective projection of Washizu's confused, ambition-haunted mind, as later will be the silent, mist-invaded no man's land expanse under bleached skies where the two men are seen riding in circles, utterly confused and disoriented. Unfamiliar spaces construct symbolism.

The Web and the Wheel

The opening sequence visuals take up the verbal metaphor contained in the original Japanese title alluding to an entrapping, insidious web. Film titles contain central images, conflated meanings or metaphorical hues. Mark Thornton Burnett argues that the former, literal translation *Castle of the Spider's Web* is more 'expressive' and effective than the latter, shorter title pointing more straightforwardly at the protagonist's bloody quest for power.[10] If both translations indeed transform the original title, metaphorical shifts are of a different nature. The first one refers to the ontological origin of evil, Cobweb Forest, the cause and primary *locus* where mysteries first appear, whereas the second points at the seat of power and subsequent effects of tyranny, when evil has definitely taken over.

Visual and aural leitmotivs, disorienting mists, unnatural light or bleached skies substantiate supernatural evil, and like a sustained cinematic metaphor or the very conceit for weirdness, subsume textual images without altering their original meaning. Textual images become an object of cinematic interpretation *per se*, so that, ultimately, the adaptation consists in creating a system of metaphorical equivalences to evoke mysteries and obliquely convey the notion of evil, the model text thus re-imagined/re-'imaged'.

The warriors then abruptly hit on the wooden hut, literally in the heart of the web and the matter, as if drawn to it by some impelling force. Here again the local and the universal coalesce. The Weird Woman (Chieko Naniwa), the androgynous being characterised by a low-key voice and marked features coined after the mask named *Yamanba* and the legendary hag of the play *Kurozuka,* is seen sitting, chanting the folly of men 'prisoners of their passions' in words and tone echoing the chorus's song, while turning a spinning wheel as if weaving man's fate.

The same whitish, fuzzy figure will later feature Miki's ghost, in a *mise en scène* drawing on Noh masks and techniques partaking of '*Mugen* style (i.e. incorporating fantasy or supernatural elements)',[11] Anthony R. Guneratne argues. The second encounter with the witch signals the third *kyü* (haste) movement, Asaji's madness and the protagonists' fall. Now encircled by the armies of lieutenant Noriyasu Odagura/Siward (Takashi Shimura), Tsuzuki's son Kunimaru/Malcolm (Yoichi Tachikawa) and Yoshiteru/Fleance (Akira Kubo), the protagonist foolishly reveals the prophecy and is finally killed by his own men, 'transfixed' by a flight of arrows, pinned to the monumental wooden wall like a derisive fly. Cinematic metaphors or conceits define the minimalist form of representation establishing the main tragic patterns and meanings: ambition, fear, guilt or absolute evil.

Neo Noir Rituals of Power

The Bad Sleep Well was the first film of Kurosawa Films Productions (made with Tomoyuki Tanaka) after the series of Toho produced films. Kurosawa wrote the script himself with Shinobu Hashimoto, Hideo Oguni, Ryuzo Kikushima and Eijiro Hisaita. If social and political ailments during post-war Occupation reconstruction are here at stake,[12] critics soon pointed at strong parallels with the play, especially as regards filial revenge themes.[13] More allusive than *Throne of Blood* or *Ran*, the film was however sensed from the start as essentially a *Hamlet*-like narrative. Triggering off the tragic concatenation of events are the dubious agreements linking the corporate world to governmental institutions.

Faithful to his commitment to 'make a movie of some social significance'[14] and chastise bribery at public level, 'the worst crimes' performed by hypocrites concealed behind respectable institutional façades, Kurosawa depicts a universe riddled with extreme psychological violence and operating on a logic of the vicious circle. Vice-President of the Housing Corporation, Iwabuchi (Masayuki Mori)/Claudius, is first among equals in this respect, when, having received an illegal rebate from Daiyru Building Trade Company president with the implicit backing of their collaborators, the government Corporation Soil Development Office, the film opens on a scandal brewing and threatening the reputation of all the officials. Koichi Nishi/Hamlet (Toshiro Mifune) is the outraged son who shrewdly managed to elbow his way right up to the top officials as the personal secretary to Iwabuchi, then marry his crippled daughter Yoshiko (Kyoko Kagawa), the vulnerable Ophelia figure, to whom he is at first indifferent, to seek revenge for the unnatural murder of his father Furuya, a senior official involved in a scandal five years before and pressed to commit suicide by his peers. Iwabuchi, the 'murd'rous, damned Dane' (5.2.277) is backed by a gang of overzealous assistants, all encapsulating social evil.

If coerced suicides are the logical consequences to corruption, carefully staged shows, lies and misrepresentations to the press[15] are the necessary correlatives. High-ranking officials involved in dubious deeds exert intimidations, duress and extreme pressures on their subordinates pressed to comply and be silent to protect their superiors. The latter are turned into dehumanised puppets, driven to depression and death, Furuya five years before, accountant Miura (Gen Shimizu) today. The chain of cause and effect – a social web – linking past and present events builds here again the tragic, circular pattern of fate. The whole system lives on an unflinching code of loyalty, which rests upon a mafia-like logic rather than plain, ethical conducts.

Nishi devises successive ploys and mousetrap-like devices to trap the guilty and disclose the truth. The opening wedding sequence, 'the kind of play ... in which to trap the conscience of the corporate president',[16] introduces characters and context, the company zealots opposed to the low, challenging world of press sneakers and 'ironical chorus' gleefully awaiting the arrest of the 'scandal trio', Administrative Officer Moriyama, Contract Officer Shirai and Chief Accountant Wada. Climax comes as a cinematic frontal shock with the arrival of the huge wedding cake shaped after the company's building, a rose seen poking out of the tragic seventh floor. Shirai (Akira Nishimura) and Moriyama (Takashi Shimura), stand gazing, aghast with fright, and the guilty are definitely self-betrayed.

Other orchestrated shows ensue: despairing Wada (Kamatari Fujiwara) about to commit suicide and ultimately rescued from the eerie volcano slopes, then made to appear as his own 'ghost' in a deserted street at night to terrified Shirai then driven to sheer schizophrenia. They are all spectral variations operating on the principle of the ghost character, even if the primary ghost figure, Furuya, never appears. Interrelated identity issues and spectral motifs form part of the film's symbolical texture.

Ghostly Selves

In the *Bad Sleep Well*, the 'something-is-rotten' effect is suggested by an elaborate blending of film noir motifs, prevalent in the 1940s–1950s, or more precisely neo noir starting in 1960, more abruptly frightening than suggestive symbolism. Raymond Borde and Étienne Chaumeton define the genre as polymorphous, borrowing from German expressionism and expounding on qualities like the 'nightmarish, weird, erotic, oneiric [*sic*], ambivalent and cruel; ... [a world showing] an incoherent, brutal atmosphere'[17] enacting 'fallible' characters, and operating on a refined cinematography supporting the view of a gloomy world. The authorities' destabilising rituals create such a brutal social atmosphere. Neo noir style is sustained throughout by hyperbolic effects: Nishi shown dramatically looming out from the volcano thick mists, systematic use of low-key lighting (Uchiro Inohara) as in Wada's 'ghost' sequence, where whole parts of shots are left in utter darkness, and a score (Sato Masaru) in full empathy with the action.

The ending is despair. Iwabuchi drugs and deceives Yoshiko into revealing Nishi's identity and the hideout where Moriyama is confined, blackmailed into disclosing the truth to the press. The setting, the ruins of a bombed munitions factory and devastated urban landscape in Tokyo, recalls 'the graveyard in *Hamlet*', Burnett suggests,[18] also a desecrated, ironic double of Wittenberg, where former students Itakura and Nishi once participated in war efforts, a symbolical locus adumbrating both the grim, collective war past and the bleak present. Ultimately time gaps are bridged. The *mono-gendai* tragedy does end in pure Elizabethan revenge tragedy style, also merging with neo noir style. Nishi is horribly assassinated – off-screen – by Iwabuchi's henchmen, drugged, his body injected with alcohol and his car thrown under the crushing wheels of a train, the fallible hero defeated. The ritualistic slaughter provides for several final declinations on the spectral theme, the protagonist now dispossessed of his life and good reputation and all hope to defeat the corrupt bureaucrats lost. Nishi becomes the ghost of social idealism, his chivalric quest for justice turned into a mere Quixote-like struggle. Real Nishi, the friend and loyal Horatio figure (Takeshi Kato) and Itakura (the protagonist) have exchanged identities to enable the latter to fulfil his revenge: the faithful double is also metaphorically dead, forever left 'to haunt the landscape as a ghost of the past'.[19]

The final shot showing Iwabuchi bowing to an invisible president, who, on the phone, has just ordered him to leave, concludes the long string of images evocative of deceptive realities and concealment, Robert Hapgood argues, the higher official 'untouched',[20] forever unattainable.

Ran, a Samurai Epic

Ran is a Franco-Japanese co-production that could only come to life after Serge Silberman from Greenwich Film Production and Masato Hara from Herald Ace had accepted the risky deal to make a film when the

Toho or the Daiei Japanese production companies had recoiled at the expected extravagant costs.

Writing a *King Lear* adaptation was not in view originally. The director was merely intrigued by the personality of warlord Motonari Mori (1497–1571), who lived with his sons during the *Sengoku-jidai* 'Age of Country at war' or feudal civil wars.[21] Mori, on ageing, decided to divide his realm among his three sons. Even more intriguing was Motoharu, Mori's second son and model for Saburo, of a rebellious nature, oddly so at a time when strong feudal, patriarchal codes would hardly allow such liberties. The story is basically the same, dialogue is simplified, and details or 'verbal lengths' are scrapped. History does not record any tragic outcome and the family lived peacefully thereafter, but the analogy with Lear naturally imposed itself and the director came to wonder 'what would have happened' if the sons had behaved like Lear's ungrateful daughters. A subtle superimposition somehow 'oddly' occurred, and gradually the two stories intermingled so that ultimately the scriptwriters, Kurosawa and his two collaborators, Hideo Oguni and Masato Ide, reading the play and rewriting the story at length were no longer able to tell which was which from Japanese real history, their imagination or Shakespeare.[22]

The opening boar hunting sequence emblematises Hidetora (Tatsuya Nakadai), placed in the filmic frame centre, his arrow pointing straight at us, as a ruthless predator. By contrast, the council gathering the Ichimonji clan, the Fool and rival clans Ayabe/Cornwall and Fujimaki/France, suggests peace and orderly hierarchy. The sons' colours are neatly disposed, yellow for Taro Takatora, the eldest son/Goneril, red for second son/Regan Jiro Masatora, and light blue for third son Saburo Naotora.

The division of the realm is allegorised in the 'strength-in unity' arrows sequence based on Mori's legend of a father attempting to demonstrate the necessity of harmony within the familial sphere. Hidetora announces his wish to yield power and advocates unity. The three arrows may be broken if taken one by one, but if bent and held together, they would be too strong to be broken on one's knee. Saburo (Daisuke Ryu) senses the mistake, and, in a powerful chiasmic image, reminds the old man of the violence ingrained in times, himself, and potentially his own sons, 'You have spilled oceans of blood! You showed no mercy, no pity … We too are the children of the age weaned on strife and chaos! … You are a fool! A senile old fool!' He is banished along with faithful Tango Hirayama (Masayuki Yui), who, as he expresses the wish to protect Hidetora without him knowing, recalls the 'banished Kent' figure (1.4.4) 'disguised' and willing to 'serve' the king even if 'condemned'.

Saburo's blunt rebuke, more self-assertive than Cordelia's subdued 'Nothing my Lord' (1.1.87), also fits the samurai Motoharu, which illustrates the characterisation merging-in technique.

Ran also means disorder, rebellion or internal chaos. Hidetora is gnawed within by remorse at his past exactions, the slaughter of Taro's wife Kaede's clan, then Jiro's wife Sué's, or Sué's brother Tsurumaru (Takeshi Nomura) saved only after Hidetora himself had gouged out his eyes. Hidetora's guilty past provides for a rational explanation to his abrupt abdication as well as his sons' ungrateful irreverence:

> How did Lear acquire the power that, as an old man, he abuses with such disastrous effects? Without knowing his past, I have never really understood the ferocity of his daughters' response to Lear's feeble attempts to shed his royal power.[23]

Critic Alan Booth saw *Ran* as a 'parable of social behaviour',[24] basically 'didactic, not cathartic'. This, incidentally, highlights Kurosawa's detached, philosophical humanism, as if mankind was watched from a distant vantage-point. The social parable image points at a blending of thematic perspectives, one universal, linked with man's archetypal aggressiveness in his quest for absolute power, and one contextual, related to *Sendoku-jidai* jungle law civil wars times when such conquest was necessarily merciless.

Tennè Kurosawa: Epic Battles

Battle sequences are shot with cameras pitched on cranes in three strategic points so as to encompass the maximum of details,[25] and the epic dimension sustained by the painterly and the cinematic. Hidetora, driven away successively from First and Second Castles, has found refuge in Third Castle, where he is assaulted by both Taro's and Jiro's armies. The Dante-esque, 'Scroll of Hell' provides for an ultimate 'vision of Apocalypse'[26] in a pandemonium of entropic violence, a general mêlée of horses, flights of arrows and muskets firing, yellow and red banners and pennants seen hysterically intermingling. Soldiers are falling dead, forming extravagant heaps of twisted, tortured corpses piling on the ground streaming with blood. As a direct echo to the play's familial treacheries, Taro (Akira Terao), is abruptly killed by Shuri Kurogane (Hisashi Igawa), Jiro's man.

Violence is however softened by internal contradictory effects. Sound is entirely suppressed in the first part of the sequence to alleviate shock as well as convey a higher perspective: 'The heavens watch such unthinkable and bloody battles and become literally mute'.[27] The distancing

effect is further enhanced by long shots preventing spectator-actor identification, 'creating a sense of detachment that positions the spectators as
distant observers of a drama of massive destruction'.[28]

Within the castle, a frantic Hidetora considers committing *seppuku* –
ritual suicide – a seemingly noble-heroic impulse immediately decon-
structed as he is shown fumbling for his lost sword in the blazing
chaos. Climax is reached as he is seen rushing out of the blaze, haggardly
lingering at the door of the keep, as if literally 'vomited' out of the
cauldrons of Hell. As he makes his way amidst the awed, silent soldiers,
he is untouched, but also unattended, Jiro (Jinpachi Nezu)'s faint sign of
help stopped by his men. In this ultimate vision of Hell, 'a logical
necessity', Stephen Prince suggests, 'There can be no turning back from
a path of evil.'[29]

Ran's is a divided world. Gentle, pious Sué (Yoshiko Miyazaki) is the
victim type ruthlessly sacrificed by her rival Kaede (Mieko Harada), who,
frozen in Noh-like masks traits like Asaji, her double, silently ruminates
her revenge, a merged-in representation of 'Centaurs' Goneril, Regan and
Edmund, all three in one, 'fox in stealth, wolf in greediness' (3.4.87), and
a direct avatar of the fiendish, cunning nine-tailed fox evoked by
Kurogane's parable.

'Is This the Promised End?' – Visual 'Endgame'

The choice of the famous transsexual actor 'Peter' – or Pita – (Shinnosuke
Ikehata) to enact the Fool, the 'ambiguous idol' acting in the tradition of
onnagata, male actors playing women's roles in Kabuki theatre,[30] was
controversial, although culturally effective. Kyoami performing
a mocking song to chastise Hidetora's incoherence on *Kyogen* rhythm,
traditionally used for Noh comic interludes seen lurching from one side to
another ('Give away his house … Give away his land … ') is also an
example of cultural merging conjuring up the play's baroque images:
'That such a king should play bo-peep/ And go the fools among' (1.4.-
157–8), or Lear's allusion to children's games, 'change places, and handy-
dandy, which is the justice, which is the thief?' (4.5.149–50) Peter's
verbal-visual interludes reflect the Fool's 'handy-dandy' jesting or abrupt
existential paradoxes, 'I am a fool, thou art nothing' (1.4.175–6). In the
final slaughter scene, the light *Kyogen* Fool takes on the general commen-
tator's voice. Saburo dies absurdly, shot by one of Jiro's men. Exhausted
Hidetora, desperately glancing at the mute sky, dies in his turn. Jiro is
killed by Ayabe's troops. Ultimately this is a godless world, altogether
devoid of soothing divine power. As Kyoami yells thrashing words to the

empty skies, 'You are laughing at us', the vibrant apostrophe echoes Gloucester's despairing chastisement of gods' flippant cruelty: 'As flies to wanton boys are we to th' gods; / They kill us for their sport' (4.1.37–8). Yet another distancing long shot, combined with a crane high angle shot, imparts the meaning of gods' deafness and man subsequently crushed by blind fate. The film takes on a metaphysical dimension.

The final scene showing Tsurumaru's lonely figure groping his way in Azusa Castle ruins, then dropping his Amida Buddha Scroll as he is reaching the fortification edge and abyss, further conveys the sense of impending doom, but now an allegory of mankind's fate: 'The blue sky is completely empty.'[31] The last shot conveys an impression of incompleteness, a vision halted, as if the ending was suspended into a questioning, as enigmatic as a final question mark. Jan Kott, who saw the play as one 'about the disintegration of the world', asserts: 'The abyss, into which one can jump, is everywhere.'[32] Such an ending conveys a nihilistic *fin de siècle* vision suggesting that what could have remained an individual story is bound to become a collective tragedy. *Ran* could then be seen as an exponential pessimistic response to the model, a stand interestingly denied by Kurosawa: ' ... in contrast to King Lear ... Hidetora reflects on his past and regrets it'.[33]

Or, is the film, as Marjorie Garber shows for *Lear*, a question that is posed and remains open, 'not foreclosed even in the direction of nihilism?'[34]

Notes

1. Akira Kurosawa, *Something Like an Autobiography*, translated by Audie E. Bock (New York, Vintage Books Edition, 1983), v–xii.
2. Mitsuhiro Yoshimoto, *Kurosawa: Film Studies and Japanese Cinema* (Durham, Duke University Press, 2000), 108–9.
3. Kenneth Rothwell, *A History of Shakespeare on Screen: A Century of Film and Television*, 2nd edition (Cambridge, Cambridge University Press, 2004), 182–9.
4. Akira Kurosawa, interviewed by the Japanese historian and film critic Tadao Sato, quoted in Roger Manvell, *Shakespeare and the Film* (New York and Washington, Praeger, 1971), 102; and (for *ge-koku-jo* period) 113, note 3. See also 105 and 108 for use of masks.
5. Donald Richie, *The Films of Akira Kurosawa*, 3rd ed. (Berkeley and Los Angeles, University of California Press, 1998), 115.
6. James Goodwin, *Akira Kurosawa and Intertextual Cinema* (Baltimore and London, Johns Hopkins University Press, 1994), 177. See also 184–5 for the borrowings to Noh-drama tripartite structure, *jo* (introduction), *ha* (destruction) and *kyū* (haste).

7. Jack J. Jorgens, *Shakespeare on Film* (Lanham, University Press of America, 1991), 157.
8. Marc Vernet, in Jacques Aumont *et al.*, eds., *Aesthetics of Film* (Austin, University of Texas Press, 1992), translated by Richard Neupert from *Esthétique du film* (Paris, Nathan, 1983), 121–3.
9. Manvell, *Shakespeare and the Film*, 104.
10. Mark Thornton Burnett, 'Kurosawa', in Mark Thornton Burnett *et al.*, eds., *Great Shakespeareans, Volume 17: Welles, Kurosawa, Kozintsev, Zeffirelli* (London, Bloomsbury, 2013), 54–91; 62.
11. Anthony R. Guneratne, *Shakespeare, Film Studies, and the Visual Cultures of Modernity* (New York, Palgrave Macmillan, 2008), 184.
12. Stephen Prince, *The Warrior's Camera: The Cinema of Akira Kurosawa* (Princeton, Princeton University Press, 1991), 175.
13. Richie, *The Films of Akira Kurosawa*, 140–1. For the wedding sequence's 'Hamlet-like *mise en scène*', see also Aldo Tassone, *Akira Kurosawa*, translated by Brigitte Branche (Paris, Flammarion, 1990), 222 and 225.
14. Kurosawa quoted by Richie, *The Films of Akira Kurosawa*, 140.
15. On the importance of the press, see Melissa Croteau, *Re-forming Shakespeare: Adaptations and Reappropriations of the Bard in Millenial Film and Popular Culture* (Balti, Moldova, Lambert Academic Publishing, 2013), 171.
16. Richie, *The Films of Akira Kurosawa*, 141.
17. Raymond Borde and Étienne Chaumeton, 'Towards a definition of film noir', translated from *Panorama du film noir* and analysed in Alain Silver and James Ursini, eds., *Film Noir Reader* (New York, Limelight Editions, 2001), 17–25 (18, 22).
18. Mark Thornton Burnett, 'New directions: *Hamlet*, Cinema, the World', in Ann Thompson and Neil Taylor, eds., *'Hamlet': A Critical Reader* (London, Bloomsbury, 2016), 139.
19. Prince, *The Warrior's Camera*, 185–6.
20. Robert Hapgood, 'Kurosawa's Shakespeare Films', in Anthony Davies and Stanley Wells, eds., *Shakespeare and The Moving Image: The Plays on Film and Television* (Cambridge, Cambridge University Press, 1994), 234–49 (240).
21. Bertrand Raison, with Serge Toubiana, 'Ran à l'épreuve du gros plan', in *Le livre de 'Ran': un film de Akira Kurosawa* (Paris, Cahiers du cinéma/Seuil/Greenwich Film Production, 1985), 11, 21 and 123. For many useful interviews and sources for the three films, see also Burnett, 'Kurosawa', 54–91.
22. Tassone, *Akira Kurosawa*, 274, quoting Kurosawa.
23. Peter Grilli, 'Kurosawa directs a cinematic *Lear*', *New York Times*, 15 December 1985.
24. Alan Booth, quoted by Richie, *The Films of Akira Kurosawa*, 216.
25. Raison, *Le livre de Ran*, 147.
26. Samuel Crowl, 'The bow is bent and drawn: Kurosawa's *Ran* and the Shakespearean arrow of desire', *Literature/Film Quarterly* 22-2 (1994), 109–16 (116).
27. Kurosawa, quoted in James Goodwin, *Intertextual Cinema*, 211.
28. Yoshimoto, *Kurosawa*, 357.
29. Prince, *The Warrior's Camera*, 288.
30. Raison, *Le livre de Ran*, 99 and 100–1 for details on *Kyogen* dancing.

31. Jan Kott, 'The Edo Lear', *New York Review of Books*, 32–7 (24 April 1986), 14.
32. Jan Kott, *Shakespeare Our Contemporary* (London, Routledge, 1988), 297 and 115.
33. Kurosawa, interviewed by Max Tessier and Aldo Tassone, 'Propos d'Akira Kurosawa', *Revue du cinéma*, 408 (September 1985), 67–70 (69).
34. Marjorie Garber, *Shakespeare After All* (New York, Anchor Books, 2005), 694.

16

NATHALIE VIENNE-GUERRIN

Zeffirelli's Shakespearean Motion Pictures: Living Monuments

The most striking memories I have of Zeffirelli's screenscape date back to the days I eagerly watched *Jesus of Nazareth* (1977) on French television in the 1970s. I was not aware at the time that the Italo-British miniseries was directed by Franco Zeffirelli and the 'Europeanness' and internationalism[1] that characterise the director's work did not matter in any way to the schoolgirl I was then. What have always remained engraved in my memory are the beautiful lights and colours, the unforgettable music (by the French composer Maurice Jarre), and the purity of the faces of the two main characters, Jesus (Robert Powell) and Mary (Olivia Hussey, who had been 'the girl on the balcony'[2] ten years before). It is with these youthful impressions still in mind that, about forty years later, I explore Zeffirelli's three Shakespearean films, *The Taming of the Shrew* (1967), *Romeo and Juliet* (1968) and *Hamlet* (1990), the success of which seems to rest on the three aspects that I had already noted as a girl and that have often since then been noticed by critics: the visual banquets that the films constitute, the memorable soundscapes that they feature and their stimulating casting choices.[3]

Indeed, Zeffirelli was one of the rare directors whose Shakespearean films have been commercially successful, which is an indicator of their popularity and accessibility.[4] 'I think I've contributed enough to the cause of reviving Shakespeare and bringing him to the attention of a mass audience' was his conclusion to an interview 'symposium' of directors in 1998.[5] For him 'culture – especially opera and Shakespeare – must be available to as many people as possible'. He wanted to 'give these things back to the people'. And for him 'the one medium that can do that' was 'the motion picture'.[6] The director who had come to be known as 'Shakespirelli',[7] and who was famous for extensively cutting the scripts of Shakespeare's plays,[8] had designed '*motion* pictures' indeed. The purpose of this chapter is to suggest that, as designer and director, Zeffirelli managed to combine movement and fixity, so that his Shakespearean films can be regarded as living monuments, landmarks that remain alive and meaningful thirty or forty years after their production.[9]

The Taming of the Shrew: 'Household Stuff' Coming to Life

In the Induction to The Taming of the Shrew, Christopher Sly asks whether the 'pleasant comedy' (Ind. 2.126) the players are going to perform is 'household stuff' (Ind. 2.116). In her edition of the play, Ann Thompson notes that the expression, which in context very probably has a bawdy meaning, literally means 'furnishings'.[10] The question remains unanswered in the text but one may guess that, for Zeffirelli, who was well-known as a designer having studied architecture, this 'household stuff' motif may have been particularly attractive. The expression has a special resonance when we consider that the two actors playing Katherine and Petruchio, Elizabeth Taylor and Richard Burton, constituted a stormy 'household' or couple at the time. In the same scene, Sly asks another question about the play to come: 'Is not a comonty [a comedy] a Christmas gambold or a tumbling trick?' (Ind. 2.128–9). Although the answer is 'No, my good lord, it is more pleasing stuff' (Ind. 2.135), and although the Induction scene is cut in the film, it seems that Zeffirelli has considered the play as a matter for 'gambold' and 'tumbling tricks' indeed.

Matter seems to come alive in this adaptation where 'household stuff' is everywhere and the basis of the most spectacular effects. The film gives life to objects and cultivates acrobatics and physical feats, which seems to echo Zeffirelli's early days when he was playing with his 'mother's materials and racing around [her] atelier'.[11] The first conspicuous living objects that we see are the cages in which a 'drunkard' and a 'wife stealer' are displayed at the centre of Padua's main square, shown through a few shots that seem to compensate for the absent Induction.

The focus on windows and shutters is then emblematic of the way matter comes to life in this film. The first window that is focused on is the frame in which a big-breasted prostitute standing on excessively high heels attracts Tranio's attention when he arrives in Padua, objectifying the woman's grotesque body.[12] The 'gambold and tumbling tricks' are illustrated in the carnival atmosphere that opens the play and the topsy-turvy world that it creates through the use of masks and props such as skeletons. The play on costumes and material stuff in general also appears when Lucentio sees Bianca, whose veil is spectacularly taken off to reveal her face in a sequence that counterpoints Tranio's bawdy attraction to the high-heeled prostitute.

The first apparition of Katherine is a close-up of one of her eyes looking down at the arrival of her sister through the interstice of shutters. The shot of this single eye framed by the shutters situates her within a household from where she observes the rest of the Paduan society but it also contributes to framing her as an object in a prison-like house. The focus on the door that remains closed when Petruchio arrives to 'wive and thrive' (1.2.55) and patiently waits for an answer while the two sisters are heard fighting and brawling inside the house, also presents Katherine's house as a private space that is going to be penetrated, a fortress that is besieged.

The relationship between Katherine and Petruchio starts as a cat and mouse and hide-and-seek game, which makes their initial confrontation spectacular. The décor is brought to life by the two protagonists who use the props as circus devices, Petruchio using a rope as a flying trapeze and the two characters climbing stairs and ladders in a farcical chase that ends up with Katherine being forced to take refuge on top of a roof, literally becoming a Katherine/'cat on a hot tile roof'. The vision of Katherine as a tightrope walker on top of this roof seems to be a literalisation of Elizabeth Taylor's playing the part of Maggie 'the Cat' Pollitt in Richard Brooks's 1958 film *Cat on a Hot Tin Roof*, as well as an illustration of the acrobatics or 'tumbling tricks' mentioned in the Induction. As the roof breaks under their weight, the two characters end up falling and struggling on a bed of wool in the barn below, a bed which Katherine had joyfully enjoyed as a space of freedom in a previous sequence, which then becomes a place of constraint and violence.

In this festive yet cruel battle of the sexes, the bed appears as a specific battlefield. Even before the bed of wool, the object first appears as Petruchio's domain when he is hosted by Hortensio (Victor Spinetti) and drunkenly falls asleep on a canopy bed. When he is woken up, a close shot of his feet wearing dirty socks with holes, presents him as a tramp who is on his way to gaining fortune. Then the bed is given particular prominence in Petruchio's house where it appears as a stage. Katherine takes refuge in a dusty canopy bed to escape Petruchio and when he wants to invade her space, she knocks him out with a pan. Petruchio then in rage destroys the bed décor, tearing the bed curtain and the bedposts, symbolically ravaging Katherine's private space. Crying on her bed once Petruchio has left the room, Katherine suddenly seems to have a comforting idea. Her resilience will lie in objects: we discover her in the next morning sequence, like a sort of Walt Disney Snow White cleaning the house with the help of the servants. Violence and healing are to be measured through the life of household stuff. For Katherine, taming Petruchio means taming his place through cleaning. The next bed sequence shows Petruchio waking Katherine up in the middle of the night to take her back to her father's. After the struggle, the bedchamber then becomes a place of negotiation.

Zeffirelli made his film a cabinet of objects that come to life. The table is another example: it too becomes a battlefield when Petruchio upturns the dinner table and all the food that was on it and that the film had carefully highlighted through a succession of shots of still life images of dishes of fruit and meat. Objects do not remain 'still' in this film, whether they are smashed to pieces by Katherine in her father's house or by Petruchio in his castle. This is confirmed during the tailor sequence when Katherine's dress which is displayed on a dummy is torn apart by Petruchio. Symbolically each of the insults he hurls at the tailor is punctuated by a physical aggression of Katherine by proxy through the dummy and the dress. Symbolically, in this tailor/Taylor scene, Katherine's clothes are torn apart and her body laid bare. Ironically and reflexively, the choice of costume had been a bone of contention in the making of the film, Taylor finally getting the costume designer of her choice (Irene Sharaff) and Burton having another one (Danilo Donati).[13]

Thus Zeffirelli's 'energetic style', which, according to Samuel Crowl has influenced Branagh's 'flamboyant realism',[14] extensively rests on the life that is given to the décor and props, Zeffirelli the director setting his design in motion. As if in a reversal of this process, his film shows that Katherine may be turned into an object or a 'movable' (2.1.196–7), especially when Petruchio is seen carrying her on his shoulder after a disturbing church scene which shows the complicity of the whole Paduan society in the whole taming process. Katherine literally becomes a property.

The materiality and physicality cultivated in *The Taming of the Shrew* go together with the theatricality of the film where many sequences constitute spectacles within the spectacle, up to the last wager sequence, staged as if it were a play within the film, with an audience watching the scene from the balconies. The Taylor-Burton couple oozes through the Katherine-Petruchio couple in this final scene, when Katherine/Liz Taylor delivers the last monologue. Zeffirelli notes in his autobiography how fiction and life overlapped:

> Full of that Welsh passion, Richard was deeply moved. I saw him wipe away a tear. 'All right, my girl, I wish you'd put that into practice'.

> She looked him straight in the eye. 'Of course, I can't say it in words like that, but my heart is there.'[15]

The two living monuments, Burton and Taylor, at that moment, prevailed over the Katherine-Petruchio duet. In a completely different way, the casting choice that Zeffirelli made for *Romeo and Juliet* transformed the film and the main characters into living monuments of another kind.

Romeo and Juliet: Fair Verona's Battle of Energies

By casting Leonard Whiting and Olivia Hussey, two completely unknown and very young actors as Romeo and Juliet, Zeffirelli seems to have aimed at the eternity and universality that anonymity may provide. If, for *The Taming of the Shrew*, Zeffirelli used two tempestuous celebrities, for *Romeo and Juliet*, he obviously chose the beauty and purity of inexperience. It is fitting that Olivia Hussey should have entitled her recent biography *The Girl on the Balcony*, thus pointing at the paradox of celebrity coming from anonymity. In her autobiography, she notes that the famous balcony had to be completely fabricated:

> he [Franco Zeffirelli] had finally settled on a beautiful sloping hillside with an ancient wall running along its crest. Ideal for Romeo's ecstatic climb ... The only drawback: there was not a balcony in sight. ... Franco simply had an entire plaster balcony built, along with a mock bedroom into which I would retreat.[16]

The balcony is never mentioned in Shakespeare's text and although Zeffirelli's film has contributed to fuelling the balcony's iconic significance, it rather looks, as is noted by Ramona Wray, like 'ramparts or battlements'.[17] On top of a Pyramus-and-Thisbe kind of wall, this 'balcony' is a space of freedom for Juliet who can walk up and down, following the movements of her heart. Zeffirelli transforms this place of fixity and constraint into a space that is cut out for movement and love impulses. While Juliet is filmed in various postures, Romeo scales the wall several times, climbing on the trees, Zeffirelli choosing to film the young man's 'athletic activity'.[18] The balcony that is symbolic of stillness becomes a stage for acrobatic movements, which testify to the youth and energy of the two lovers. Olivia Hussey comments on the physicality of the sequence that left Leonard Whiting 'bruised and battered', and she cleverly asks: 'how could kissing be this much work?'[19] Kissing is definitely a lot of work in *Romeo and Juliet*.

This treatment of the balcony is emblematic of the way Zeffirelli, again, animates still lives in an adaptation that throws action into relief. The colourful costumes for which Zeffirelli is so well-known are themselves infused with life and become meaningful acting props. For example, the cap that is worn by Tybalt seems to provide him with the cat's ears that mirror his name. The skull-shaped mask that Mercutio plays with during the Queen Mab speech ominously announces his fate. The veil worn by the Nurse when she comes to meet Romeo in the middle of Verona's square becomes a 'sail' (2.3.91), with which Romeo's friends mock her. Mercutio, before the deadly duel, puts his white handkerchief on his face, talking through it, transforming it into an ominous shroud. Objects are meaningfully energised, be it to ironically announce the fatal ending.

The bedchamber sequences also take their meaning from the setting. The first dialogue between Juliet and her mother takes place in Lady Capulet's chamber. The mother's red-coloured canopy bed is the background of the whole scene, thus suggesting that Juliet is to be married soon. From the beginning to the end of the film, Juliet is visually associated with a bed. The love bed in which Romeo and Juliet are seen waking up, naked, in a sequence that created a stir at the time,[20] reveals the youth, purity and physicality of the young lovers' passion, which contrasts with what we see of the cold relationship between Juliet's parents. It is the same bed, surrounded with white veils, that will become her mock-death bed, the stage of a theatrical death. Then the bed will turn into a living 'monument' before eventually exhausting all the lovers' energy.

The bed that is the space of Eros and Thanatos is emblematic of the struggle of energies that the film manages to create. Once the prologue, delivered by Laurence Olivier's uncredited voice, has set a tone of solemnity, the film cultivates energy and action. The hustle and bustle created by the thumb-biting scene in the central square of Verona shows the power of destruction that the 'ancient grudge' (Prol. 3) may have through the décor being ravaged. When Romeo arrives once the fray is over, he is seen alone, walking up a quiet and deserted street, which strikingly contrasts with the previous chaotic market sequence. The physicality of Mercutio's performance of the Queen Mab speech, followed by the festive atmosphere of the Capulet's ball, then contrasts with the love energy that is expressed by the two main characters, especially through the focus on their hands.[21] Throughout the ball sequence Zeffirelli dramatises the struggle between positive and negative energies, shots of Tybalt's angry face counterpointing shots of the beauteous lovers' faces. The 'What is a youth' song[22] that is sung and heard in the background delivers a reminder of the transitory nature of youth and an intimation of mortality that disturb the viewers' reception of the lovers' first embraces. The beautiful and peaceful music composed by Nino Rota contrasts with the unsettling and ominous lyrics by Eugene Walter which point to the fragility of love and life: 'Death will come soon to hush us along', the song warns.

The 'impetuous fire' of youth that the song refers to is illustrated in the central unforgettable duel scene. This very long sequence stages a corrida-like fight, in which Tybalt cuts a lock of hair from Mercutio, which becomes his trophy. The duel is dizzying thanks to circular camera movements and by enhancing the physicality of the fight that has the characters run and jump in an endless chase. What makes the scene memorable is Mercutio's death which is made all the more pathetic as the viewers on screen think he is just playing the part of a dying man. Mercutio's death thus provokes laughter instead of lamentation before Romeo and Benvolio finally realise that Mercutio is a 'grave man' (3.1.98). This discrepancy between death and the laughter it mistakenly provokes reveals the theatricality of the scene, which constitutes a spectacle within the spectacle. At that moment, the laughter and crying that the film cultivates overlap to provoke a tragic feeling of discomfort in the audience. Thus, the positive energy of the balcony scene is contrasted with the negative energy of the duelling episode. The bedchamber scene that stages the battle of the lark and the nightingale (3.5.1–36) restores the energy of love and the naked bodies of the two young protagonists are here to conjure up the force of life opposing the deadly damage of hate. But throughout the end of the film, Zeffirelli's shots of objects such as candles or torches point to the vanity of the lovers' energy, their two bodies being finally turned into two golden statues at the end of the film. The lovers themselves become monuments or works of art, which ensures their eternal life through the viewers' memory.

Hamlet: A Labyrinth of Fury

In 1990, twenty-two years after *Romeo and Juliet*, Zeffirelli brought Shakespeare back to the screen. It seems to be a very long gap but Zeffirelli had lived with Shakespeare throughout his career whether it be in theatres or opera houses. The monumental book that was published on his career in 2010, *Franco Zeffirelli: Complete Works: Theatre/Opera/Film*, shows that since his revelatory discovery of Olivier's *Henry V*, Zeffirelli had spent his whole life with Shakespeare. The director relates the beginning of his Shakespearean dreams to the figure of Laurence Olivier.[23] The oedipal interpretation of *Hamlet*, conspicuous in the

Gertrude (Glenn Close)/Hamlet (Mel Gibson) couple, may echo that in Olivier's 1948 film of the play. The physical, sexualised confrontation in the closet scene and the many kisses between mother and son make the incestuous motif very clear and provide an oedipal motive for Hamlet's fury.

Zeffirelli's casting choices for this version of *Hamlet* are, again, highly significant. In 1990, Mel Gibson was already known for his parts in *Mad Max* (dir. George Miller, 1979) and the first two *Lethal Weapon* films (dir. Richard Donner, 1987 and 1989). His playing Hamlet is thus both paradoxical and logical. Hamlet's deferring action is at odds with the image of the violently efficient Martin Riggs but the motif of madness that is inherent in Hamlet's part can be related both to the famous cop known for his psychopathic and suicidal trends and to 'Mad' Max. Glenn Close, on the other hand was famous at the time for her part as a sexual psychopath in *Fatal Attraction* (dir. Adrian Lyne, 1987). While with *Romeo and Juliet* Zeffirelli aimed at a young audience, with *Hamlet*, his casting choice aims to attract viewers who enjoy action films and thrillers so that Hamlet's supposed inertia is infused with action.

The location that is chosen, a dark, grey monumental medieval castle, becomes the labyrinth where Hamlet's unsettling fury expresses itself. Zeffirelli explained that the colours he cultivated in *The Taming of the Shrew* and *Romeo and Juliet* would have been inappropriate for *Hamlet*: 'Colour is devastating here, but in this way: I keyed the whole movie to mostly grays and ash colours, a "medieval-primitive" look, the look of a society that is brutal and made of stone.'[24] Filmed from various angles and at various scales, the castle is made of rooms, doors, stairs, balconies, wall hangings and dark corners that are reminiscent of the labyrinthine abbey in *The Name of the Rose* (dir. Jean-Jacques Annaud, 1986), all the more so since Hamlet's environment is packed with books. The maze of doors, corridors and passages made of a mixture of rock and wood allow the director to multiply eavesdropping scenes in a world where surveillance is key. The place allows for the many spying sequences, which emphasise the theatricality of the film. This castle seems to be cut out for spying; so much so that Hamlet's father's ghostly appearance and vanishing seem to be a mere replication of the way his son himself appears and disappears from the view throughout the film. When Polonius, at the beginning of the film, catches a glimpse of Hamlet who is standing on the battlements against a beautiful blue sky and the next second no longer sees him, the viewer realises that the son too is a ghost, an evanescent figure who is going to feed as much doubt and fear as his father. This evanescence is made

220

possible by the labyrinthine structure of the castle in which one gets lost as much as one gets lost in Hamlet's mind.

By choosing Mel Gibson, Zeffirelli enhanced the attractiveness of the character. Most of the monologues are shot in close-ups that throw the actor's beautiful blue eyes in relief. The blue of Hamlet's eyes is one of the few colours that come out in the film, making 'the effect ... even more vivid'.[25] Thus, the film creates a Hamlet that is both intellectual and physical, a body and a mind. The piles of books that surround the character present him as a mind who cares about 'words, words, words' (2.2.195), but the sweat on his face that is shown in numerous close-ups also reveals the physicality of the part. Hamlet going up and down stairs and corridors, thrilled and awed by the idea of revenge that haunts him, shows physical signs of exhaustion even before the final duel.

In the labyrinth of Hamlet's fury, the spaces where things get clearer are the theatrical spaces of the mousetrap and of the duel. The way Zeffirelli represents the play-within makes it obvious that the world of Elsinore is made of characters who watch and are watched in turn. The film perfectly shows that the spectacle is as much in the audience as it is on the stage. Hamlet's theatrical 'acting' abilities are made more and more evident as the film progresses, *acting* being a substitute for *action*. When he arrives with the comedians, he is shown wearing a multicoloured costume and seems to be a member of their company. Later he uses a table as a stage where, with a fool's cap on his head, he puts on a show for Claudius (Alan Bates) and his followers. The final duelling sequence is the moment that takes all the society out of the labyrinth: the place becomes a rectangular wooden stage, delineating the space of the fight, and Hamlet is shown playing a part, giving a performance, playfully provoking Laertes and asking for his mother's applause and admiration. Hamlet the actor probably best appears in this sequence, which leads to catastrophe but shows us the way out of a realm of folly and fury.

The absence of the Fortinbras plot from the film reduces the play to its domestic dimension. All the violence that is expressed in the film comes from inside and is carried out by Hamlet who grapples his friends by the throat, brutally rejects Ophelia, brandishes a sword whenever he is angry, assaults his mother in a quasi-rape scene, blindly murders Polonius (Ian Holm) and finally ragingly kills Claudius, with sword and poison. The sweat that almost never leaves his face is the sign of the labyrinth of fury in which he is stuck, until a wooden horizontal space finally liberates him from the stifling monumental castle he is in. Ramona Wray rightly notes the 'claustrophobic' effect that the film creates.[26] The

huge labyrinth in which Hamlet is seen struggling and suffering transforms him into a mouse that is eventually relieved to escape its trap. In
the same way, Ophelia's death appears as a liberation from this labyrinth
of fury when she is seen joyfully running in a green landscape to finally
drown in a river, not far from the sea which will bring Hamlet back to
her. The blue sky and the blue sea are like hopeful horizons in the film,
which contrast with the earthly vault in which the film starts. The first
image that we see of Hamlet is his hand, sprinkling some earth on his
father's tomb, in an anticipation of the gravedigger scene. The vault will
be the place where, as if he were buried alive, he delivers the famous 'To
be or not to be' monologue. The final image shows that he dies like an
actor on stage and that a wooden scaffold rather than an earthly vault
will be the character's monument.

Many critics have noticed that Zeffirelli's career as a designer influenced
his films. This chapter hopefully shows that far from being mere visual
decoration, the designs that are at the heart of his films are infused with life
and reinvigorate the vision of the plays. Zeffirelli's 'fabric' of his vision was
not 'baseless'. The architecture and design of his films make them monuments. There is a lot of art in this matter. There is a lot of life in these
monuments.

Notes

1. On this 'Europeanness', see the chapter by Tom Matheson (with Russell Jackson
   and Robert Smallwood), 'Franco Zeffirelli', in John-Russell Brown, ed., *The
   Routledge Companion to Directors' Shakespeare* (London and New York,
   Routledge, 2008), 526–47 (544): 'his work challenged a language-based British
   theatrical establishment with the visual traditions of the European opera house,
   insisting on the physicality of performance and the freedom of actorly
   invention . . . '.
2. See Olivia Hussey, with Alexander Martin, *The Girl on the Balcony*
   (New York, Kensington Books, 2018).
3. For a visual record of Zeffirelli's work, see the monumental volume by
   Caterina Napoleone, ed., *Franco Zeffirelli: Complete Works: Theatre/Opera/
   Film* (London, Thames and Hudson, 2010).
4. See Robert Hapgood, 'Popularizing Shakespeare. The artistry of Franco
   Zeffirelli', in Lynda E. Boose and Richard Burt, eds., *Shakespeare The
   Movie. Popularizing the Plays on film, TV and Video* (London and
   New York, Routledge), 80–94.
5. 'Shakespeare in the cinema: a film directors' symposium with Peter Brook, Sir
   Peter Hall, Richard Loncraine, Baz Luhrmann, Oliver Parker, Roman Polanski
   and Franco Zeffirelli', *Cinéaste*, 24.1 (1998), 48–55 (55).
6. 'Breaking the classical barrier: Franco Zeffirelli interviewed by John Tibbetts',
   Literature/Film Quarterly, 22.2 (1994), 136–40 (138–9).

7. The nickname meets Garrick's original Italianization of Shakespeare's name as 'Shakespearelli', see Fiona Ritchie and Peter Sabor, eds., *Shakespeare in the Eighteenth Century* (Cambridge, Cambridge University Press, 2012), 215.

8. See Ace G. Pilkington, 'Zeffirelli's Shakespeare', in Anthony Davies and Stanley Wells, eds., *Shakespeare and the Moving Image. The Plays on Film and Television* (Cambridge, Cambridge University Press, 1994), 163–79.

9. On Zeffirelli's 'influence and legacy', see Ramona Wray, 'Franco Zeffirelli', in Mark Thornton Burnett, Courtney Lehmann, Marguerite H. Rippy and Ramona Wray, eds., *Great Shakespeareans Vol. XVII. Welles, Kurosawa, Kozintsev, Zeffirelli* (London and New York, Bloomsbury, 2013), 181–4.

10. Ann Thompson, ed., *The Taming of the Shrew* (Cambridge, Cambridge University Press, 1984), 66.

11. *Franco Zeffirelli. The Autobiography* (London, Arena Books, 1987), 5.

12. On this spectacular figure of a courtesan, framing the action of the film, see Carol Chillington Rutter, 'Looking at Shakespeare's women on film', in Russell Jackson, ed., *The Cambridge Companion to Shakespeare on Film*, 2nd ed. (1986; Cambridge, Cambridge University Press, 2007), 245–66 (254–5).

13. On this battle of costumes, see Zeffirelli, *Autobiography*, 214–15.

14. 'Branagh's flamboyant realism is so obviously indebted to Zeffirelli's lush and energetic film style', in Samuel Crowl, 'Zeffirelli's *Hamlet*: the golden girl and a fistful of Dust', *Cinéaste*, 4.1 (1998), 56–61 (56).

15. Zeffirelli, *Autobiography*, 216.

16. Hussey, *The Girl on the Balcony*, 67.

17. Wray, 161.

18. Ibid.

19. Hussey, *The Girl on the Balcony*, 67, see also Hussey's long interview in a Folger Shakespeare Library 'Shakespeare Unlimited' podcast, www.folger.edu/shake speare-unlimited/olivia-hussey?fbclid=IwAR2kisbcYdvu1QLbAnNXsX2kFzHYI_jvVTydTr4dnwuAhcVsazmHUNca4y4 (accessed 11 October 2019).

20. Claude Barma's 1973 French TV version, which is much indebted to Zeffirelli's film, would also use nudity. The film is available at www.ina.fr/video/CPF86651356 (accessed 19 January 2019).

21. See Peter S. Donaldson, '"Let lips do what hands do": male bonding, eros and loss in Zeffirelli's *Romeo and Juliet*', in *Shakespearean Films/Shakespearean Directors* (1990; London, Routledge, 2013), 145–88.

22. *Fakespeare*, 2 March 2015, available at www.youtube.com/watch?v=zCQMlyXMRJE (accessed 19 January 2019).

23. On this moment of revelation see Zeffirelli, *Autobiography*, 60–1.

24. Tibbetts, 'Breaking the classical barrier', 139.

25. Ibid.

26. Wray, 171–4.

17

SARAH HATCHUEL

Kenneth Branagh: Mainstreaming Shakespeare in Movie Theatres

'The Man who would be Olivier': this was the cover title used by *Time Magazine* in November 1989 to describe a young Belfast-born stage actor who had just made his debut as screenwriter and film director of a new version of *Henry V*, a play that had been famously directed on the big screen by Laurence Olivier in 1944. Branagh thus invited comparisons with the legendary English actor-director right from the start of his career. He has often acknowledged in interviews that Olivier was an inspiration to him; he has portrayed Olivier in the film *My Week with Marilyn* (Simon Curtis, 2011), directed *Sleuth* (2007), a remake of a 1972 Mankiewicz film starring Olivier, and performed the role of Archie Rice in a 2016 West End production of Osborne's *The Entertainer*, a play that served as an Olivier vehicle on stage and on screen. Like Olivier in 1947, Branagh was knighted in 2012. However, *Times'* title was less revealing of what Branagh himself wanted to become than of what journalists and the public wished to create – a new heir in a line of Shakespearean kings. Branagh certainly fulfilled this hope as he eventually acted in and directed more Shakespeare plays than any other filmmaker before him; yet he also defied what was expected from a Shakespearean actor-director. First, he used the codes and genres of Hollywood cinema to make the plays entertaining and available to a younger, more popular audience. Second, he not only adapted Shakespeare but also ventured into directing Hollywood blockbusters, as well as more intimate projects on stage and screen, injecting Shakespearean echoes into a new range of productions. Through his taste for popular, mainstream movies, his bold self-made trajectory that carried him repeatedly in and out of the 'Establishment', and his blue-collar origins (his father was a joiner in Belfast, who moved his family to Reading during the Troubles in the 1970s) – all of which he emphasises in his 1989 autobiography *Beginning*, in his published scripts and multiple interviews – Branagh has contributed to redefining relations between Shakespeare and Hollywood, between the art house and the multiplex, and between theatre and cinema.

From Theatre to Cinema

Branagh started his professional journey as a stage actor, trained at the Royal Academy of Dramatic Art in London. In 1984, he joined the Royal Shakespeare Company where he portrayed the RSC's youngest Henry V under Adrian Noble's direction, before creating his own theatre company, Renaissance, in order to gain artistic freedom. However, from the early stages of his career, Branagh alternated between roles on stage and on screen. He had his lucky break as Billy, a young working-class Protestant in Graham Reid's *Billy* teleplays, and soon learnt the basics of filmmaking, surrounding himself with trusted fellow actors and crew – Brian Blessed, Richard Briers, Judi Dench, Gerard Horan, Derek Jacobi, Michael Maloney, Emma Thompson, and Jimmy Yuill, with Patrick Doyle for the scores and Tim Harvey for the designs – with whom he would regularly work on his filmic projects, thus importing into film the special feel and rapport of a theatre company. The making of each film includes an important phase of rehearsals as in the theatre – a communal experience which is then reflected in the emphasis on family in the works themselves.[1] His Shakespearean films bear the aesthetic and interpretative influence of previous stage productions in which Branagh was involved as an actor, with the RSC (playing Henry V and *Love's Labour's Lost*'s King of Navarre in 1984, as well as Hamlet in an uncut production in 1992–1993) and with Renaissance (*As You Like It*'s Touchstone, *Much Ado*'s Benedick and Hamlet in 1988).[2] From the early days of his Renaissance company, Branagh declared his wish not only to bring Shakespeare to the people but also to turn the stage productions into films: *Twelfth Night*, which he directed for the stage in 1987, was subsequently recorded and broadcast by Thames Television.

Branagh's fascination with the energetic movement of film may at first be thought as opposed to the ethos of theatre. However, if his films avoid static staginess, they always present theatrical effects in the sense of amplified, operatic forms – fluid movements using Steadicam (a camera held by the operator in a harness, allowing smooth shots while moving), swirling circle shots, impressive long takes, symmetrical shots in which a central figure is flanked by two characters in profile (reflecting oppositions or tensions), festive or fairy-tale environments with songs, dances, masks and disguises. There has been much negative criticism of Branagh's cinema, which

225

appropriates Shakespeare's plays into a highly stylised universe rooted in a pseudo-historical reality: it has been called too literal, too emphatic, too musical, too narcissistic, too manipulative and/or too conservative. One cannot deny, however, that his films have given a boost to Shakespeare's visibility from 1989 onwards, triggering a powerful new wave of screen adaptations. If Branagh believes in epic momentum, textual clarity, colloquial delivery, visual audacity and unashamed romantic force, this energy very often serves the Shakespeare play-texts. By promoting international casting and natural acting styles, the films strive to make us hear the words in fresh new ways.

Referencing Mainstream Films and Genres

Branagh's five Shakespearean films to date – *Henry V* (1989), *Much Ado About Nothing* (1993), *Hamlet* (1996), *Love's Labour's Lost* (2000) and *As You Like It* (2006) – mobilise various mainstream genres, from the western to the epic saga, from the thriller to the war film, and are filled with allusions to film classics such as Orson Welles's *Citizen Kane*, Alfred Hitchcock's *Vertigo*, or Michael Curtiz's *Casablanca*. *Love's Labour's Lost*, for instance, was turned into an American musical *à la* Busby Berkeley, with a synchronised swimming sequence evoking the aquatic ballets of Esther Williams and with songs by Cole Porter, Irving Berlin and George Gershwin that were first heard in *Top Hat* (1935) or *Shall We Dance* (1937). Shakespeare's iambic pentameters are even explicitly associated with the rhythm of tap-dancing.

Branagh's highly intertextual movies reach the 'third degree' theorised by Laurent Jullier: they mix references that viewers may spot but without generating ironic distance or parodic effects (second degree) and, more crucially, without giving up on emotion (first degree).[3] While calling out to our filmic culture, Branagh paradoxically uses film genres to offer a very personal view of the plays. He favours the creation of a realistic and coherent story world, but on some occasions does not hesitate to subordinate the text to a general vision, for instance rethinking *Hamlet* as an epic and wintry saga reminiscent of David Lean's *Doctor Zhivago*, where flowers grow in winter, Hamlet's father rests in a snowy orchard and Ophelia drowns herself in a supposedly frozen river. Whether we consider these choices as inconsistencies[4] or distancing devices, they are signs of Branagh artistically shaping the plays around themes that can be found all through his filmography. Often isolated in vast spaces and confronted with the power of nature (fire, ice, sun, water) and reminders of impending death, Branagh's heroes are endowed with memories and thoughts through flashbacks and mental images; they undergo an initiatory quest for a lost state of harmony, nostalgically attempting to restore a sense of community after – shocks of separation or loss.

Henry V and *Hamlet*: Questioning Olivier's Legacy

In *Henry V*, Hal has to give up the warm world of the taverns when he becomes king. The war against France comes to amplify this departure from a previously carefree life. Branagh uses intimate close-ups and flashbacks to delve into the king's mental space and establish the friendship that he shared with Falstaff, Pistol and Bardolph. During the execution of the latter, flashbacks and close-ups of the king, who vainly tries to conceal his tears, paradoxically create empathy towards the executioner rather than the victim. Henry is presented as an earnest and conflicted youth: a Hamlet-like figure filled with doubts regarding the legitimacy of war and of his power, he becomes the tragic victim of the prelates' conspiracy to invade France as a diversion to protect the Church's financial interests.

In this interpretative context that constructs a path of fall and redemption, the comic altercation between Pistol and French soldier Le Fer (4.4) is replaced with a brutal and bloody battle, the longest and most outstanding sequence in the film. Branagh's film stresses the atrocities of war by showing blood, mud, wounds, impaled bodies and looting. Damp, foggy weather intensifies hardships, while slow motion turns the battle of Agincourt into a chaotic and dreamlike sequence verging on nightmare, dilating time and adding power to the combatants' blows. Agincourt becomes a quasi-eternal fight that symbolises every other armed conflict. Branagh's *Henry V* was shot in England at a time when films expressing the disillusion of warfare were influenced by the Falklands war. But through scenes that show the solidarity between men, united in their fighting, Branagh's film makes war disgusting and heroic, hellish and glorifying, repulsive and attractive. As Chris Fitter notices, 'the structure ... owes much ... to Vietnam movies of the 1980s, particularly its moral ambiguity: war is hell but it heroizes'.[5]

Branagh ends the battle with the now-famous *Non nobis* sequence in which the king, followed by his soldiers, crosses the battlefield in one uninterrupted four-minute tracking shot with a score that builds into a crescendo of voices and orchestra. As soldiers start to sing the *Non nobis* hymn, Henry takes Falstaff's dead Boy on his shoulder and makes his way among the carnage of the battlefield. Carrying the youth like a cross, Henry is turned into a Christ-like figure bearing sin and misery on his back. The camera then cuts close on Henry's blood-stained face and the king's head drops as if in shame. Yet, again, it is through Henry's eyes, the eyes representing royal power, that all the wasteful carnage is observed. The film has, indeed, been criticised for the reactionary nature of its worldview, its legitimisation of (royal) leadership and its private mode of fundraising.[6] However, one also needs to recognise the ideological balance that the film achieves. While Shakespeare's play creates ambivalence by oscillating between parodic dissent and epic speeches, Branagh's film never fluctuates in tone but at the same time denounces and glorifies conflicts through a clash between terrible images of slaughter and swelling music of triumph.

For his 1996 *Hamlet*, contrary to Olivier who, in 1948, drastically cut the text to turn the play into a Oedipal domestic tragedy, Branagh conflated the three existing versions (Quarto 1, Quarto 2 and Folio) to offer an epic, monumental and cosmic four-hour production, taking full advantage of the centrifugal qualities of cinema. Branagh's film is full of sparkling colours and includes a hall of mirrors highlighting duplicity, histrionics and situations repeating themselves. The film is set within the tradition of the Hollywood epic through its international cast of well-known stars, its length, landscapes, number of extras, and even its 'Intermission'. The impression of vastness is also enhanced by the film format: *Hamlet* was filmed using a 70 mm photographic format instead of the traditional 35 mm. Emotional details can thus be caught in extreme close-ups, as the entire frame is sometimes filled by an ear, an eye or a mouth. Faces become landscapes, and intimacy itself is turned into epic.

By making visual the verbal dilemmas of Shakespeare's play, Branagh gives greater importance to swashbuckling action. For instance, Branagh's Hamlet is seen stabbing Claudius at prayer: in an almost subliminal flash, a dagger is plunged into Claudius' ear – but the viewers are quickly jolted back into a reality in which Hamlet has not moved. Branagh plays on magnitude, not only by presenting the conflated text but also by stressing the play's military dynamics via the gleaming rooms, neat uniforms, fencing sessions and Fortinbras' conquering *coup*. The film constructs a world of discipline and hierarchy, violence and indifference towards suffering. Ophelia becomes a mistress abandoned by her lover (their sexual relationship is made explicit in flashbacks): she suffers from the incarceration and callous mistreatment typical of an overtly militarised nation. After Old Hamlet's murder, which is seen as a destruction of domestic bliss through various nostalgic flashbacks in which the family is playing together or enjoying dinner, the Ghost appears as a warrior in full armour, a representation which clashes with the filmic tradition that emphasises his ethereal or pitiful aspects.

Even one of Hamlet's soliloquies, 'How all occasions do inform against me,' (which ends 4.4. in the Second Quarto text) is turned into an exhortation to war. Hamlet's rising voice rings out while his body disappears in the distance. The effect is huge, relying on its impulse and momentum, on its strength and evidence. This moment in which Hamlet asserts his new resolution to act ('My thoughts be bloody or be nothing worth') recalls the epic sequence in *Gone With The Wind* (1939) in which Scarlett O'Hara proclaims her determination to survive ('As God is my witness, I'll never be hungry again!'). In both films, the camera races backwards in a similar way just before the Intermission – turning Scarlett smaller and smaller under the tree at Tara; and Hamlet into a mere dot within the snowy landscape where Fortinbras's army marches.

This immensity emphasises the hero's isolation. Space, like time, is dilated.[7] The film *In The Bleak Midwinter*, which Branagh directed a year prior to making *Hamlet*, makes this idea explicit: when Fadge unveils her concept for the theatre set of an amateur production of *Hamlet*, she says: 'We must make the design all about Space. People in space, things in space, women in space, men in space.' In his 1994 *Mary Shelley's Frankenstein*, man is also lost in infinite spaces of white ice. For such *tableaux*, Branagh was inspired by German romantic paintings, notably *Traveller Above the Sea of Clouds* (1818) by David Caspar Friedrich, with its representation of a man alone in a wild, snowy landscape. Hamlet, like Victor Frankenstein, is turned into an insignificant black dot, melting into powerful nature. Extreme backward moves serve to open spaces for the prince to realise he is either a 'king of infinite space' or some mere 'quintessence of dust'.[8] Branagh here uses a specific shot chosen by Olivier to film the king's speeches in his 1944 *Henry V*. Olivier thought that the camera had to be at a remove from the character when the vocal delivery reached its peak, in order to accommodate the actor's rhetorical projection and gestural expansiveness.[9] With this signature shot, Branagh insists upon the warlike aspects of Hamlet's soliloquy and on his 'bloody thoughts'. Thus, while Branagh had played his Henry V as a self-doubting Hamlet, he performed Hamlet as a swashbuckling action hero reminiscent of Olivier's own Henry V. Olivier's influence and that of the tradition of Shakespearean performance are always there – just not where one may expect them.

When Branagh illustrates Barnardo's words 'When yon same star that's westward from the pole' with a shot of the sky, and those of Horatio 'But look, the morn … / walks o'er the dew' with a shot of the rising sun, these illustrations might be deemed superfluous but they free the film from the interior space of Elsinore and present the actions of men through a macrocosmic lens. The same artistic vision can be found at the end of the 1993 *Much Ado About Nothing*. The last crane shot allows for a flight towards the intensely blue sky, expressing the futility of the film's events compared to celestial beauty, before carrying the audience out of the story with a last fade to black.

Filming the Comedies

Contrary to other Shakespearean film *auteurs*, Branagh has directed Shakespearean comedies, a genre somehow neglected as its humour and clowns are often considered too outdated and anchored in the Elizabethan period. Branagh's *Much Ado About Nothing*, filmed under the Tuscan sun, mixes the musical (the camera follows the characters whirling in the garden just as in Robert Wise's *The Sound of Music*, while Branagh's Benedick splashes in the fountain *à la* Gene Kelly) with the popular romantic film and the screwball comedy (Branagh and Thompson, married at the time, reproduce the witty bantering of Katharine Hepburn and Spencer Tracy, recalling how much this Hollywood genre actually owes to Shakespeare's battles of the sexes).

The film starts with white words on the black screen – lyrics from the song 'Sigh No More, Lady' recited by Thompson's Beatrice – allowing the viewers to tune in to the language and its particular rhythm. The opening image then pans from Leonato's painting of the beautiful land-scape to the landscape itself, suggesting that the film will make words and art come to life. By moving from darkness to light, from text to image, the film suggests how cinema may revitalise a play. As the opening credits unroll, we see the soldiers arriving on horseback, all lined up as in John Sturges' *The Magnificent Seven*, bouncing on their saddles as if anticipating their upcoming sexual encounters. Close-ups in slow motion of the horses' breasts and nostrils, of the hooves hitting the ground, of a waving flag, then shots of the men's bathing and of the women's dressing up, all contribute to convey energy and sensuality.

Though aesthetically very pleasing, the film has occasioned some criticism regarding its cultural politics. By adding a scene shot from Claudio's point of view, which shows how easy it is to confuse Margaret with Hero at her window meeting with a man, the film presents Claudio as a too likeable youth, who thought in earnest that his wife-to-be was cheating on him. At the same time, Keanu Reeves' villainous Don John was perceived as a closeted gay man having his oily body massaged by

Borachio, problematically linking homosexuality with treachery.[10] Finally, the well-intentioned colour-blind casting has one unfortunate consequence: Denzel Washington's Don Pedro ends up single at the end of the play, as if he could only be rejected as a black man.[11]

If Branagh's *Much Ado About Nothing* is located in a kind of timeless Shakespeare fairyland, his *Love's Labour's Lost* is placed just before World War II, with voice-over black-and-white sequences (narrated by Branagh) parodying the newsreels of the time. The study retreat proposed to his friends by the King of Navarre thus presents Branagh's vision of the 1930s as both an escape and 'a stolen, magical, idyllic time which nevertheless had a clock ticking'.[12] The context brings an explanation of the play's peculiar ending: when the war breaks out, the couples must separate and the men atone for their mistakes. They reunite not 'a twelvemonth and a day' later, but six years later on VE Day. Branagh's adaptation of the play as a 1930s musical providing a hopeful vision of British endurance during the war has been seen as escapist nostalgia denying political realities.[13] As one of the newsreels shots indicates that VE Day takes place not on 8 May 1945, but on 11 November, the day when World War I ended, the film thus merges the two world wars, generating historical indeterminacy and, again, shaping the story to fit an auteuristic vision and give the *feel* of a period and place, without necessarily thinking through all the cultural and historical consequences.

Impression is also at the core of *As You Like It*: Branagh creates a Japanese environment, but a legendary one seen through a western prism, especially since the shooting took place in West Sussex. The film opens with a Kabuki piece (Japanese traditional theatre) but the show is soon interrupted by Duke Frederick's violent *coup* (recalling Fortinbras' irruption in the 1996 *Hamlet*) which destroys the stage set as if the world of war and politics brutally replaced the world of make-believe. The film celebrates nature and the pastoral genre in its regular shots of the sun, waterfalls, rivers, trees, leaves, flowers, cobwebs. In this forest of Arden, almost every shot (in low angles) starts by focusing on the sky and the tops of the trees, before meeting the characters below. The action in the wood thus always begins with an idea of freedom, and unfolds beneath cosmic benevolence and radiance. But grim realities are not hidden either: the two enemy brothers fight in the mud under the rain, and life in the woods is not always as idyllic as expected by Celia and Rosalind. The film shows what remains hidden in the play-text – the *coup* organised by Duke Frederick, Orlando's brother attacked by a lioness, or the Duke's final conversion. By giving flesh to these events, Branagh keeps validating all the reports voiced in the play. As with his *Much Ado*, this is a world where doubts over a character's account are not encouraged.

The camera revolves fluidly around the characters, unites the small community within long shots in which they can all be seen together, or slowly tracks forward to catch emotions on faces. Celia is repeatedly framed by Rosalind and Duke Frederick to highlight her dilemma about staying loyal either to her best friend or to her father; and is seen between Rosalind and Orlando, far in the background, to signal that she will be literally left behind, swapped for Orlando in Rosalind's affections. The camera follows Rosalind and Orlando in their first scene together in the forest, constructing a sequence-shot of several minutes, the length of which paradoxically emphasises the theatricality of the actors' movements and voices through the bold display of cinematic virtuosity. The play on theatrical illusion reaches its peak during the end credits when Rosalind appears for her Epilogue, but this time as the actress behind the part, being handed drinks, wandering between the film crew and the modern-day cars before disappearing behind the door of her private van. The last words of the film belong to the director who wraps up everything with 'And ... cut!' asserting the make-believe nature that links film and theatre, as well as Branagh's position as *auteur*.

From Cinema to Filmed Theatre

Because *Love's Labour's Lost* and *As You Like It* were not commercial successes, Branagh could not raise funding for the film of *Macbeth* that he had planned to direct with his newly founded Shakespeare Film Company. However, the project came to fruition through another channel when Branagh played and co-directed (with Rob Ashford) *Macbeth* during the 2013 Manchester International Festival in a small deconsecrated church. The pacey production evoked Branagh's *Henry V* with its muddy and bloody battlefield, which had been inspired by the 1984 RSC stage *Henry V* directed by Adrian Noble – in which the exhausted English army was lined up under a large canvas protecting them from a downpour. The production first ran from 3 to 20 July 2013, and was then transferred to New York at the Park Avenue Armory from 31 May to 22 June 2014, where a larger audience could be accommodated.

The Manchester performance was broadcast by National Theatre Live on a giant screen in Manchester and in a few cinemas in the UK; the recorded version was then shown in cinemas worldwide at the end of 2013 and beginning of 2014. A local, immersive theatrical experience was thus fixed, mediated and distributed globally, the live broadcast in cinemas capturing some aspects of the social event and sense of occasion that theatre-going represents. The many image feeds and soundtracks were mixed together live, so that the cast never knew which camera was broadcasting at any one moment and, therefore, whether they were seen by the cinema audience or not – just as they did not know if they were the focus of spectators' gazes in the theatre.

The Branagh/Ashford *Macbeth* was a show that certainly anticipated a future cinematic experience from the start – with its star-filled quality, cinematic and almost balletic rhythm, violent fighting, non-diegetic music (i.e. music from outside the story world) composed by Patrick Doyle, down to the rain that fell on the muddy ground of the battlefield. Beyond the interpolated battle that stood as the second scene, moments that Shakespeare's play does not show were fully displayed. The 'dagger of the mind' was at first a cross of light on the muddy ground, but did not remain virtual: two of them, one on each side of the nave, were seen suspended in mid-air, glowing and guiding Macbeth towards the apse where Duncan slept. The audience also witnessed Macbeth's blasphemous stabbing of Duncan in the back – a scene supposed to happen off-stage.

Branagh seems to have learnt from this NT Live experience: when he founded the Kenneth Branagh Theatre Company to put on six plays at the Garrick Theatre in London for the 2015–2016 season, he formed a partnership with Picturehouse Entertainment to broadcast live three of the six productions – Shakespeare's *The Winter's Tale* and *Romeo and Juliet*; Osborne's *The Entertainer* – to cinemas worldwide. Just as Branagh injects theatricality into his films, he likewise imports cinematic devices onto the stage: in his 2015 *The Winter's Tale*, Leontes' family gathers around the Christmas tree to watch home movies on a cinema screen, while Antigonus' exit 'pursued by a bear' is spectacularly rendered by the projected image of a giant, roaring bear. After many creations in the theatre and in the cinema, Branagh has now made it his 'brand' of combining both media through his own 'Branagh Theatre Live'.

Shakespearean Echoes

Like Olivier, Branagh did not adapt *Othello* but starred in another director's *Othello* (Olivier played the Moor in Stuart Burge's 1965 version; Branagh played Iago in Oliver Parker's 1995 production). However, we may wonder if *Othello* does not haunt Branagh's filmography in subtle ways, resurfacing in films that critics do not label 'Shakespearean'. The Hollywood thriller *Dead Again* (1991) is thus centred on the murder, in her bed, of a spouse who sparked off her foreign husband's jealousy, while the Marvel super-hero production *Thor* (2011) works on the malevolent manipulation of a close relative: Loki poisons with lies the ear of his brother (and heir-apparent of the Asgard throne) in order to lead him to his fall. According to Pierre Berthomieu, *Thor* appears as a 'Shakespearean blockbuster', which also takes up many aesthetic motifs of Branagh's *Hamlet* and *Henry V*.[14]

As Jennifer Holl argues, 'To be a Shakespearean celebrity is to be both star and fan, or rather, Shakespeare's star fan ... reeling in Shakespeare from otherwise elitist heights and grounding him in the everyday, accessible forum of popular celebrity.'[15] Branagh as a Shakespeare fan comes through in *In the Bleak Midwinter*, a 1995 black-and-white film he wrote and directed: Joe Harper (Michael Maloney), an unemployed and idealistic actor, puts on *Hamlet* in a forsaken village's disused church and rejects the tempting offer of playing in a big-budget Hollywood sci-fi film to perform the gloomy Dane on stage. In *All is True* (2018), a film directed from a script by Ben Elton, Branagh embodies Shakespeare himself during the last years the playwright spent with his wife and daughters in Stratford-upon-Avon. Between fact and fiction, through intimate sequence shots lit like Rembrandt paintings, Branagh finds a subtle, melancholic way of playing Shakespeare: he neither glorifies nor debunks the myth, but faces the mysteries and contradictions of an ordinary bourgeois patriarch who could create such momentous art. Placing gender dynamics at the front and befitting the #MeToo generation, the film suggests that Shakespeare lost his young son Hamnet because he had failed to imagine his daughter Judith as a poet.[16]

Since Branagh is a Shakespearean celebrity in the eyes of the public and the media, each new filmic endeavour is perceived through a Shakespearean lens. Upon the release of his *Cinderella* (2015), pressed to talk about the Shakespearean themes he saw in the story, Branagh recalled how Shakespeare himself borrowed motifs from fairy tales and linked *Cinderella* with the cruel family context of *King Lear*.[17]

Through his 'respect for both the textual richness of Shakespeare's plays and the visual possibilities of cinema',[18] Branagh's cinema merges tradition and modernity; it also synthesises, as Samuel Crowl aptly argues, 'Olivier's attention to the spoken text with Welles' fascination with camera angle and editing and Zeffirelli's visual and musical romanticism',[19] but it has also found its own culturally synthesising voice, as he has straddled 'rival legacies ... : Protestant and Catholic in Belfast; English and Irish in Reading; and Stratford and Hollywood in his film career'.[20] Its specificity is perhaps not only to have revitalised

Shakespearean adaptations at the end of the twentieth century but to have fuelled his Shakespearean projects with his Hollywood endeavours (his *Hamlet* would not have been the same without the previous *Frankenstein*) and to have, in return, injected Shakespearean motifs into Hollywood scripts that celebrate the creative energy inspired by Shakespeare. Through his ceaselessly renewed 'vaulting ambition' of bringing Shakespeare to the people, Branagh has constructed over the years the ideologically complex persona of a working-class Shakespearean entrepreneur.

Notes

1. Douglas Lanier, *Shakespeare and Modern Popular Culture* (Oxford, Oxford University Press, 2002), 157–60.
2. Sarah Hatchuel, *A Companion to the Shakespearean Films of Kenneth Branagh* (Winnipeg, Blizzard Publishing, 2000), 33–64.
3. Laurent Jullier, *L'écran post-moderne: un cinéma de l'allusion et du feu d'artifice* (Paris, L'Harmattan, 1997), 19.
4. Bernice W. Kliman, 'The unkindest cuts: flashcut excess in Kenneth Branagh's *Hamlet*', in Deborah Cartmell and Michael Scott, eds., *Talking Shakespeare* (Basingstoke, Palgrave, 2001), 151–67.
5. Chris Fitter, 'A tale of two Branaghs: *Henry V*, ideology and the Mekong Agincourt', in Ivo Kamps, ed., *Shakespeare Left and Right* (New York and London, Routledge, 1991), 270.
6. Ian Aitken, 'Formalism and realism: *Henry V* (Laurence Olivier, 1944; Kenneth Branagh, 1989)', *Critical Survey*, 3.3 (1991), 260–8; Curtis Breight, 'Branagh and the prince, or a "royal fellowship of death"', *Critical Quarterly*, 33.4 (1991), 95–111.
7. The reorganisation of scenes through editing can generate extra time, suggesting for instance that Claudius has already spent a certain amount of time in deep thought before starting to pray aloud. See Russell Jackson, 'Kenneth Branagh's film of *Hamlet*: the textual choices', *Shakespeare Bulletin*, 15.2 (Spring 1997), 37–8.
8. Pierre Berthomieu, *Kenneth Branagh: traînes de feu, rosées de sang* (Paris, Jean-Michel Place, 1998), 93.
9. See Anthony Davies, *Filming Shakespeare's Plays* (Cambridge, Cambridge University Press, 1988), 28.
10. Celestino Deleyto, 'Men in leather: Kenneth Branagh's *Much Ado about Nothing* and romantic comedy', *Cinema Journal*, 36.3 (Spring 1997), 91–105.
11. Courtney Lehmann, *Shakespeare Remains: Theater to Film, Early Modern to Postmodern* (Ithaca and London, Cornell University Press), 177.
12. Quoted in Ramona Wray and Mark Thornton Burnett, 'From the horse's mouth: Branagh on the bard', in *Shakespeare, Film, Fin de Siècle* (Basingstoke, Macmillan, 2000), 174.

13. Ramona Wray, 'Nostalgia for Navarre: the melancholic metacinema of Kenneth Branagh's *Love's Labour's Lost*', in James M. Welsh *et al.*, eds., *Shakespeare into Film* (New York, Checkmark Books, 2002), 193–9; Katherine Eggert, 'Sure can sing and dance: minstrelsy, the star system, and the post-postcoloniality of Kenneth Branagh's *Love's Labour's Lost* and Trevor Nunn's *Twelfth Night*', in Richard Burt and Lynda E. Boose, eds., *Shakespeare, The Movie II* (London, Routledge, 2003), 72–88.

14. Pierre Berthomieu, *Hollywood: le temps des mutants* (Aix-en-Provence, Rouge Profond, 2013), 478–82.

15. Jennifer Holl, 'You Shakespeare: Shakespearean celebrity 2.0', in Christy Desmet, Natalie Loper, Jim Casey, eds., *Shakespeare/Not Shakespeare* (London: Springer Nature, 2017), 203–19 (205).

16. Special thanks to Samuel Crowl without whom I could not have seen *All is True* before submitting this chapter.

17. WSJ/Video, 'Cinderella and Shakespeare: crafting fairy Tales' (3 October 2015), www.wsj.com/video/cinderella-and-shakespeare-crafting-fairy-tales/ 6AC0C33D-6070-4C96-A9E7-E621BF54BB6A.html.

18. Mark White, *Kenneth Branagh* (London, Faber and Faber, 2005), 97.

19. Samuel Crowl, 'Flamboyant realist: Kenneth Branagh', in Russell Jackson, ed., *The Cambridge Companion to Shakespeare on Film*, 2nd ed. (Cambridge, Cambridge University Press, 2007), 226–42 (228).

20. Samuel Crowl, *The Films of Kenneth Branagh* (Westport, Praeger, 2006), 2.

18

POONAM TRIVEDI

Remaking Shakespeare in India: Vishal Bhardwaj's Films

Shakespeare's presence in India can be traced back to over 200 years. He is also to be found very early (1923) in Indian cinema which began in 1913. Hundreds of Indian cineastes have since drunk from this well-spring. A recent filmography lists 140 films based on Shakespeare, including many with scenes, citations and afterlives, in as many as thirteen languages and a variety of film genres over nearly 100 years.[1] All these films have deployed Shakespeare in diverse innovative ways. Yet none of these films or their creators, though successful in their own time, has achieved the recognition and international acclaim that has been accorded to Vishal Bhardwaj, the director of a trilogy of films in Hindi: *Maqbool* (*Macbeth* 2004), *Omkara* (*Othello* 2006) and *Haider* (*Hamlet* 2014). Suddenly, Vishal Bhardwaj's Shakespeare films and Bollywood by default have become the subject of intense critical comment and analysis and are recognised as the global face of Indian cinema, so much so that he has been called Hindi cinema's 'Renaissance man',[2] stimulating a new wave of international interest in Bollywood/Indian movies and renewing and spearheading fresh performative engagements with Shakespeare in India.

At first glance, Vishal Bhardwaj seems an unlikely candidate for these Shakespearean adventures: he is not a product of the English Literature schooled generations, being brought up in the small towns of North India. As matter of fact, he came to Shakespeare late, as an adult, admittedly hating him at school – Shakespeare was 'scary'. But a chance encounter through Charles and Mary Lamb's *Tales from Shakespeare* ignited his interest, motivating him to return to re-reading the plays, and discovering the depths of the drama therein: he now confesses to finding a kind of close intimacy, a deep consonance, a 'connection from our previous births' with Shakespeare. 'Now I can happily live my life in Shakespeare', he has admitted recently (*The Indian Express* 'Adda' 5 October 2018) and has announced his intention to film a trilogy on the comedies next. Filming Shakespeare, as all would agree, is an

act of bravado, it rarely makes money at the box-office. Bhardwaj has taken
on the risk three times and executed it with a certain audacity or (the word
which he has notoriously played around with in *Haider*) with a 'chutzpah',
telling Shakespeare's stories intertwined with another plot of his own. He
has done it with a surehanded, perceptive manner taking the liberty to
locate the tragedies in contemporary India, to interpolate and infuse them
with signature Bollywood elements, but with a clear loyalty to the play: 'If
I don't remain true to the spirit of the play, I'd be a fool. That is what has
worked for the past 400 years',[3] re-textualising the plays with a sensitivity
and sophistication that even academic critics have had to admit that the
way Bhardwaj 'connect[s] the live wires of Shakespeare's culture to contemporary Indian culture and practice ... makes the play live in ways that
many American and British adaptations of Shakespeare on film just don't
get' (James Shapiro, *Interview*, *The Review Monk* 17 May 2015).[4] Vishal
Bhardwaj's affinity to Shakespeare was best summed up in a quip by Ian
McKellen, that he should be renamed 'Bardwaj'![5]

Bhardwaj's films simultaneously straddle the global and the local. They
remain close to the original in plot and detail while ringing true to his
relocations. His critical interpolations, filling out the back stories of the
characters, foregrounding the dormant and giving space to the repressed,
especially with regard to the women, do not just re-locate into another
cultural milieu, but re-formulate the dynamics and impact of the genre,
modifying the endings of the tragedies. This has the effect of downplay-
ing the larger than life tragic heroes, but radicalising the women. Though
his films are very much part of Bollywood, with many characterising
elements such as song and dance, family setups, weddings, emphasis on
rituals, etc., they are nevertheless generically reprised and modified like
his Shakespearean source. They are full-scale commercial productions
that attempt to marry the literary in style and design, and by being
embedded in contemporary Indian culture, they make bold comments
on Indian power politics. Music, in songs and as background, plays
a critical role in interpreting the narrative, with the lyrics often laced
with wry humour and irony. And in all three films poetry/verse, in its
many dimensions, surfaces repeatedly. Lines from other Indian poets or
his own filter through, the lyrics of the songs and the dialogues have
a poetic flavour, and the innovative visualisation of Shakespeare's images
reveals a poet's sensibility at work. Not only is Vishal Bhardwaj
a director, but also script-writer, music director, producer and aspiring
poet too; he exerts total control over his output and has appropriately
been called an auteur.

Passion Play: *Maqbool*

As has been noted, 'One of Bhardwaj's greatest strengths is his readiness to rebalance Shakespeare, giving new speeches to the silent and bolstering relationships.'[6] This arises partly from the advantages which accrue to the intercultural Shakespeare film, which, divested of the burden of blank verse, is better able to hone the language and meanings in consonance with the new location. It is also provoked by Bhardwaj's own third gen-erational post-coloniality and non-metropolitan upbringing which has freed him from the lingering 'reverence' for Shakespeare which continues to beset many Indians. Bhardwaj thrives on the liberties he takes: 'I want to produce an original work ... Shakespeare was my assistant, Unpaid assis-tant!' (*The Review Monk* 17 May 2015). In his first film *Maqbool* (2004), a relocation of Scotland's clan factionalism into the Mumbai underworld of 1990s, a period of gang wars, drug dealing and extortion presided over by Abbuji/Duncan and his right-hand man Maqbool/Macbeth, Vishal Bhardwaj retains most of the characters but interpolates to expand and restructure relationships and clarify obscurities of the original. Instead of two sons, Duncan is given a daughter, Sameera, who is in love with Guddu/Fleance, who later becomes the inheritor of the gang. This creates a more immediate moral coherence and structural neatness than Shakespeare's own use of Fleance – possibly as a compliment to King James I, said to be his eighth-generation descendent. The most radical bolstering, however, is to make Nimmi/Lady Macbeth, Duncan's mistress, who is having an affair with Maqbool. Not only does this shift the dynamics of the motivation of the regicide, but when sexual desire is added to ambition, she becomes 'the throne herself'[7] for Macbeth. It also fleshes out the suggestion in the text that Lady Macbeth uses her sexual hold over her husband to subdue his scruples and agree to kill Duncan to fulfil her ambitions too. The film foregrounds this dimension: Nimmi, in a wily manner with smiles and tears, uses every occasion to pursue and seduce Maqbool – she herself is repulsed by Abbuji's old and obese corporeality and disenchanted by his failure to get her into films. She literally forces Maqbool at gunpoint to admit his attraction to her, a liaison visualised in Bollywood-like terms, with the pair high up on a rocky promontory, overlooking the panorama of the sunshot sea spread out before them, interspersed with a voice-over of a bitter-sweet song.

However, if Nimmi destroys, she also redeems Maqbool. Unlike Lady Macbeth, she is also generative and procreative. In what is the most potent interpolation in the film, Nimmi gives birth and her new-born becomes a vital trigger in the movement towards a fully tragic catharsis and ending.

In the play, the image of the babe is a trope which signifies pervasively: its absence is a symbol of the moral sterility of the Macbeths, its nakedness and vulnerability liable to provoke a storm of pity and its prematurity is a forewarning of vengeance towards Macbeth. In Bharadwaj's film, the live presence of a new-born babe harnesses and encapsulates all these several functions. At the end, with Nimmi dead, his gang decimated and the law closing in upon him, Maqbool rushes to the hospital to pick up his new-born son before fleeing the country. On reaching the ward he spies through the glass in the door the baby being lovingly cradled by Sameera and Guddu. Like the naked babe of Macbeth's imagination, 'Pity like a naked new-born babe ... shall blow the horrid deed in every eye / That tears shall drown the wind ... ' (1.7.21, 24–5), Maqbool is overcome with pity at the sight of his vulnerable new born, who has just found its nurturers; his own horrid life of blood shed is blown into his eyes in a moment of anagnorisis; a self-realisation of the futility of his blood-lust overwhelms him. He withdraws, dropping his gun in an act of sur-render, leaving what looks like a tear on the glass. He walks out in a reverie only to be shot down by Boti/Macduff. Since Nimmi's child was premature, it also encapsulates the functions of the babe 'from his mother's womb / untimely ripped' (5.10.15–16) who was predicted to be the one to vanquish Macbeth, here his own child. In the play, Macbeth dies fighting, his head cut off and displayed to the new king. In the film, in a more cathartic, positivist mood, Maqbool's head rolls with his eyes slowly closing. The camera tilts and blue skies and spiritual music cine-matically signal 'the time is free' (5.11.21). The gangster hero-villain is seen from the inside: Shakespearean contradictions are filled out with the 'emotional realism'[8] of Indian cinema. Vishal Bhardwaj's cinematic trans-positions re-interpret. His visualisations of the famed images re-textualise and the scenario re-configures the ending of Shakespearean tragedy.[9]

The other inspired transposition in *Maqbool* is of the witches/weird sisters as a duo of canny but comic cops with a predilection for drawing horoscopes and making predictions. Naturalising Shakespeare's superna-tural for today's audiences is a challenge on stage or on screen. Again Bhardwaj, very surely and successfully, roots this in a gamut of contem-porary terms. Inspectors Pandit and Purohit, are conniving and corrupt, seeming to be hand in glove with the gangsters, but like the witches, 'juggling fiends', they spout an equivocal view of duty and dharma in striving to maintain law and order: '*Shakti ka santulan*'/a balance of power, by letting fire and water confront and confound each other, '*Aag ko paani ka dar bahut bada hai*'. In their canny wisdom they take on shades of the wise fools of Shakespeare, especially when, like the Porter, they are caught urinating into the night rain.

If Shakespeare was commenting on his own cultures of blood-soaked violence, Vishal Bhardwaj does not miss the opportunity to expose the traumas plaguing his own city in *Maqbool*. Mumbai, mentioned several times as the beleaguered beloved '*mehbooba*', was in the 1990s being held to ransom by underworld Dons, like Chota Rajan, Dawood and Haji Mastan, who also interfered in the film industry (as is shown in a few sharp sequences), subventing and supplying film production through their ill-gotten gains. Police and politicians too were in their grip, alternately manipulated and manipulating as shown in the film.

Power Play: *Omkara*

Omkara (2006), Vishal Bhardwaj's second Shakespeare film, is a more polished and assured version which transposes Venice and Cyprus into the mafia-ridden rural hinterlands of Uttar Pradesh controlled by a wily politician, Bhai Saab/the Duke and his henchman fixer, Omi/Othello. Dolly/Desdemona, the college-going daughter of Bhaisaab's reputed law-yer, elopes with Omi on the eve of her wedding and Langda Tyagi/Iago, Omi's comrade in arms, is so alienated at being passed over for a promotion that he vows revenge. While *Maqbool* was promoted very gingerly as 'a loose adaptation of Shakespeare' by Bhardwaj, its critical success abroad emboldened him later to market *Omkara* openly as 'an adaptation of Shakespeare's *Othello*' with the promos positioning the film within an international tradition of adaptations including those by Orson Welles. *Omkara* is closer to the original text than *Maqbool*, with fewer interpolations. Omi, however, is given a family and home: we are taken to his village, to his father's house and meet the grandmother who goes about arranging his wedding, and Indu/Emilia, his 'sister' by con-vention. The effect of this is not a simple domestication but instead a rooting down, a positioning in an everydayness which creates a persuasive authenticity. The family and community ties which enmesh Omi, Iago and Indu ballast and suggest a rationale for Iago's 'motiveless malignity', making Omi's jealousy more understandable and the betrayal by Langda more vicious. Omi is family, 'Bhaiya' (brother) – not just master; Dolly, 'Bhabhi' (sister-in-law) dignified by a familial honorific, making her killing more tragic and wasteful. And Indu's avenging fury towards her husband at the end almost inevitable.

The other well-known Bollywood convention, of interspersing songs, however, is more instrumental in *Omkara*: in Bhardwaj's hands it amplifies, fills-out, interprets and comments on the narrative. *Omkara* has more songs than the other two Shakespeare films and in another, more subtle, multi-layered mode of transposition, it not only acculturates the play's many songs but also brings in others to bear centrally on the adaptation. The title song for instance, 'Omkara, *'Dham, dham dhram dhariya re, sabsee bade lariya re, ... Omkara*/Omkara, the greatest warrior, who subdues all', overlaid on to the first shootout between Omkara and a rival politician's goons, works to underline the 'heroic' in Omi. Since it is based on a triumphal folk song from North India, the *'aalah'* which extolled the valour of legendary warriors of local narratives, the rhythms, beats, lyrics and diction of this song exalt Omkara, investing him with some of General Othello's larger than life status even while the direction underplays him as a cool and nifty young muscleman. Again, the opening song, *'Naina ki mat maaniyo re, naino ki mat suniyo re ... naina thag lenge ... das lenge*/Don't listen to the eyes, don't trust them, they will betray you' which is voiced over the visual flashback narration of Dolly's infatuation with Omi, both simultaneously presents and critiques this unfolding of love, forewarning of the tragedy to come. Based on a Sufi tune, of high notes sinking into low ones, and sung by Rahat Fateh Ali Khan, a renowned Sufi singer from Pakistan, like all Sufi songs, it warns against the deceptive attractions of this world, and extorts the lover to look for the truth behind the image. And though Desdemona says she sees Othello's 'visage in his mind' (3.253) it is a fatal attraction engendered through (as Othello puts it) a 'greedy ear' (1.3.148). In fact, all the songs in *Omkara* are integrated into the narrative, extending it and commenting on it. Even what is usually considered a detachable 'item' number, the courtesan's song and dance (reprised drinking song), here resounds with the central theme – passion: *'Beedi jalaee le jigar se piya, maa badi aag hai*/ Light the fag with my heart, love, it is aflame with passion.'[10]

Music is second nature to Vishal Bhardwaj, 'my soul' as he puts it. And it is the key to his sensibility, reflected in his close responsiveness to the rhythms and cadences of Shakespeare's plays: 'that's why subconsciously I connect so well' with Shakespeare, he says (*The Review Monk* 17 May 2015). Bhardwaj started as a music director, but began directing films so that he could compose his own kind of music and songs, integral to the narrative. Music in *Othello* has both a literal and symbolic role: ceremonious instrumental and vocal music punctuates the play. It is, as what is described by David Lindley, the 'surrounding variety of these musics'[11] in the text, which is picked up by Vishal Bharadwaj and re-written in Indian terms or notes. *Omkara* is his most successful adaptation because here visuals, words and music come together. This elucidation and amplification of the manifold suggestiveness of the text is also to be found in his other films, for example in the witches' incantations, the songs of Ophelia, the gravediggers' songs and the 'Mousetrap'.

Race and colour, the most topical issues in addressing *Othello* today, are seen in terms of caste and class differences and somewhat down-played in *Omkara*. Omi is relatively dark complexioned but only a half-brahmin. Vishal Bhardwaj gives a different spin to the tragic. In the case of Kesu/Cassio – a fair-skinned, English-speaking, college-going young-ster – class differences provoke jealousy. Omi's betrayal, though, is fraternal, instigated by his confidant 'brother in arms' Langda, whose first name happens to be 'Ishwar' (God). Good and evil are mixed up and fate takes its toll.

Passion and Politics: *Haider*

Haider (2014), the final film of the trilogy, is the most ambitious in its adaptation. It not only builds up the back story, but also intertwines it with that of the politically beleaguered state of Kashmir traumatised by terrorism and insurgency. Vishal Bhardwaj neatly dovetails the two: Haider/Hamlet is sent away from Kashmir to study to prevent him from falling into the hands of radicalising militants. He returns to find his doctor father missing, 'disappeared', his home blown up and his mother befriended by his father's brother. Haider takes up the challenge to find his father, the search unravelling the state of surveillance, deten-tion and torture of civilians by the army in the state. His soliloquy in his antic disposition, 'To be or not to be ... ' (3.1.58–92) is projected as a disquisition on the divided fate of all Kashmiris, '*Hum hain ki hum nahi*/do I exist or do I not?' His attempts at revenge for his father's betrayal get him embroiled with insurgents and counter insurgents all of whom are hunted by the army. All the major scenes and episodes of the play are worked in, though, at times it feels as though Kashmir gets the better of *Hamlet*.

Interestingly, we meet King Hamlet in the guise of Hilal Meer, a doctor who thinks nothing of bringing home a wanted terrorist for emergency surgery (this costs him his life and hearth), and whose idealism is mir-rored in the poetry from Faiz that he is wont to sing, '*Gulon mein rang bhare baad-e-nau bahar chale / Chale bhi aao ki gulshan ka karobar chale /* Let the blossoms fill with colour, let the breeze ruffle the spring / Come along, my love, awaken the garden to life.' The ghost too therefore is given a back story: he is a double agent, an alter ego, Rooh Daar (spirit keeper) who was imprisoned with the father but miraculously survives to tell the tale to young Haider. But the character who grows the most with the 'back stories' is the mother, Ghazala/Gertrude. Gertrude in Shakespeare is opaque, we know her only through others, she rarely speaks for herself. In *Haider*, she is given space: we are shown her loneliness, her sense of neglect in the face of her doctor husband's dedication towards his profession, her consequent leaning towards her brother in law, her inadvertent role in the husband's arrest, her fierce protectiveness towards her son, her attempts to save him at the end. So much does Gertrude grow in Bhardwaj's adaptation that she threatens to overshadow Hamlet – part of his mystery and his function of avenger rubs off on her.

For it is through Ghazala that the tragic denouement takes place – she blows herself up to force her son to abjure revenge and surrender – reiterating the message for the moment: 'Revenge does not set us free ... Freedom lies beyond revenge.' Haider walks away leaving a badly mutilated Khurram (Claudius) screaming for the mercy of death. This ending is prefigured in an early scene where Ghazala is first seen conducting a primary school lesson on 'What is a home? ... it is sharing and caring ... ' a pointed reference to the larger question which haunts the entire film: is Kashmir a home, a nurturing space which must be saved at all costs, or like Denmark, a 'rotten state' with a contest for sovereignty entailing surveillance, detention and bloodshed? This disintegrating notion of home – like the blowing up of Ghazala's house and then the gravediggers' hideout at the end – becomes a metonymy of the combustion in Kashmir.

Bollywood has traditionally fought shy of tackling politics and sexuality upfront: Bhardwaj takes on both in *Haider*. A large part of the alienation of Haider is the pull of his attractive and possessive mother, the sexual tension suggestively played out in his gestures like kissing her on the nape of her neck and applying kohl to ward off the evil eye while she is dressing for her wedding to Khurram.

'Is It a Crime to Read Shakespeare in This Country?'

So invested is Bhardwaj in Shakespeare that he has even ventured a parody – of the temptation scene between the Macbeths – in his lesser known film, *Matru ki Bijli Ka Mandola* (*Matru's Friend Bijli Shifts her Affections*, 2013) in a complex intertextual and self-reflexive interpolation. This film is a satirical exposé of land scams and development politics in which a rich businessman, Mandola, seeks to hoodwink villagers into selling off their fertile fields for building glitzy malls. His free-spirited daughter, Bijli, who is engaged to be married to the abetting politician's son, suddenly realises that she loves instead her childhood village friend, Matru. On the eve of the wedding, she is found reading Shakespeare's *Macbeth*; Matru joins her and they read together, realising that 'fair and foul' are truly mixed up for them, and wonder how to get out of this cleft stick. Discovering that they are being spied upon by the bridegroom and his cronies, they decide to scare them and, taking their cues from the Macbeths, they begin to plot and mimic the murder of the groom on the wedding night. Like Lady Macbeth, Bijli takes the lead saying she will first add sleeping pills to the bridegroom's drink, and when he lies unconscious, she will pull out the dagger from under the pillow, cut him to bits, and then shout murder! Matru adds that he will implicate the guards by drugging them and placing the dagger in their hands. Swept along in this fantasy of 'solely sovereign sway and masterdom' (1.6.68) the young lovers dance and dream of sailing away together. Lady Macbeth's temptation of her husband into 'a river of blood' from which there is no return is here inverted into a comic prank which will supposedly save the couple from an unwanted marriage.

Bhardwaj further spins this episode into an auteuristic self-referential stance. Shakespeare's lines are recited in English: his name is pronounced several times; his image, pictured on the cover of the book, is glimpsed twice, along with a full bookshelf alongside the pool where Bijli is sitting. 'Textual Shakespeare' is fore-grounded and the episode declares itself as an act of reading, and re-writing. It concludes on a comic but self-reflexive note: when the surreptitious lovers are caught and confronted by Bijli's furious father who is brandishing a gun, they plead the reading of Shakespeare as a defence for spending time together, with the retort: 'Is it a crime to read Shakespeare in this country?' An apologia and justification are voiced not only on behalf of the errant lovers, but more crucially for the director, Vishal Bhardwaj himself, who is unusual in his predilection towards Shakespeare with three full length films in ten years, more than any other Indian director. His work with Shakespeare has been critiqued as catering to the Anglophone class in India and conducted with an eye to cashing in with the West. But in this relentlessly Bollywood-ish comedy, with the interpolated Shakespearean fragment, Bhardwaj delights in playing around both with the bard and himself.

Yet Vishal Bhardwaj is no mere story teller, he is at heart a poet too, with a recently published book of poems in Urdu with English translations. As he has put it, both music and poetry are in his blood – his father was also a poet and musician who wrote lyrics for films in the 1970s and

1980s. He himself grew up during the age of the *ghazal* (an Urdu poetry form) in the 1980s, when the form underwent a renaissance with many famed singers being accorded the popularity of rock stars. He says he was so intoxicated by Urdu poetry that he made huge efforts to read great poets of the tradition, and then taught himself the grammatical intricacies of the form to be able to compose proper Urdu poetry. For a long time, he was a closet poet being finally pushed into publication by his mentor, Gulzar, an established poet and lyricist in his own right. This slim collection entitled *Nude Poems* (2018)[12] lays bare many dimensions of Bhardwaj's sensibility: as one of his verses/*sher* says 'Indeed, I search for myself in vain / Having lost myself within me' (Ghazal 7, verse 2, page 15). What is immediately striking is how most of the poems effortlessly blend passion and politics: i.e. the central theme of Urdu poetry, the pain of loss and unrequited love, along with observations on the contemporary situations. And his use of English words, alongside the Urdu and Hindi, reflects his belief that poetry should reflect the times. Though he says that he has read very little English poetry, yet resonances and even a direct citation of Shakespeare occur: 'So slowly does time drag / Like a tale told by an idiot' (Ghazal 12, verse 2, page 25). And the first *nazm* (a more informal verse form) 'I' gives voice to Hamlet's ghost, part of which was recited by Rooh Daar, the alter ego persona of Old Hamlet in *Haider*, on being questioned on his religion: 'I was the one, I am the one ... / River am I, also a tree / Sky I am, the earth too / Temple am I, also a harem / Shia I am, Sunni too / In the hands of the pandits / Like a diya for a prayer / On the forehead of a Qazi / A mark of obeisance / On the chest of the pastor / a swinging cross / I was the one, I am the one' (55). This poem, which is fast acquiring a visibility through online sharing, and emerged out of *Hamlet*, is Bhardwaj's indictment of the volatile communal politics troubling Kashmir and other parts of India.

As significant, if not more, than these immediate references to Shakespeare, are the poetic inflexions which inform all aspects of Bhardwaj's adaptations. They are there in his interpretation, his structuring, his dialogues, his visualisation, his songs and music. If looking deep into the life of things, especially the underside and the unstated, handled with a nuanced delicacy is the characteristic of poetry, then many instances of it emerge in the films. To note a few: Nimmi's yearning for legitimacy at the very end, 'our love was pure wasn't it?' in *Maqbool*; Indu's fierce retaliatory action in slashing her husband's neck; Dolly's poignant attempts to learn a Western love song in *Omkara*; Haider's dilemma, not of 'not to be', but of whether to believe his mother or not; Khurram's covert attraction to Ghazala; Arshie/Ophelia's madness symbolised as enmeshed in the unravelled wool of the scarf she lovingly knitted for her father in *Haider*. The films sensitively frame the submerged and subterranean states of the characters. It is this larger poetic humanity and sensibility, along with his intimate grounding in music, which enables Bhardwaj to pick up the ineffable, the associative and the unsaid of Shakespeare's works. His keen ear for rhythms and inflections produces a sharply etched language and diction which rings true to the idiomatic registers of the locations, be it Bambaiya Hindi and refined Urdu in *Maqbool*, rustic street lingo with choice expletives in *Omkara*, or authentic Kashmiri accents in *Haider*, quite unlike the sanitised synthetic language of most Bollywood films. His dialogues often have the pithiness and flair of an Urdu *sher*/couplet (characterised by a layered collocation of meaning and suggestiveness), they are being detached and posted in online blogs and social media as memorable verse. His aesthetics and visualisation too are marked by lyrical but controlled frames. All these go towards creating a particular synthesis of poetry and cinema, where narrative movement is interspersed with in-depth moments, giving extra interpretative layers to the lens.

Vishal Bhardwaj's Shakespeare films may be seen as work in progress: from the hesitant *Maqbool* to the confident *Haider*, his style and sensibility have evolved over ten years. Yet, as he has confessed in the preface to his book of poems, he still feels 'half, half/*aadha*/*aadha*', incomplete within himself, dissatisfied with his output as poet, director and musician, but continues to have a 'lust', a 'dream' to better himself. Like Kurosawa, he has been more appreciated in the West than at home where his films have received a mixed reception. Seen by many as not quite Shakespeare, and by others as not Bollywood enough – 'why couldn't *Omkara* end with the marriage?' was a common response. They have also been critiqued for their pungent diction, seen as too localised for a pan-Indian accessibility, and for a one-sided partial picture of Kashmir, which was also called anti-national and anti-army. Despite the international critical esteem, his films have just managed to recoup their investment: they have not broken the box-office. Critics have noted that his films adapted from literary texts have been more successful than his other films (he has adapted two stories of Ruskin Bond). We can hope that Bhardwaj will trust his own literary-poetic-musical instincts and continue to create meaningful interventions with Shakespeare. As he recently announced, 'Shakespeare is my trump card, whenever I am drowning ... I will bring up my trump card'.[13] He has said that he will next make a trilogy on the comedies – these are eagerly awaited.

Notes

1. See Poonam Trivedi and Paromita Chakravarti, eds., *Shakespeare and Indian Cinemas: 'Local Habitations'* (New York, Routledge, 2019).

2. Amy Rodgers, 'Vishal Bhardwaj', *Shakespeare Bulletin* 34.3 (2016), 500.

3. Vishal Bhardwaj, Interview with Raja Sen, 'Today Othello, tomorrow Hamlet', 27 July 2006, Rediff.com www.rediff.com/movies/2006/jul/27vishal.htm (accessed 26 April 2019).

4. 'Decoding Shakespeare', interview Vishal Bhardwaj with James Shapiro at New York International Film Festival, 17 May 2015, *The Review Monk*, https://thereviewmonk.com/ (accessed September 2018).

5. Zenia D'Cunha, 'Can't imagine my life without Shakespeare: Sir Ian McKellen in conversation with Firstpost', 23 May 2016, www.firstpost.com/entertainment/cant-imagine-my-life-without-shakespeare-sir-ian-mckellen-in-conversation-with-firstpost-2795078.html (accessed December 2018).

6. Antony Howard, 'Hamlet in Kashmir', 17 February 2015, The bba Shakespeare blog, https://blogs.warwick.ac.uk/bbashakespeare/entry/hamlet_in_kashmir/ (accessed March 2017).

7. Vishal Bhardwaj, 'Preface', *Maqbool: The Original Screenplay with English Translation* (Noida, Harper Collins, 2014), vi.

8. Sudhir Kakar, *Intimate Relations: Exploring Indian Sexuality* (New Delhi, Penguin, 1990), 30.

9. See Poonam Trivedi, '"Woman as avenger": Indianising the Shakespearean tragic in the Films of Vishal Bhardwaj', in *Shakespeare and Indian Cinemas: 'Local Habitations'*, for a longer discussion.

10. See Poonam Trivedi, 'Singing to Shakespeare in Omkara', *Renaissance Shakespeare: Shakespeare Renaissances*, Proceedings of the Ninth World Shakespeare Congress (Newark, University of Delaware Press, 2014) for a longer discussion.

11. David Linley, *Shakespeare and Music* (London, Arden Shakespeare, 2006), 153.

12. Vishal Bhardwaj, *Nude Poems*, translated by Sukrita Paul Kumar (Noida, Harper Collins, 2018).

13. Vishal Bhardwaj, in conversation with Jonathan Gil Harris, 'The Hindu lit for life', session on *Nude Poems*, 27 February 2018, www.youtube.com/watch?v=VwiilgN_oac (accessed December 2018).

FURTHER READING

Introduction

Some General Works

Boose, Lynda E. and Richard Burt, eds., *Shakespeare the Movie: Popularizing the Plays on Film, TV and Video* (London, Routledge, 1997).
Buchanan, Judith, *Shakespeare on Silent Film. An Excellent Dumb Discourse* (Cambridge, Cambridge University Press, 2009).
Burnett, Mark Thornton and Ramona Wray, eds., *Shakespeare, Film, Fin de Siècle* (Basingstoke and New York, Macmillan and St. Martin's, 2000).
Shakespeare and World Cinema (Cambridge, Cambridge University Press, 2013).
Burt, Richard, ed., *Shakespeare after Shakespeare: An Encyclopedia of the Bard in Mass Media and Popular Culture* (Westport, Greenwood, 2007).
Burt, Richard and Lynda E. Boose, eds., *Shakespeare the Movie II* (New York, Routledge, 2003).
Crowl, Samuel, *Shakespeare at the Cineplex. The Kenneth Branagh Era* (Athens, University of Ohio Press, 2003).
Davies, Anthony, *Filming Shakespeare's Plays. The Adaptations of Laurence Olivier, Orson Welles, Peter Brook and Akira Kurosawa* (Cambridge, Cambridge University Press, 1988).
Davies, Anthony and Stanley Wells, eds., *Shakespeare and the Moving Image. The Plays on Film and Television* (Cambridge, Cambridge University Press, 1994).
Donaldson, Peter S., *Shakespearean Films/Shakespearean Directors* (1990; London: Routledge, 2013).
Henderson, Diana E., ed., *A Concise Companion to Shakespeare on Screen* (Malden, Blackwell, 2006).
Jackson, Russell, *Shakespeare and the English Speaking Cinema* (Oxford, Oxford University Press, 2014).
Jorgens, Jack J., *Shakespeare on Film* (Bloomington, Indiana University Press, 1977).
Lanier, Douglas, *Shakespeare and Modern Popular Culture* (Oxford, Oxford University Press, 2002).
Levenson, Jill L. and Robert Ormsby, eds., *The Shakespearean World* (London and New York, Routledge, 2017).

Rothwell, Kenneth S., *Shakespeare on Screen, A Century of Film and Television* (Cambridge, Cambridge University Press, 1999).
Shaughnessy, Robert, ed., *The Cambridge Companion to Shakespeare and Popular Culture* (Cambridge, Cambridge University Press, 2007).
Welsh, James M., Richard Vela and John C. Tibbetts, eds., *Shakespeare into Film* (New York, Checkmark Books, 2002).
Willis, Susan, *The BBC Shakespeare Plays, Making the Television Canon* (Chapel Hill, University of North Carolina Press, 1991).

1 Shakespeare and the Film Industry of the Pre-Sound Era

JUDITH BUCHANAN

Further Reading

Ball, Robert Hamilton, *Shakespeare on Silent Film: A Strange Eventful History* (New York, Theatre Arts Books, 1968).
Buchanan, Judith, *Shakespeare on Film* (Harlow, Pearson, 2005).
  Shakespeare on Silent Film: An Excellent Dumb Discourse (Cambridge, Cambridge University Press, 2009).
  '"Now, where were we?", ideal and actual lecturing practices in early cinema', in A. Davison and J. Brown, eds., *The Sounds of Early Cinema in Britain* (Oxford, Oxford University Press, 2012), 38–54.
  'Literary adaptation in the silent era', in Devorah Cartmell, ed., *Blackwell Companion to Literature, Film and Adaptation* (Oxford, Wiley-Blackwell, 2012), 17–32.
  'Collaborating with the dead, playing the Shakespeare archive, *or* how to avoid being pushed from our stools', in B. Cronin and N. Preuschoff, eds., *Adaptation as a Collaborative Art, Process and Practice* (Basingstoke, Palgrave Macmillan, 2019).
Burrows, John, *Legitimate Cinema: Theatre Stars in Silent British Films 1908–1918* (Exeter, Exeter University Press, 2003).
Guneratne, A. R., *Shakespeare, Film Studies, and the Visual Cultures of Modernity* (Basingstoke, Palgrave Macmillan, 2008).
Howard, Antony, *Women as Hamlet: Performance and Interpretation in Theatre, Film and Fiction* (Cambridge, Cambridge University Press, 2007).
Jackson, Russell, 'Staging and storytelling, theatre and film: *Richard III* at Stratford, 1910', *New Theatre Quarterly* 62 (May 2000), 107–21.
Keil, Charlie, *Early American Cinema in Transition: Story, Style and Filmmaking, 1907–1913* (Wisconsin, University of Wisconsin Press, 2001).
McKernan, Luke and Olwen Terris, eds., *Walking Shadows: Shakespeare in the National Film and Television Archive* (London, British Film Institute, 1994).
McKernan, Luke, 'A scene – *King John* – now playing at Her Majesty's Theatre', in L. Fitzsimmons and S. Street, eds., *Moving Performance: British Stage and Screen, 1890s–1920s* (Trowbridge, Flicks Books, 2000), 56–68.
Pearson, Roberta E. and William Uricchio, *Reframing Culture: the Case of the Vitagraph Quality Films* (Princeton, Princeton University Press, 1993).

Thompson, Ann, 'Asta Nielsen and the mystery of *Hamlet*', in Lynda E. Boose and Richard Burt, eds., *Shakespeare the Movie. Popularizing the Plays on Film, TV and Video* (London, Routledge, 1997), 215–24.

Commercially/Publicly Available Silent Shakespeare Films

a *Play On! Shakespeare in Silent Film* (BFI DVD)
Seven of the films on this BFI DVD feature a Laura Rossi score. All ten include a commentary by Judith Buchanan.

  i *King John* (BMBC: dir. W-K.L.Dickson, 1899), starring Tree.
  ii *The Tempest* (Clarendon: dir. Percy Stow, 1908), cast unknown.
  iii *A Midsummer Night's Dream* (Vitagraph: dirs. J. Stuart Blackton and Charles Kent, 1909), starring Billy Ranous, Maurice Costello, Julia Swayne Gordon and Florence Turner.
  iv *King Lear* (FAI: Gerolamo Lo Savio, 1910), starring Novelli and Bertini.
  v *King Lear* (Vitagraph: 1910), starring Billy Ranous – no musical accompaniment included.
  vi *Twelfth Night* (Vitagraph: dir. Charles Kent, 1910), starring Turner, Kent, Swayne Gordon.
  vii *The Merchant of Venice* (FAI: dir. Gerolamo Lo Savio, 1910), starring Novelli and Bertini.
  viii *Richard III* (Co-operative Film Company: dir. F. R. Benson, 1910), starring Benson and Constance Benson.
  ix *The Winter's Tale* (Milano: 1913) – no musical accompaniment included.
  x *Romeo and Juliet* (Living Pictures for Pathé: 1924) starring Gwen Ffrangcon-Davies and John Gielgud – no musical accompaniment included.

The DVD also includes an extended montage of clips from other silent Shakespeare films held by the British Film Institute.

b *Othello* (Kino): Includes Five Silent Shakespeare Films

  i *Othello* (Wörner-Filmgesellschaft: dir. Dimitri Buchowetzki, 1922), with Jannings and Krauss.
  ii Duel Scene from *Macbeth* (AMBC, 1905).
  iii *The Taming of the Shrew* (Biograph: dir. D. W. Griffith, 1908), starring Florence Lawrence and Arthur V. Johnson.
  iv *Romeo Turns Bandit/Roméo se fait bandit* (Pathé: dir. Bosetti, 1910), with Max Linder.

v *Desdemona* (Nordisk: dir. August Blom, 1911), starring Valdemar Psilander and Thyra Reimann.

c The Thanhouser Collection, Vol. 7 (Thanhouser Company Film Preservation Inc.). Includes Three Silent Shakespeare Films

i *The Winter's Tale* (Thanhouser: dir. Barry O'Neil, 1910), starring Martin Faust.

ii *Cymbeline* (Thanhouser: dir. Frederick Sullivan, 1913), starring Florence LaBadie.

iii *King Lear* (Thanhouser: dir. Ernest Warde, 1916), starring Frederick Warde.

These are also freely available on the Thanhouser website. *The Winter's Tale* includes a commentary by Judith Buchanan.

d *Richard III* (Kino): Includes One Silent Shakespeare Film with an Ennio Morricone Score

i *Richard III* (Shakespeare Film Company: dir. James Keane, 1912), starring Frederick Warde.

2 Adaptation and the Marketing of Shakespeare in Classical Hollywood

DEBORAH CARTMELL

Barnes, Jennifer, *Shakespearean Star: Laurence Olivier and National Cinema* (Cambridge, Cambridge University Press, 2017).

Bazin, André, 'Adaptation, or the cinema as digest' (1948), in James Naremore, ed., *Film Adaptation* (London, Athlone, 2000), 19–17.

Bortolotti, Garry R. and Linda Hutcheon, 'On the origin of adaptations: rethinking fidelity discourse and "success"—biologically', *New Literary History*, 38.3 (2007), 443–58.

Buhler, Stephen M., 'Ocular proof, three versions of *Othello*', *Shakespeare in the Cinema Ocular, Proof* (New York, SUNY Press, 2001), 11–33.

Cartmell, Deborah. *Adaptations in the Sound Era, 1929–37* (New York, Bloomsbury, 2015).

French, Emma, *Selling Shakespeare to Hollywood: The Marketing of Filmed Shakespeare Adaptations from 1989 into the New Millennium* (Hatfield, University of Hertfordshire Press, 2006).

Geist, Kenneth L., *Pictures will Talk: The Life and Films of Joseph L. Mankiewicz* (New York, Da Capo, 1978).

Geraghty, Christine, *Now a Major Motion Picture: Film Adaptations of Literature and Drama* (Lanham, Rowman & Littlefield, 2007).

Jackson, Russell, *Shakespeare Films in the Making: Vision, Production and Reception* (Cambridge, Cambridge University Press, 2007).

Keyishian, Harry, 'Shakespeare and the movie genre, the case of *Hamlet*', in Russell Jackson, ed., *The Cambridge Companion to Shakespeare on Film*, 2nd ed. (Cambridge, Cambridge University Press, 2007), 72–86.

Nicoll, Allardyce, *Theatre and Film* (London, George G. Harrap, 1936).

Pearlman, E., '*Macbeth* on film, politics', in Anthony Davies and Stanley Wells, eds., *Shakespeare and the Moving Image: the Plays on Film and Television*, (Cambridge, Cambridge University Press, 1994), 250–60.

Rothwell, Kenneth S., *Shakespeare on Screen. A Century of Film and Television* 2nd. edition (Cambridge, Cambridge University Press, 2004).

Stam, Robert, 'Introduction, the theory and practice of adaptation', in Robert Stam and Alessandra Raengo, eds., *Literature and Film: A Guide to the Theory and Practice of Film Adaptation* (Oxford and Malden, Blackwell, 2003), 1–52.

Turner, E. S., *The Shocking History of Advertising* (Harmondsworth, Penguin, 1952).

Willson, Robert F. Jr., *Shakespeare in Hollywood, 1929–1956* (Madison, Fairleigh Dickinson University Press, 2000).

3 Shakespeare 'Live'

PETER HOLLAND

Aebischer, Pascale, Susanne Greenhalgh and Laurie E. Osborne, eds., *Shakespeare and the 'Live' Theatre Broadcast Experience* (London, Arden Shakespeare, 2018).

Barker, Martin, *Live to Your Local Cinema: The Remarkable Rise of Livecasting* (Basingstoke, Palgrave Macmillan, 2013).

Buchanan, Judith, '"Look here, upon this picture": Theatrofilm, the Wooster Group *Hamlet* and the film industry', in Gordon McMullan and Zoe Watts, eds., *Shakespeare in Ten Acts* (London, British Library, 2016), 197–214.

Doran, Gregory, 'Director's commentary', on *King Lear* (DVD, London, RSCLive, 2017).

Doran, Gregory and John Wyver, 'Director's commentary', on *Richard II* (London, DVD, RSCand Opus Arte, 2014).

Findlay, Polly, 'Director's commentary' on *The Merchant of Venice* (DVD, RSCLive, 2015).

Friedman, Michael D., 'The Shakespeare cinemacast: *Coriolanus*', *Shakespeare Quarterly*, 67.4 (2016), 457–80.

Greenhalgh, Susanne *et al.*, 'Live cinema relays of Shakespearean performance', *Shakespeare Bulletin*, 32.2 (2014), 255–78.

Holland, Peter, '*Richard II* on screens', in Joseph A. Candido, ed., *The Text, the Play, and the Globe* (Madison, NJ, Fairleigh Dickinson University Press, 2016), 155–72.

Holland, Peter, 'Filming theatre, a tale of two *Merchants*', in Kenneth Graham and Alysia Kolentsis, eds., *Shakespeare On Stage and Off* (Montreal, McGill University Press, 2019), 171–85.

Kauffmann, Stanley, 'Notes on theater-and-film', *Performance* 1.4 (1972), 104–9.

Osborne, Laurie E., 'Speculations on Shakespearean cinematic liveness', *Shakespeare Bulletin*, 24.3 (2006), 49–65.

Stone, Alison, 'Not making a movie: the livecasting of Shakespeare stage productions by the Royal National Theatre and the Royal Shakespeare Company', *Shakespeare Bulletin*, 34.3 (2016), 627–43.

Sullivan, Erin, '"The forms of things unknown": Shakespeare and the rise of the live broadcast'. *Shakespeare Bulletin*, 35.4 (2017), 627–62.

Wyver, John, *Screening the Royal Shakespeare Company: A Critical History* (London, Bloomsbury/Arden Shakespeare, 2019).

4   Shakespearean Cinemas/Global Directions

MARK THORNTON BURNETT

Andrew, Dudley, 'Islands in the sea of cinema', in Kevin Rockett and John Hill, eds., *National Cinemas and World Cinema* (Dublin, Four Courts, 2006), 15–28.

Burnett, Mark Thornton, Hamlet *and World Cinema* (Cambridge, Cambridge University Press, 2019).

Collick, John, *Shakespeare, Cinema and Society* (Manchester and New York, Manchester University Press, 1989).

Dickson, Andrew, *Worlds Elsewhere*: *Journeys Around Shakespeare's Globe* (London, Bodley Head, 2015).

Dionne, Craig and Parmita Kapadia, eds., *Native Shakespeares*: *Indigenous Appropriations on a Global Stage* (Aldershot, Ashgate, 2008).

Graft, Joe de, 'Interview', in Bernth Lindfors, ed., *Africa Talks Back*: *Interviews with Anglophone African Writers* (Trenton and Asmara, Africa World Press, 2002), 69–88.

Joubin, Alexa Alice, *Chinese Shakespeares*: *Two Centuries of Cultural Exchange* (New York, Columbia University Press, 2009).

Lo, Jacqueline, *Staging Nation. English Language Theatre in Malaysia and Singapore* (Hong Kong, Hong Kong University Press, 2004).

Massai, Sonia, *World-Wide Shakespeare*: *Local Appropriations in Film and Performance* (London and New York, Routledge, 2005).

Pidduck, Julianne, *Contemporary Costume Film* (London, BFI, 2004).

Trivedi, Poonam and Paromita Chavravarti, eds., *Shakespeare and Indian Cinemas*: *'Local Habitations'* (London and New York, Routledge, 2018).

5   The Comedies

RAMONA WRAY

Burnett, Mark Thornton, '"We are the makers of manners", The Branagh Phenomenon', in Richard Burt, ed., *Shakespeare after Mass Media* (New York, Palgrave, 2002), 83–106.

Crowl, Samuel, *Shakespeare at the Cineplex*: *The Kenneth Branagh Era* (Athens, Ohio University Press, 2003).

Jackson, Russell, 'Shakespeare's comedies on film', in Anthony Davies and Stanley Wells, eds., *Shakespeare and the Moving Image*: *The Plays on Film and Television* (Cambridge, Cambridge University Press, 1994), 99–120.

Hopkins, Lisa, 'Comedies of the green world, *A Midsummer Night's Dream*, *As You Like It*, and *Twelfth Night*', in Heather Hirschfeld, ed., *The Oxford Handbook of Shakespearean Comedy* (Oxford, Oxford University Press, 2018), 520–36.

Howard, Jean E., *The Stage and Social Struggle in Early Modern England* (London and New York, Routledge, 1994).

Hulbert, Jennifer, Kevin J. Wetmore Jr. and Robert L. York, *Shakespeare and Youth Culture* (New York, Palgrave, 2006).

Lanier, Douglas M., 'Shakespearean comedy on screen', in Heather Hirschfeld, ed., *The Oxford Handbook of Shakespearean Comedy* (Oxford, Oxford University Press, 2018), 470–86.

Laroque, François, 'Shakespeare's festive comedies', in Richard Dutton and Jean E. Howard, eds., *A Companion to Shakespeare's Works: The Comedies* (Oxford, Blackwell, 2003), 23–46.

Rackin, Phyllis, 'Shakespeare's cross-dressing comedies', in Richard Dutton and Jean E. Howard, eds., *A Companion to Shakespeare's Works: The Comedies* (Oxford, Blackwell, 2003), 114–36.

Waller, Gary, 'Much joy, some terror: reading Shakespeare's comedies today', in Gary Waller, ed., *Shakespeare's Comedies* (London and New York, Longman, 1991), 1–28.

6   The Environments of Tragedy on Screen: *Hamlet, King Lear, Macbeth*

PETER KIRWAN

Burnett, Mark Thornton, 'Figuring the global/historical in filmic Shakespearean tragedy', in Diana E. Henderson, ed., *A Concise Companion to Shakespeare on Screen* (Malden, Blackwell, 2006), 133–54.

Calibi, Maurizio, *Spectral Shakespeares: Media Adaptations in the Twenty-First Century* (New York, Palgrave Macmillan, 2013).

Crowl, Samuel, *Screen Adaptations: Shakespeare's* Hamlet (London, Bloomsbury, 2014).

Davies, Anthony, *Filming Shakespeare's Plays: The Adaptations of Laurence Olivier, Orson Welles, Peter Brook, Akira Kurosawa* (Cambridge, Cambridge University Press, 1988).

Griggs, Yvonne, *Screen Adaptations: Shakespeare's* King Lear (London, Methuen, 2009).

Hatchuel, Sarah, Nathalie Vienne-Guerrin and Victoria Bladen, eds., *Shakespeare on Screen:* Macbeth (Mont-Saint-Aignan, PURH, 2013).

Hatchuel, Sarah, Nathalie Vienne-Guerrin and Victoria Bladen, eds., *Shakespeare on Screen:* Othello (Cambridge, Cambridge University Press, 2019).

Howard, Tony, *Women as Hamlet* (Cambridge, Cambridge University Press, 2009).

Huang, Alexa, 'Shakespeare on film in Asia', in Jill L. Levenson and Robert Ormsby, eds., *The Shakespearean World* (London and New York, Routledge, 2017), 225–40.

Jackson, Russell, *Shakespeare and the English-Speaking Cinema* (Oxford, Oxford University Press, 2014).

Lehmann, Courtney, 'Out damned Scot: dislocating *Macbeth* in transnational film and media culture', in Richard Burt and Lynda E. Boose, eds., *Shakespeare the Movie II* (New York, Routledge, 2003), 231–51.

Lehmann, Courtney, 'Grigori Kozintsev', in Mark Thornton Burnett, ed., *Great Shakespeareans: Welles, Kurosawa, Kozintsev, Zeffirelli* (London, Bloomsbury, 2013), 92–140.

Miller, Gemma, '"He has no children": changing representations of the child in stage and film productions of *Macbeth* from Polanski to Kurzel', *Shakespeare*, 13.1 (2017), 52–66.

Rowe, Katherine, '"Remember me": technologies of memory in Michael Almereyda's *Hamlet*', in Richard Burt and Lynda E. Boose, eds., *Shakespeare the Movie II* (New York, Routledge, 2003), 37–55.

Wray, Ramona, 'The butcher and the text: adaptation, theatricality and the Shakespea(re)-told *Macbeth*', in Ann Thompson, ed., Macbeth: *The Stage of Play* (London: Bloomsbury, 2014), 261–81.

7   Two Tragedies of Love: *Romeo and Juliet* and *Othello*

VICTORIA BLADEN

Burnett, Mark Thornton, *Shakespeare and World Cinema* (Cambridge, Cambridge University Press, 2013).

Casey, Jim, 'Hyperomeo and Juliet: postmodern adaptation and Shakespeare', in Christy Desmet, Natalie Loper and Jim Casey, eds., *Shakespeare/Not Shakespeare* (London, Springer Nature, 2017).

Darragi, Rafik, 'The perfect, impossible love: three Egyptian film adaptations of *Romeo and Juliet*', *Critical Survey*, 28.3 (2016), 175–80.

Davies, Anthony, '"An extravagant and wheeling stranger of here and everywhere". Characterising *Othello* on film: exploring seven film adaptations', *Shakespeare in Southern Africa*, 23 (2011), 11–19.

Donaldson, Peter S., '"In fair Verona": media, spectacle and performance in *William Shakespeare's Romeo + Juliet*', in Richard Burt, ed., *Shakespeare After Mass Media* (Basingstoke, Palgrave, 2002), 59–82.

García-Periago, Rosa M., 'In search of a happy ending: the afterlife of *Romeo and Juliet* on the Asian screen', *Journal of the Spanish Association of Anglo-American Studies*, 38.1 (June 2016), 185–200.

Hatchuel, Sarah and Nathalie Vienne-Guerrin, eds., *Shakespeare on Screen:* Othello (Cambridge, Cambridge University Press, 2015).

Jackson, Russell, *Shakespeare Films in the Making* (Cambridge, Cambridge University Press, 2007).

Lehmann, Courtney, Romeo and Juliet: *The Relationship between Text and Film* (London, Methuen, 2010).

Thompson, Glen, '*Otelo Burning* and Zulu surfing histories', *Journal of African Cultural Studies*, 26.3 (2014), 324–40.

Trivedi, Poonam and Paromta Chakravarti, eds., *Shakespeare and Indian Cinemas: 'Local Habitations'* (New York, Routledge, 2019).

Yoshihara, Yukar, 'Tacky "Shakespeares" in Japan', *Multicultural Shakespeare: Translation, Appropriation and Performance, The Journal of the University of Lodz*, 10.25 (2013), 83–97.

8   'Sad Stories of the Death of Kings': *The Hollow Crown*
and the Shakespearean History Play on Screen

KINGA FÖLDVÁRY

Andrews, C. '*Richard III* on film: the subversion of the viewer', *Literature/Film Quarterly*, 28.2 (2000), 82–94.
Cartelli, T. 'Shakespeare and the street: Pacino's *Looking for Richard*, Bedford's *Street King*, and the common understanding', in Richard Burt and Lynda E. Boose, eds., *Shakespeare The Movie II: Popularizing the Plays on Film, TV, Video, and DVD* (London and New York, Routledge, 2003), 186–99.
Cook, Hardy M., 'Jane Howell's BBC first tetralogy: theatrical and televisual manipulation', *Literature/Film Quarterly*, 20.4 (1992), 326–31.
Coursen, H. R. 'Filming Shakespeare's history: three films of *Richard III*', in Russell Jackson, ed., *The Cambridge Companion to Shakespeare on Film* (Cambridge, Cambridge University Press, 2007), 102–19.
Donaldson, Peter S., 'Cinema and the kingdom of death: Loncraine's *Richard III*', *Shakespeare Quarterly*, 53.2 (2002), 241–59.
Hatchuel, Sarah and Nathalie Vienne-Guerrin, eds., *Shakespeare on Screen*: Richard III (Rouen, Publications des Universités de Rouen et du Havre, 2005).
Hatchuel, Sarah and Nathalie Vienne-Guerrin, eds., *Shakespeare on Screen: The Henriad* (Rouen, Publications Publications des Universités de Rouen et du Havre, 2008).
Lennox, Patricia, '*An Age of Kings* and the "normal American"', *Shakespeare Survey*, 61 (Cambridge: Cambridge University Press, 2008), 181–98.
Loehlin, James. N., '"Top of the world, ma": *Richard III* and cinematic convention', in Richard Burt and Lynda. E. Boose, eds., *Shakespeare The Movie II: Popularizing the Plays on Film, TV, Video, and DVD* (London and New York, Routledge, 2003), 173–85.
Manheim, M. 'The English history play on screen', in Anthony Davies and Stanley Wells, eds., *Shakespeare and the Moving Image: The Plays on Film and Television* (Cambridge, Cambridge University Press, 1994), 121–45.
Pilkington, Ace G., *Screening Shakespeare from* Richard II *to* Henry V (Newark, University of Delaware Press, 1991).
Royal, D. P., 'Shakespeare's kingly mirror: figuring the chorus in Olivier's and Branagh's *Henry V*', *Literature/Film Quarterly*, 25.2 (1997), 104–10.
Smith, Emma, 'Shakespeare serialized: *An Age of Kings*', in Robert Shaughnessy, ed., *The Cambridge Companion to Shakespeare and Popular Culture* (Cambridge, Cambridge University Press, 2007), 134–49.
Smith, Peter J., '"To beguile the time, look like the time": contemporary film versions of Shakespeare's histories', in Richard Dutton and Jean E. Howard, eds., *A Companion to Shakespeare's Works*, Vol. 2, *The Histories* (Oxford, Blackwell, 2003), 146–69.
Wiseman, S., 'The family tree motel: subliming Shakespeare in *My Own Private Idaho*', in Richard Burt and Lynda E. Boose, eds., *Shakespeare The Movie II: Popularizing the Plays on Film, TV, Video, and DVD* (London and New York, Routledge, 2003), 200–12.

9 The Roman Plays on Film

PETER J. SMITH

Berkoff, Steven, Coriolanus *in Deutschland* (Oxford, Amber Lane Press, 1992).

Blumenthal, Eileen, *Julie Taymor: Playing with Fire: Theatre, Opera, Film* (New York, Harry N. Abrams, 1999).

Cartmell, Deborah, *Interpreting Shakespeare on Screen* (Basingstoke, Macmillan, 2000).

Davies, Anthony and Stanley Wells, eds., *Shakespeare and the Moving Image: The Plays on Film and Television* (Cambridge, Cambridge University Press, 1994).

Hartley, Andrew James, *Shakespeare in Performance*: Julius Caesar (Manchester, Manchester University Press, 2014).

Hatchuel, Sarah, *Shakespeare, from Stage to Screen* (Cambridge, Cambridge University Press, 2004).

Hatchuel, Sarah and Nathalie Vienne-Guerrin, eds., *Shakespeare on Screen: The Roman Plays* (Mont-Saint-Aignan, Publications des Universités de Rouen et du Havre, 2009).

Hodgdon, Barbara and W. B. Worthen, eds., *A Companion to Shakespeare and Performance* (Oxford, Blackwell, 2005).

Logan, John, Coriolanus, *Screenplay* (New York, New Market Press, 2011).

Miller, Anthony, '*Julius Caesar* in the Cold War: the Houseman-Mankiewicz film', *Literature/Film Quarterly*, 28 (2000), 95–100.

Ormsby, Robert, *Shakespeare in Performance:* Coriolanus (Manchester, Manchester University Press, 2014).

Rothwell, Kenneth S. and Annabelle Henkin Melzer, *Shakespeare on Screen* (New York and London, Neal-Schuman Publishers, 1990).

Taymor, Julie, *Titus, the Illustrated Screenplay* (New York, Newmarket Press, 2000).

Willis, Susan, *The BBC Shakespeare Plays: Making the Televised Canon* (Chapel Hill, University of North Carolina Press, 2002).

10 Screening Shakespearean Fantasy and Romance in *A Midsummer Night's Dream* and The Tempest

ANTHONY GUY PATRICIA

Babbington, Bruce, 'Shakespeare meets the Warner Brothers: Reinhardt and Dieterle's *A Midsummer Night's Dream*', in John Batchelor, Tom Cain and Claire Lamont, eds., *Shakespearean Continuities, Essays in Honour of E. A. J. Honigmann* (New York, Macmillan, 1997), 259–74.

Burnett, Mark Thornton, 'Impressions of fantasy: Adrian Noble's *A Midsummer Night's Dream*', in Mark Thornton Burnett and Ramona Wray, eds., *Shakespeare, Film, and Fin de Siècle* (Basingstoke and New York, Macmillan and St. Martin's, 2000), 89–101.

Coplica, Gabriela Iuliana and Ligia Pîrvu, 'Screening a *Dream*', in Odette Blumenfeld and Veronica Popescu, eds., *Shakespeare in Europe: Nation(s) and Boundaries* (Iasi, Editura Universitatii Alexandru Ioan Cuza, 2011), 223–47.

Ellis, Jim, 'Conjuring *The Tempest*: Derek Jarman and the spectacle of redemption', *GLQ, A Journal of Lesbian and Gay Studies*, 7 (2001), 265–84.

Ford, John R, '"A marvail's convenient place": Trading spaces in *A Midsummer Night's Dream*', *Publications of the Mississippi Philological Association* (2005), 60–5.

Forsyth, Neil, *Shakespeare the Illusionist, Magic Dreams, and the Supernatural on Film* (Athens, Ohio University Press, 2019).

Hatchuel, Sarah and Nathalie Vienne-Guerrin, eds., *Shakespeare on Screen*: A Midsummer Night's Dream (Rouen, Publications de l'Université de Rouen, 2004).

Holderness, Graham, '*A Midsummer Night's Dream*, film and fantasy', in Linda Cookson and Bryan Laughrey, eds., *A Midsummer Night's Dream* (Harlow, Longman, 1991), 63–71.

Holland, Peter, 'Magical realism, raising storms and other quaint devices', in Silvia Bigliazzi and Lisanna Calvi, eds., *Revisiting* The Tempest: *the Capacity to Signify* (Basingstoke and New York, Palgrave Macmillan, 2014), 185–201.

Hopkins, Lisa, *Shakespeare's* The Tempest: *The Relationship Between Text and Film* (London, Methuen Drama, 2008).

Jackson, Russell, *Shakespeare Films in the Making*: Vision, Production, and Reception (Cambridge, Cambridge University Press, 2007).

Lefait, Sébastien, 'Prospera's looks: adapting Shakespearean reflexivity in *The Tempest* (Julie Taymor, 2010)', *Literature/Film Quarterly*, 43.2 (2015), 131–45.

Mori, Yukiko, 'The females and the non-humans in Julie Taymor's *The Tempest*', *Gender Studies*, 14.1 (2015), 1–11.

Sibley-Esposito, Clare, 'Becoming-Ariel: viewing Julie Taymor's *The Tempest* through an ecocritical lens', *Babel, littératures plurielles*, 24 (2011), 121–34.

11 Questions of Race: *The Merchant of Venice* and Othello

RUSSELL JACKSON

Bulman, James C., *Shakespeare in Performance*: The Merchant of Venice (Manchester, Manchester University Press, 1991).

Donaldson, Peter S., '"Haply for I am black": Liz White's *Othello*', in *Shakespearean Films/Shakespearean Directors* (Boston, Unwin Hyman, 1990), 127–44.

Edelman, Charles, ed., *Shakespeare in Production*: The Merchant of Venice (Cambridge, Cambridge University Press, 2002).

Hatchuel, Sarah and Nathalie Vienne-Guerrin, eds., *Shakespeare on Screen*: Othello (Cambridge, Cambridge University Press, 2015).

Hodgdon, Barbara, 'Race-ing *Othello*, re-engendering white-out, II', in Richard Burt and Lynda E. Boose, eds., *Shakespeare the Movie, II: Popularizing the Plays on Film, TV, Video, and DVD* (London and New York, Routledge, 2003), 89–104.

Jackson, Russell, *Shakespeare in the Theatre*: Trevor Nunn (London, Bloomsbury/ Arden Shakespeare, 2019).

Romain, Michael, 'Work in progress: a Dialogue with Jonathan Miller', in *A Profile of Jonathan Miller* (Cambridge, Cambridge University Press, 1992), 21–94.

Thompson, Ayanna, *Passing Strange. Shakespeare, Race and Contemporary America* (Oxford, Oxford University Press, 2011).

Introduction to E. A. J. Honigmann, ed., *Othello*, revised edition (1997; London, Bloomsbury/Arden Shakespeare, 2016).

Taylor, Neil, 'National and racial stereotypes in Shakespeare', in Russell Jackson, ed., *The Cambridge Companion to Shakespeare on Film*, 2nd ed. (Cambridge, Cambridge University Press, 2007), 267–79.

Tynan, Kenneth, ed., Othello. *The National Theatre Production* (London, Rupert Hart-Davis, 1966).

Vaughan, Virginia Mason, Othello. *A Contextual History* (Cambridge, Cambridge University Press, 1994).

12 'A Wail in the Silence': Feminism, Sexuality and Final Meanings in *King Lear* Films by Grigori Kozintsev, Peter Brook and Akira Kurosawa

COURTNEY LEHMANN

Brook, Peter, *The Quality of Mercy. Reflections on Shakespeare* (New York, Theatre Communications Group, 2013).

Burnett, Mark *et al.*, eds., *Great Shakespeareans, Volume 17: Welles, Kurosawa, Kozintsev, Zeffirelli* (London and New York, Bloomsbury Arden Shakespeare, 2013).

Kurosawa, Akira, *Something Like an Autobiography*, translated by Audie E. Bock (New York, Vintage Books Edition, 1983).

Moore, Tiffany, *Kozintsev's Shakespeare Films: Russian Political Protest in* Hamlet *and* King Lear (Jefferson, NC and London, McFarland, 2012).

13 Violence, Tragic and Comic, in *Coriolanus* and *The Taming of the Shrew*

PATRICIA LENNOX

Brooke, Michael, BFI Screen on-line notes on *Spread of the Eagle*. www.screenonline.org.uk/.

Buchanan, Judith, *Shakespeare on Film* (London and New York, Pearson, 2005).

Cartelli, Thomas and Katherine Rowe, eds., *New Wave Shakespeare* (Malden, Polity, 2007).

George, David, ed., Coriolanus, *1687–1940* (Bristol and New York, Continuum, 2004).

Haring-Smith, Tori, *From Farce to Metadrama: A Stage History of* The Taming of the Shrew, *1594–1983* (Westport, CT and London, Greenwood, 1985).

Hatchuel, Sarah and Nathalie Vienne-Guerrin, eds., *Shakespeare on Screen: the Roman Plays* (Mont-Saint-Aignan, Publications des Universités de Rouen et du Havre, 2009).

Holland, Peter, *English Shakespeares: Shakespeare on the English Stage in the 1990s* (Cambridge, Cambridge University Press, 1989).

Jackson, Russell, ed., *The Cambridge Companion to Shakespeare on Film*, 2nd ed. (Cambridge, Cambridge University Press, 2007).

Kendrick, James, *Film Violence: History, Ideology, Genre* (London and New York, Wallflower Press, 2009).

Logan, John, Coriolanus, *Screenplay* (New York, New Market Press, 2011).

Ormsby, Robert, *Shakespeare in Performance:* Coriolanus (Manchester, Manchester University Press, 2014).

Rutter, Carol, ed., *Clamorous Voices: Shakespeare's Women Today* (London, The Women's Press, 1988).

Solomon, John, *The Ancient World in the Cinema* (New Haven, Yale University Press 2001).

Vance, Jeffrey, *Douglas Fairbanks* (Berkeley and Los Angeles, University of California Press, 2008).

Willis, Susan, *The BBC Shakespeare Plays: Making the Television Canon* (Chapel Hill, University of North Carolina Press, 1991).

14 The Shakespeare Films of Orson Welles

EMMA SMITH

Buchanan, Judith. *Studying Shakespeare on Film* (Harlow, Pearson, 2005).

Callow, Simon. *Orson Welles: The Road to Xanadu* (London, Jonathan Cape, 1995).
Orson Welles: Hello Americans (London, Jonathan Cape, 2006).
Orson Welles: One Man Band (London, Jonathan Cape, 2016).

Conrad, Peter. *Orson Welles: The Stories of his Life* (London, Faber, 2003).

Guneratne, Anthony R. *Shakespeare, Film Studies, and the Visual Cultures of Modernity* (New York, Palgrave Macmillan, 2008).

Thornton Burnett, Mark and Ramona Wray, eds. *Screening Shakespeare in the Twenty-First Century* (Edinburgh, Edinburgh University Press, 2006).

Welles, Orson, with Peter Bogdanovich and Jonathan Rosenbaum. *This is Orson Welles* (London, HarperCollins, 1993).

15 Kurosawa's Shakespeare: Mute Heavens, Merging Worlds or the Metaphors of Cruelty

ANNE-MARIE COSTANTINI-CORNÈDE

Goodwin, James, *Akira Kurosawa and Intertextual Cinema* (Baltimore and London, Johns Hopkins University Press, 1994).

Guntner, J. Lawrence, '*Hamlet, Macbeth* and *King Lear* on film', in Russell Jackson, ed., *The Cambridge Companion to Shakespeare on Film*, 2nd ed. (Cambridge, Cambridge University Press, 2007), 120–40.

Kurosawa, Akira, *Something Like an Autobiography*, translated by Audie E. Bock (New York, Vintage Books Edition, 1983).

Kurosawa, Akira, Ran, *The Original Screenplay and Storyboards* (Boston and London, Shambhala, 1986).

Kurosawa, Akira, Throne of Blood/Kumonosu-Djo, Seven Samurai *and Other Screenplays*, translated by Hisae Niki (London, Faber, 1992).

Richie, Donald, *The Films of Akira Kurosawa* (1965) 3rd ed. (Berkeley and Los Angeles, University of California Press, 1998).

Yoshimoto, Mitsuhiro, *Kurosawa, Film Studies and Japanese Cinema* (Durham, Duke University Press, 2000).

16 Zeffirelli's Shakespearean Motion Pictures: Living Monuments

NATHALIE VIENNE-GUERRIN

Cartmell, Deborah, 'Franco Zeffirelli and Shakespeare', in Russell Jackson, ed., *The Cambridge Companion to Shakespeare on Film* (Cambridge, Cambridge University Press, 2000), 212–21.

Crowl, Samuel, 'Zeffirelli's *Hamlet*: the golden girl and a fistful of dust', *Cineaste*, IV.1 (1998), 56–61.

Donaldson, Peter S., '"Let lips do what hands do": male bonding, eros and loss in Zeffirelli's *Romeo and Juliet*', in *Shakespearean Films/Shakespearean Directors*, (1990; London, Routledge, 2013), 145–88.

Hapgood, Robert, 'Popularizing Shakespeare. The artistry of Franco Zeffirelli', in Lynda E. Boose and Richard Burt, eds., *Shakespeare The Movie. Popularizing the Plays on film, TV and Video* (London and New York, Routledge), 80–94.

Holderness, Graham, *Shakespeare in Performance*: The Taming of the Shrew (Manchester, Manchester University Press, 1989).

Hussey, Olivia, with Alexander Martin, *The Girl on the Balcony* (New York, Kensington Books, 2018).

Matheson, Tom, with Russell Jackson and Robert Smallwood, 'Franco Zeffirelli', in John Russell Brown, ed., *The Routledge Companion to Directors' Shakespeare*, (London and New York, Routledge, 2008), 526–47.

Napoleone, Caterina, ed., *Franco Zeffirelli: Complete Works: Theatre/Opera/Film*, (London, Thames and Hudson, 2010).

Pilkington, Ace G., 'Zeffirelli's Shakespeare', in Anthony Davies and Stanley Wells, eds., *Shakespeare and the Moving Image*: The Plays on Film and Television (Cambridge, Cambridge University Press, 1994), 163–79.

Wray, Ramona, 'Franco Zeffirelli', in Mark Thornton Burnett, Courtney Lehmann, Marguerite H. Rippy and Ramona Wray, eds., *Great Shakespeareans Vol. XVII: Welles, Kurosawa, Kozintsev, Zeffirelli* (London and New York, Bloomsbury, 2013), 141–84.

Zeffirelli, Franco, *The Autobiography* (1986; London, Arena Books, 1987).

17 Kenneth Branagh: Mainstreaming Shakespeare in Movie Theatres

SARAH HATCHUEL

Berthomieu, Pierre, *Kenneth Branagh: traînes de feu, rosées du sang* (Paris, Jean-Michel Place, 1998).

Branagh, Kenneth, *Beginning* (London, Chatto and Windus, 1989).
  Hamlet *by William Shakespeare: Screen Play, Introduction and Film Diary* (London, Chatto and Windus, 1996).
Cook, Patrick J., *Cinematic* Hamlet. *The Films of Zeffirelli, Branagh and Almereyda* (Athens, University of Ohio Press, 2011).
Crowl, Samuel, *Shakespeare at the Cineplex. The Kenneth Branagh Era* (Athens, University of Ohio Press, 2003).
  The Films of Kenneth Branagh (Westport, Praeger, 2006).
Eggert, Katherine, 'Sure can sing and dance: minstrelsy, the star system, and the post-postcoloniality of Kenneth Branagh's *Love's Labour's Lost* and Trevor Nunn's *Twelfth Night*', in Richard Burt and Lynda E. Boose, eds., *Shakespeare, The Movie II* (London, Routledge, 2003), 72–88.
Hatchuel, Sarah, *A Companion to the Shakespearean Films of Kenneth Branagh* (Winnipeg, Blizzard Publishing, 2000).
Jackson, Russell, 'Kenneth Branagh's film of *Hamlet*: the textual choices', *Shakespeare Bulletin*, 15.2 (Spring 1997), 37–38.
White, Mark, *Kenneth Branagh* (London: Faber and Faber, 2005).
Wray, Ramona and Mark Thornton Burnett, eds., 'From the horse's Mouth: Branagh on the Bard', in *Shakespeare, Film, Fin de Siècle* (Basingstoke, Macmillan, 2000), 165–78.

18 Remaking Shakespeare in India: Vishal Bhardwaj's Films

POONAM TRIVEDI

Cabaret, Florence, 'Indianising *Othello*: Vishal Bhardwaj's *Omkara*' in Sarah Hatchuel and Natalie Vienne-Guerrin, eds., *Shakespeare on Screen, Othello* (Cambridge, Cambridge University Press, 2015).
Dionne, Craig and Parmita Kapadia, ed., *Bollywood Shakespeares* (New York, Palgrave Macmillan, 2014).
Gruss, Sussane, 'Shakespeare in Bollywood? Vishal Bhardwaj's *Omkara*', in Sara Sackel, Walter Gobel and Noha Hamdy, eds., *Semiotic Encounters, Text, Image and Trans-Nation* (Amsterdam and New York, Rodopi, 2009).
Henderson, Diana, 'Magic in the chains, *Othello*, *Omkara* and the materiality of gender across time and media', in Valerie Traub, ed., *The Oxford Handbook of Shakespeare and Embodiment, Gender, Sexuality and Race* (Oxford, Oxford University Press, 2016).
Huang, Alexa, ed., 'Asian Shakespeares on screen: two films in perspective', *Borrowers and Lenders*, IV. 2 (2009), special issue edited by Alexa Huang, www.borrowers.uga.edu/7158/toc.
Mookherjee, Tarini, 'Absence and repetition in Vishal Bhardwaj's *Haider*', *Cogent Arts & Humanities* (2016), 3, 1–10, http//dx.doi.org/10.1080/23311983.2016.1260824.
Thornton Burnett, Mark, *Shakespeare and World Cinema* (Cambridge, Cambridge University Press, 2013).
Trivedi, Poonam, 'Filmi Shakespeare' in Manju Jain, ed., *Narratives of Indian Cinema* (Delhi, Ratna Sagar, 2009). (First published in *Literature/Film Quarterly*, 35, 2 (2007).)

FILMOGRAPHY

The filmography lists versions of Shakespeare's plays referred to in the chapters. Details are given as: title, director(s), nationality and year of release. Where the play in question is not self-evident from the title, it is identified in square brackets.

For a full filmography of Shakespeare films from the silent era and beyond, see the (open access) online International Database of Shakespeare on Film, Television and Radio from the British Universities Film and Video Council (BUFVC), at: http://bufvc.ac.uk/shakespeare.

Alegres Comadres, Leilia Hipólito (Brazil 2003) [*The Merry Wives of Windsor*]

All is True, Kenneth Branagh (UK 2018)

All Night Long, Basil Dearden (UK 1962) [*Othello*]

As You Like It
  Paul Czinner (UK 1936)
  Christine Edzard (UK 1992)
  Kenneth Branagh (UK/USA 2006)

The Bad Sleep Well, Akira Kurosawa (Japan 1960) [*Hamlet*]

The Banquet, Xiaogang Feng (China 2000) [*Hamlet*]

Broken Lance (USA 1954) [*King Lear*]

Caesar Must Die (Cesare deve morire), Paolo and Vittorio Taviani (Italy 2012)

Chimes at Midnight, Orson Welles (aka *Falstaff*, Spain/Switzerland 1964) [*Henry IV*, parts 1 and 2]

Cigán, Martin Šulík (Czech Republic 2000) [*Romeo and Juliet*]

Coriolanus, Ralph Fiennes (UK 2011)

Dhadak, Shashank Khaitan (India 2018)

Dead Poets Society, Peter Weir (USA 1989) [*A Midsummer Night's Dream*]

Desdemona, August Blom (aka *For aabent Tæppe*, Denmark 1912) [*Othello*]

A Double Life, George Cukor (USA 1948) [*Othello*]
Forbidden Planet, Fred M. Wilcox (USA 1956) [*The Tempest*]
Gnomeo and Juliet, Kelly Asbury (UK/USA 2011)
Go!, Isao Yukisada (Japan 2001) [*Romeo and Juliet*]
Goliyon Ki Rasleela Ram-Leela, Sanjay Leela Bhansal (India 2013)
   [*Romeo and Juliet*]
Hamile: the Tango 'Hamlet', Terry Bishop (Ghana 1965)
Hamlet
   Cecil Hepworth (UK 1913)
   Eleuterio Rodolfi (Italy 1917)
   Svend Gade (Germany 1920)
   Laurence Olivier (UK 1948)
   Grigori Kozintsev (USSR 1964)
   Tony Richardson (UK 1969)
   Franco Zeffirelli (USA/UK/France 1990)
   Kenneth Branagh (UK/USA 1996)
   Michael Almereyda (USA 1999)
Henry V
   Laurence Olivier (UK 1944)
   Kenneth Branagh (UK 1989)
Huapango, Ivan Lipkies (Mexico 2004) [*Othello*]
In the Bleak Midwinter, Kenneth Branagh (UK 1995) [*Hamlet*]
Jarum Halus, Mark Tan (Malaysia, 2008) [*Othello*]
Julius Caesar
   Joseph L. Mankiewicz (USA 1953)
   Stuart Burge (UK 1970)
King of Texas, Uli Edel (TV movie, USA 2002) [*King Lear*]
King John (UK 1899)
King Lear
   Grigori Kozintsev (USSR 1970)
   Peter Brook (UK 1971)
Kiss Me Kate, Jack Cummings (USA 1953) [*The Taming of the Shrew*]
Kohlhiesel's Daughters, Ernst Lubitsch (Germany 1920) [*The Taming of
   the Shrew*]
The Lion King, Roger Allen and Rob Minkoff (USA 1994) [*Hamlet*]
Love's Labour's Lost, Kenneth Branagh (UK/France/USA 2000)
Macbeth
   Vitagraph (USA 1908)
   Orson Welles (USA 1948)
   George Schaefer (USA 1960)
   Roman Polanski (UK/USA 1971)

Justin Kurzel (UK/France/USA 2015)
Kit Monkman (UK 2018)
Macbeth on the Estate, Penny Woolcock (UK 1997)
Makibefo, Alexander Abela (France/Madagascar 1999)
Maqbool, Vishal Bhardwaj (India 2004) [*Macbeth*]
Master Will Shakespeare, Cyril Tourneur (USA 1936)
Men of Respect, William Reilly (USA 1991) [*Macbeth*]
The Merchant of Venice, Michael Radford (USA/Italy/UK/Luxembourg 2004)
A Midsummer Night's Dream
   Max Reinhardt/William Dieterle (USA 1935)
   Peter Hall (UK 1969)
   Adrian Noble (UK 1996)
   Michael Hoffmann (USA/Italy/UK 1999)
   Christine Edzard (as *The Children's' Midsummer Night's Dream* (UK 2001)
Much Ado about Nothing
   Kenneth Branagh (UK/USA 1993)
   Joss Whedon (USA 2013)
My Kingdom, Don Boyd (UK 2001) [*King Lear*]
My Own Private Idaho, Gus Van Sant (USA 1991) [*Henry IV*, parts 1 and 2]
O, Tim Blake Nelson (USA 2002) [*Othello*]
Omkara, Vishal Bhardwaj (India 2006) [*Othello*]
Ophelia, Claire McCarthy (USA 2018) [*Hamlet* and *Romeo and Juliet*]
Otelo Burning, Sara Blecher (S. Africa 2011)
Othello
   William V. Ranous (USA 1908)
   Franz Porten (Germany 1908)
   Ugo Falena (Italy 1909)
   Arrigo Frusta (as *Othello the Moor* (Italy 1914)
   Dmitri Buchowetski (Germany 1922)
   Orson Welles (USA/Morrocco/Italy/France 1952)
   Sergei Yutkevich (USSR 1955)
   Stuart Burge, from John Dexter's stage production (UK 1965)
   Liz White (USA 1980)
   Janet Suzman (S. Africa 1988)
   Oliver Parker (USA/UK 1995)
Otello, Mario Caserini and Gaston Velle (Italy 1906) [from Verdi's opera]
Private Romeo, Alan Brown (USA 2012)
Prospero's Books, Peter Greenaway (Netherlands/France Italy/Japan 1991)
Ran, Akira Kurosawa (France/Japan 1985) [*King Lear*]

The Real Thing at Last, L. C. Mac Bean (UK 1916) [*Macbeth*]
Der Rest ist Schweigen, Helmut Käutner (West Germany 1959) [*Hamlet*]
Richard III
  F. R. Benson (UK 1910–1911)
  Laurence Olivier (UK 1955)
  Richard Loncraine (UK 1995)
Romeo and Juliet
  István Kató Kiszly (Hungary 1921)
  George Cukor (USA 1936)
  Renato Castellani (Italy/UK 1954)
  Franco Zeffirelli (Italy/UK 1968)
  Baz Luhrmann (as *William Shakespeare's 'Romeo+Juliet'*: USA 1996)
  Carlo Carlei (Italy/Switzerland/UK 2013)
Romeo.Juliet, Armando Acosta (USA 1990)
Romeo y Julieta, Miguel M. Delgado (Mexico 1943)
Romeo i Dzhulyetta, Lev Arnshtam and Leonid Lavrovsky (USSR 1955)
  [Prokofiev's ballet]
Scotland PA, Billy Morisette (USA 2001) [*Macbeth*]
Shakespeare in Love, John Madden (UK/USA 1999)
Shakespeare Must Die, Ing K (Thailand 2012) [*Macbeth*]
She's the Man, Andy Fickman (USA 2006) [*Twelfth Night*]
Souli, Alexander Abela (France/Madagascar 2004) [*Othello*]
The Taming of the Shrew
  Sam Taylor (USA 1929)
  Franco Zeffirelli (Italy/USA 1967)
Tempest, Paul Mazursky (USA 1982)
The Tempest
  Derek Jarman (UK 1980)
  Julie Taymor (USA 2011)
10 Things I Hate About You, Gil Junger (USA 2002) [*The Taming of the Shrew*]
Titus, Julie Taymor (USA/Italy 1999)
Throne of Blood, Akira Kurosawa (Japan 1957 [*Macbeth*]
To Be or Not to Be, Ernst Lubitsch (USA 1942) [*Hamlet*]
Tromeo and Juliet, Lloyd Kaufman (USA 1996)
El Triunfo, Mireia Ros (Spain 2006) [*Hamlet*]
Twelfth Night, Trevor Nunn (UK/Ireland/USA 1996)
Warm Bodies, Jonathan Levine (USA 2013) [*Romeo and Juliet*]
West Side Story, Robert Wise (USA 1960) [*Romeo and Juliet*]

Television/Video Versions

Note: For ongoing series from the RSC, Stratford, Ontario and and Shakespeare's Globe see the companies' websites.

An Age of Kings, Peter Dews (BBC, UK 1960) [sequence from *Richard II* to *Richard III*]

Coriolanus
 Claudio Fino (RAI, Italy 1965)
 Elisha Moshinsky (BBC, UK 1984)
 Christian Schiaretti (Théâtre National Populaire – Villeurbanne, France 2006)
 Royal Shakespeare Company (UK 2018)

Filming Othello, Orson Welles (ZDF, Germany 1978)

Hamlet, Gregory Doran (UK 2009)

The Hollow Crown (2 series, various directors; BBC, UK 2012 and 2016) [Sequences from *Richard II* to *Henry V* and 1–3 *Henry VI* to *Richard III*]

Macbeth
 Trevor Nunn (UK 1979)
 Gregory Doran (RSC, UK 2001)
 Rupert Goold (UK 2010) screen adaptation of his Chichester production

Othello
 Tony Richardson (BBC, UK 1955)
 Trevor Nunn (UK 1989)

The Merchant of Venice
 Jonathan Miller/John Sichel (London Weekend TV, UK 1973)
 Trevor Nunn/Chris Hunt (BBC, UK 2001)

The Tempest, Rodney Bennett (BBC, UK 1980)

The Taming of the Shrew, Jonathan Miller (BBC, UK 1980)

Kiss Me, Petruchio, Christopher Dixon (New York Shakespeare Festival/ PBS (USA 1981)

Romeo and Juliet, Alvin Rakoff (BBC UK 1978)

RomeoxJuliet, Fumitoshi Oizaki (Japan 2007) [Anime series, produced by Gonzo Media Group]

Shakespeare Re-Told (BBC, UK 2005) [*Macbeth, A Midsummer Night's Dream, Much Ado About Nothing, The Taming of the Shrew*]

Shakespeare: The Animated Tales (BBC, UK/Russia 1995–1996) [animated versions of twelve plays with voice-over casts of British actors speaking Shakespeare's texts]

INDEX

Note: Performance versions of Shakespeare's plays are listed under the play's title by date and medium (film, stage, etc.). Where applicable, the new title of the version is noted in brackets.

INDEX

Cambridge Companions To ...

AUTHORS

Tennessee Williams edited by Matthew C. Roudané

August Wilson edited by Christopher Bigsby

Mary Wollstonecraft edited by Claudia L. Johnson

Virginia Woolf edited by Susan Sellers (second edition)

Wordsworth edited by Stephen Gill

Richard Wright edited by Glenda R. Carpio

W. B. Yeats edited by Marjorie Howes and John Kelly

Xenophon edited by Michael A. Flower

Zola edited by Brian Nelson

TOPICS

The Actress edited by Maggie B. Gale and John Stokes

The African American Novel edited by Maryemma Graham

The African American Slave Narrative edited by Audrey A. Fisch

African American Theatre edited by Harvey Young

Allegory edited by Rita Copeland and Peter Struck

American Crime Fiction edited by Catherine Ross Nickerson

American Gothic edited by Jeffrey Andrew Weinstock

American Literature of the 1930s edited by William Solomon

American Modernism edited by Walter Kalaidjian

American Poetry Since 1945 edited by Jennifer Ashton

American Realism and Naturalism edited by Donald Pizer

American Travel Writing edited by Alfred Bendixen and Judith Hamera

American Women Playwrights edited by Brenda Murphy

Ancient Rhetoric edited by Erik Gunderson

Arthurian Legend edited by Elizabeth Archibald and Ad Putter

Australian Literature edited by Elizabeth Webby

The Beats edited by Stephen Belletto

British Black and Asian Literature (1945–2010) edited by Deirdre Osborne

British Fiction: 1980–2018 edited by Peter Boxall

British Literature of the 1930s edited by James Smith

British Literature of the French Revolution edited by Pamela Clemit

British Romantic Poetry edited by James Chandler and Maureen N. McLane

British Romanticism edited by Stuart Curran (second edition)

British Theatre, 1730–1830 edited by Jane Moody and Daniel O'Quinn

Canadian Literature edited by Eva-Marie Kröller (second edition)

Children's Literature edited by M. O. Grenby and Andrea Immel

The Classic Russian Novel edited by Malcolm V. Jones and Robin Feuer Miller

Contemporary Irish Poetry edited by Matthew Campbell

Creative Writing edited by David Morley and Philip Neilsen

Crime Fiction edited by Martin Priestman

Dracula edited by Roger Luckhurst

Early Modern Women's Writing edited by Laura Lunger Knoppers

The Eighteenth-Century Novel edited by John Richetti

Eighteenth-Century Poetry edited by John Sitter

Emma edited by Peter Sabor

English Dictionaries edited by Sarah Ogilvie

English Literature, 1500–1600 edited by Arthur F. Kinney

English Literature, 1650–1740 edited by Steven N. Zwicker

English Literature, 1740–1830 edited by Thomas Keymer and Jon Mee

English Literature, 1830–1914 edited by Joanne Shattock

English Melodrama edited by Carolyn Williams

English Novelists edited by Adrian Poole

English Poetry, Donne to Marvell edited by Thomas N. Corns

English Poets edited by Claude Rawson

English Renaissance Drama edited by A. R. Braunmuller and Michael Hattaway (second edition)

English Renaissance Tragedy edited by Emma Smith and Garrett A. Sullivan Jr.

English Restoration Theatre edited by Deborah C. Payne Fisk

The Epic edited by Catherine Bates

Erotic Literature edited by Bradford Mudge

Made in United States
Orlando, FL
16 January 2023